外国语言文学与文化研究文库
WAIGUO YUYAN WENXUE YU
WENHUA YANJIU WENKU

The International Symposium on the Orient VS. the Occident: Cultural Exchanges and Influences

东方与西方：文化的交流与影响国际学术研讨会论文集

朱安博/主编

首都经济贸易大学出版社
·北京·

图书在版编目(CIP)数据

东方与西方:文化的交流与影响国际学术研讨会论文集/朱安博主编.
—北京:首都经济贸易大学出版社,2016.8
ISBN 978-7-5638-2545-5

Ⅰ.①东… Ⅱ.①朱… Ⅲ.①东西文化—文化交流—国际学术会议—文集
Ⅳ.①G115-53

中国版本图书馆 CIP 数据核字(2016)第 196234 号

东方与西方:文化的交流与影响国际学术研讨会论文集
Dongfang Yu Xifang: Wenhua De Jiaoliu Yu Yingxiang Guoji Xueshu Yantaohui Lunwenji
朱安博 主编

责任编辑 刘欢
封面设计 小尘
出版发行 首都经济贸易大学出版社
地 址 北京市朝阳区红庙(邮编 100026)
电 话 (010)65976483 65065761 65071505(传真)
网 址 http://www.sjmcb.com
E-mail publish@cueb.edu.cn
经 销 全国新华书店
照 排 首都经济贸易大学出版社激光照排服务部
印 刷 北京九州迅驰传媒文化有限公司
开 本 710 毫米×1000 毫米 1/16
字 数 370 千字
印 张 21
版 次 2016 年 8 月第 1 版 2016 年 8 月第 1 次印刷
书 号 ISBN 978-7-5638-2545-5/G·382
定 价 40.00 元

目　录

外语教学研究

文学与文化研究

语言学与翻译研究

外语教学研究

以应用能力培养为导向的新型校本教学模式之构建

首都经济贸易大学外国语学院　白云红

本文为首都经济贸易大学教改立项(02491454210165)部分研究成果

摘　要:目前大学英语的教学要求是以英语的实际使用为导向,以培养学生的英语应用能力为重点,围绕这一要求而开展的大学英语教学改革正在进行之中。如何构建更加有效的校本教学模式,从而提高学生英语应用能力成为笔者以及同仁们在教学过程中不断探索的课题。

关键词:应用能力培养;新型教学模式;克拉申假说;输出驱动假设

Abstract: In accordance with the new edition "College English Teaching Guide", College English teaching is to be application-oriented, with the focus on fostering students, competency of using the language. College English teaching reform centering on the requirements is well under way. And it proves to be a lasting researching topic among all the language teachers that they have to figure out how to construct a more effective school-based teaching model, thus helping students put into a better use of the language.

Key Words: fostering language competency; new teaching model; Krashen' s Hypothesis; output-driven hypothesis

教育部高等学校大学外语教学指导委员会制定的《大学英语教学指南》征求意见稿(以下简称指南)明确指出大学英语的教学目标是培养学生的英语应用能力,增强跨文化交际意识和交际能力,同时发展自主学习能力,提高综合文化素养,使他们在学习、生活、社会交往和未来工作中能够有效地使用英语,满足国家、社会、学校和个人发展的需要。

大学英语教学目标分为基础、提高、发展三个等级。在三级目标体系中,基础目标是针对大多数非英语专业学生的学习基本需求确定的。就笔者目前所授课程学生对象而言,大部分应该达到这个基本要求,即:能够基本满足日常生活、学习和未来工作与自身密切相关的信息交流的需要;能够基本正确地运用英语语音、词汇、语法及篇章结构等语言知识;能够基本理解语言难度中等、涉及常见的个人和社会话题进行简单的口头或书面交流；能够借助网络资源、工具书或他人的帮助，对中等语言难度的信息进行处理和加工，理解主旨思想和重要细节，表达基本达意；能够使用有限的学习策略；在与来自不同文化的人交流时，能够观察到彼此之间的文化和价值差异，并能根据交际需要运用有限的交际策略。

根据指南设定的大学英语教学目标，各高等院校陆续着手进行以“应用型”人才培养目标为导向的教学模式的探索研究，我校也不例外。因此，如何在新形势下更好地培养符合社会需求的人才也成为我校教师研究的重要主题之一。

一、教学改革过程中问题的呈现

多年来，传统的教学模式已呈现出不少弊端，大部分学生习惯于课上记笔记，被动参与英语学习，而不是积极参与到课堂活动中去。大学英语教学也长期存在着“重输入、轻输出”的问题。“教师为主体”的课堂教学模式不再适应于当今的英语教学与学习形势，然而对于“以学生为中心，教师为主导”的新型英语教学模式，学生们不能短时间内完全适应这种改变。因此，构建有效的新型教学模式并非易事，需要教师充分了解学生需求，理清不同时段的教学目标，尽力设计满足学生需求的各种教学活动，但最重要的是如何激发学生积极参与到构建新型教学模式过程中来。

目前，任课教师充满热情地投入到教学改革中，尝试不同教学形式，设计多种教学活动，但如何通过各种努力取得最大效果，构建出具有长效的教学模式，这需要广大同仁齐心合力，分别把自己在教学实践过程中得到学生广泛欢迎的有效做法加以归纳、总结、升华，形成我校具有校本特色的教学模式。

二、教学改革中构建新型教学模式实践活动的理论基础

（一）

多年的大学英语教学改革从以前的“听说领先”到最近的应用语言能力的培养，无不在强调学生使用语言的能力，最新的教学指南涵盖了听说、写作不同的层面的学生能力培养。大学英语学习目标的定位在于使学生在未来的学习、工作中有效使用语言进行国际交流、跨文化交际。

（二）

在教学改革过程中，美国著名语言学家克拉申的假设理论对我们摸索教学改革实践模式有很大的指导意义。克拉申认为单纯主张“输入假说”对英语学习是不够的，学习者需要的是“可理解输入”（Comprehensible input），有效的语言输入必

须包括“i+1”。如果语言习得者目前的语言能力为i，语言输入则需要略高于i，即i+1，而且这种i+1的输入必须在意义上是可以理解的。“输入假说”还提出了一个观点，语言的使用能力不是被老师教出来的，而是外语习得者通过长时间地接触大量的可理解输入之后自然形成的。

教师在教学过程中要多提供给学生接触真实的语料的机会，如先听后说，先读后写；这是克拉申的自然顺序假设（Natural Order Hypothesis）所给予我们的启示。克拉申的情感过滤假说（Affective Filter Hypothesis）表明情感因素起着对输入进行过滤的作用；情感因素因人而异。学习的情感因素会阻碍或加速语言的习得。只有在最佳情感条件下，才会产生真正的习得。最佳情感条件包含三个方面：学习者有强烈的学习动机、学习者充满信心和学习者心情舒畅、焦虑感适中。

（三）

文秋芳教授2013年在《外语界》发表的研究成果探讨了其提出的“输出驱动假设”（output-driven hypothesis）在大学英语教学中应用的可能性。假设的具体主张包括：（1）就教学过程而言，输出比输入对外语学习的内驱力更大，输出驱动不仅可以促进接受性语言知识运用，而且可以激发学生学习新语言知识的欲望。（2）就教学目标而言，培养说、写、译类表达性语言技能更符合社会需求，因此说、写、译等表达性技能为显性考核目标，听、读类接受性技能仅为隐性目标；根据社会就业的实际需要，学习者可以从说、写、译中选择一种或几种输出技能作为自己的学习目标。

三、以应用能力培养为导向的新型校本教学模式探索

学生应用能力的培养应贯穿在教学过程中，其中在教学活动的设计上，教师应做到有理有据，活动的目标应设定明确，并应该在教学活动后做到及时的总结。

（一）基于输入假说的课堂活动模式探索

根据输入假说理论，教师在课堂上给学生提供可理解的输入材料，但输入量应以学生可接受为限，另外需要关注输入材料对学生今后的学习所产生的意义。笔者认为有效的可理解输入材料需要具备如下特征：教师引出的输入材料话题要有趣味性、现实性，要能激发学生主动参与课堂活动的兴趣；i+1理论中，超出学生理解范围的语料难度不能过大，适当的时候教师需要讲解，以便使学生有更好的理解，从而不会影响学生学习的积极性；教师引出输入语料的方式可以多样化，尽量以学生更为接受的形式呈现，如视频、音频、时尚英文杂志、原版真实语料等；融洽的师生关系能够提升学生学习效果，学生在相对轻松的学习环境中享受到低情感

过滤氛围时,才能使其语言的学习不会受到诸如动机、自信心以及焦虑程度的影响。

克拉申认为,学习者的消极情感因素强、情感过滤水平越高时,他们对语言输入的吸收量就低;但如果学习者处于积极的情感中、情感过滤水平越弱时,他们便能够积极地内化语言的习得。因此,在教学过程中,教师需要充分考虑到情感因素对学生语言习得的影响,从而避免不必要的干扰因素,使学生的语言学习效果不断加强。

(二)“输出驱动假说”指导下的教学实践活动模式

语料输入的终极目标是学生能够有效输出(口语或者写作的输出),利用所输入的材料进行有效内化后进行语言的交流与互动。

传统的教学模式下,课堂上与课本内容相关的学习是以学生课下复习课文,教师课上教授难点及其他语法、语言点的模式进行的。而顺应改革的要求,输出驱动假说指导着更多的教师们尝试例如“任务型教学”(task-based approach)的形式进行相关内容的学习。课前学生以小组为单位接受输出型的任务:与课文背景知识相关的话题或旨在发展学生批判性思维的延伸性话题等。教师在布置任务时需要考虑学生英语水平的差异,延伸性的话题难度要适度,否则学生无法进行有意义的语言输出。

针对学生输出能力的培养需求,笔者在课堂上开展了多种教学实践活动。针对口语能力的训练,教学活动遵循了“以读促说”(read for speaking)、“以听促说”(listen for speaking)以及“以写代说”(write for speaking)等形式让学生进行口语训练。学期结束后,通过学生的反思日记对该学期的口语实践进行总结,并对下一个学期的设计进行思考。“以读促说”的活动展开基本围绕所学读写教程的话题内容,“以听促说”围绕《新视野大学英语视听说教程》及课外相关主题音频、视频材料展开,学生参与度较好。围绕视听说课本的口语活动,在听的基础上,给予学生适当的输入帮助,或采用学生一起进行头脑风暴的形式,集思广益。对课外相关主题的音频、视频材料而言,让学生听过两遍后回答相关的问题。因为手里没有该文字材料,学生反而表现出更大的兴趣,认真听后根据所理解的内容进行产出。

四、结语

综上所述,基于“输入假说”和“输出驱动假说”的理论支持,我们逐步意识到大学英语教学需要采取“输入为基础,输出为驱动”的教学策略。输入与输出并重的原则要体现在日常教学实践活动中。笔者通过教学观察发现目前倡导的“以学生为中心”也要量力而行，因为该教学理念成功实施与否还得参照教学对象的实际英语水平。

大学英语教学改革历史久矣，每次顺应形势变化的教学改革实践都为教育者们提供了进一步探索教学效果的依据。笔者所进行的实践探索都是基于本校学生实际英语水平而展开，其目的在于构建更加切合实际的本校教学模式，能够有效地使学生提高英语应用能力水平。改革的艰辛并非个人力量能够承担，我们需要各个层面教育者们达成共识，齐心协力地探索出适应我校乃至我国大学生英语学习的有效途径，摒弃长期存在的学生学习英语的弊端，让学生真正地摆脱应试教育，不受任何牵绊地提高英语实际应用能力。笔者认为，英语学习的改革需要彻底地进行：学生应用能力的提高不仅仅是大学英语教师的责任，而是从学生一开始接触英语学习，教育者们就要把应用能力摆在首位。而这需要彻底改变中国英语教育传统的教学理念及方法，只有这样才能避免社会人士所看到的“中国的学生学习英语费时、费力，却收效低”的现象出现。

参考文献：

[1]教育部高等教育司．大学英语课程要求(修订稿)，2015.

[2]Krashen S. *The Input Hypothesis: Issues and Implications* [M]. London: Longman, 1985.

[3]文秋芳．输出驱动假设在大学英语教学中的应用：思考与建议[J]．外语界，2013(6).

试析文化导入在二语习得过程中的影响
——以二外日语教学为例

首都经济贸易大学外国语学院　杜娟

摘　要:语言和文化密不可分,文化在语言习得过程中起着十分重要的作用。本文试以二外日语教学为例,分析日本文化导入在二外日语语言习得过程中的积极作用。主要表现为两方面:一、从激发学生学习动机的角度看,在枯燥的纯语言知识的讲授过程中,如果融入了文化的介绍、讨论,可以有效增加学生的学习兴趣,以使其保持学习的积极性和持续性;二、从跨文化交际的角度看,把文化背景知识融入语言教学将会更好地促进二语习得过程中的正迁移,有效避免负迁移,使跨文化交际得以顺畅进行。

关键词:语言;文化;动机;跨文化;迁移

语言和文化密不可分。跨文化交际学的奠基人霍尔曾经指出:语言是文化的一部分,也是传播文化最有效的途径之一,两者相互依存相互影响。每一种语言都有其存在的特定的文化背景,无法脱离文化而存在。只有根植于文化背景下的语言才是有生命的、厚重的语言,一旦割离,就无法了解该语言使用民族的心理特征和思维想法。早在二十世纪四五十年代,美国的语言教学专家查尔斯·弗里斯(C. C. Fries)(1945)和罗伯特·拉多(Robert Lado)(1957)就主张在外语教学中对文化予以足够的重视;随着中国改革开放的发展和对人才培养方针的改变,语言教学和文化教学之间的关系也越来越受到国内外语教学工作者的重视,如胡文仲、高一红(1997)、戴炜栋、张红玲(2000)等。从二语习得教学实践来看,如果单纯偏重于语音、词汇、语法句型等语言形式学习的话,一方面令学习者倍感单调枯燥,从而导致其学习动机降低;另一方面,这种模式学习的结果在语言实践中也常常表现为跨文化交际时的语言信息或非语言信息的偏误及由此产生的交流误解和摩擦。因此,要真正掌握一种语言,就必须了解它所依存的文化背景,在教学过程中导入文化内容。本文以二外日语教学为例,尝试分析日本文化导入在二外日语语言习得过程中的积极作用。

一、现阶段二外日语教学特点

长期以来，日语教学在我国高校的课程设置中，主要分为两大部分：一是专业日语教学；二是非专业日语教学，这部分主要分为英语专业的二外日语和其他专业的日语选修性课程。本文的讨论对象主要是英语专业的二外日语教学。专业日语教学课程设置时数多，基本周课时在10～14小时；课程类别丰富，除了精读、泛读、视听说等专门语言形式的学习以外，还在不同学期单独开设日本概况、文化、社会、经济等专题性质的课程；以日语为专业的学生主体，学习意愿强，投入时间和精力较多，且来自于母语以外其他语种的干扰较小。与此相比，二外日语教学呈现出以下特点：

（一）课时少，内容多，进度快

二外日语是英语专业必选的课程之一，学生基本为零基础起点学习。从一个语言体系进入到另一个完全不同的语言体系的学习，在初学阶段需要投入大量的时间和精力来适应并习得。但是在现阶段，我国高校的二外日语课程的课时较少，大概每周2～4个课时，开设学期为3到4个学期。近几年教改之后，二外日语的课程时数受到压缩，每周时数和开设学期数都不同程度地减少了。然而，无论从语言实践的技能要求来看还是从学生考研需求来看，学生需要掌握的内容并没有较大幅度地缩减，教和学两方面的任务不可谓不重。许多学生因此不得不花大量财力物力，在社会培训机构学习，而高校的教师和学习资源却闲置浪费。

（二）课程内容设置单一

由于课时数受限，传统的二外日语课程内容设置比较单一。教学多采用传统的结构分析法和语句翻译法，教学重点放在日语知识的传授上，强调语音、词汇、语法句型三要素的掌握，对于日本文化相关内容的导入缺乏重视或无暇顾及。和专业日语的专项课程系统讲解相比，大部分是在单词的讲解过程中，蜻蜓点水似的作以简要介绍。

（三）学生的学习动机不足

选择日语作为二外的学生的学习动机主要有娱乐型、信息考试型、自身提高型、学习工作型、文化型等8种①。但是，经过一段时间的学习，由于授课方式的单一、单纯语言学习的枯燥、学习难度的增加、时间分配不够等多方面原因，学生的学习动机后续力量不足，学习劲头下降，学习状态开始出现浮动。

---

① 参考王婉莹(2005)，以下将在2.2做详细说明。本文中，由于文化的内涵和外延较广，笔者更倾向于把娱乐型、美食型动机一并纳入文化型动机内。

(四)来自母语和英语的双重干扰较大

日语专业的学生在进入大学之前,二语习得以英语为主。但是进入大学以后,专业语言的高标准要求和强化训练使英语的语言干扰降到了最低,对于日语学习的干扰主要来自母语的语言和文化迁移。而对于以日语作为二外的英语专业的学生来说,由于其母语的语言文化背景加之长期学习的英语语言文化背景,在二外日语习得过程中,所受的干扰常常是双重的。例如,发“ベッド”等外来语的音时,受到英语影响,常常加入长音,误读作“ベード”。

下文将结合现阶段上述二外日语教学特点,具体分析文化导入在日语二外习得过程中的影响。

二、文化导入在激发学生学习动机中的影响及其对策

单纯语言技能的训练和学习会使学习者的学习缺乏新鲜感,学习动机后续乏力,弱化教学效果。而文化的导入会调动学习者的兴趣,使其长久地保持高涨的学习劲头。

(一)动机在语言学习中的重要性

关于日语学习的动机研究,日本研究者守谷智美(2002)有详尽综述。此外,日本国内以及我国的日语学习动机研究也分别以不同地区、不同文化背景学习者为对象进行了多角度的调查。尽管结论不尽相同,但动机对外语学习的重要性以及不同动机所体现的不同作用却是毋庸置疑的。动机是学习者的内部动因,会直接影响学习者的努力程度,有助于学习者实现长远学习目标。当然,动机的强弱也会随着学习的进程发展受到外界因素影响而发生变化,因此需要不断地激发和保持。

(二)二外日语学习的动机类型

英语专业的学生一般进入大二或大三学年之后,开始学习第二外语,学期数大概是二到四个学期。王婉莹(2005)曾以在京三所高校二外日语学生为对象进行了动机调查,并将其分为娱乐型(听歌曲、玩游戏、看动画)、信息考试型(通过报纸、杂志等获取信息或是参加考试)、自身提高型(开拓视野、提升自信)、学习工作型(学习、留学、工作等)、文化型(对日本或中日文化差异感兴趣)、竞争型(可提高自身竞争力)、可行型(易学、有用途)、美食型(喜欢日本料理)共8个大类,并指出“信息考试型”“自身提高型”“文化型”对动机的影响程度较大。如果说“信息考试型”“自身提高型”动机的激发主要来自于学习者的自觉和自省,那么“文化型”动机的激发则主要来源于教学中的文化导入。

(三)文化导入和学习动机激发的关联性

张占一(1990)把语言教学中的文化、背景知识按功能分为知识文化和交际文

化两大类。其中知识文化是指一个民族的政治、经济、教育、宗教、法律、文化艺术等文化知识；交际文化则是指两个文化背景不同的人进行交际时，那些影响信息准确传达的语言和非语言因素。从二外日语教学实践来看，学习者学习日语的文化型动机主要来源于对知识文化的渴求。在学习日语之前，学习者通过各种媒介一般对日本文化（如社会、经济、文学、文化生活、民族特性等）已经有了或多或少的了解，希望通过日语语言的学习，增加和拓展对日本文化的理解的深度和广度。但是，由于对文化导入的重视程度不够，兼之受到课时的限制，课堂上能够涉及的知识文化的讲解无法满足学习者的需求。此外，长时间的语言知识讲授和机械的替换练习以及学习难度的增加，都会导致学习者学习动机的减弱，具体表现为学习内容单一枯燥、课堂气氛沉寂死板、学习者乏味走神等。教学实践表明，如果在语言知识讲授的过程中，导入相关的知识文化，不仅能吸引学生的注意力、激发学生的学习兴趣，也会加深学生的记忆、活跃课堂气氛、强化教学效果。比如，《标准日本语（中级上册）》第 11 课课文题目为“漫画とアニメ”，这是“90 后”学生十分感兴趣的大众文化现象之一，并且他们在这方面的了解甚至比教师还要多。笔者尝试在课堂上导入以漫画、动漫为代表的日本大众文化的介绍和讨论，收到了良好的反馈和教学效果。

（四）知识文化导入的对策

对课时极其有限的二外日语学生来说，教师如何把语言教学与知识文化教学融为一体至关重要，可以尝试从以下几个方面和渠道进行日语知识文化的讲解和普及：(1)教师结合教材，利用多媒体等教辅设备进行有目的的知识文化的传授和讲解；(2)教师提前制定学习任务，并要求学习者在预习阶段通过各种媒介完成对某一文化背景或现象的调查了解，并在课堂上用简短的时间进行结果报告；(3)开设第二课堂，以“请进来、走出去”的方式，利用课余时间请专家来校做日本文化专题讲座，或组织学生参加兄弟院校、日本国际交流基金会主办的日本文化活动。除此之外，在知识文化导入的过程中，要注意以下几点：(1)引导学生形成文化比较意识，重视讲解的系统性，而非简单的现象列举；(2)注意量和度的把控，教师应充分考虑文化导入与语言学习的比例分配，避免授课时的喧宾夺主，可以把知识文化的学习更多地放在第二课堂进行。

三、文化导入在跨文化交际时的影响及其对策

如果说知识文化的导入能够更多激发学生的学习动机的话，那么交际文化的导入则能够有效避免中日跨文化交际时的负迁移现象。由于中日在地缘文明上同

属东方文化,且在历史的发展过程中,中国文化的输入对日本文化有很大的影响,以至于很多人认为中日文化同源,从而想当然地用母语的心理和思维方式进行跨文化交际而忽略了中日交际文化的差异性。事实上,日本由于其封闭的地理环境、纵式的社会结构以及在此基础上形成的独特的思维模式和民族特性,日本文化尤其是其交际文化(如民族特性在语言上的反映)和中国文化的差异很大。二外日语的学习者往往受到母语文化及英美文化的影响,在跨文化交际时存在语用错误,造成交流受阻或者引起误会和摩擦。

(一)日语呈现的独特的民族性和思维方式

日语是日本民族的语言。它不像英语和中文等语种,不受国界和民族的限制,能够较多地融合当地的文化,其特殊性就在于只有生活在日本境内的大和民族才使用。因此,其语言、民族和文化是有机的统一结合体,日本人的民族性和思维方式就很直观地反映到日语表达方式上来,如群体优先和等级意识、自我的隐遁、以和为贵、体察文化及以心传心等。

(二)日本民族性和思维方式在语言上的具体表现特征

1. 群体优先、等级意识、内外有别

①群体优先

日本人具有强烈的群体优先①和等级意识。比如,在讲座、座谈等场合进行提问或发言时,由于参加人员分别来自不同的单位或部门,一般要进行简单的自我介绍。除了名字外,所属单位也是不可缺少的信息项,如“××大学の……です”(我是××大学的……)。反观以中文为母语的发言者,通常都省去自我介绍环节,而直奔主题地进行提问或发言。而在英语世界里,这种附加所属单位的自我介绍亦非习惯要求。

②等级意识

强烈的等级意识不仅造就了发达的日语敬语体系,也使得具体的表达中某些表达成为禁忌。类似评价性的话语只能用于上对下、长对幼,否则极易造成失礼。如“先生は教授法がお上手ですね”(老师,您教得真好)、“先生、お疲れ様でした”(老师,您辛苦啦)等等。在我们的母语课堂上,上述赞许性的话语经常会听到,也不会带来任何违和感。但是,在日语和日本文化的世界里,这种对上级或长辈的评价即便内容是积极正面的、语言是恭敬的,也会因为下对上的评价而造成听话人的不悦,因此在使用上要慎之又慎。这时从自己的角度出发,选择“いい勉強になり

① 参考王秀文(2005)。

ました”(我学到了很多)、“ありがとうございました”(谢谢老师)等,就会比较安全。①

2. 自我的隐遁

二外日语初学者在进行日语表述时,受中文和英语主语优先的影响,作为主语的“わたし”“あなた”几乎会出现在每句话的开头,这是极不自然的表达。因为,动辄以“わたし”开头会给人过分强调自我的感觉,往往被视为不礼貌、缺少教养之辈,②因此第一人称常常是省略的。而“あなた”也只有在面对陌生人不知其身份和姓名的情况下才会使用。一般来说,日语经常以亲属称谓或是身份名称代替第一人称,如父母对孩子自称“お父さん/おかあさん”,哥姐对弟妹自称“お兄さん/お姉さん”,老师对学生自称“先生”等;第二人称亦同样选择名字加“さん”、亲属称谓或是身份职位名称来代替第二人称,如××さん、お父さん、社長、車掌さん等,上对下、长对幼有时甚至直呼其名。在句法结构上,由于授受表达、敬语等也能够区别人称,所以在此类表达中,也经常省略第一人称和第二人称。③

3. 以和为贵

由于长期生活在日本列岛,日本民族单一,生活环境封闭,因此他们十分重视人际交往的和睦。以和为贵的民族特性表现在语言上,具体体现为:

①表达的暧昧性

如“いい”、“結構”这两个词根据使用的具体语境,既可以表达“好,可以”的意思,也可以表达“够了,不要了”的意思。

②话语的柔软委婉性

如在谈话中的“あいづち”现象。日本人的交谈中常常会有“はい”、“そうですね”、“なるほど”等表达。表面上,这些词句的意思都是对对方言语的认同,但这仅是一种言语上的附和,而不代表说话人真的同意,其使用目的在于营造一个同一融洽的谈话氛围,表明“自己正在聆听对方的话,请接着说”,而上述表达之后出现否定的观点是很常见的现象。在拒绝对方的时候,日本人也不直接说不,而是采取先表示感谢或肯定,然后再婉拒的形式。如“せっかく…のに、本当に残念に思いますが、また今度いいですか。”

---

① 对于长辈或上级,也很少直接询问涉及对方意愿、希求的内容。因此,“~たいですか”“~がほしいですか”等是不对上级或长辈说的,否则就会失礼。此外还有其他因等级意识造成的禁忌表达,由于篇幅有限,不再一一列举。

② 参考李兆忠(2010)。

③ 参考刘慧云(2008)。

4. 体察文化、以心传心

由于日本生活环境的封闭及民族的单一,日本人的生活方式具有高度同一性。在这种环境里生活的日本人在心理上很善于协调,具有极强的默契感,崇尚以心传心、体察别人话语的言外之意。如在室内,当有人问到“寒くないですか”(你不冷吗?),以日语为母语的听者就会起身把开着的窗户关上,因为他/她从说话者的话语里,体察到了对方感觉到寒冷的信息,并迅速地做出应对。但是非母语的听者常常只捕捉到字面意思,简单地把对方的询问理解为自己是否觉得冷,从而直截了当说“はい、寒くないです”(不,我不冷)。如此,话者和听者在信息的表述和接收上就出现了不对称,极易造成交际时的尴尬。

如上所述,如果学习者在二外习得过程中只看到了中日文化相同的一面而忽视了最为关键的差异的话,就会造成虽然语法正确但是依然无法顺畅交流的窘境。因此,在二语教学中,需要教师适时地指出目标语言交际文化的具体表达和特征。

(三)交际文化导入的对策

与知识文化教学的导入的系统性、独立性、主题化相比,交际文化导入的过程一般分散于语言教学的整个过程中,并且很难脱离语言单独讲授,需要和语言教学有机地结合于一体。因此可以采取以下方式培养学生跨文化交际的能力:①在教学中“见缝插针”地对学生进行讲解和提醒,培养学生对交际文化知识的敏感性,并进行阶段性的总结;②采用对比法,通过比较中日两种文化之间的差异,使学生加深对目标语文化的理解,加强文化对比的意识,从而指导具体的语言表达;③通过课堂角色扮演等语境教学和争取社会语言实践,使学生亲身感受跨文化交际时的摩擦、挫折带来的挫败及顺畅交流带来的成就感,从而能够自主自觉地适度文化移情,更好地体会文化的差异性;④教师也应进行自我提高,不断加强跨文化交际的意识和能力。

四、结语

本文从二外日语教学的实际着手,尝试分析了日本文化导入在二外日语语言习得过程中的积极作用:一、知识文化可以激发学生学习动机,增加学习兴趣,保持其学习的积极性和持续性;二、从跨文化交际的角度看,把交际文化知识融入语言教学将会更好地促进二语习得过程中的正迁移,有效避免负迁移,使跨文化交际得以顺畅进行。同时,亦从教学实践的角度,提出了知识文化和交际文化导入时的对策。在国际化全球化飞跃发展的当今时代,传统的日语教学所侧重的单纯语言知识学习既无法满足学生的知识渴望,也无法更完善地指导学生的语言实践,因此教学内容和教学方法的改革势在必行且任重道远。作为课堂主导者的教师,更应有意识地丰富自己的知识架构、主动自觉地把语言外的文化要素和教学结合起来。

参考文献:

[1]王婉莹. 大学非专业学生日语学习动机类型与动机强度的定量研究[J]. 日语学习与研究,2005(3).

[2]张占一. 试议交际文化和知识文化[J]. 语言教学与研究,1990(3).

[3]戴炜栋,张红玲. 外语教学中的文化迁移及其对外语教改的启示[J]. 外语界,2000(2).

[4]胡文仲,高一红. 外语教学与文化[M]. 长沙:湖南教育出版社,1997.

[5]王秀文. 跨文化交际与日语教育[J]. 日语学习与研究,2005(3).

[6]守谷智美. 第二言語教育における動機付けの研究動向——第二言語としての日本語の動機付け研究を焦点として[J]. 言語文化と日本語教育,2002(5).

[7]李兆忠. 暧昧的日本人[M]. 北京:九州出版社,2010.

[8]刘慧云,向洁. 海外研修中的中日语言跨文化比较研究[M]. 北京:国防工业出版社,2008.

研究生英语汉英翻译练习的应对策略

首都经济贸易大学外国语学院　高建平

摘　要：本文以非英语专业研究生英语课内汉英翻译练习为着眼点，从英语教学的基本规律出发，探讨如何增强该类练习的教学效果，使翻译这一迄今为止仍被广泛使用的古老外语教学法，能够更加适应现代课堂外语教学。

关键词：汉英翻译；外语教学；研究生英语

Abstract: With the aim of revitalizing some of the positive factors in the traditional Grammar-translation approach to cope with related contemporary pedagogical problems, this paper analyzes the Chinese-English translation exercise strategies that can be optimized and utilized in the context of EFL teaching at the Non-English-Major graduate level.

Key Words: Chinese-English translation; EFL; Graduate English

一、汉英翻译练习使用中的现存问题

笔者长期从事非英语专业研究生英语教学工作，而汉译英翻译练习是该工作中一直令人困扰的问题之一。该问题的主要表征有两类：其一，学生对此类练习很少表现出兴趣，练习完成率较低。其二，在完成的译文中，语言质量差强人意。

在很多研究生综合英语类教材中，汉英翻译练习均为必备环节之一；而据笔者了解，很多学校乃至具体到研究生导师，都对其培养的研究生的外语实用技能，比如汉英翻译技能，抱有相当高的期望。但现实情况却是，不少一年级新入校的非英语专业研究生，对课后的汉英翻译练习具有较强的畏难情绪，一些学生不能完成该部分作业，或者上网搜索答案应付了事。此类作业的完成情况远不及 Presentation 类甚至写作类练习。

与此相伴而生的另一个问题是，学生的译文质量往往非常差，其中充斥各种词汇、句法错误；生硬的"中式英语"也非常常见。笔者过去一直把这些问题笼统地归因为学生英语综合运用水平还待提高，直到发现了一个具有较高一致性的现象：如果把同一学生的作文抑或 Presentation 作业中的语言质量，在剔除特定内容要求的前提下，与其翻译练习的语言质量进行对比，在很多情况下前者的语言质量会明显优于后者。无论选词的地道程度,还是句式的适切性,翻译练习中学生的表现似乎均不及他们在作文中的表现。该现象促使笔者对汉英练习进行了比较彻底的反思,并通过逐步探索形成了目前的应对模式。在笔者不断实践和改进中,取得了比较满意的效果,在很大程度上缓解了这一问题造成的困扰。

二、翻译法在研究生英语教学层面的潜在作用

我们都知道所谓"Pedagogy of Translation"和"Pedagogical Translation"的区分,前者指翻译教学,而后者指用于教学的翻译练习。笔者这里旨在集中探讨后者。众所周知,"语法翻译外语教学法"(the Grammar-Translation Approach,简称为翻译法)是传统上经典的外语教学法之一。尽管由于各种原因,从19世纪末以来该教学法一直饱受争议,但至少有两条该方法的相关具体原则还是得到公认的。其一,语法翻译法最初并非针对儿童外语教学而创制,也并非针对缺乏系统语法知识的普通成人,它初始的适用对象是教育背景良好并且经典语法知识丰富的外语学习者。其二,该方法强调从母语向目标语的翻译练习,该练习的实质是提高学习者目标语的精确性(豪厄特:1984)。

现在我们需要重新审视一下我们的教学对象,以及他们所存在的迫切需要解决的问题。首先,非英语专业研究生显然并非儿童。从语言学习的内在规律角度,其实很容易发现他们和青春期之前的儿童外语学习者具有很大的不同。例如,他们对语音、语调的模仿能力从整体上看肯定不如后者;他们对语言的机械记忆能力同样不及后者。尽管如此,但他们在外语学习方面仍具有儿童学习者所不可企及的优势因素。首先,作为已完成本科学习的研究生,他们对母语语法的掌握肯定应该远胜后者。这里所说的对语法的掌握,并非限于外在的语法规则,而是指在口笔语交流中,使用者对语法规则的运用能力,即使用者对合乎通用语法规范的语言的驾驭能力。显然,从整体上讲研究生对语言的驾驭能力,也就是对通用语法的掌握程度要好于儿童,两者口笔语的语言质量和交流能力的差异即为佐证。另一方面,由于成人分析能力的提高,辅以语言使用经验的累积,他们对语言使用规则——也就是语法——的作用机理应该比后者有更好的把握。从某种程度上来说,他们在语言学习中可以更为理性、更为有效地利用语言规则进行归纳和推广,从而取得举一反三、事半功倍的效果。至少他们不必像后者那样依赖感性、模仿和机械记忆,或者说,他们可以利用抽象的语法规律,更为高效地把握具体的语言现象。而他们的这些特点,恰恰符合上文中提及的翻译法的适用原则。

其次,目标语语言质量低是我们不得不面对的严重问题。尤其在研究生这一

公众所预期的高素质群体之中,翻译译文的质量直接影响到各种层次的学术交流效果,很多时候会影响到稿件的接受与否以及修改周期。以近期被媒体广泛关注的一个热点事件为例,一位中国学者的论文因为一个单词(Creator)的误用,遭到了国外诸多媒体及业内人士的“群殴”,并最终导致《公共科学图书馆》(*Plos One*)杂志不得不撤稿并致歉。而该问题的根源,居然仅仅是因为在对一个词的翻译过程中,忽略了对其文化内涵的考证,即译文出了偏差。今天课堂里的研究生,明天可能就会成长为学界精英。如果今天不打牢目标语语言质量的基石,将来就有可能影响他们的学术成长。从更广的角度来说,语言质量还会直接影响交流对象对语言使用者的形象评价。很难想象一个满嘴语误、满篇语病的学者能给参加交流的同行留下良好的学术印象,至少交流的效率也会大打折扣。

回到前面提到的语法翻译法的两条原则,我们可以清楚地看到它恰恰与研究生外语学习者在年龄及学术背景方面具有较高的契合度,并且根据该方法的设计初衷,也可能有助于解决目前普遍存在的目标语语言质量低下的问题。当然,我们不能走向另一个极端,抛弃近年来交际法以及意念法等新近发展起来的外语教学理论之中的积极因素。我们也无意全盘恢复语法翻译法,毕竟在信息及媒体技术如此发达的21世纪,如果不能与时俱进地利用现代教学技术在外语教学领域所带来的种种便利,也是很大的损失。笔者所强调的只是发挥其契合教学对象自身情况,可以帮助解决教学效果中存在问题的潜在的积极因素。具体地说,就是要参照其重视理性分析、强调目标语质量的积极理念,更好地利用研究生英语综合课上的汉英翻译练习。

三、汉英翻译练习的原则

翻译练习的特性使其可以直观地呈现两种语言对同一语义的不同表达方式。语法翻译法尽管受到不少诟病,但对翻译自身所具有的这一特性则少有质疑。因此,笔者认为利用好翻译练习的关键就是充分运用好它可以很好地呈现两种语言的对比效果这一特性。有鉴于此,我们应该强调如下四个原则。

其一,练习中要强调语境对比,不可断章取义。其实语法翻译法被人诟病的主要原因之一就是,传统上的语法翻译法是以典型句子为单位的翻译教学法,往往给人以忽略语境的印象。比如裴剑波(2003)给“教学翻译”(也就是语法翻译法中的翻译)罗列的“十宗罪”中的大部分其实都与各种层级的语境相关。此处之所以要把语境作为第一原则,就是要对传统的语法翻译法加以优化,使其更好地适应现代教学要求。笔者所使用的研究生英语教材之中,课后汉英翻译练习多数都与课文关系密切，并且该密切关系不仅存在于形式层面，还存在于内容层面。这就使处理翻译练习时强调语境不会流于形式，因为课文提供了学生所需要的大部分语境信息——既有内容背景，又有相关语言结构的使用场景。教学过程中所需要强调的只是提醒学生充分加以运用。

其二，在明确语境的前提下，要强调英汉词汇，或更准确地说是两种文化中某一概念所对应的不同表达法的对比，尤其要强调在文化层面上就所谓对等概念进行对比。教师应该提醒学生注意词汇的色彩和内涵，从而更精确地传达信息。

其三，要强调句法层面英汉结构的对比。教师要提醒学生某一信息在不同语言中完全可能通过不同的语言单位进行表达。例如，汉语原文中的时间状语（比如名词性结构）可能会转变成译文中的动词时态，通过动词的曲折变化全部或部分地传达原意。这一层面对比的核心作用有二：一是明确原文信息需要整体转换成目标语，而不能从词汇、短语等低级语言单位层面进行对应转换；二是帮助学生熟悉目标语的句法特点，提升其句法层面的语言质量。另外，如遇段落翻译，亦须提醒学生语义的传递不应受到原文中语句分割的影响，应通盘考虑目标语的语篇习惯。

其四，在上述三种对比之中，都必须强调原文语义的真实传达，即形式必须服从于内容，而不能以译文形式之美为由，牺牲原文信息。之所以单列此为独立原则，是因为笔者在前文提到的一个有趣现象，即同一学生作文的语言质量要好于翻译质量。有些学生在自主表达（比如作文）时，会牺牲原来想表达的意思来迁就目标语的语言形式。这时，尽管其语言貌似地道流畅，但往往只不过是对某一范文例句的近似机械的照搬而已。这种“貌合神离”的语言学习，只会使学习者语言形式和实际表达内容走向脱节，长此以往必将影响其正常交流技能的培养。而汉译英练习，因其明确了需要传达的具体信息，从而为帮助一些学生克服这一问题提供了很好的平台。

四、汉英翻译练习的具体操作过程及注意事项

首先，借鉴翻转课堂的理念，在通过课文讲解之后，教师把课后翻译练习分解成不同任务模块，根据学生情况分配任务。任务可以是某句话或某几句话的翻译。任务可以落实到个人，也可以落实到小组。任务分配主要考虑学生水平和班内学生人数两个因素。一般应给予一周左右准备时间，之后要求学生根据上面提到的四条原则，在班上讲解任务句、段的翻译。要求做 PPT，并在空间允许的情况下，要求在同一张幻灯片上呈现原文、学生译文和参考译文（参考译文由教师提前提供，供学生完成翻译后进行对比）。经过笔者实践发现，通过这一方法，翻译练习的完

成率有了很大提高。由于提供了展示平台,多数学生的潜能得以发挥,并在一定程度上激发了他们的学习兴趣和积极性。

其次,教师为学生提供必要支持。首先教师要在课文讲解时尽可能结合语境透析相关语言现象,使学生初步具备运用相关语言结构实现翻译的能力。此外,教师还要提前讲解翻译练习的上述四条原则。对于研究生层面的学生,提前明确某一练习的原则和设计初衷,取得其对任务的理解,往往会得到他们更好的配合。这一点在笔者所任课的不同班级中都得到了印证。当然,不同层次的学生可能对此会有不同反应,具体实施时须根据具体情况灵活处理。但总的原则应该是,对于成年学生,应予以充分信任,调动其元认知能力,积极参与到教学活动中来。另外,教师还需要为学生提供参考译文。亦可以提前告知学生该译文并非最佳译文,希望他们能对其有所改进。这一做法对调动学生特别是程度较好学生的探索积极性有很好的效果。

此外,在学生讲解时强调学生—学生、学生—教师之间的互动,就翻译的细节或整体随时进行讨论。学生的讲解要求双语,尽可能鼓励其更多地使用目标语。如果讲解中出现关键讹误,在氛围许可又不打断讲解学生思路的前提下,如果为了提高效率,可以由教师加以提醒,或根据情况请持不同意见的同学评论。如果时间允许,笔者个人感觉讲解完成后由教师进行归类总结效果会更好,但需要教师做大量笔记,并且由于需要重建某一具体语境,有可能会占用较多时间。对于非典型讹误,如需要可课后个别讲解。由于加入了互动环节,翻译练习所需时间较传统方法要长很多,因而教师点评一定力求精当,抓住系统性、代表性问题即可。

五、汉英翻译练习的应用前景

只要贯彻学生为中心的原则,采取灵活多样的形式,汉英翻译练习同样会受到学生的欢迎。结合学生之间、师生之间的互动和教师的精当点评,该类练习不但可以深化学生对相关内容的理解,还可以切实提高学生的语言质量。总之,一种教学方法的理念是否过时,不能机械地看它的产生年代或名称,亦不可人云亦云,而要具体问题具体分析,看它是否存在符合教学对象实际情况的积极因素。只要有甄别、有扬弃地运用,翻译法同样有其用武之地。

参考文献:

[1]李靖民. 浅谈综合英语课上的英汉翻译教学[J]. 中国翻译,1996(2).

[2]李忠华. 大学英语翻译教学:现状与对策[J]. 外语与外语教学,2007(9).

[3]裴剑波．论教学翻译对翻译教学的十种不良影响[J]．高教论坛,2003 年 2 月(1)．

[4]束定芳．中国外语教学理论研究(1949—2009)[M]．上海:上海外语教育出版社,2009.

[5]Howatt,A. *A History of English Language Teaching*[M]. Oxford:OUP,1984.

[6] Stevens, P. *New Orientations in Teaching of English* [M]. Oxford: Oxford University Press,1977.

A Study on Expanding Patterns in Classroom Interaction

首都经济贸易大学外国语学院　杨郁

Abstract: Classroom discourse analysis has attracted more and more attention from both linguistics and educationalists. Classroom discourse analysis is defined as "the analysis of spoken language as it is used in classroom among teachers and learners" and "an analysis of the processes of classroom interaction by means of a close examination of audiovisual records of interaction". This thesis, as might be expected, attempts to test and investigate the typical structure of classroom discourse in College English intensive reading class context. The model used in the thesis is the classroom discourse model proposed by Sinclair and Coulthard (1975), who argued for a rank scale of classroom discourse analysis. This rank scale is composed of five ranks: lesson, transaction, exchange, move and act, which are related in a "consist-of" relationship. A descriptive analysis of sample classroom discourse in College English class will be given and some new findings in the structure of classroom discourse will be explored. From the structure and classes of five ranks, this thesis pays more attention to a study on expanding patterns in classroom interaction.

Key Words: classroom discourse analysis; structure of classroom interaction; patterns

I　Classroom Discourse Analysis: Literature Survey

Discourse analysis as a field of linguistic enquiry has received an enormous amount of attention over recent years. Carter R. (1993:22) gives the definition of discourse as "any naturally occurring stretch of language occurring in context." Discourse analysis is defined as "a variety of procedures for examining chunks of language, whether spoken or written." (Allwright and Bailey: 1991) And Michael Stubbs (1986: 1) considers discourse analysis as "the linguistic or sociolinguistic analysis of naturally occurring discourse or text, spoken or written." Roughly speaking, it refers to attempts to study the organization of language above the sentence or above the clause, and therefore to study larger linguistic units, such as conversational exchanges or written texts. It follows that discourse analysis is also concerned with language in use in social contexts, and in particular with interaction or dialogue between speakers'. Classroom discourse analysis, as Allwright and Bailey (1991:61) put it, involves the analysis of spoken language as it is used in classroom among teachers and learners. Van Lier (1988:122) describes classroom discourse analysis as "an analysis of the processes of classroom interaction by means of a close examination of audiovisual records of interaction." Hatch (1992:1) defines discourse analysis as "the study of the language of communication—spoken or written." The system that emerges out of the data shows that communication is an interlocking social, cognitive, and linguistic enterprise.

Most studies of the classroom are inevitably concerned with how teachers and pupils interact; that is, with aspects of teacher-pupil dialogue, conversation or discourse.

Appealing to linguistics, the language functions of classroom discourse should be, first of all, noted; nevertheless, the language function that is of primary interest here is not the universal functions of language identified as statement, question and command or the detailed function of surface formal ordering within the sentence discussed by Halliday (1970). "It's rather the level of the function of a particular utterance, in a particular social situation and at a particular place in the sequence", as Sinclair and Coulthard put it. (1975:13) In the classroom, the teacher uses language to perform a good many functions: telling things to students, eliciting students' answers, organizing the teaching-learning process, evaluating the things that students do, and the like. The students also contribute to the classroom discourse by answering the teacher's questions, bidding to be nominated, acknowledging the teacher's directives and so on. The use of language in the classroom is seen as a means to construct an ongoing discourse and the function of an utterance is identified by its relation with other utterances preceding or succeeding it. Thus, in the classroom discourse analysis, to recognize the function of an utterance is to see whether the utterance is, for instance, intended to elicit a response, whether it is a feedback to a preceding response, or whether it is intended to mark a boundary in the discourse.

II Birmingham Model Adopted & Modifications

Discourse analysis "follows from the evolution in descriptive linguistics of analytical procedures for the description of suprasentential structures (see van Dijk 1972,1977, 1985;Grimes 1975; Dressler 1978), as well as from ethnographic and sociolinguistic investigations into the structure of interaction (Hymes 1962,1964;Gumperz and Hymes 1972)". (see Chaudron, 1988: 13) In 1970's, the so-called Birmingham group, the members of which include J. Sinclair, M. Coulthard, M. Ashby, and I. Forsyth, embarked on the project "the English used by Teachers and Pupils", which is a major step made in the discourse analysis of L1 classroom on British elementary school classrooms with minority children. As Michael McCarthy (1991) puts it, "the Birmingham model is certainly not the only valid approach to analyzing discourse, but it is a relatively simple and powerful model which has connections with the study of speech acts but which at the same time, tries to capture the larger structures", and Sinclair and Coulthard found in the language of traditional native-speaker school classrooms a rigid patter, where teachers and pupils speak according to very fixed perceptions of their roles and where the talk can be seen to conform to highly structured sequences. This model is originally built on the basis of one type of interaction only, namely classroom interaction of a fairly traditional nature. It is important to keep this in mind, in as much as this type of discourse is characterized by a comparatively rigid structure, well-defined objectives, and an unequal distribution of status, and therefore of rights and obligations, among participants. After several years of hard work, the Birmingham Group published their findings in Sinclair and Coulthard (1975), in which they "incorporate both the linguistic and sociolinguistic traditions in their conception of classroom interaction a hierarchically structured system of ranks, analogous to the rank scale approach to sentential linguistic description" (see Halliday, 1961) and in their system, they argue for a hierarchy of rank scales for classroom discourse: Lesson, Transaction, Exchange, Move and Act, each of which constitutes the elements of the rank above, according to the rank-specific structural rules.

A lesson is marked by some observable markers, which signal the beginning or ending of a lesson. A transaction is a major stage of the lesson marked linguistically by characteristic expressions and intonation patterns such as "Right", "Ok", "Then", etc. An exchange is a sequence of moves. For example, a typical eliciting exchange is made up of three moves: initiating, responding and following up. A move is rather similar to Bellack's "teaching cycle", and can be subdivided into acts. An act is the smallest unit in the rank system. So far, 22 acts have been identified as elicitation, informative, direct, reply and so on. This system, as Sinclair and Coulthard (1975) claim, can cope with nearly all kinds of classroom discourse, and present a systematic description of classroom discourse. A full account of the system is to be included in the second chapter as the theoretical model for the analysis on the College English classroom discourse.

The work began in 1970 as a research project to investigate the structure of verbal interaction in classrooms, and from the start the aim was to anchor this study within the discipline of linguistics and to use tried linguistic techniques on new data. The Birmingham description is located within the major British linguistic framework of the time that derives its theoretical basis from Halliday's classic article "Categories of the theory of grammar".

A first assumption of "category" description is that the analytic units can be arranged on a rank-scale which implies that units are related in a "consist-of" relationship with smaller units combining with other units of the same size to form larger ones. The structure of each unit is expressed in terms of permissible combinations of units from the rank below, the structure of a clause for example being described in terms of nominal, verbal, adverbial and prepositional groups. Therefore, Sinclair et al. propose "a new level, discourse, with its own rank scale, to cope with the structure of classroom interaction": Lesson, Transaction, Exchange, Move and Act. (Coulthard, 1981: 120 - 123) Coulthard et al. see "the level of discourse as lying between the levels of grammar and non-linguistic organization" as follows (Sinclair and Coulthard, 1975: 5):

One of the preliminary steps to be taken, in any type of discourse analysis, is to collect the discourse data that systems are meant to describe. To analyze the classroom discourse, it is required that we should do data collection and transcription of classroom interaction between students and teachers. Discourse analysts typically use transcripts from audiotape or videotape recordings as their database. Many of them work from videotaped data for the reason that non-verbal information such as eye gaze, body orientation and movements may seen as communicative signals. The data on which our analysis is based on are collected from teacher-student interactions via transcriptions of videotaped College English intensive reading classes taught to groups to up to about 40 students in graduate flipped English class setting. In collection our classroom data, careful data collections have been done to incorporate a variety of lessons by different types of teachers to different types of lessons, and moreover, texts, teaching materials, teachers' sex, teachers' age, class size and grades have been taken into consideration.

Ⅲ Analysis of Classroom Discourse in Graduate Flipped English Class Setting and New Findings

These specific questions will be further discussed and answered:

(1) Does Sinclair and Coulthard's model fit in the College English Intensive Reading class? If so, to what extent does it do? If necessary, could the model in the College English class be somewhat modified?

(2) How is flipped English classroom discourse typically structured?

(3) What are the educational applications and how does it function in practicing oral English in the current study?

To the great extent, flipped English classroom discourse is highly structured in the rank scale. And from the data transcription and the descriptive analysis, it is found that such variables as teacher's age, teacher's sex, class size, teaching style have little influence on the overall structure of the classroom discourse.

The classifications of acts in Sinclair and Coulthard's model depend on acts realizations and functions. In the process of description of classroom discourse, it is found that the 22 acts in Sinclair and Coulthard's model are insufficient in the practical descriptive analysis in College English intensive reading class context. And then the following 8 new acts are recommended in the model based on the same standard of classifications.

- * Self-respond (s-resp)
- * Turn-transfer (t-t)
- * Cooperation (co)
- * Explanation (expl)
- * Broken-reply (b-rep)
- * Self-confirm (s-cf)
- * Confirm (cf)
- * Interruption (inter)

(1) Self-respond Act: Self-respond act is usually bound to an elicitation exchange. It typically follows the preceding elicitation act. It is realized by statement (a

linguistic response). Its function is to respond to the preceding elicitation made by the teacher himself or herself and to make clear his or her point to the students.

(2)(3) Turn-transfer Act and Cooperation Act: Turn-transfer act is realized by a pause or by slowing down the pace of utterance. Cooperation act is realized by statement (a linguistic response). These two acts frequently occur together in pair. They are also concerned with a contribution to the classroom discourse. As far as the function is concerned, however, they are not the kind of turn-takings caused by pupil bid to signal a desire to contribute to the discourse or teacher nomination to call or give permission to a student to contribute to the discourse. Instead, they are the kind of turn-taking where the teacher or the student or the students signals the end of a turn non-verbally, typically when the teacher provides an incomplete linguistic cue expecting the student(s) to complete the reply or when the student provides the reply but not complete for the student is not sure of the answer or even does not know the answer expecting the teacher to provide the answer.

(4) Explanation Act: Explanation act is an act performed by a teacher to explain what has been discussed above, usually functioning to make his or her point clear by giving a definition or an explanation. It usually follows the preceding follow-up move in the teaching-elicit exchange and occurs with a self-respond act at the same time.

(5) Broken-reply Act: Broken-reply Act is an act performed by a student or students in the responding move in the teaching-elicit exchange when an elicitation is made by a teacher and a reply provided by the student functions merely as a clue for the teacher to give the complete answer. It usually happens together with turn-transfer act and cooperation act. The structure follows as elicitation-broken-reply/turn-transfer-cooperation.

(6) Self-confirm Act: Self-confirm act is an act performed by a student or students to confirm the answer that the teacher provides and repeat the answer relatively or in chorus. It typically follows the preceding follow-up move in teaching-elicit exchange.

(7) Confirm Act: Confirm Act is an act performed by the teacher to confirm that the preceding reply is right or not with the whole class.

(8) Interruption Act: Interruption Act is an act performed when a teacher or a student interrupts the discourse in the classroom context. When a teacher needs to interrupt the talk or to point out errors the students makes in his or her reply, or when

the student interrupts the teacher when he or she needs to request a clear reply from the teacher or request a permission to talk.

Findings of New Exchanges

(1) Confirm Exchange:

Confirm exchange refers to confirmation exchange, which is usually bound to teacher-elicit exchange. If functions for the teacher to confirm with all the students or a student nominated by him or her that the question he or she has asked is right or not. And follow-up move seldom occurs after responding move; when it occurs occasionally, it typically functions as an evaluation (e) or comment (c) act. For example,

T: Is that right? (c-f)

SS: Right. (rep)

T: Excellent. This paragraph is an introduction to the topic. (com/s) (Text I, 90 – 92)

(2) Self-confirm Exchange:

Self-confirm exchange refers to self-confirmation exchange, which usually consists of responding move and follow-up move. It typically functions as a repetition by the student or all the students to the preceding follow-up move in the teacher-elicit exchange. The follow-up move usually is realized by a comment(c) act.

(3) Self-respond Exchange:

Self-respond exchange seems to be an elicit exchange, but the difference lies in the fact that the initiating move is not realized by a tag question but an incomplete statement in an affirmative sentence using the rising tone with a pause for students to reply. For the statement needs a reply, which may be a difficult question for students to answer, the teacher slows the pace with a pause to expect his or her students to answer. However, the teacher responds to the question himself or herself after a while.

Ⅳ Applications in Postgraduate English Teaching

Classroom discourse analysis has largely been investigated in the field of classroom research. (Stubbs, 1986; Allwright, 1981; Van Lier, 1988; Allwright and Bailey, 1991; Numan, 1992) Classroom research refers to the investigation centered on the processes of teaching and learning as they occur in classrooms. Much classroom research is actually concerned with studying classroom dialogue: in terms of teachers' questioning strategies, pupils' responses to teachers' questions, the kinds of exploratory discussion amongst groups of pupils working on tasks, and son on; if not immediately concerned with studying the dialogue itself, much work nevertheless draws its data from such sources. And much other work admits that it ought to be concerned with teacher-pupil interaction, or that study of teacher-pupil interaction would be required to provide empirical substance to theoretical points. (Michael Stubbs, 1986) In recent years a much grater role has been attributed to "interactive features of classroom behaviors", such as turn-taking, questioning and answering, negotiation of meaning, and feedback, in contrast to a more traditional view of teaching and learning which "conceptualizes classroom instruction as the conveyance of information" from the knowledgeable teachers to the "empty" and passive learner. (Chaudron, 1988: 10 – 12) Interaction is viewed as significant because it is argued that: (1) only through interaction can the learner decompose the structure and derive meaning from classroom events; (2) interaction gives learners the opportunities to incorporate structures into their own speech (the scaffolding principle); (3) the meaningfulness for learners of classroom events of any kind, whether thought of as interactive or not, will depend on the extent to which communication has been jointly constructed between the teacher and learners. (Allwright, 1984; Breen, 1985)

Classroom discourse analysis could be of great use in the study and practice of classroom teaching since it can suggest an analytical method and supporting activities, which can be used to aid understanding of the process of classroom teaching.

With a more accurate picture of natural discourse, we are in a better position to evaluate the descriptions upon which we base our teaching, the teaching materials, what goes on in the classroom, and the end products of our teaching, whether in the form of spoken or written output. The Birmingham model to analyze the College English Classroom discourse has been used and confirmed in the classroom discourse analysis. "The Birmingham model is certainly not the only valid approach to analyzing discourse, but it is a relatively simple and powerful model which has connections with the study of speech acts such as were discussed, and they found in the language of traditional native-speaker school classrooms a rigid pattern; where teachers and pupils spoken according to very fixed perceptions of their roles and where the talk could be seen to conform to highly structured sequences. "(McCathy,1991:12 – 17)

Studying teacher-student talk as a discourse system would, for example, provide one way of studying how classroom knowledge is "framed" and structured. Only by studying how teachers control the classroom discourse itself can one then study how this also controls the transmission of educational knowledge. Thus, several important questions were asked in Classroom Interaction (Malamah-Thomas, 1987: 20), "what kind of classroom interaction, what kind of participation of teacher and learner, are most likely to provide conditions whereby the exercise of individual learner initiative can lead to effective learning?" To answer these critical questions, the analysis of classroom discourse is of great necessities.

(a) How questions are asked: by first giving the question item, the teacher supplies clues to the right answer, then check whether the pupil can understand. It follows the pattern: Initiation-Response-Evaluation.

(b) How students are nominated: the tone used by teachers is encouraging and non-demanding.

(c) How students' errors are dealt with: the teacher interprets the student to tell him or her inappropriateness in the answer and asks to put it right, or confirms with the class that the answer is inappropriate.

(d) How the teacher gives feedback to students' answers: by telling them to what extent they get the answers right with encouragement.

(e) What kind of roles the teacher plays in the classroom: the classroom discourse displays three roles of teachers. The teacher as a controller, who controls not only what the students do, but also "who speaks when"—in other words, the teacher should determine goals and objectives and select and develop materials and activities; the teacher as an assessor, who not only notifies students of occurrence of errors, and helps them to put their answers right, but organizes feedback to students' performance so that they can see the extent of their success or failure; the teacher as an informer, who provides relevant information and conceptualize content for them. To sum up, the teacher is considered as course developer.

(f) What kind of pattern of teaching goes on in the classroom: the class is teacher-centered for the time being, since it is the teacher who dominates the class for the most of the time.

(g) What the general classroom atmosphere is like: the teaching and learning activities should go on in an encouraging and non-demanding manner.

V Expanding the Patterns of Classroom Interaction

It should be clear at this point that the way in which the patterns of communication are established and maintained in language classrooms is not random. Teachers, by virtue of the ways they use language, have the authority to retain control over both the content and structure of classroom communication. Sometimes, teachers tightly control the topic they hold in class for the special purpose of teaching; that is, they control the relevant information of discussion to the topic, who may participate in the discussion, when and in what form. At other times, they grant varying degree of control to their students by allowing them to choose the topic of discussion, discuss freely in a certain degree, choose the time and sequence to speak and participate. Therefore, the patterns of classroom communication depend largely on how teachers use their classroom language to control the content and structure of classroom activities.

Actually, establishing and maintaining the patterns or the structure of classroom interaction is, to a greater or lesser degree, to find an appropriate way to make teachers and students a "joint venture". (Johnson, 1995: 145) that is, teachers control the content and structure of classroom interaction, and students interpret and respond to what teachers say and do.

If teachers wish to promote classroom interaction in language classroom, they need to allow for greater variability in the patterns of classroom interaction so as to maximize students' linguistic and interactional competencies and create more opportunities for students to participate in classroom event for the ease of classroom language teaching and learning and language acquisition. Trueba (1989) claims it is the teachers' responsibility to adjust their instruction practices to the competencies of their students in order to provide appropriate and effective classroom instruction. (Johnson, 1995: 146)

Some proposals will be advanced in the paper to promote interaction in the language classroom: the prerequisite is that teachers must establish an atmosphere in the classroom that is encouraging, supportive, and accepting of any and all student contribution. This means accepting student contributions not as right or wrong answers but, as Hymes (1981) suggests, as an indication of where students are, what students understand, and how they have made sense of what they are learning. First of all, teachers should enact ways in which they make it possible for learners to participate in classroom interaction that are beyond their current linguistic ability level, which represents an important source of comprehensible input for language acquisition in that they provide language that is adjusted to students' current level of language proficiency and enable them to participate in meaningful interaction. When teachers do so, they have joint responsibility with students for the interaction or task, support as they make sense of the new information, adapt that support to match students' linguistic and interactional competencies, provide opportunities for students to acquire necessary language skills and to foster their participation.

Second, teachers should have the ability and responsibility to make the classroom activities predictable. When the students know exactly what is expected in the language class and have opportunity to make full preparations before the class or in class, they are more willing to participate in the language classroom interaction. Making classroom activities predictable means giving students great opportunity to prepare for what teachers expect their students to say and do in class. If teachers give the opportunity for students to use language to express themselves clearly and encourage them to do so in public, students will be encouraged to participate in class activities and their language ability will surely be enhanced.

Third, teachers should create more opportunities for students work in small groups or in pair. Barnes (1969) proposes that "small group activities are more conducive to using language for learning since they tend to distance teacher's control over the patterns of communication". Moreover, small group activities enable students to take a more active role in what they are learning, as well as have more opportunities to contribute to and help formulate the information that is generated and learned. However, several factors must be taken into consideration. The first factor is students' feeling of competence. The extent to which students are willing to participate in and contribute to small group activities depends on how they think their contributions will be received. To some extent, "these perceptions are linked to the perceived status and abilities of individual group members." That is, if a student is perceived by his or her peers as more competent, group members may be more likely to defer to this student, thus limiting their own opportunities for interaction and influence in the group. And teachers can bolster up students' feelings of competence by consistently accepting their contributions and showing that they value those contributions by making them part of the instructional content. The second factor is establishing common ground. Students should know and have experienced some information in common before they are given the opportunities to filter the new information in class. Students in small group can be free to reunderstand and reorganize new information with their peers, otherwise they will only learn to imitate and memorize what teachers tell them instead of making good sense of the information on their own. The third factor is focusing students' attention on specific ideas, concepts, or elements of the instructional content. Teachers should focus students' attention on what is important in their lectures and the features of the information and meanwhile teachers should encourage their students to bring about their own questions on the new information and understand it. The fourth factor is the pace of teaching. Teachers should give more time to their students for thinking about the new information and using the language during small group learning. Thus, ample time should be allotted for students to use new language information as a carrier to express themselves before being asked in public.

Reference

[1] Allwright, Dick & Bailey, Kathleen M. *Focus on the Language Classroom: An Introduction to Classroom Research for Language Teacher* [M]. Cambridge: Cambridge University Press, 1991.

[2] Allwright, Dick. *Observation in the Language Classroom* [M]. London: Longman, 1988.

[3] Barnes, D. *Language in the Secondary Classroom.* In Language, the Learner and the School. Harmondsworth: Penguin Books, 1976.

[4] Carter, R. *Introducing Applied Linguistics* [M]. London: Penguin, 1993.

[5] Chaudron, Craig. *Second Language Classrooms: Research on Teaching and Learning* [M]. Cambridge: Cambridge University Press, 1988.

[6] Coulthard, R. M. *An Introduction to Discourse Analysis* [M]. London: Longman, 1981.

[7] Coulthard, R. M. & Montgomery, M. *Studies in Discourse Analysis.* London: RKP, 1981.

[8] Coulthard, R. M. & Carmen R. C. *Texts and Practices: Reading in Critical Discourse Analysis*[M]. London:RKP,1996.

[9] Halliday, M. A. K. *An Introduction to Functional Grammar*, 2nd ed. London: Edward Arnold,1994.

[10] Hatch, E. *Discourse and Language Education* [M]. Cambridge: Cambridge University Press,1992.

[11] Hymes, D. *Functions of Language in the Classroom*[M]. New York: Teachers College Press,1981.

[12] MaCarthy, Michael. *Discourse Analysis for Language Teachers* [M]. Cambridge: Cambridge University Press,1991.

[13] Numan, David. *Second Language Teaching and Learning*[M]. Boston: Heinle & Heinle Publishers,1999.

[14] Stubbs, M. *Educational Linguistics*[M]. Oxford: Basil Blackwell,1986.

[15] Van Lier, Leo. *The Classroom and the Language Learner: Ethnography and Second Language Classroom Research*[M]. London: Longman,1988.

An Investigation into Intercultural Literacy of Chinese College Students

首都经济贸易大学外国语学院　郝钦海

Abstract: The essence of the language education is to cultivate cultural literacy. And intercultural literacy is what foreign language education is intended to achieve. This paper is aimed to offer some advice on how to foster the intercultural literacy in foreign language teaching based on the analysis of a survey conducted among college students on intercultural awareness, intercultural communication competence and intercultural knowledge in order to perfect foreign language education.

Key Words: intercultural literacy; intercultural awareness; intercultural communication competence; foreign language teaching

I　Introduction

The 21st century witnesses a dramatically changing world in the process of globalization, with countries more interconnected with and interdependent on each other. Globalization refers to supranational ideas and processes which are borderless, beyond nations or states, resulting in the situation where the world's economies, societies and cultures are getting more and more interlinked (Anne h., 1999). Since social, cultural and community contexts shape every aspect of education and influence the very nature and form of education, "education must operate within prescribed parameters and deliver certain outcomes" (Daphne Meadmore et al, 1999). Therefore, in the context of globalization, globalizing education should be more concerned about the cultivation of intercultural literacy. Intercultural literacy is defined as the understandings, attitudes, competencies and identities which enable effective participation in a cross-cultural setting. As such it is presented as a crucial literacy for the globalised world of the twenty-first century.

Ⅱ Literature Review

Some scholars did some research on intercultural literacy in language education. Cakmak (1989) argues that "A contextually adaptable agenda for promoting intercultural literacy through English can be adapted in different contexts to generate various communicative activities." MacLauchlan (1992) introduced an English language literacy project which is an extension program of the University of Regina, formally known as the Cross Cultural Intergenerational Pilot Project. Boschetto (1983) introduced a way of promoting intercultural literacy in the Michigan Technological University that was American foreign language students and foreign students enrolled at the institution to be paired for tutoring in cultural facts and awareness. In China, the paper by Zhou Xiaolin (2002) shows that the reform in the syllabus, teaching materials and teacher training is key to cultural literacy. Qi Mingjun (2006) recognizes the role of the critical intercultural literacy in foreign language education. Liu Juan (2007) provides several suggestions on cultivating the college students' intercultural communicative awareness.

However, up to now, no paper focuses on the present situation of Chinese students' intercultural literacy. Therefore, based on the survey of students' intercultural literacy, this paper is intended to offer some advice on foreign language education to enhance students' intercultural literacy, which is helpful to language education and students' cultivation of all-rounded quality.

Ⅲ Methods

In order to shed light on the present situation of Chinese college students' intercultural literacy, we conducted a survey involving 183 students altogether, with 76 male and 107 female students. They are sophomores in several colleges in Beijing, and willing to participate in the survey. These students have finished College English level 1 and 2, and are now studying level 3. So they all have been studying English for nearly twelve years.

Following the theoretical framework originating from Young Yum Kim's structural model of factors influencing intercultural adaptation and guided by Gao Yihong's idea of "going across" and "going beyond" cultures proposed as two levels of intercultural communication competence development, we designed a questionnaire, listing in it 40 items in three categories: intercultural awareness, intercultural communication competence as well as intercultural knowledge. The students are expected to choose one correct answer from the four choices under each item. The following table demonstrates the content of the questionnaire:

Table 1: the content of the questions

	intercultural awareness	items	intercultural communication competence	items	intercultural knowledge	items
content	intercultural psychology	1	gifts acceptance and giving	3	system of government	1
	value system	1	dating and appointment	1	geography	2
	ethnocentric attitude	1	nonverbal communication	7	literature	2
	collectivism/individualism	1	verbal communication	9	history	1
	behavior	1	lady priority	2	race	1
	problem recognition	1	paying a visit/receiving a guest/table manners	5		
Total		6		27		7

From the table, it is obvious that the questionnaire mainly covers the content of the first two sublevels of the cognitive and behaviorist aspects, namely. the "going across" level as Gao proposed. The affective aspect is closely related to intercultural awareness, attributed to "going beyond" level. The questions originate mainly from three kinds of resources: 1, intercultural communication experience of the students and teachers; 2, intercultural communication experience of the native speakers of the target culture who are teaching in China; 3, the findings of some researches.

The questionnaires were distributed to 183 students who were required to answer the questions of the survey in class for about 60 minutes. All the sample questionnaires were returned and all are credible.

Ⅳ Results and Findings

After collecting the questionnaire, analysis were made about the difficulty and problems students have in intercultural communication. As is shown in Table 2, the most striking finding can be traced to intercultural awareness. The mistakes students make nearly account for half of the questions, implying the weakness in and the shortage of the knowledge of intercultural awareness may be one of the major factors to affect students' promotion in intercultural literacy. Despite the fact that they have been engaged in the study of English for at least 12 years, the participants in the research are not successful in fostering their intercultural awareness and often fail to respond appropriately in a intercultural communication contexts. It illustrates the claim made by Gao Yihong (2002) that, whether corresponding courses are offered or not, it is not a easy job in language education to cultivate intercultural awareness in a short time. Only exposed to and involved in the target culture for quite a long time, can we reach the stage of "going beyond" cultures.

Table 2

items \ results \ type	average amount of mistakes	percentage of mistakes
intercultural awareness	3.04	50.71%
intercultural communication competence	10.76	39.85%
intercultural knowledge	2.82	40.29%

The result also reflects the idea of "habitus" theory. In Bourdieu's work (1977), habitus can be defined as a system of durable and transposable "dispositions" (lasting, acquired schemes of perception, thought and action). The individual agent develops these dispositions in response to the determining structures (such as class, family, and education) and external conditions (fields) they encounter. So to foster cultural awareness, educational institute should make efforts to reform the structure of education. In terms of foreign language education, the atmosphere and condition of language and culture aqcuisition play a significant role in it.

Table 3 demonstrates the first three items in which student got the lowest score. As is shown in the table, about half of the students are not psychological well-being in intercultural communicative context. When talking to native speakers of other cultures, they tend to be introvert and behave themselves in shyness, fearing to address others or be addressed to. Without doubt, it is closely related to Chinese culture where modest is highly valued, individualism is constrained and people are encouraged not to be prominent among others.

Table 3

	Number of students with wrong answers	Percentage
Intercultural psychology	92	50. 27%
Problem recognition	84	45. 90%
Collectivism/individualism	82	44. 80%

With regards to the next two items, almost the same percentage of students are found to have intercultural communication failure in the corresponding contexts. Unaware of the difference between native culture and other cultures, they are not alert to the problems existing in their communication, thus failing to adjust themselves to the specific situation. Furthermore, although Chinese culture advocates collectivism and in western culture, individualism enjoys the priority, team work and cooperation is highly thought of both in western and Chinese cultures. However, many students have the misunderstanding that only individualism is boosted in the target culture.

From what have been discussed above, it is self-evident that to overcome those problems in language learning, intercultural literacy should be enhanced by paying more attention to those problems and taking greater measures to sharpen their intercultural awareness and facilitate their acquisition of the target culture.

V Discussion and Suggestions

Educators have called for basing language instruction on a definition of language as ideological social practice, rather than autonomous linguistic skills (Gee, 1992; Street, 1984, 1995). As a social practice, language always involves linguistic skills, but the skills are consequences of participating in the social practice, or discourse, as a member of the cultural community. Language skills cannot be taught in isolation of a discourse-practice with the hopes of transferring them into some future participation in the practice. Instead, you must engage in the communicative activity and develop sociolinguistic as well as psycholinguistic knowledge in how the language functions in cultural contexts of experience. Therefore, the learning and teaching are to be shaped and transformed for the cultivation of intercultural literacy.

"In foreign language and culture acquisition the notion of intercultural literacy would mean that only by accumulating shared symbols in L2 and C2 and in L1 and C1 learners will be able to communicate effectively with members of a foreign language community." (Maria W. ,2003) Intercultural literacy is now the goal of foreign language education. Both the objectives of a global approach and the fact that China is facing economic integration call forth the implementation of cultivating students' intercultural literacy, if not in all school subjects at least in foreign language teaching. However, the approach to achieve it differs greatly. The foreign culture approach focuses on the target country culture (C2) and neither references to the home culture (C1) nor to relations between C2 and C1 are made. The intercultural approach supposedly replaced the foreign cultural approach in the 1980s (Risager 1998), its main focus is on C2 but it also deals with C1 and the relations between the two. These relations include aspects of dominance, and intercultural attitudes leading to the exchange of ideas, information, and interpersonal actions between persons from different groups or nations. Kramsch calls it "dialectic", meaning a dialogue between two conflicting viewpoints. It is the dialogue that allows for reaching a common ground, when differences are recognised and accepted (1993). Teaching of culture becomes, then, an "*interpersonal process*" (1993) that leads to an understanding of what is foreign.

What has to be stressed is that in foreign language education we should place emphasis on national identity and as comparisons between C2 and C1 are incorporated this presumably develops a *reflective attitude* towards C1 in learners. additionally notes that it includes a reflection on both cultures, C1 and C2, thus establishing a "sphere of inteculturality" as Kramsch proposes (1998).

Intercultural literacy is an urgent need in today's world of global interdependency. A contextually adaptable agenda for promoting intercultural literacy through English can be adapted in different contexts to generate various communicative activities. Teachers and students can collaborate to work towards becoming intercultural citizens, based on age, needs, experiences, levels, and interests. Intercultural literacy should promote conversation between Chinese and Western cultures. Through an intercultural English language curriculum Chinese and Western cultures engage in dialogue and verbal and nonverbal means become meaningful for exchanging ideas and alternate world views. Language use becomes efficient, enjoyable, and purposeful as students perceive that even a foreign language is only a tool for various learning.

The establishment of intercultural communication atmosphere is of great importance. With the help of ICT, it is possible for Chinese learners of English to be exposed to the authentic or simulated intercultural contexts and to be directed to access to TV program, internet, videos to get intercultural knowledge. Intercultural critical literacy with print and media texts easily shared with today's digital technologies is essential in our increasingly multicultural and international lives in which our acts of language, literacy, and media often create divisions and dislikes, instead of providing opportunities to negotiate shared meaning through our cultural differences.

References

[1] Anne H. & Jo-Anne F. *Globalisation, postcolonialism and educational change*. In Peter, Bruce and Daphne. *Understanding education context and agendas for the new millennium.* Australia: Person Education, 1999.

[2] Bourdieu, P. *Outline of a Theory of Practice* [M]. Cambridge University Press, 1977.

[3] Boschetto, S. M. *Foreign Students and the Tutoring Practicum: Intercultural Literacy for Students of Language and Culture beyond the Classroom*, 1983.

[4] Ben W., Jasin P. & Ross B. *Culture and Education*, 2007.

[5] Cakmak, S. *English Literacy Redefined: Promoting Intercultural Literacy through English as a Search for Better Cross-Cultural Understanding and Communications.*

[6] Peter, Bruce, Daphne. *Understanding Education: Contexts and Agendas for the New Millennium* [*M*]. Australia: Person Education, 1999.

[7] Gee, James. *What is Literacy?* In P. Shannon (Ed.), *Becoming Political: Readings and writings in the politics of literacy education*, 21 – 41. Portsmouth, NH: Heinmann, 1992.

[8] Kim, Y. Y. *Becoming intercultural: An Integrative Theory of Communication*

Research[M]. (International and Intercultural Communication Annual, Vol. 8) Beverly Hills, Calif. :Sage Publications, Inc. ,2001.

[9] Kramsch, Claire. *Context and Culture in Language Teaching* [M]. Oxford: Oxford University Press, 1993.

[10] Kramsch, C. *The privilege of the intercultural speaker.* In M. Byram and M. Fleming (Eds), *Language Learning in Intercultural Perspective: approaches through drama and ethnography*, 16 – 31. Cambridge: Cambridge University Press, 1998.

[11] MacLauchlan, B. *Bringing Our Stories Home.* An English Language Literacy Project of the Intercultural Grandmothers Uniting, 1992.

[12] Maria W. , 2003, Towards Intercultural Literacy in a Polish FL Classroom http://elt. britcoun. org. pl/elt/r_ilit. htm

[13] Risager, Karen. *Critique of textbook criticism.* In Dorthe Albrechtsen, Birgit Henriksen, Inter M. Mees og Erik Poulsen (eds.), *Perspectives on Foreign and Second Language Pedagogy.* Odense: Odense University Press, 1998.

[14] Street, B. *Literacy in theory and practice*[M]. New York: Cambridge University Press, 1984.

[15] Street. B. *Social Literacies: Critical approaches to literacy development, ethnography, and education*[M]. New York: Longman, 1995.

[16]高一虹. 语言文化差异的认识与超越[M]. 北京:外语教学与研究出版社,2000.

[17]高一虹. 跨文化交际能力的培养:"跨越"与"超越"[J]. 外语与外语教学,2002(27).

[18]刘娟. 大学英语教学与跨文化素养的培养[J]. 大理学院学报,2007(30).

以应用能力为导向的大学英语口语教学

首都经济贸易大学外国语学院　刘燕梅

摘　要:提高大学英语应用能力是北京市教委根据本市大学英语教学改革发展的需求,提出的新一轮大学英语教学改革的要求。据此,教委还推出相应的大学英语应用能力口语测试(TEP:Test of English Proficiency Oral)。为提高大学生英语口语表达能力,也为应对考试,笔者在课堂教学上进行了一些有针对性的改革。

关键词:应用能力;口语教学;教学改革;国际化人才培养

Abstract: The new round of college English reform launched by Beijing Educational Committee generates the idea of enhancing college students' application competence. Therefore, TEP (Test of English Proficiency Oral), a test aims to boost students' oral English proficiency appeared. In order to meet the new requirement and improve students' oral ability, some new classroom teaching activities have been putting into action.

Key Words: application competence; oral English teaching; teaching reform; cultivation of internationalized human resources

一、背景

作为英语综合能力的重要组成部分,大学生英语口语应用能力越来越受到社会各方面的关注。令人感到沮丧的是,虽然我们的教师花费了大量的时间和精力用来改善、提高学生的口语表达,但口语教学却一直是我国大学英语教学的薄弱环节。摆脱"哑巴英语",走出"虽然学英语多年,但不能用英语自由表达自己想法"的尴尬局面已成为广大英语教师在当今形势下不得不思考并积极探索的问题。

中国社会正处于一个前所未有的机遇多多的时代,无论是从习近平总书记提出的"一带一路"出发,还是我国中长期发展规划的角度考虑,提高大学英语应用能力都是一个亟待解决的问题。为探索接轨国际、立足国情、契合校情的改革发展之路,绘制好学校未来五年的发展蓝图,实现我校建设"国内一流"、"国际知名"财经大学的战略目标,外国语学院也在去年出台了"首都经济贸易大学公共外语应用能力培养改革实施方案(草案)(2015)",草案中明确提到"以学生的有效跨文化交际能力培养为核心,着力提高学生的听力、口语、写作、翻译等语言应用能力和学术英语交流能力,进一步提高学生的中西人文素养,适应国际化背景下社会和经济发展的需要。”

由此可见,在课堂教学中加强学生的口语学习,提升学生的口语表达能力不但顺应潮流,也满足国家、社会和学生职业生涯发展的需求。借北京市教委于2013年6月推出的大学英语应用能力口语测试这一契机,为提高大学生英语口语表达能力,也为应对考试,笔者在课堂教学上进行了一些有针对性的改革。

二、我校英语口语教学现状

作为北京市属重点院校,首都经济贸易大学的大学英语教学一直处于改革的最前沿。早在2007年,外国语学院教师就根据“大学英语课程教学要求”(2007)制定了针对首都经济贸易大学学生的公共外语学习大纲。本着更新教学内容、优化课程体系的改革宗旨,从2007年开始,我校的大学英语课一直采用“2+2+1”新框架构思,即将大学英语课程学习分为读写、听说和课外自主学习三个部分,教学重心放在读写和听说上,每周安排两个学时的读写和两个学时的听说课程,让学生根据自己的需求安排另一个学时的自主学习。这种教学模式兼顾课堂教学与学生自主学习,能够从教学内容和课程体系的角度兼顾到学生的语言基础和语言运用能力两个方面的需求,并能让学生根据自己的情况安排学习。这一课程模式已经是在当时新出台的“大学英语课程教学要求”(2007)的基础上制定的。

在每周两节的听说课上,教师以外语教学与研究出版社的《新视野大学英语视听说教程》为教材,让学生根据每一单元不同的主题进行相应的听说练习。受限于学生人数、学生水平和教学内容等诸方面的因素,课堂教学实际上还是听为主、说为辅。虽说每学期都有相应的口语考试,但是内容也基本是课本内容的重现,没有达到真正的口语考试的水平。

然而随着时代的进步、社会需求的变化和学生英语学习情况的更迭,运行了8年的大纲和教学模式也需要进行调整以达到适应形势的需求。国家教委在2015年提出的“大学英语教学指南”(征求意见稿)明确提出了对口语表达能力的要求:

基础目标:能就日常话题用英语进行简短但多话轮的交谈;能对一般性时间和物体进行简单的叙述或描述;能就某一主题进行简单的讨论;经准备后能就所熟悉的话题做简短发言,表达结构清楚,语音、语调、语法等基本符合交际规范。能在交谈中使用基本的会话技巧。

提高目标:能用英语就一般性话题进行比较流利的会话;能较好地表达个人意

见、情感、观点等;能陈述事实、理由和描述事件或物品等;能够就熟悉的观点、概念、理论等进行阐述、解释、比较、总结等,语言组织结构清楚,语音、语调基本得体。能较好地使用口语表达技巧。

发展目标:能较为流利、准确地就一般或专业性话题进行对话或讨论;能用简练的语言概括篇幅较长、有一定语言难度的文本或讲话;能在国际会议和专业交流中宣读论文并参加讨论。能参与商务谈判、产品宣传等活动。能恰当地使用口语表达技巧。

三、我的课堂

根据学生英语水平的变化和新的英语学习要求,我对教学班的口语课堂教学进行了调整:每周一次的听说课上用一节课时间来完成视听说课本上的教学任务,一节课完全交给口语课堂。以课程导入、课堂互动、创造语言环境、自主学习、合作学习、四六级考试和社会上其他学生关注的热点考试、新闻和跨文化交际等为切入口,目的是在课堂上就给学生实操的机会,提高口语表达能力。除此之外,在读写课和听力课上也抓住一切机会给学生增加口语练习的机会。

依托先进的信息技术,尤其是网络技术,充分利用教室内外、校内外等多方面资源,增加学生练习英语口语的机会。在过去的一年中,我的听说课在兼顾基本的会话技能、听说技巧和跨文化语言表达策略的讲授的情况下,尽可能多地提供机会让学生练习口语表达;把原来的课本听力内容放到课下,借助网络听力学习平台完成课本上听力练习;根据需求在课堂上下辅以 CCTV、CRI、VOA、BBC、National Geography、电影、电视片段等原声视听材料。通过改善教学检测手段,加大平时口语成绩的方法,为学生提高口语表达助力:增加平时口语表达的内容,通过在两年学习的不同阶段要求学生进行背诵、复述、课堂个人展示、对话、讨论、小辩论、新闻评述等课堂活动,强化口语学习;把握时代脉搏,抓住每年“两会”的契机,为学生提供与时俱进的英语政治、经济、社会新闻;利用学校和各个院系大力开展第二课堂的机会,鼓励并指导学生参加校内校外的英语竞赛、口语活动,力争通过多渠道激励学生用英语进行口语表达,进而达到提高英语口语水平的目的。

根据学生年龄特点和喜好,我把每周的视听说课按照不同教学目的精细划分为课前文化导入、相关主题信息、主题词汇拓展、听力技巧训练、精听练习、主旨深化、创造性思维训练和效果检测几大部分,通过包括师生、学生之间的问答、讲授、试听、对话、讨论、复述和辩论等环节的课堂活动让学生达到有效提高听说技能的目的。

提倡合作学习。我在课上通常让学生通过开展两人或四人小组活动,搭建起互助交流的英语学习平台。这种课堂活动既解决了学生多,老师不能兼顾,致使一大部分学生无事可做的问题,也促进了学生之间的合作学习。大部分学生都很认可并适应这种轻松、对等的交流方式,学生之间的平等对话和交流互动给予了他们自信;没有了焦虑感的学习氛围,使学生们更经常地感受到自己和同学的进步,提高了自信心,也增强了学习英语的主动性。

四、问题

通过一段时间的改革,我的英语口语课堂教学内容充实了,教学手段丰富了,学生的学习积极性也有了不同程度的提高,这是可喜的一面。但是与“大学英语教学指南”(征求意见稿)明确提出的对口语表达能力的要求还是有差距的,而且随之也产生了一些问题。

首先,大量的补充材料的介入,虽然填补了课本的不足,但是也很大地冲击了课本的讲授,有时甚至无法完成教学大纲上要求的内容。这在现行的考试系统和内容下,对学生的成绩或多或少都有一定影响。

其次,大量的课堂口语活动对学习自觉性和自主性不强的学生来说,非但没有促进,反倒纵容了他们的惰性,影响了他们的英语学习。

第三,作为传统的教师,很多必须借助高科技手段和现代信息技术才能利用的音频、视频资料的获得耗费了我很大的精力,也占用了很多的备课时间。

尽管存在着这种或那种的问题,我还是认为我的改革尝试是成功的。提高学生的英语水平,加强学生口语表达能力是大学英语多年来坚持不懈的目标。2010年颁布的《国家中长期教育改革和发展规划纲要(2010—2020)》关于高等教育人才培养目标的论述里指出,在“培养高素质专门人才和拔尖创新人才”的基础上,鼓励高等教育的国际交流合作,为“适应国家经济社会对外开放的要求,培养大批具有国际视野,通晓国际规则,能够通晓国际事务和国际竞争的国际化人才”。

我在听说课上施行的这些教学改革实践虽然还不足以让学生的英语表达在短时间内达到大幅提升,但教学内容和模式的变革至少能使学生提高英语学习的兴趣,引导并培养学生对英语口语的关注,鼓励学生进行更高、更深层次的学习探索,进而逐步提高学生英语语言应用能力。

参考文献:

[1]国家中长期教育改革和发展规划纲要(2010—2020年)

[2]大学英语课程教学要求(2007)
[3]大学英语教学指南(2015)(征求意见稿)
[4]首都经济贸易大学"十二五"规划(2015)
[5]首都经济贸易大学公共外语应用能力培养改革实施方案(2015)(讨论稿)

L' enseignement de la deuxième langue étrangère en milieu institutionnel chinois: vers un apprentissage "pour la vie"

首都经济贸易大学外国语学院　栾婷

中文摘要:高校英语专业第二外语课一直是英语专业学生的必修课,在教育部设置的英语专业本科培养方案中有明确要求。而法语作为仅次于英语的世界第二大通用语,在第二外语课上受到学生格外的青睐。目前,第二外语(法语)课程平均开设三个学期,每周2~4课时。课程使用国人自编的教材,课堂活动以语法讲解和句型操练为重点,忽视学生的交际能力和跨文化能力,导致学生对法语及法语课的兴趣日益减少,教学效果欠佳。课程结束后,学生再也不愿继续自主学习法语。为了改善这一状况,必须重新定义第二外语(法语)的教学目标,即从教授语法调整为培养学生的跨文化能力及自主学习能力。课上以听说活动为主线,配以中西文化对比;大量使用原版材料,为学生创造交际环境;课下开设法语第二课堂,组织文化交流活动,举办法语角,定期开办文化讲座、讨论……这样的课程新颖、有趣、实用,将极大吸引学生,使法语学习成为他们一生的兴趣,即使课程结束,也会坚持自主学习。

法语摘要: L' apprentissage d' une deuxième langue étrangère est obligatoire pour les étudiants spécialisés en anglais, qui est leur première langue étrangère. Parmi des nombreux choix proposés par les institutions, la langue française est souvent la préférée des étudiants. Le cours du français deuxième langue étrangère dure trois semestres (12 mois au total), à raison de deux à quatre heures par semaine. Les manuels les plus utilisés sont les manuels "traditionnels" qui mettent l' accent sur la grammaire et les exercices structuraux, en négligeant les compétences communicatives et socio-culturelles des étudiants. Les enseignants, eux, utilisent également les méthodes traditionnelles. Tout cela rend la langue française "difficile, monotone, inutile" et le cours de français "ennuyeux" chez les étudiants. Les cours terminés, ils n' ont plus envie de continuer à apprendre le français, même si des occasions leur sont offertes.

Pour améliorer cette situation, il faudrait redéfinir les objectifs de l' enseignement de la deuxième langue étrangère: il ne doit pas s' agir d' "acquérir" quelques règles grammaticales, mais il devrait viser à améliorer les compétences interculturelles et les compétences d'auto-apprentissage des étudiants. Pour ce faire: les contenus et les modalités de cours doivent être adaptés: prendre en considération des connaissances culturelles, organiser des visites, des rencontres, des conférences thématiques, introduire en cours les documents authentiques (chanson, roman, film...), utiliser les activités ludiques et le travail en groupe, profiter de l'internet pour des échanges avec les francophones et des exercices interactifs en ligne... Un tel cours, vif et ludique, intéressera et motivera les étudiants, de telle sorte qu'ils garderont un intérêt pour la langue française et continueront à l'apprendre après leurs études universitaires et même pour toute leur vie.

Introduction

Le cours de deuxième langue étrangère est un cours obligatoire pour les étudiants spécialisés en anglais, qui est leur première langue étrangère. Parmi des nombreux choix proposés par les institutions, la langue française est souvent la préférée des étudiants. Pourtant, par des raisons multiples, le cours du Français Langue Etrangère est considéré comme "ennuyeux" et il manque d'efficacité. Dans ce présent texte, nous allons d'abord voir le statut de ce cours de deuxième langue étrangère, puis analyser les difficultés actuelles à partir d'une enquête. A la fin, je propose de guider les étudiants vers un apprentissage "pour la vie". C'est également pour moi un moyen d'améliorer l'efficacité de l'enseignement.

I. Qu'est-ce que la deuxième langue étrangère?

En Chine, sauf dans quelques écoles des langues très rares, les élèves apprennent une seule langue étrangère de l'école primaire jusqu'au lycée. C'est l'Anglais. L'Anglais est aussi une matière obligatoire dans le Gaokao, le bac chinois. A l'Université, l'Anglais reste la seule langue obligatoire. Mais ceux qui ont choisi l'Anglais comme spécialité doivent apprendre une deuxième langue étrangère. Donc, quand on parle de l'enseignement de la deuxième langue étrangère, il s'agit des cours de langue autre que l'Anglais pour les étudiants spécialisés en anglais.

Quelles sont les langues offertes, comme deuxième langue étrangère? Cela dépend des universités. D'après les informations publiées sur le site internet des universités, les langues que l'on trouve le plus souvent sont le français, le japonais, et le russe. Le français, parce que c'est souvent le "chouchou" des étudiants, grâce à l'image romantique de la France et de sa culture; le japonais, parce que c'est proche de la langue chinoise et les BD et les dessins animés japonais sont très populaires chez les jeunes étudiants; le russe, c'est plutôt lié à l'histoire de la Chine du temps de l'ancienne Union Soviétique. Dans les années 90, on a formé beaucoup d'enseignants de russe, qui travaillent maintenant dans des établissements chinois. Mais aujourd'hui, le russe est moins important et donc moins reconnu chez les étudiants. A part cela, on trouve aussi l'espagnol, le coréen, l'allemand ou l'italien que les universités proposent aux étudiants comme seconde langue étrangère.

Les cours durent souvent 3 ou 4 semestres, à raison de 2 à 4 heures par semaine. Le cursus varie selon les établissements. Dans les universités qui prennent en compte les compétences de langues des étudiants, le nombre de cours est plus important, soit plus de 250h en deux ans. C'est le cas de l'Université des Langues Etrangères de Pékin, de l'Université des Affaires Etrangères, etc; dans d'autres université comme par exemple l'université de l'Economie et du Commerce de Pékin, ou l'Université Centrale des Finances, les étudiants ont moins de cours de langues, parce qu'ils apprennent aussi l'Economie, la Finance, les statistiques, etc. Par conséquent, les cours de langues sont moins importants.

II. Situations actuelles du cours de deuxième langue étrangère

Avant de continuer, on pourrait sans doute se demander: pourquoi exige-t-on une deuxième langue étrangère aux étudiants d'anglais ? Cette décision relève du Ministère de l'Education Chinois en 1949. On pensait que si les étudiants en anglais connaissaient une autre langue étrangère, ils seraient plus compétents dans l'usage de l'anglais. Mais maintenant, le temps change, les situations des cours de deuxième langue étrangère changent également. D'un côté, c'est un cours obligatoire, de l'autre côté, les étudiants ne l'acceptent plus forcément volontier, et l'efficacité des cours est loin d'être satisfaisante. Je prends l'exemple du français deuxième langue étrangère. J'ai fait une enquête auprès des 80 étudiants qui ont choisi le français comme deuxième langue étrangère dans mon établissement. On relève 3 paradoxes:

D'abord, il n'y a qu'un étudiant qui n'aime pas la langue française, mais 17 avouent qu'ils n'aiment pas le cours de français, parce que le français est "trop compliqué" et "trop difficile". En plus 80% ne sont pas satisfaits de leur niveau de langue. Il est donc temps de réfléchir sur le contenu du cours, les méthodes d'enseignement et l'efficacité des cours.

Deuxièmement, l'intérêt et la curiosité pour la langue et la culture françaises constituent la première motivation d'apprentissage. Mais au fil du temps, cet intérêt diminue. Cela explique pourquoi les étudiants consacent de moins en moins de temps sur le français. On peut donc se demander: comment maintenir l'intérêt des étudiants pour cette langue, et les pousser à travailler plus en dehors des cours ?

Enfin, c'est la culture française qui les attire le plus, mais pas la langue elle-même; Ce qu'ils attendent le plus de nos cours de français, c'est de pouvoir communiquer avec les francophones, mais pas comprendre la grammaire française ou lire les textes en français. Pourtant, la grammaire occupe toujours la place la plus importante dans l'enseignement. Comment, alors, réajuster nos cours pour satisfaire les besoins et les attentes des étudiants ?

III. Vers un apprentissage "pour la vie".

Compte tenu du statut et de la situation actuelle de l'enseignement de la deuxième langue étrangère, je propose un cours de deuxième langue étrangère orienté vers un apprentissage pour toute la vie. Qu'est-ce qu'un apprentissage pour la vie ? Les étudiants ont toute leur vie et leur carrière devant eux. Ils commencent à apprendre une deuxième langue étrangère à l'université. En tant qu'enseignant, si on ne pense qu'à ces 250 h de cours, on risque de tomber facilement dans l'enseignement de la grammaire avec la méthodologie traditionnelle. Ainsi, au bout de 2 ans, les étudiants n'ont plus d'intérêt ni d'envie pour cette langue. Leurs études s'arrêtent là. A mon avis, les études à l'université ne devraient pas être la fin de l'apprentissage de la 2e langue étrangère, mais en être le début. Avec les cours, ils vont connaître la langue, aimer cette langue, garder même augmente l'intérêt pour cette langue, si bien qu'ils vont continuer à l'apprendre après les études universitaire et pour toujours. L'apprentissage de la 2e langue étrangère, ce n'est pas l'affaire de 3 ou 4 semestres, mais c'est un plaisir pour toute la vie.

Pour parvenir à ce but, pour que le français soit l'ami des étudiants pour toute la vie, beaucoup de changements doivent être opérés. Faute du temps, je voudrais partager avec vous simplement deux points que je trouve extrêmement importants: maintenir l'intérêt des étudiants, et satisfaire les attentes sur la culture.

3.1 Intérêts pour l'apprentissage

En ce qui concern l'intérêt des étudiants pour la langue, l'enquête nous montre déjà que c'est la plus grande motivation des étudiants, en plus en chinois nous avons un proverbe: l'intérêt est le meilleur professeur. Mais au fur et à mesure, l'intérêt diminue, puis disparaît. C'est vraiment dommage. Bien sûr les raisons sont multiples, on pourrait en discuter la prochaine fois. Ici, je propose seulement deux "moyens" que je trouve nécessaires pour sauvegarder l'intérêt des étudiants:

—Eviter l'image "difficile" de la langue. Cela est surtout important pour le cours de français. Tout le monde dit que le français est difficile, et comme l'enquête nous montre, cette difficulté empêche les étudiants à continuer à apprendre le français. Mais en fait, quand on apprend une nouvelle chose, rien n'est simple. La difficulté ne devrait pas être l'excuse de la mauvaise performance; si un enseignant répète toujours que "oui, c'est vrai que le français est difficile", c'est comme si il dit aux étudiants "vous avez raison de ne pas bien apprendre le français". Donc, l'enseignant devrait éviter et nier fermement cette affirmation, même s'il le pense. L'enseignant doit donner une impression plutôt favorable de la langue française. Quand les étudiants comprennent, on les félicite en disant: "Vous voyez, c'est simple!". Quand ils ont du mal à comprendre, on les encourage et on les aide à trouver les astuces d'apprentissage.

—Créer une ambiance joyeuse et soulagée en classe. Cela nous rappelle facilement la fameuse école privée chinoise des langues "New Oriental". Son énorme succès vient surtout de ses cours "amusants", "attirants" et "efficaces". Les enseignants y sont très ouverts et cherchent tout le temps à faire rire les apprenants. Les apprenants, eux, adorent leurs enseignants "drôles", et sont très attentifs et actifs pendant le cours. Bien que cette école de langue, à but purement lucratif, soit critiquée de temps en temps par sa distraction excessive lors d'enseignement, on ne peut jamais nier qu'une bonne relation enseignant-étudiant et étudiant-étudiants ainsi qu'une bonne ambiance en cours favorise grandement l'apprentissage des étudiants. Au moins ils aiment les cours et veulent y assister. C'est la base d'un apprentissage "avec plaisir", contrairement à l'apprentissage "par obligation".

Avec une bonne ambiance en classe, avec une bonne humeur, sans trop de pression, les étudiants vont tomber vraiment amoureux de la langue française et surtout de nos cours de français. L' apprentissage sera aussi plus spontané et efficace. Cette expérience va devenir un beau souvenir de leur vie universitaire, si bien qu' ils vont volontiers apprendre le Français après la fin de leurs études, quand des occasions leur sont offertes.

3.2 Désir pour connaître la culture

Pour ce qui concerne les attentes sur la culture, ce n' est pas facile à comprendre. Avec l' ouverture de la Chine et la mondialisation, les jeunes chinois ont une forte envie de connaître le monde. La langue étrangère est une sorte de fenêtre ouverte sur sa culture correspondante. En plus la culture française est aussi réputée et attirante que sa langue. Pourtant beaucoup d' enseignants pensent que l' introduction de la culture en classe est une perte de temps. C' est une idée dangereuse, parce qu' en fait, de nos jours, On ne peut plus jamais apprendre une langue sans parler desa culture. Les compétences interculturelles sont parfois plus importantes que les compétences linguistiques. Donc la culture francophone devrait occuper une place importante dans l' enseignement. On pourrait travailler la culture en cours, et organiser des activités culturelles en dehors de cours.

En cours, j' ai demandé aux étudiants de faire des exposés sur la comparaison entre les cultures française et chinoise; on travaille souvent sur les stéréotypes; j' introduis souvent des documents authentiques en cours. En dehors du cours, j' organise beaucoup d' activités culturelles. Par exemple, des visites guidées de l' Institut Français de Pékin, participation à la soirée bretonne à Pékin; des conférences thématiques, par exemple sur la cuisine française, sur la francophonie, l' éducation française, l' œnologie, les systèmes de numération comparés, etc... On pourrait aussi organiser des rencontres avec des francophones, des professeurs qui ont séjourné longtemps dans les pays francophones, des étudiants en français d' autres universités, ou des gens qui utilisent le français dans leur travail, des soirées françaises, etc, etc... Quand il s' agit de la culture, il y a des milliers de choses à faire ! Et ces activités sont souvent très bien reçues par les étudiants. Grâce à ces activités, les étudiants développent aussi leurs compétences interculturelles qui les accompagneront pour toute la vie.

Conclusion

L' enseignement, c' est un art. Il est constitué des détails cachés dans chaque activité en classe, chaque parole prononcée par l' enseignant, ou chaque réflexion et auto-réflexion sur l' enseignement. Tous ces details méritent d' être travaillés de façon minutieuse. Tout ce dont nous avons parlé en haut, ce sont aussi des détails. Si les enseignants prennent soin de leurs cours et des attentes des étudiants, l' efficacité du cours sera bien différente.

“慕课”时代大学英语教学探讨

首都经济贸易大学外国语学院　潘速

摘　要：慕课（Massive Open Online Courses：大规模网络公开课程）时代的到来，为传统大学英语教学带来巨大的挑战和深刻的变革。慕课将传统课堂的教学活动转变为以现代信息技术和互联网为平台的虚拟课堂，教学设计和教学评价不再是经验式和主观式的，而是通过大量事实数据进行归纳，真正做到客观性和多元化。高效的课堂和新的教学理念为当今大学英语教学改革提供了机遇和挑战。

关键词：慕课；大学英语；教学

Abstract: With the coming of the age of Massive Open Online Courses, great challenges and revolution are being done to the traditional college English teaching. MOOC transfers the traditional teaching activities into a virtual classroom with modern information technology and the internet as its platform. The design and assessment of teaching are no longer empirical and subjective. On the contrary, with substantial collections of practical statistics, objectivity and diversification are realized. This kind of efficient classroom and the brand – new teaching concept bring opportunities and challenges to the revolution of college English teaching.

Key Words: Massive Open Online Courses, ; college English; teaching

一、引言

MOOCs（“慕课”）是近年来涌现出来的一种在线课程开发模式。它发端于过去的那种发布资源、学习管理系统以及将学习管理系统与更多的开放网络资源综合起来的旧的课程开发模式。通俗地说，慕课是大规模的网络开放课程，它是为了增强知识传播而由具有分享和协作精神的个人组织发布的、散布于互联网上的开放课程。2012 年被《纽约时报》称为“慕课元年”。多家公司专门提供慕课平台，Coursera、edX 和 Udacity 是其中最有影响力的“三巨头”，前两个均已进入中国。2013 年到 2014 年，中国一些知名大学也纷纷参与到这场在线教育的运动中。北京大学、清华大学、上海交通大学、复旦大学等国内一流院校加入到国际慕课运行的平台,这对于推动中国开放教育的发展,乃至重塑整个高等教育都有可能带来重要的影响。

二、慕课特点分析

MOOCs 一般是由国际名校向全球学习者免费开放的课程,其授课形式和班级授课制相似,不过班级被拓展到网络空间,整个地球就是一间巨型教室。其主要特点如下:(1)课程具有时效性(一般开课 2 ~ 12 周,许多 MOOCs 结束后,未注册者不能访问该课程);(2)每周均有作业,学习者需要在规定的时间内完成,且实施同伴互评;(3)课程具有强交互性(教师与学习者之间互动、视频与学习者之间互动、学习者之间互动);(4)提供学员学习档案;(5)完成课程且成绩达到一定要求者授予"课程完成证书"(Statement of Accomplishment)(马武林、李晓江,2013:87)。相比较而言,国家精品课程、视频公开课、资源共享课在"教学"功能上逊色很多。

此外,MOOCs 关键特性还有三点:(1)微视频;(2)自动评分系统,可以将教授参与作业评价的工作量降到最低;(3)学习者相互回答问题的论坛,发挥集体智慧的优势。微视频一般控制在 15 分钟之内,且视频播放过程中会插入问题供学习者回答,类似闯关游戏,学习者可以多次尝试作答,直至回答正确,一般系统都会给出相应的解释。该功能一方面防止学生思想开小差,另一方面帮助学习者消化教学内容。所有 MOOCs 视频均配有英文字幕,部分课程配有多语种字幕。主要培养学习者的批判性思维能力,同伴互评的重点没有放在语法和词汇上,而是考察学习者是否独立进行批判性思维。学习者要对同伴的作业根据要求进行反馈,收到同伴反馈意见后修改自己的作文,再次提交,接受同伴的最终评价,系统会计算出同伴评价结果的平均分,形成本次作业的最终成绩。学生最终成绩由 4 次作业和 3 次测试构成,测试在课程进行中以反思形式出现。

MOOCs 的蓬勃发展离不开其内在优势。方便、灵活、价格低廉,并且模拟了一套比较完整的教学模式,包括课堂互动参与、反馈、答疑、作业、课程安排及专为学生间交流学习经验而建立的论坛。通过网络学习,学生们能接触到平时难以获得的高质量讲课。但慕课也有其内在缺陷。某一门课程以同一种方式向数以千计甚至数以万计的学生授课,没有照顾到学生的个体差异。没有传统的课程学分、毕业、考证的压力,很容易半途而废,学习的效果也会受很大的影响。

三、MOOCs 为我国大学英语教学带来的机遇

大学英语教学一直是我国高等院校改革的重点。大学英语是我国高等院校所

占学分比例最高的单一课程，一直是教学改革的试验田。2007 年颁布的《大学英语教学课程要求》（简称《课程要求》），提出实施“基于计算机和课堂的大学英语教学模式”，根据英语语言的特性，通过多模态呈现方式，刺激学生多种感官参与语言学习，提高学习效率。教育部曾设立大学英语教学改革专项课题，引导各高校实施“基于计算机和课堂的大学英语教学模式”，全面推进信息技术与大学英语课程整合。

慕课时代的到来为大学英语教学改革带来了极好的契机。MOOCs 最大优势是使名校名师的名课程全球免费共享，从而使学习者能够自定步调学习课程内容。学有余力的在校学生亦可学习自己感兴趣的课程，完成作业，参与全球网络社区讨论课程内容，交流自己的学习体验。在通用大学英语越来越难以受到学生重视的今天，MOOCs 为我国大学英语教学带来了机遇：

（一）根据学习者 MOOCs 学习情况，适当调整课堂教学内容。

许多学习者由于语言障碍无法完成国际 MOOCs 学习，这给我国英语教学又一次敲响了警钟。MOOCs 的特点之一是允许学习者自定步调开展学习，但是我国大学生以及毕业生（在职人员）由于语言障碍无法完成 MOOCs 学习，说明我国的英语教学还需要改进。一方面我们有必要在课堂上对学生进行答疑，解决学生在学习 MOOCs 过程中遇到的问题；另一方面，需要通过调研找出学生在学习 MOOCs 过程中遇到的具体语言障碍，在课堂教学过程中给予适当的强化。此外，由于 MOOCs 对作业的评价主要通过同伴反馈（Peer review）来实现，学生非常期望自己的老师能够对自己所做的作业给予评价，而不是全部来自同伴。

（二）依托国际 MOOCs，激励学生学好大学英语。

语言障碍是阻止大半的学生完成 MOOCs 学习的主要原因。教师可以抓住这个机遇，鼓励学生通过国际 MOOCs 学习来检验自己的英语水平，开展需求导向语言学习，激发学生学习大学英语的兴趣。学生将学习 MOOCs 过程中遇到的问题带到课堂，通过同伴协商解决，或通过咨询教师解决。

（三）根据 MOOCs 课程需要，适当调整大学英语课程体系。

最近几年，关于我国大学英语教学内容改革的呼声四起。出现多种主张与专家所在的学校不同有很大关系。可以考虑根据学校的具体情况，给学生开设“大学通用英语 + 大学英语后续课程”相结合的大学英语课程体系。各个高校可以对本校学习 MOOCs 的学生进行调研，根据学生需求调整课程体系。

（四）借力国际 MOOCs，提升学生的英语语言水平。

通过国际 MOOCs 的学习，我国学习者不但可以检验自己的语言水平，而且可以进一步提升自己的语言水平,同时提升自己的专业知识和人文素养。MOOCs使高校几乎不需要承担任何费用就可以把海外专家"请来"授课,提升学生的就业竞争力。高校在进行大学英语课程设置时,可以综合考虑本校学生的具体情况,把某些MOOCs直接搬过来为我所用(转变为本校学分课)。学生在课下自主学习某一门MOOCs,教师课上答疑,通过"翻转课堂"教学模式(Flipped Classroom Model)提升学生的英语水平,然后教师组织本校学生的考核,通过考核给予相应的学分,考核不通过者,可以参与该课程下一轮学习,再参加本校考核,考核通过给予学分。

四、MOOCs对大学英语教学的挑战

随着MOOCs的普及,我国的大学英语教学面临新的挑战。MOOCs是典型的以学生为中心进行教学设计的课程,直接挑战我国以教师为中心的大学英语课堂教学模式。MOOCs通过营造全英文学习环境、提供经典学习资源、实施师生在线交互和生生在线即时交互,来提升教学质量,创建优质外语课程。另一方面,大学英语的课程内容也受到挑战。我国对大学英语的定位是"培养学生的英语综合应用能力,特别是听说能力,使他们在今后学习、工作和社会交往中能用英语有效地进行交际,同时增强其自主学习能力,提高综合文化素养以适应我国社会发展和国际交流的需要"(教育部高教司,2007)。一般情况下,普通院校大学英语主要由《综合英语》和《视听说》构成,在内容选材上偏重于培养学生的人文素养。对学生的个性化学习需求训练明显不足,影响学生的后续发展。而MOOCs则不同,在Coursera平台已有486门英文课程,涉及多个专业,而且课程在不断增加中。MOOCs课程的重要定位还在于免费的非学分性课程,这无疑也对单调、枯燥而又权威的学分课构成了挑战。

五、结语

本文主要探究了慕课时代的到来给我国大学英语教学所带来的机遇和挑战。挑战是多方面的,包括大学英语的教学质量、课程内容、评价方式等。但与此同时,机遇也应运而生,比如可以依托国际MOOCs,激励学生学好大学英语,探究个性化教学,同时利用网络学习环境及海量资源促进教师专业发展。外语教学的实践者必须有充分的思想准备,迎接新挑战,与此同时寻求更好的发展机遇。

参考文献:

[1]陈冰冰.MOOCs课程模式:贡献和困境[J].外语电化教学,2014(3).

[2]教育部高教司．大学英语课程教学要求[M]．上海:上海外语教育出版社,2007.

[3]马武林、李小江．国际 MOOCs 对我国大学英语后续课程建设的启示[J]．现代教育技术,2013(11).

英语听说教学原则与研究生交际能力的培养

首都经济贸易大学外国语学院　曲文洁

摘　要:本文以听说教学原则为理论基础,以提高学生的语言交际能力为宗旨,从不同层面分析了听说教学的实施和运用,着重阐述了在听说这一教学过程中,教师的职责以及教师在课堂上如何回应学生的方式方法,同时,也为听说课程的师生互动活动提出了一些措施,以便教师更加有效地、有的放矢地进行听说教学,切实提高研究生的听说交际能力,以顺应社会的需求。

关键词:听说法;倾听;模仿;转换;交际能力

Abstract:This article analyses teaching practice in listening and speaking from different levels based on the teaching theories for the purpose to improve students' communicative competence . It also emphatically elaborates the responsibility of the teacher and how the teacher responds to the students questions in listening and speaking in the process of teaching. At the same time, It also puts forward some measures and activities for listening and speaking courses of interaction between teachers and students in order to make teachers have a definite object in view of the teaching of listening and speaking, make teaching more effectively, improve the graduates communicative ability and make them adapt to the social needs.

Key Words:listening; speaking; imitation; conversion; communicative competence

一、引言

近几年社会对研究生的英语要求越来越高,尤其对听说能力的要求已经成为一些大学毕业生择业的门坎,提高学生的听说交际能力在近几年的英语教学改革中也往往被作为重点提出,这些年经过师生的共同努力也取得了一些成效,但是,似乎离社会和学生的要求总是有那么一段距离,那么,如何做、怎样做才能更有效地提高教学水平和研究生的听说能力,使学生在真实且有意义的交际语境中具备熟练运用语言的实际能力,在有意义的语境中恰当、得体地表达自己,在社会语言场中轻松和有效地进行交际,便显得非常重要。注重对语言运用及语言交际能力的培养是研究生听说英语教学的最终目的。

二、听说策略

听和说二者密不可分，但是，形式上却是完全不同的两个行为过程。听是吸收的过程、输入的过程，说是表达的过程、输出的过程，因此，有效的听说策略不仅对口语非常重要，而且，这一过程对语言知识获取亦很重要（Pickard，N. 1996）。在课堂教学中，我们应该尽量为学生营造一个虚拟的听力环境，帮助学生提高听力技能。

（一）自信心的建立

很多学生害怕听力，一是因为材料难，例如，语速快，另一原因是学生不切实际的期望，例如，他们希望听懂每一个单词。但是，如果教师选材合理、教学方法得当，上述问题还是可以帮助学生建立听的自信心的。在建立学生的自信心方面，语言学家布朗和尤尔（1983）提出了以下4个方面：1、说话者，例如，说话的人数、语速、复杂度、口音；2、内容，其中包括文体、听者的动力；3、学习者的学习动机；4、手段，例如，视听内容或打印材料。基于上述4个方面，教师可有针对性地筛选材料，如果说话者口音重且语速快，那么教师要求学生的反馈可以简单些，学生能回答出概要就可以，例如，“What is the speaker talking about？”“Do you agree？”；但如果材料比较容易，那么，问的问题就可以详细一些了。让学生多接触英语也可以帮助他们建立信心，例如，听英语广播、看英语电视剧、英语电影以及随处可见的英语广告、英语标识等。“参与性的听”（面对面的对话、讨论）和“非参与性的听”（听英语讲座、广播节目等）都能够训练学生的听力，然而，教师在授课过程中，要注意：既要让学生泛听，也要让他们精听，即，学生既要学会听懂大概的内容，也要学会听懂具体的内容；在听的过程中，要鼓励学生模仿和学习，让学生学会记顺序号、填表、给图片对号入座、给所听的内容画画，以上活动教师可以根据学生的水平有选择地进行操作。在培养和提高学生听力技能时，教师务必要求学生做到如下几点：专心致志、精神集中、适当、有效的反应，基于所听到的内容教师要进行提问以强化学生的记忆、培养思考能力。

听完一段材料后，教师可以采取以下措施来加强和提高听力能力：

- 提出问题来检验学生的听力。
- 检测学生对已讨论过的事物的理解力。
- 让学生分组讨论并分享他们对于某个话题或论点的不同看法。（赫奇，2001）

当然,要提高听力能力来自于日常的点点滴滴的训练,作为教师,不但要尽可能地在课堂上为学生提供各种各样的听力语言材料,还要为学生提供在课堂上说的机会,并鼓励学生不要放过一切说英语的场合。

(二)倾听策略

言语的有效运用以听力为基础,教师的回答与学生交流应依托于对一方表达的仔细倾听。学生需要在讲话和语言运用中树立信心,通过适当的有感情的反应暗示教师已在倾听他们讲话,能够鼓励他们这样做。当他们意识到他们的活动有意义而且能够影响交流,他们就会获得自信。需要注意的是,课堂上,如何清楚地表示出对学生的注意以及向他们表明他们的话很有价值,教师可以采取以下方法:

- 用眼睛交流等非语言的表达信号,如微笑、点头、手势来表达理解。
- 做出相关的解释、提问或回答。
- 要听懂潜在的信息。学生有时以口头表达或许有些困难,但可能显现在其非语言表达信息中。
- 记住以前讨论中的有关要点。

下面的做法表明教师没有专心倾听学生,是应该避免的,它们包括:

- 在学生问问题时,表现出要走或准备离开的样子。
- 发出无兴趣的、离题的噪声或评论。
- 打断或结束学生的话语。
- 听不出有隐含意味的话。
- 不肯花时间倾听学生。

倾听是最重要的交流技能之一,教师良好的倾听习惯对帮助学生提高他们的听力技能起着重要的作用,教师和学生同样需要细心而专注地倾听,这样才能够使学生的听力技能和理解力达到更高的水平,并在讨论中使重大议题得到更为清晰的概念,否则,有听力困难的学生会失去获得理解和更深层知识的机会。为了培养学生的听力技能,教师不但需要创造一个有效听的环境,还要创造一个倾听的环境。

(三)有效运用言语的策略

练习听说不是单纯意义上的活动,而是要通过运用大量不同的说话方式来提高语言能力。外语教学实践中,许多教师都强调提高口语,但做法因人而异,效果大不相同。尽管做法上千差万别,概括起来主要不外乎采取两种不同的提高口语途径:1. 通过语言练习和背诵提高外语口语;2. 通过课内外言语实践提高外语口语。培养口语的类型有:讲故事、体现想象力的游戏和戏剧、大声朗读、陈述事件、阐述观点、陈述经历、解释选择项(就观点给出原因并加以解释)。由于培养学生不同类型的语言表达是为了不同的目的,因此,课程中也应该包含其他各种活动。例如,角色扮演是学生语言能力提高的比较重要的传媒工具,其活动类型很多,从依据某种信息而进行的对话到比较复杂的剧目表演。通过角色扮演,学生练习了新的词汇,培养了新的观念和思想并与他人交流语言。Skehan(1989)认为学生通过角色扮演来培养语言能力。此过程同时也与认知发展密切相关,在角色扮演过程中,学生讨论剧目的选择,商量题目,练习词汇,构思人物和故事情节,解决冲突,分享构想,大量技能的开发也应运而生。通过讨论,阐述各自观点,在可行性构思中进行选择,协商不同观点,评价剧目质量,设置剧目主题及故事情节。鼓励学生学习在多人小组中进行表达,这是听说教学中的重要组成部分。另外,每一堂课前,拿出10分钟左右的时间让学生做自我陈述也是锻炼学生口语的一个极佳的办法,在自我陈述过程中,学生发现了自我,找回了自信。

在口语教学中,教师的提问也非常重要,问什么、不问什么都直接影响教学效果,作为教师,我们要和学生谈论什么呢?我们怎样才能帮助他们扩展,培养使用不同类型语言呢?这一点,教师一定要认真思考。通常教师可以采取以下措施来训练不同类型的讲话:

- 提问开放性问题(问题要用一句话或多句话来回答而非仅用“是”或“不是”)。
- 询问学生的意见和主张。
- 鼓励学生问问题。
- 师生共同进行非正式的交流,如有关宠物、朋友、最喜欢的电视节目、爱好等。

下面的问话和与学生交流是没有一点成效的,例如,教师问:“Did you do anything exciting yesterday?”有些学生大概知道最简单的回答是:“Nothing”。这样一来,谈话就进行不下去了,提问题的类型是否正确、运用鼓励是否恰当、激励谈话的不同类型,是培养学生语言表达的重要组成部分。学生需要学习的语言形式不止一类,这些形式的价值体现在不同的环境中。在学校或公共场所里,师生需要通过共同交流、讨论、计划、构思和设计活动来鼓励听和说。有些学生可能对讲话缺乏信心,那就要鼓励他们讨论日常生活中所熟悉的事,对于那些不愿说话的学生,鼓励他们在较小的小组里讲话是一个有效的办法。注意要提问学生能回答出来的问题,这能够帮助学生获得勇于大声说话的自信。

三、交际能力的培养

听说教学与交际能力的培养是不可分割的,所谓交际能力(communicative competence)就是理解和传达意思的能力。它主要包括语言能力、社会语言能力和筹划能力。语言能力指掌握语言规则的能力,既掌握基本的语言语法和词汇方面的知识,又能够准确地理解和表达所需要的语言知识。社会语言能力是指说话人能够根据说话时的场合和各自的身份以及社会习俗等,使用恰当的语言来进行交际(Widdowson,H. G. 1978)。话语能力是根据不同的交际场景,通过口头语言或书面语言来进行交际。筹划能力指说话人用非语言手段如"you see"、"Oh"等犹豫时的填补词使交际有效地进行下去。听说教学正是在强调培养学生的交际能力这一前提下进行的,其交际性不仅体现在"听"、"说"的语言交际功能上,它更注重培养考生"活"的语言交际能力,而不是"死"的语言知识。

四、结语

语言的表达能力和理解能力常常体现在听和说上,是学生未来学习和工作的重要技能,而获取广泛的语言技能的这一过程与思考力、理解力、预测力、理论化以及推理能力的提高密不可分,在缺乏语言环境的情况下,如何培养和提高学生的听说能力,实在是很值得深究的问题,我们不应光满足于课程和教材的改革,而应该以学生为本,从细微处入手,认真思考并研究教学方法,帮助学生掌握学习方法,充分利用课堂上的每一分钟,为学生营造好的英语环境,创造更多的说话机会,使英语听说课上得更具有时效性,从而最终达到"善学者,师逸而功倍"之境界。

参考文献:

[1]Brown,G & Yule G. *Discourse Analysis*[M]. Cambridge,London:CUP,1983.

[2]Pickard,N. *Out-of-class Language Learning Strategies.* [J]. ELT journal 50\2:150\9.

[3]Skehan,P. *Individual Differences in Second Language learning*[M]. London:Edward Arnold,1989.

[4] Tricia Hedge. *Teaching and Learning in the Language Classroom* [M]. Shanghai Foreign Language Education Press,2001.

[5] Widdowson, H. G. *Teaching Language as Communication* [M]. Oxford University Press,1978.

外语学习倦怠与激发动机的教学策略研究

首都经济贸易大学外国语学院　王春花

摘　要：本文分析了外语学习中出现的倦怠现象与学习动机的关系，文章通过借鉴动机研究理论，结合教学实践，探讨了如何通过引起并维持注意、促进相关、树立信心、产生满足等激发动机成分的教学策略，帮助学生消除外语学习中的倦怠现象。

关键词：倦怠现象；学习动机；教学策略

Abstract: This article probes into the relationship between the language learning burnout and motivation. Based on motivational theories, it discusses strategies to reduce burnout through stimulating or remaining Attention, Relevance, Confidence and Satisfaction in language teaching.

Key Words: burnout syndrome; motivation; teaching strategy

一、外语学习中的倦怠现象

心理学家认为，倦怠是一种心理状态，是指从业人员因压力过大而出现的精力耗竭、待人冷漠和个人成就感降低等症状（杨涛，2015:15）。学习倦怠是学习者个体在学习活动中产生的心理状态。国内外教育者的研究证实了学习倦怠的存在并对其进行了深入的研究。王和契克森米哈（1991）发现青少年认为学习和作业是最不值得做的事情，学生反应在学习和写作业时感到内在动力不足和负面的体验，他们感到沮丧、被动、无聊、孤独、离群。施耐德等（1995）在研究中也发现学生倾向于认为大部分的教学活动枯燥无趣（德尔涅依，2005:89）。外语学习中的倦怠现象也普遍存在。笔者在一次关于课堂活动的问卷调查时发现，大部分学生表示对课后练习、测验、复述课文等有利于巩固语言知识的活动容易产生厌倦；但对语言能力要求较高的更具创意和思想性的活动，当他们不能流畅表达时又产生挫败感，这些消极的心理状态反映出了外语学习中倦怠的特征。在教学中我们不难发现，无论学生对英语如何感兴趣，过于细碎的课后练习都难维持他们的注意力，甚至对他们感兴趣的演讲、电影、演示和音频等教学材料，在面对重复时，兴趣也会降低。研究表明，学习倦怠的形成和发展与学习者个体因素和学习活动相关因素有着密切的联系。

二、外语学习倦怠与动机的关系

杨涛(2015:25)把外语学习倦怠定义为:学习者由于外语学习活动的内容、过程或结果与学习者本人在这些方面的预期存在差异而产生的,以耗竭、对外语学习的冷漠态度和在外语学习方面降低的自我效能感等与颓废相关的消极情感为主要表征的心理综合征。他还认为外语学习倦怠与外语学习活动密切相关,具有动态性,当外语学习者发现其可能二语自我与现实二语自我间的差异长期存在,并难以消除时,外语学习倦怠就有可能出现并不断发展。杨涛在定性研究中,通过对受试者课堂行为描述的分析,发现学习者对外语学习环境的消极态度会影响其外语学习动机状态,导致外语学习倦怠特征的出现。不过他同时发现,对外语学习环境有积极评价的学习者,也可能由于缺乏成就感(降低的自我效能感,比如总是不能流畅地用英文表达)产生外语学习倦怠。

研究表明,动机是与情境相关的,教育领域的认知理论将动机解释为人类对理解、奋斗、卓越、成功、进步以及自我不断挑战的需要;社会学习理论认为动机既来自个体内在的头脑(他的思想、计划、对自己能力的认识),也来自外部环境(达到既定目标的可能性、达到目标后可能的回报);人本主义认为影响人的所有因素都会引发或影响动机,包括思想、情感和环境的各个方面(斯腾伯格、威廉姆斯,2003:322-323)。

越来越多的外语教育研究者非常关注学习动机在语言学习教学中的作用。外语学习动机研究者既关注二语短期学习过程中动机的发展,也关注语言长期学习过程中学习者动机的波动变化。加德纳(Gardner)的社会心理学理论(social psychological construct)阐述了语言态度、动机行为及语言成就的关系。其中特别强调了从态度到动机行为的中介变量如目标凸显度、效价及自我效度。他认为外语学习者在学习过程中会有两类动机结构:语言学习动机和课堂学习动机(杨涛,2015:37),二语学习者的学习目的倾向决定了他们学习的努力程度,他将焦虑、自我效能和学习效果等相关内容全部列入动机内在结构中。他虽然强调动机的多层面性,但也倾向于将动机定义为选择和努力程度。约翰·舒曼从神经生物学的角度对二语习得进行了研究,认为情感因素是外语学习的驱动力。他的模型核心成分是刺激评价(stimulus appraisal),它的5个维度是新颖度、吸引度、目标意义、参与潜能、自我和社会形象(德尔涅依,2005:61)。德尔涅依(DÖrnyei)和奥托(OttÓ')(process model of 12 motivation)的二语动机过程模型提出了强调过程导向的动机研究,他认为动机是指学习者对学习行为的选择、坚持和努力。在外语学习活动中由于受到社会和课堂教学因素的影响,学习者的这些选择、坚持和努力程度都会发生变化,即外语学习动机变化。他指出二语学习的某些削弱性动机因素有可能会导致动机缺乏(amotivation),他引用 Vallerand(1997)的论述指出动机缺乏的原因可能有 4 类:认为自己缺乏进行相应行为的能力;认为缺少有效的策略;认为要达成目标所需的努力程度过高;认为所需完成的任务过于庞大,自己的努力无足轻重(杨:32)。外语学习动机消极变化是外语学习倦怠的主要症状之一,而学习者对外语学习环境的态度是影响学习者动机状态的重要因素,因此,在外语教学中采用激发动机的教学策略有助于消除学习中的倦怠现象。

三、ARCS 模型所建议的激发动机的教学策略

凯勒将动机定义为“人们为了接近或避免某些经历或目标所作出的选择以及努力的程度”(徐锦芬:67)。他(1983、1984)认为学生的动机(或价值观)以及他们的期待(如效能期待和结果期待)会影响他们用于学习任务上的注意和努力的程度。成就(或不能取得成就)的结果和学习者对其表现的归因也会影响未来的学习动机。因此,他提出了激发学习者动机必须满足动机的 4 个条件 ARCS,A 即注意(attention),R 即相关(relevance),C 即信心(confidence),S 即满足(satisfaction)以及这个模型所建议的激发动机的教学策略(转引自 M. P. 德里斯科尔,2008:282)。

表 1　ARCS 模型所建议的激发动机的教学策略

动机成分	相应的策略
引起并维持注意	• 通过运用新奇或意想不到的教学方法吸引学生的注意。 • 用可唤起神秘感的问题来激发持久的好奇心。 • 通过变化教学呈现来维持学生的注意。
促进相关	• 通过阐明(或让学生确定)教学如何与个人目标相关以提高对有用性的知觉。 • 用自学、领导和合作的场合来提供将学习者的动机和价值观加以匹配的机会。 • 通过在学习者原有经验基础上进行教学来增加熟悉感。
树立信心	• 通过澄清教学目标和目的而创设一种积极的成功期待。此外,允许学习者设置自己的目标。 • 给予学生成功完成挑战性目标的机会。 • 让学习者合理地控制自己的学习

续表

动机成分	相应的策略
产生满足	• 通过给学习者提供运用新学的技能的机会以引起自然后果。 • 在自然后果缺失时,可以运用积极后果策略,如口头表扬、真实的或符号性的奖励。 • 通过保持一致的标准并将结果与期待相匹配而确保公平。

上述的 ARCS 教学策略在实践中得到了检验,当促进相关的策略用于教学中时,学生的动机有所增强。这一理论同样适用于外语教学。

四、激发动机的教学策略在外语教学实践中的应用

在应用语言学领域,很多学者一直在强调加强语言课堂的学习自主性,提高学习者的学习动机。教学实践中,我们不难发现,能够自主学习者本身就具有强烈的学习动机,而且学生对学习成败的归因与学习动机有着紧密的联系。研究发现,当学生具有内部而非外部定向时,会表现出更强的动机。这意味着他们倾向于将学习任务视作由技能决定的,并因此受个人控制。外部定向的学生倾向于相信他们在学习任务上的成功是由机会而不是由他们可控制的手段决定的,因此这些学生不易卷入学习任务。把凯勒的刺激动机的教学策略运用于外语教学情境中,可以减少学习过程中的倦怠现象,激发学习兴趣,培养学生的自主学习能力。

(一)通过设计不同的课堂任务引起注意、减少倦怠

在教学实践中,教师可以根据不同的语言输入,通过设计不同的课堂任务引起学生的注意,如《现代大学英语·精读 1》*The Boy and the Bank Officer* 一课中,open 这个词出现了多次:He was holding an open savings-account book and wearing an expression of open dismay. I opened the account myself, so why can't I withdraw any money? I had my opening. 教师可以通过任务来唤醒学生的好奇心和学习兴趣,可以先让学生用 open 造句以检验他们对这个词的掌握情况,继而要求学生关注并分析该词在课文语境中的用法和意义。如果教师不给任务,学生很容易一带而过,因为这并不影响他们对课文的理解,但是他们会失去欣赏这种简洁而优雅的语言风格的机会,从而影响他们语言输出的地道性。在外语学习中,许多学生习惯把词汇学习看成背课文后面的单词表,有的学生甚至靠反复抄写来学习单词,他们习得词汇的方式停留在"读音 + 拼写 + 词义",很少意识到词汇其他方面的知识,缺乏对词汇的深度加工,导致所学词汇不能有效地储存和提取,语言输出的地道性不够。

教师要引导学生关注教材中某些容易被他们忽视的表达,促使学生在具体语境中理解和欣赏语言,通过教师的不断引导,学生会意识到对接受性词汇和产出性词汇应采取不同的学习策略。在教学中将策略训练任务与具体的教学内容相结合,能够促使学生的元认知能力在学习语言的过程中得到发展。学习者通过琢磨和分析语言得到关于语言的形式、结构及其他方面的元语言知识。学生在处理课后关于词汇搭配、同义、反义、语用知识等练习时更有耐心,减少词汇学习带来的倦怠感。

(二)通过增加适当教学材料促进相关,激发学习兴趣

语言能力的发展取决于运用外语进行大量自主的交流,受到社会现实的影响,外语课堂教学不可能传授语言的全部,因此语言教学除了对目标语的呈现和练习外,还应该包括社会现实。教师针对学习者的背景,为他们提供一些课外学习资源、并给予他们一定的学习技巧和策略上的指导,使外语学习与学习者的现实生活相关联,促进学习者的学习动机。比如 BBC 提供的一档学习节目 NEWS,仅需两到三分钟的音频,里面涉及很多激发学生兴趣的话题,尤其是那些与我们的现实生活相关的话题,诸如票贩子(Ticket Touts)、咖啡成瘾(Coffee Addiction)、3D 打印机(Print Your Gun)、微博(Microblog)、机器人厨师(Robert Chef)、粮食浪费问题(Food Wasted)、北京的雾霾(Air Pollution in Beijing)、空中花园(Garden in Clouds:北京的违章建筑)、极端天气(Climate Violence)、钉子之路(Road of Nails:关于印度尼西亚首都发生的机修工为了招揽生意雇人往路面上撒钉子)等许多学生熟悉的现实生活中的现象,这些语言输入可以激发学生运用目标语表达的欲望和学习语言的兴趣。通过这样的活动使学生认识到:语言运用是语言学习的动力,语言本质上就是实用的和社会的,学习语言仅仅掌握它的语言特征是不够的,学习者还应该知道如何恰当地使用这门语言。大学阶段的外语学习不同于其他学科的学习,需要重视外语教学的特殊性,学习者首先需要学习并接受一种外来语言和文化,它是一种接受性学习,需要学习者大量地诵读、记忆、模仿、操练才能获得大量语料储备,这是认知建构过程的必然途径,也是进行有意义的语言交流的前提。在教学中适当增加真实材料并设计交际性强的课堂活动有助于激发学生的学习兴趣,保持学生的学习动力,培养学生的融合型学习动机(常俊跃,2015:79)。

(三)通过培养学生的学习策略,帮助学生树立信心

应用语言学领域的研究表明:学习效果好的学生经常会采取某些特定的策略来改进学习,增强记忆和提高应用能力。美国的 5C《21 世纪外语学习目标》要求强化学习策略。《目标》认为,传授学习策略应该是教学不可或缺的有机组成部分(周文娟,2014:55)。因此教师需要通过课堂教学过程向学生传授这些策略。元认知知识是不同类型的学习中所经历的心理过程中的知识，包括对学习者个人、学习任务和学习策略三方面的知识。学习者能够意识到自己的心理过程，包括怎样的学习任务引起了困难，哪些方法更有利于记忆信息、如何解决不同的问题。因此，元认知知识影响着对学习策略类型的选择。强烈的学习动机是培养学生元认知能力不可缺少的内部条件，学习任务的完成依赖于学习者的积极性和主动性。在处理教材内容时，教师要明确地提出认知任务，学生需要明确不同的认知任务有不同的目的要求和特点，在结合教材主题推荐语言材料时，尽量注意材料的趣味性和学习价值，使学生在完成任务的过程中体会到学习外语的乐趣，认识到学习外语的意义。能够激发和调动学习者强烈的内在动机的任务，也能促使他们在学习过程中充分发挥主体作用。在语言学习的过程中，学习者的学习态度、自信心和自我意识在元认知意识产生的过程中相互作用，促进认知技能更有利地发展。班杜拉认为，自我效能信念知觉是个体对自己组织和执行达成给定成就所需行动力的信念，它影响人们选择执行的行动进程，影响在制定的活动中投入多大的努力，影响在面对阻碍和失败时能坚持多久，影响他们从逆境中恢复的能力，影响他们的思维方式是自我阻碍的还是自我帮助的，影响他们在应对高负荷的环境要求时体验到多大的压力和抑郁，以及影响他们所能实现的成就水平（转引自 M. P. 德里斯科尔，2008：269）。

在语言实践中，能否顺利完成学习任务影响着学习者维持持续的学习动机。因此实践过程中的目标设置至关重要。研究认为，设置具体的目标（每天用 20 分钟朗读并复述课文）优于设置一般的目标（像操母语者一样流利使用英语）。设置近期目标比设置长远目标能更大程度地提高自我动机和行为表现。教师在设计任务活动时要关注学习者的不同学习风格、语言能力、语言学习的阶段性等，使学习者在完成任务的过程中提高认知能力，如语音识别能力、模仿力及感受力；归纳、概括、总结能力；灵活运用语言知识和文化背景知识的能力；发展获取信息、整合知识的能力、建构适合学习者个人的学习方法；发展整合能力、合理利用教材的能力；拓展思维的深度和广度、增强逻辑思维能力；发展学生利用原有知识进行联想、归纳、对比、推断、演绎等解决问题的能力。在完成某一特定任务时某种特定的能力获得提高能够帮助学生理解具体目标与一般目标、近期目标与长远目标的关系，能够激发学习者的学习动力。学习者对自己在任务难度和结果关系中的信念是动机的另一来源。

外语教学仅仅向学习者灌输知识结构和行为模式是不够的，还要使学习者认识到他们应该对自己的学习负责，在学习过程中关注自己收集、处理、分析和储存信息的方式,认识到他们既不是知识的被动接受者,也不是脱离于学习过程的独立个体,而是各种学习过程的参与者。在外语教学中,教师还要考虑学生的独特性,如他们的语言天赋、能力、情感因素、学习进度、学习风格、发展阶段等,通过采取保护学生自主性、提供选择性、建设性反馈、创造自我指导的机会等评价方法去提高学生的学习动机。动机和学习者自主是一种动态的关系,学习者自主有利于促进学习者的动机。在学习过程中让学生体验到带有现实生活特点的问题解决的复杂性能增强学生的动机。

(四)通过加强学生语言体验的活动,促使学生产生满足

认知语言学家认为,语言知识源自语言运用(Knowledge of language emerges from language use),语义、句法、形态、语音中的概念和结构都是建立在人们在具体的运用场景中对具体话语的认知之上的。对于句法行为(syntactic behavior)和语义理解中的规约化的细微差异(conventionalized subtleties)的详细分析可以建立起一种语法模型,既可用于解释高度普遍的语言行为模式,也可用于解释特殊的语言行为模式。当代语言学家认为"语言存在于使用者的心智之中"。基于体验哲学的认知语言学研究语言与知识的获得和使用中的思维过程,反对行为主义和"刺激-反映"论,分析人类思维、储存信息、理解话语和说话过程中所使用的认知策略从而揭示思维的结构和组织。

元认知体验既可以是对"知"的体验,也可以是对"不知"的体验。"知"的体验会给学生带来满足感和自豪感,但"不知"的体验却会使学生感到沮丧,产生焦虑感。注重语言输出的教学模式能够促使学生从"不知"的体验过渡到"知"的体验。文秋芳认为,调动学习积极性的最好方法就是创造机会让学生主动寻求知识盲点以激发弥补盲点的欲望(文秋芳,2008)。教学过程中的小组讨论、课堂演示、角色扮演等合作式课堂活动,能够帮助学生不断发现自己的"知识盲点",在教师和同学的帮助下他们积极弥补这些盲点。这些活动调动学生参与课堂活动的积极性,使学生在与同学的合作中将焦虑降到最低。

五、结论

外语教学中学生对外语学习环境的态度是影响学习者动机状态的重要因素之一。凯勒的引起注意、促进相关、树立信心、产生满足的刺激动机的教学策略关注学生的好奇心和兴趣、目标和目标定向以及自我效能信念等动机来源的要素,强调认知过程在情感生成与发展中的重要性。因此,有助于减少甚至消除外语学习过程中的倦怠现象。

参考文献:

[1]Zoltan Dornyei. *Teaching and Researching Motivation*[*M*]. 北京:外语教育与研究出版社,2005.

[2]杨涛. 外语学习倦怠与动机关系研究[M]. 北京:科学出版社,2015.

[3]常俊跃. 英语专业基础阶段内容依托教学改革研究[M]. 北京:北京大学出版社,2015.

[4]周文娟. 大数据时代外语教学理念与方法的探索与发现[M]. 上海:上海交通大学出版社,2014.

[5]杨立民. 现代大学英语·精读1、2[M]. 北京:外语教学与研究出版社,2011.

[6]文秋芳. 输出驱动假设与英语专业技能课程改革[J]. 外语界,2008(2):2-8.

[7]M·P·德里斯科尔. 学习心理学[M]. 王小明等译. 上海:华东师范大学出版社,2008.

[8]徐锦芬. 大学外语自主学习理论与实践[M]. 北京:中国社会科学出版社,2007.

[9]斯腾伯格,威廉姆斯. 教育心理学[M]. 张厚粲译. 北京:中国轻工业出版社,2003.

An Exploration of Classroom Teaching Mode for English Language Undergraduates in MSU

首都经济贸易大学外国语学院　王宏玉

摘要:一个突出的现象是美国密歇根州立大学课堂管理与国内首都经济贸易大学课堂管理特征存在明显差异。因此,大学课堂管理全球化的新挑战正面临所有高校老师,这一挑战对于使学生积极参与课堂教学意义深远。此文旨在说明如何建立积极活跃的课堂及为创建新的课堂管理提供一些有意义的举措,这些课堂管理策略来源于本人在密歇根州立大学做访问学者的经历及研究探索,希望对我校及国内大学课堂管理有所借鉴。由于访学时间短暂及有限的观察和研究,本文具有一定的局限性。

关键词:课堂管理;活跃的课堂;课堂管理策略

Abstract: A salient phenomenon is that the features of classroom teaching management in MSU America are obviously different from those of CUEB in China. A new challenge of globalization of university classroom management is confronting all the teachers, which will be beneficial in order to actively engage students in classroom teaching in China. This paper is intended to provide some significant strategies on how to establish positive classrooms and create a new classroom management in universities in China based on personal experience and exploration as a visiting scholar in MSU and thus will shed some light on classroom management both in CUEB and other universities in China. This paper has some limitations due to a short period of time and limited observation and research.

Key Words: classroom management; positive classroom; classroom strategies

Ⅰ　Introduction

1. Current Problems

Nowadays, in some classrooms of universities in China, it is common that some students especially sophomores and juniors lack self-disciplines. For instance, some students were late or absent for class; some were texting and playing games with mobile phones; some were even sleeping in class; some are unprepared; some were daydreaming... Such examples of disruptive behaviors are endless, which mainly result from poor classroom management. So positive classroom management should be established and constitutes a big challenge for university teachers and calls for immediate innovation.

What is classroom management? It is a term used by teachers to describe the process of ensuring that classroom lessons run smoothly despite disruptive behavior by students. The term also implies the prevention of disruptive behavior. It is probably the most difficult aspect of teaching for many teachers. According to Moskowitz & Hayman (1976), once a teacher loses control of their classroom, it becomes increasingly more difficult for them to regain that control. For example, my colleague once quarreled with a student in a rage in class in that he listened to music loudly in the hot zone and since then, her class was out of control. It is evident that poor classroom management skills result in a lower rate of academic engagement in the classroom. According to Allen, J. D. (1986), from the student's perspective, effective classroom management includes clear communication of behavioral academic expectations as well as a cooperative learning environment. That's why many teachers establish rules and procedures at the beginning of the school year in order to achieve a good result of classroom teaching. According to Gootman (2008), rules give students concrete direction to ensure that our expectation becomes a reality. But in CUEB, classroom rules and teaching syllabus are established and shown to the students but are not printed for students as a must of necessary reading, moreover, the requirements are not detailed and implementation are too obscure.

2. Positive Classrooms

As a teacher, teaching should involve learning to manage a classroom of students, learning to teach students with different learning styles, learning to provide an environment where children are intrinsically motivated to do their best, learning to contend with mountains of paperwork. (The Classroom of Choice, p. 3) Positive classrooms are developed by Dr. Robert DiGiulio who sees positive classroom management as the result of four factors: how teachers regard their students (spiritual dimension), how they set up the classroom environment (physical dimension), how skillfully they teach content (instructional dimension), and how well they address student behavior (managerial dimension).

Ⅱ Student-teacher relationship

One prominent feature in Classroom environment is referred to dynamic relationships that characterize student-educator interactions. What I witnessed in MSU showed this point. Three language classrooms in my study were places where people usually spoke politely to one another, and appeared to cooperate in a common effort. One teacher is Sue who taught level 307(Ⅱ), another is Ellne Spino teaching level 307(Ⅰ), the other is Paula who taught level 807, who taught language teaching in educational department.

At the beginning of class or before class, polite formulas or small talk were class routine of the whole semester. There were times when students forced teachers to reveal what they were doing and as the students worked to develop area of self-determination. Sometimes, teachers were quite direct with students. Both students and teachers seemed to prefer keeping their conflicts in the shadows.

The construction of harmonious student-teacher relationship must be a result of actions of all participants, not teacher alone. Specific actions of classroom are the focus of study, which can be seen and heard in the insular classroom. The interactive construction of relationship, and indeed all aspects of life in classroom take place within that miniature society.

Manke, Mary Phillips stressed four key ideas about classroom power:

(1) Power belongs to both teacher and students just as teachers have interactional resources that affect how students act, students use their own resources to shape teacher's behavior. For this point, in the three classes group presentation done by leading discussants focused on not only scheduled articles but also summaries of another three articles related the same topic from each person and in turn, students sometimes challenged teachers for some provoking questions.

(2) Human interaction creates a context in which further interaction occurs. The actions of participants are shaped by the actions of those around them—both teacher and students. In the three classes I observed, students imitated the teacher's and other students' mode of teaching and added some changes by themselves. In this way students and teachers learn from each other. Academic atmosphere was established gradually from all kinds of forms of interactions.

(3) Teachers and students bring their own agendas to the classroom—agendas with potential for significant conflict. The teacher's agenda, as I saw it, came from their culture understanding of what university classrooms are supposed to be about. Teachers "have power"; they exercise control over students because their control leads to students' learning, thus, teacher's contributions to the building of power. The students' agenda rose from one aspect of their culture's view of what adulthood is a time of compliance. The students have an agenda of maintaining their action and thus it is possible for them to find learning contributes to having a sense of achievement. For this point, MSU professor Paula set a good example by voting for the articles which should be included in the schedule for study and exam.

(4) Some of the resources teachers and students use as they build a structure of power relationships can be found in the area of discourse, teachers (and students) choose from an array of interactional resources as they construct classroom power relationships. (Classroom power relations, 1997, p. 7) In the three classes. Syllabus and learning materials are the first important and put on line by Angel System for every student several days before the classes start. Thus the teaching goal and what the students are expected to do and achieve can be seen clearly.

Other Ways to Develop Positive Relationships with Students:

(1) Smile.

(2) Use humor appropriately.

(3) Be able to laugh at yourself.

(4) Provide adequate space for each student.

(5) Make sure students are always safe—physically and emotionally.

(6) Listen to students in and outside of the classroom.

(7) Attribute the ownership of ideas to those who initiated them. (The Classroom of Choice, p. 53, 2013)

During the period of my observing classes in MSU, I experienced that students and teachers developed a harmonious relationship and constructed more relaxing atmosphere full of discussions and negotiations by means of interaction to each other. Two or three students each time took over teacher's role to lead the discussion and some aggressive students often dominated the classroom, and tried to manipulate the teacher's role to create a physical environment. In this class, group presentation for 20 ~ 30 minutes is part of the teacher's plan as scheduled before the start of the term in three hours credit. In this case, teacher and students are at equal position of transmitting knowledge based on mutual understanding and respect. In some cases, students became actively involved in such discussion to the point that they took over the floor, controlled the distribution of turns to talk, assigned task to each group and influenced the definition of knowledge in the discussion by means of negotiating with classmates and teacher.

Ⅲ Classroom Environment

The key elements of classroom environment to be emphasized involves group cohesiveness and interpersonal relations, group norms and student roles, the teacher's leadership styles, and the process of facilitation, as well as the main phases of a proactive, motivational teaching practice within a process-oriented framework. What is the significance of trying to create a more pleasant classroom environment? How can a motivating classroom environment be created. One of the most prominent features of the classroom environment is the quality of the relationships between the students. That is cohesiveness. The quality of teaching and learning is completely different depending on whether the classroom is characterized by a atmosphere of trust and support or by a competitive, provocative atmosphere.

What is of importance for the students, however, is not so much how the teacher intends the object of learning to come to the fore, but how the teacher structures the conditions of learning so that it is possible for the object of learning to come to the fore of the learners' awareness. (Classroom Discourse and the Space of Learning, p. 4) Both academic and physical environments are significant. In all classrooms of MSU, wireless net, multimedia computer and projector central conditioner are basic. Spacious classroom for different number of students are provided with movable chairs for small sized classroom offering a good opportunity for students to group together and switch members easily. Secondly, classroom walls with window shutters are decorated with all kinds of famous dictums and information bulletin board. You can easily find state newspaper, weekend newspaper, vending machine, drinking fountain small kitchen in each building. All sorts of clubs, seminars, art festivals, sports facilities and recycled activities are scattered everywhere on campus, which constitute instructive environment to develop all-around students consciously and subconsciously.

Ⅳ classroom activity management

Through one semester of observation, most commonly used activities are as followed:

Taking time with class-building activities is an investment, not only in building and maintaining positive relationships for their own sake, but also in preparing students for one of the most effective teaching strategies: cooperative learning. According to Erwin, Jonathan, not only does cooperative learning result in higher achievement and greater long-term retention of what is learned, it also tends to result in

- Higher-level reasoning (critical thinking);
- Process gain (more new ideas, strategies, and solutions generated);
- Transfer of what is learned from one situation to another;
- Positive attitudes toward the subject being studied;
- Time on task. (The Classroom of Choice, p. 76 – 76).

So Cooperative learning is most addressed by the language teacher in the classes observed. Students are divided into several groups of two or three to work together before class as a team for one topic from one or two articles in the agenda. In class, this team as leading discussants with a previewed question list under the teacher's revision, manipulated the whole class, and the other students were grouped randomly by three or four to discuss the questions randomly arranged in the question list. During the first half an hour of cooperation and interaction mainly among students, the teacher was mainly listening, observing and sometimes questioning the students' idea and supporting the students to get reasonable answers or explaining more deeply about a certain aspect of the topic.

Another salient activity in class is peer interaction: peer interaction through tasks is an important feature of communicative classrooms. It complements teacher-fronted interaction by providing a context for practice and meaningful use of the target language and greater opportunity for individual production. Thus, it may facilitate acquisition through learner production, feeding-back, and noticing of form. (Jenefer Philp, Susan Walter and Helen Basturkmen, 2010) Through peer interaction, students learn more from each other and share some knowledge together. After students' presentation, the teacher makes final summary and discusses more about the difficult or debatable questions. Usually the data analysis and findings of the research are the most challenging part which will be discussed more under the teacher' s leading and guiding. The whole class is full of interactions between students and students, teacher and students. Thus, the task-based language teaching is accomplished. The other frequently-used activities are included:

Know-Want-Learned (KWL). This is a well-known strategy for beginning a new unit of study. Students are first asked what they know about a particular topic. This helps the teacher determine how much prior knowledge students have about the subject they' re about to study helping her connect new information into what they already know.

Inquiring Minds. This process helps students work in teams of three or four focus on a class reading assignment, learn important questioning skills, and engage higher level thinking skills.

Information Gap: This creates the need and desire to speak/write and the curiosity to listen/read. Information gap activities are those in which students are given different bits of information. By sharing this separate information they can complete a task.

Jigsaw: the best way to learn something is to teach it to others (p. 82 – 85).

Graffiti: Benefit of allowing students to get out of their seats and move around the room to have students offer solutions to problems.

All Hands on Deck. This strategy, explained by Paula Rutherford (1998), promotes participation by all students, focuses students on a topic to be studied, and helps uncover students' prior knowledge about the topic to be studied.

Pairs Discuss. This activity, described by Johnson and Holubec (1993), is a great follow-up to teacher-guided practice on a particular skill. Once the teacher gives an assignment, partners take turns answering a question or doing a problem while the other partner coaches and gives feedback.

V Student behavior

Student discipline and classroom management have always been a concern for teachers, administrators, and teacher educators (classroom discipline in American schools, 1998, p. 2). Simply punishing "misbehaving" students to "take responsibility for their actions", as many teachers advocates classroom management do, in important aspects misses the point. In an atmosphere of trust, caring, and empathy, learners can open their hearts and minds to new knowledge, change old patterns of behavior, and develop a vision of how they can relate in caring, responsible ways to the world (Classroom Discipline in American Schools, p. 263).

Empowerment strategies help increase student success and achievement in classroom. When teachers provide a number of opportunities for students to gain power, these students will work harder on their assignments, and behavioral problems will be reduced significantly, if not completely eliminated.

Dozens of specific strategies are emphasized that teachers can use to provide students with responsible ways to meet their need for power by (1) giving students a say in the classroom, (2) helping students gain recognition, and (3) adopting other classroom procedures designed to help students gain personal empowerment in school.

In the three classes I observed, there were no problems of disruptive behaviors. Students carried out their tasks in class and out of class carefully. Attendance each time will be signed by students. Group presentation was done successfully full of discussions and negotiations of knowledge. Homework of doing a project or writing a paper and quizzes were submitted on line on time. Spino asked students to do a quiz and handed in class notes each time. Students seemed satisfied with these. One common and obvious phenomenon is that some students ate snacks in class from now and on, which interfered class attention and focus on the lesson.

Ⅵ Giving Students Recognition

"Feedback is one of the greatest sources of intrinsic motivation" (Jensen, 1998, p. 67). The individual grade was composed of several parts. Peer feedback refers to their rating sheets including the following criteria:

1. Attended team meetings.
2. Carried out team responsibilities.
3. Treated other team members with courtesy.
4. Communicated effectively with other team members.

I felt that using this system was the fairest way to allow them to do group projects and still have individual accountability. Peer recognition is adopted by teachers all the time.

At the end of a unit or at the end of a week, month, or semester, have students give recognition to each other. One way to do this is to have the students write their name on an envelope and place a blank piece of paper in the envelope. Have the students sit in a circle and pass their envelopes to the person to their right. Each student takes the piece of paper out of the envelope and writes down a strength that they recognized in that student during the last unit, week, semester, or year.

Ⅶ Conclusion

Based on the experience of being a visiting scholar in MSU for a year, a conclusion can be drawn that positive classroom is the keystone of many universities. Student and teacher relation is very relaxing and harmonious. Small talk and praising words from the teacher before class make the atmosphere soothing. Secondly teaching content is rich and colorful but surrounding the key thread along with effective on-line Angel System. Cooperative learning, students presentation, and group discussion dominate the classroom. Considerable reading work and individual learning before class seem much more crucial than that in class learning. Normal classroom learning activities are impossible without previewing. What's more, standard, detailed teaching syllabus and policy at the beginning of each semester is the indispensable condition to regulate students to follow the teacher for learning. In addition, credit system and no make-up examination as well as university culture guarantee students to succeed in completing school work well. To sum up, good policies and learning atmosphere, advanced net technology, harmonious student-teacher relationship, colorful campus beneficial activities render classroom management successful.

Reference

[1] Moskowitz, G. , Hayman, J. L. , Jr. *Success Strategies of Inner-city Teachers: A Year-long Study*. Journal of Educational Research, 69:283 – 289.

[2] Allen, J. D. *Classroom Management: Students' Perspectives, Goals, and Strategies*. American Educational Research Journal, 23, 437 – 459.

[3] Gootman, Marilyn E. *The Caring Teacher's Guide to Discipline: Helping Students Learn Self-control, Responsibility, and Respect*, K-6. 2008:36.

[4] Ronald E. Butchart & Barbara McEwan. *Classroom Discipline in American*

Schools Problems and Possibilities for Democratic Education [M]. State University of New York Press, 2013.

[5] Erwin, Jonathan C. *The Classroom of Choice: Giving Students What They Need and Getting What You Want*, 2013.

[6] Mary Phillips Manke. *Classroom Power Relations Understanding Student-Teacher Interaction*, Lawrenc Erlbaum Associates. London: Mahwah New Jersey, 1997.

[7] Marton, Ference, Tsui, Amy. *Classroom Discourse and the Space of Learning*, 2013.

[8] Jenefer Philp, Susan Walter and Helen Basturkmen. *Peer Interaction in the Foreign Language Classroom: What Factors Foster a Focus on Form?* Applied Language Studies and Linguistics, Vol. 19. 4, November 2010, 261 – 267, University of Auckland, Auckland, New Zealand.

美国高等教育国际化的经验与启示

首都经济贸易大学外国语学院　王鹏

摘　要:高等教育国际化是高等教育发展的一种趋势,也是我国高等教育发展的新方向。美国在这方面积累了不少经验,包括树立全球化与国际化的思想观念、以政策法规方式规范高等教育国际化、重视国际化的教学内容、推动教学主体在国际间交流、积极开展国际合作等。为我国建立有中国特色的高等教育国际化体系提供了借鉴。

关键词:美国;高等教育;国际化

高等教育国际化既是当今世界高等教育发展的全球性趋势,也是国际社会和国际组织积极推动的一项活动。随着全球化的深入,高等教育国际化已从边缘逐渐成为高校管理、规划、培养目标和课程设置的一个中心因素。高等教育国际化主要包括三个方面的内容:一是课程中的国际内容;二是与培训和研究有关的学者和学生的国际流动;三是国际的技术援助与合作计划。具体来说,就是加强教育的国际交流合作,积极向世界开放国内教育市场并充分利用国际教育市场。众所周知,美国是高等教育最发达的国家,其高等教育国际化有很多值得我们借鉴的地方,本文则从介绍美国高等教育国际化的经验入手,希望能对我国高等教育国际化的发展有所助益。

一、美国高等教育国际化的历程

美国的高等教育有近一个世纪的国际化经验。高等教育国际化在不同时期往往呈现不同的表现形式。美国首次国际化尝试开始于十九世纪二三十年代的出国留学。之后,共历经了4次高等教育国际化的浪潮:第一次是在第二次世界大战以前;第二次发生于20世纪70年代,大众普遍认为,吸收其他国家的知识会促进世界和平;第三次发生于20世纪90年代,是对当时国际化和科技发展的一种回应;第四次发生于21世纪以来,也是国际化浪潮最显著的一次,人们普遍认识到国际化对本土安全有着明显的启示。

二、美国高等教育国际化的经验

(一)树立全球化与国际化的思想理念

美国是一个重视高等教育国际化的国家。全美州立院校联合会在其敦促加快教育国际化的报告中指出:“学生应接受正确反映全世界社会、政治、文化和经济的全方位的国际化教育”,“教育界应改变‘只扫门前雪’的封闭的教育观念,积极研究全球性问题,通过国际教育交流项目、技术支持等方式,加强同外部世界的联系。”美国著名的高等教育专家克拉克曾明确指出:“我们需要一种超越赠地学院传统的新的高等教育观念,这种观念实际上就是高等教育要面向世界,或者说高等教育要国际化。”由于具有全球化与国际化的观念,尤其重视高等教育国际化,使美国高等教育国际化一直处于世界前列。

(二)完善高等教育法规及规范高等教育国际化发展

完善的高等教育法规为美国的高等教育国际化打下了坚实的基础和创造了良好的操作平台。美国的高等教育国际化是其全球化发展战略在教育上的反映,它以法规和政策的形式将高等教育国际化的要求固化和规范起来,使之成为国家意志,从而保持了国际化原则的延续性和稳定性。美国 1948 年出台了《美国新闻与教育交流法》,1958 年出台了《国防教育法》,1966 年又通过了《国际教育法》。2000 年,美国颁布的《美国 2000 年教育目标法》则主要强调教育的国际化,明确提出采用“面貌新、与众不同的方法使每个学生都能达到知识的世界级标准”。这些教育法律的相继颁布与实施,为美国高等教育国际化的发展提供了法律保障,这也是美国高等教育国际化始终处于国际前列的重要原因。有了政策和法规的支持,美国政府、各种社会组织及高等学校等就可以通过设置奖学金或项目基金的方式,直接支持高等教育国际化,吸引来自世界各地的留学生,为美国的经济发展提供了大量的人才储备。例如,国务院的“教育与文化教育交流”、“富布莱特项目”以及 2001 年 1 月 17 日教育文化事务署宣布设立的用以资助美国本科生出国学习的“本杰明·吉尔曼国际奖学金项目”、国防部的“国家安全教育项目”、联邦教育部的“高等教育法第 6 款项目”和“富布莱特 - 海斯项目”等就是这样。

(三)加强国际理解教育

国际化不仅意味着了解和掌握国外的语言文字,更重要的是要形成从全人类利益出发、以全球观点考虑问题、理解国际社会、关心和宽容异国文化的品性和风范。目前,美国 50 个州中有 34 个州制定了旨在指导和鼓励开展全球教育的章程,其余各州正在对有关规则进行讨论。

美国各高校近年来也普遍加强了国际知识的教学,以培养具有国际战略眼光的人才。为了推出国际知识的教学,诸如国际关系、比较政治、比较经济体制、国际法、国际组织等课程早已进入高校。有研究表明,77%的四年制院校开设了国际教育内容的课程,其中47%的院校开设历史与文明,35%开设世界历史与文化,29%开设其他国际教育内容,而20%多一点开设非西方历史、文明和文化,例如东方文化、非洲文化、中东文化等。美国大学一方面通过开设相关课程加强学生对非西方文化的了解;另一方面还对传统课程进行了修订,一些科目如历史学、政治学、经济学、社会学、比较语言学、文学等,以前都仅限于西方世界的有关事件和成就,现在已扩大了范围,在内容上涵盖了整个世界。

(四)积极开展国际间的交流与合作

高等教育国际化的目的就是强化国际高等教育的交流与合作。美国通过开展跨国教育合作、在海外设立分支机构、建立合作伙伴和以研究为基础的合作等方式,推动高等教育在国际间的交流。一是开展跨国教育合作。美国高校重视与国外同行开展国际合作,主要方式是某一美国大学与一所或多所外国大学共同开展学术合作项目,其中包括合作研究、共同研究、合作培训、联合办学、共同开发项目等。二是在海外设立分支机构。美国还积极在海外创办分校,探索与其他国家合作办学的道路。1985年,美国在中国创办的南京大学中美文化中心成绩显著,它是由南京大学和美国约翰·霍普金斯大学合作举办的教学和研究机构的统一体,每年招收具有硕士学位或类似水平的中美学生各50名,中美教授各自用本国语言授课,以两国的政治、经济、文化、外教、历史、法律和国际问题为主要内容,培养从事中美事务的专门人才和有关领域的教学研究人员。三是伙伴合作和以科技为基础的合作。高等教育的伙伴组织可以加速为国际化提供资源,包括与其他高等教育机构更全面的合作、创建基于网络的资源,以分享关于全球化和国际事务的内容与视角、发布例行的国际内容,以及对超越地域和国界事务的政策与法律事务更加专注等。

三、美国高等教育国际化对我国的启示

全球化是指技术、经济、知识、人类、价值和观念的潮流以各种不同的方式对每个国家的历史、传统和文化所产生的影响作用,而高等教育国际化则是每个国家对应全球化浪潮所做出的独特反应之一,是把国际的和跨文化的理念整合到院校的教学、研究和服务的功能中去的过程。高等教育国际化改革已经成为一个国家经济全球化的重要组成部分和全球化程度的重要参考指标,我们应该从教学、研究和

服务三个方面来推进我国高等教育国际化改革。

(一)教育教学体系国际化

首先,积极引进国际化教材。尽管国内优秀教材众多,其知识体系的逻辑性强,学科体系的结构清晰,有利于学生知识的整体把握,但与美国大学以培养学生创新精神、研究能力为教学目标的教材设计有很大的差异,因此,国内大学应该积极引进国外原版教材,增加国际性、跨国文化等内容,强化学生国际视野和国际意识的培养。其次,加强国际性课程建设。国际性课程是指教师在国际框架下讲授某一学科的知识,旨在培养学生对国际化和多元文化环境的适应能力,可以通过增设与国际事务相关的课程,或者加大传统课程中国际知识和国际主题的内容,并及时将前沿国际研究内容纳入课程。再次,学习借鉴国际教学方法。国内大学过分注重课堂教学,注重概念、理论和知识点的掌握和逻辑思维的培养,缺乏对教学实践活动的设计和研究,因而在教育质量方面与美国相差很大。我们应该认真学习和借鉴包括美国在内的西方发达国家大学的教学经验,关注学生实践能力的培养和创新意识的建立,积极鼓励开展社会实践活动和参加各种社会活动,引导学生参与教师的科研活动,提高学生发现问题、分析问题和解决问题的能力。

(二)科学研究平台国际化

我国高校与世界一流大学相比,国际化科研工作尚处于起步阶段,国际化科研氛围不够浓厚,国际化科研意识尚未建立,国家层面的重大国际合作学术科研交流还很缺乏,居于国际前沿水平的学科或专业也很少,参与科研团队建设的国际知名学者数量仍不多。因此,必须着力建设国际化的科学研究平台,通过发挥重点建设学科的带动作用开展学科建设中的国际科研合作与交流工作。同时,拓宽科学研究的视野,充分利用发达国家先进的科学研究成果、经验与人力智力资源,提高我国高校科学研究的总体实力和水平,从而实现高等教育跨越式发展。

(三)社会服务机制国际化

社会需求是高等教育发展的最大动力。当前,经济全球化和教育国际化对高等教育发展提出了更新更高的要求,也为高等教育的发展提供了有利的机遇。坚持以服务求支持,以贡献求发展,才能肩负起促进社会经济发展的历史任务。我国高校应主动适应经济发展的需要,把学校发展融入到经济全球化和社会大发展的时代背景下,主动积极地为经济建设、社会发展和文明进步服务,从而建立有效的国际化社会服务机制。首先,培养高素质的国际化人才是增强我国在经济全球化中竞争实力的有效手段,我们要充分发挥高等教育机构在国际化人才培养中的重要作用。其次,拓展服务经济社会发展的能力,积极开展与国际知名公司企业的交流合作，寻求建立稳定的科技合作关系，实现大批高科技含量科研成果的产业化，从而取得良好的社会效益和经济效益，带动社会经济的发展，促进高校学科建设与人才培养。再次，在专业建设中体现国际化的特色。要根据社会发展需要、国家产业结构调整和学校的自身特点，加强同行业、企业乃至人才市场、劳动力市场的密切联系，进一步拓宽专业口径，应用国际观念和信息技术加快专业建设和发展，调整专业定位，以信息化带动专业建设现代化。

参考文献：

[1]杨保成，苏艳红．美国高等教育国际化的特点、经验与启示[J]．黄河科技大学学报，2011.

[2]昊坚．当代高等教育国际化发展[M]．北京：人民出版社，2008.

[3]谌莉，刘晓虹．美国高等教育国际化的经验与反思[J]．世界教育信息，2005(1).

[4] Hans de Wit, Jane A. Knight. *Quality and Internationalization in Higher Education*[M]. OECD Publishing, 1999: 14, 16.

[5]汪霞，钱小龙．美国高等教育国际化的现状、经验及我国的对策[J]．全球教育展望，2010.

学习者个体差异对二语习得的影响

首都经济贸易大学外国语学院　吴琨

摘　要：近年来大量研究表明学习者个体差异对二语习得，尤其是学习成效起着重要的作用。个体差异研究已经成为二语习得领域一个重要组成部分。本文着重分析、介绍了个体差异的4个主要方面即年龄、学能、动机和学习策略对二语习得的影响，并讨论了这些因素对外语教学的启示。

关键词：二语习得；个体差异；年龄；学能；动机；学习策略

Abstract: In recent years, more and more studies show that individual differences play a significant role in second language acquisition, especially in the achievement of the language acquisition made by learners. Individual differences research has become an indispensible part of SLA. The paper mainly introduces and analyses the four key aspects of individual differences namely age, language aptitude, motivation and learning strategies and their impact on SLA. It also discusses implications of IDs for language teaching.

Key Words: second language acquisition; individual differences; age; language aptitude; motivation; learning strategies

多年来二语习得领域的研究者们一直在探讨为什么在相同的环境下第二语言的学习者在语言最终的学习成效上存在显著差异。究其原因，在语言学领域可以说是语言迁移现象、僵化、过度归纳等的影响；而在非语言学领域，学习者的个体差异和语言学习成效有着直接的关系。因此对个体差异的研究就显得尤为重要。基于这一点，本文着重讨论了学习者个体差异的4个主要方面年龄、学能、动机及学习策略，以及它们对外语教学的启示。

一、年龄

关于二语习得年龄的研究一直致力于回答这样的问题：学习外语是否有最佳年龄，即语言学习的关键期？许多研究者都在考察一种普遍的观点，即儿童学习外语要优于成年人。这一观点的理论依据是关键期假设理论，此理论始于20世纪60年代，即人类只有在2岁到青少年初期这段时间具备学语言的能力，过了这段时期,这种学习语言的能力会明显减弱。但有趣的是研究的结果却无法令人信服。相反有些研究结果还证明年龄大是一个优势。如哈利(Harley,1986)研究中加拿大学生学习法语,斯诺(Snow)和赫夫纳格尔(Hoefnagel,1978)关于英语成人学习者和儿童学习者学习荷兰语的实验结果证明,如果成人和儿童用同样的方法在同样的环境下学习外语,成人在最初的语音规则和句法结构的掌握上均优于儿童。但这些研究所证明的是在语言习得初始速度上成人的表现优于儿童。而在约翰逊(Johnson)和纽伯特(Newport,1989)的研究中,46 名受试者是生活在美国的中国和韩国学习者,研究的结果是二语习得的起始年龄对最终的学习成效具有预测作用。辛格尔顿(Singleton,1989)的研究证明习得起始年龄小的儿童二语习得更易取得更大的成效。他们的研究及其他的研究说明语言习得有关键期,但这是从最终的学习成效来考察的,仍然还存在疑问。这些研究的结果是如此的复杂而自相矛盾。克拉申等(Krashen、Scarcella 和 Long,1979)提议如果长效学习和短效学习区分开来,那么年龄对二语习得的影响会有一个清晰的脉络,即年龄大的学习者学得快而年轻的学习者学得更好。长效学习研究表明从长远来看年轻学习者的外语水平最终会高于年龄大的学习者,尤其是在语音方面。只有年龄非常小的学习者的语音才会达到英语本地人的水平,而过了青春期之后语音很难达到与本族语相当的水平。就语音习得而言,年龄的影响毋庸置疑。而短效学习研究表明年龄大的学习者在掌握句法和构词方面速度较快,但这种优势将随着时间的推移而消逝。即成人在语言习得的最初阶段优于儿童,但最终儿童取得的成效高于成人。这些是年龄问题研究取得的共识性结论。对于最佳年龄期,研究者们有着不同的看法。笔者以为,不论人们如何阐述关键期假设理论,外语学习是服务于每个人不同的目的的。如果学习者打算以外语作为一种流利使用的交际工具,并且计划花几年的时间来学习,那么最好从儿童期开始,这样他们有可能成为流利的语言使用者。如果只是想对某种语言有个了解,那么他们可开始得晚些。年龄不同,学习方式应做相应的调整,而教师也应变化教学方式来满足学生的不同要求。另外对于成人学习者来说,教师不应过分强调他们语音的准确性,进行过多的纠音,这会挫败他们学习的动力;而应该把重点放在是否可以运用外语清晰地表达思想,是否可以进行流利的交流上,毕竟语言是我们用以交流的工具。年龄只是人们从生理的角度研究外语学习的生理因素,对二语习得有影响,但不是主要的。

二、学能

个体差异研究的第二个重要方面是学能研究。学能是指学习者学习外语所需要的认知能力或学习外语能力倾向。学能是相对稳定的,它不是通过训练或实践可以改变或提高的。有些人这种能力较强而有些人则较弱。抛开年龄和动机等因素,我们都承认个体学习的速度和水平是不同的。这种差异可归因于众多因素中的一个——学能因素。早在五六十年代,研究者们通过卡罗尔等(Carroll 和 Sapnos)的现代语言能力测试(MLAT,1959)或是皮姆斯勒语言能力 Battery(1966)来考察学习者的学能。Carroll(1981)认为学能由几个相互独立的能力构成,即语音解码能力、语法敏感性、语言学习归纳能力和联想记忆能力。这些能力与二语习得有着直接的联系,对学好外语是有帮助的。如语音解码能力可帮助辨别和记住发音,这种能力强的学习者语音就学得快;具有良好语言分析能力的人比较容易发现和归纳语言规律等。同样斯凯恩(Skehan,2002)认为学能在二语习得的不同时期起着不同的作用。语音解码能力在习得的输入加工接触起作用;语言分析能力在中央处理阶段发挥作用;记忆能力则在语言检索和输出时产生作用。这些学习能力帮助学习者提高学习速度,降低学习难度,对学习效果有着直接的预测作用(戴运财,2006)。而在研究学习者能力和教学处理的相互关系方面,Cronbach(克朗巴哈)最早提出了能力倾向处理交互模式。根据这个模式,当教学策略或教学步骤和学习者能力相匹配时,学习者能取得最优化的学习效果(杨连瑞,2009)。

三、动机

二语习得研究表明一些学习者比另一些学习者学得更好、达到更高的程度是因为他们有着强烈的动机。这种动机和成功之间的直接关系首先由加德纳等(Gardner 和 Lambert,1972)提出。他们在动机对二语习得的作用方面做了广泛的研究。以此为基础,他们把动机分为两大主要类型:融合型动机和工具型动机。融合型动机指学习外语是为了与另一文化背景说这种语言的人进行交流,为了认识目标语文化、语言,尊重目标语社会。具有这种动机的学习者对目标语、文化、民族有着真正的兴趣并且有着融入其社会的强烈愿望和认同感。工具型动机则指学习者学习语言是因为它有利于某些实际的目标,如找工作、出国留学、通过等级证书考试等。通过研究,Gardner(1972)总结到融合型动机对培养交际技能尤其重要。而这种动机对正规学习的重要性同样不可忽视。Cook(库克,1996)相信学习者越崇拜目标语文化,在课堂上学习会越成功,表现越好。似乎对于二语习得的长期目标来说融合型动机更优于工具型动机。然而在其他情形下,如果目标语如英语是作为外语来学习的,例如 Gardner 的菲律宾学生,工具型动机则极为有效。这种相矛盾的结论可能源于目标语在学习者所处社会中起到的作用不同。而近几年对动机的研究又有了新的发展。研究者们对融合型动机赋予了新的解释。其中多内的研究最具开创性。他(2005)认为应该重新定义融合型动机的认同感,所认同的国家或文化不应该是某一个国家或文化,而是外语在学习者心目中的理想位置,这种叫理想外语自我。这个自我是学习者所向往的,而精通外语是学习者心目中的愿景。实现这个愿景就会给学习者带来学习的动力。有着这种愿景或理想自我的学习者会愿意出国留学、工作、旅游,关心国际风云,愿意和不同国家和文化背景的人交往。因此融合型动机的这些外在的表现源自学习者对理想外语自我的认同(王初明,2010)。

但不论怎么说,如果学习者既无融合型动机又无工具型动机,他会发现学习目标语是困难的,语言教师也同样认为教授没有任何学习动机的学习者很难。在教师看来,学习者应该带着对目标语言和文化的浓厚兴趣和强烈好奇心走进语言课堂,他们渴望学习到尽可能多的语言文化知识。而现实与理想相去甚远。从某种程度上讲,学习者动机的增强是依赖于教师的。学习者对教师及课程的看法将会影响他们的动机,而动机又会最终影响他们学习的成败。Gardner(1972)写道动机由两个因素组成——对学习环境的态度如教师或课程等以及融合性(包括教师在语言教授过程中如何对待目标语文化因素等)。显然他的观点强调了教师在二语习得过程中所起的重要作用。教师在课堂上的一切言行可以或是激发学习者学习动力或是使学习者失去动力。因此,教师最好对学习者不同动机了然于心或至少应该意识到学习者是有不同动机的。这样他们才能够顺利解决课堂上的问题。对教师来说重要的是增强学习者的动机并使他们能够保持。因为动机可把学习者引向成功,而成功反过来会提升他们的动机。要达到这种目标,在课堂上需要考虑几个因素。库克等(Cook 和 Schmitt,1991)认为课堂活动、教师的肯定和学习内容都对动机有极大的影响。因此,教师的言行、教授的内容、输入的语言信息都应符合学习者的动机。这些对提高动机并最终影响他们语言学习成败起着重要作用。在正规课堂教学中,教师对学习者的影响是不可替代的。

四、学习策略

Cohen(科恩,1998)认为学习策略是指学习者为了提高学习而进行的有意识的行为活动。他们通过储存、记忆、回忆、运用等来加强语言学习和运用。学习策略可以包括几个方面,着重于新信息的学习过程中为增进理解对信息进行分析和组织,学习完成后对它进行评估以决定是否需要进一步的行动。学习策略既可用于学习词汇这样的简单任务,也可用于语言理解和产出的复杂任务(J. C. Richards, J. Platt, H. Platt, 2000:260)。对于策略的分类主要有两种观点。一种是由 O' Malley

(奥玛利)和 Chamot(查莫特,1990)提出的,认为策略可分为元认知策略、认知策略和交际策略。另一种是 Oxford(奥克斯福德,1990)的二分类法,即直接策略(包括记忆、认知、补偿策略)和间接策略(即元认知、情感和社交策略)。早期的策略研究源于探究好的学习者策略,从而得出能够帮助弱势学习者的普遍策略。而由此引发的问题是弱势学习者是否能够通过运用介绍给他们的策略而提高学习的效果呢?大量研究表明结果并非如此。因为学习效果的好坏除了我们上述因素的影响,在学习策略层面,从某种程度上说是有关学习者策略选择的问题,而策略的选择又由年龄、动机、个人喜好、学习风格等诸多因素决定。

策略研究的另一个领域是学习策略培训。根据 Cook(1996)、Oxford (1990)和 Bailystok(比亚利斯托克,1990)的观点,策略培训的目的是帮助学习者了解他们能够采用的所有策略而不是教授他们一些特别的技巧。研究者对策略培训进行了各种认证,但结果各不相同。O'Malley 和 Chamot(1990)通过对学生的策略培训发现训练学习者运用学习策略可促进外语学习。在我国这方面的研究中,朱维芳(1999)对 57 人进行策略培训。结论是只有 31% 的学生反映有收获,多半学生认为效果不显著。王立非、范琳、刘津开等的实验结果是策略培训能够促进外语学习。Ellis(埃利斯,1994)曾提出疑问诸如应该接受哪些策略?策略培训是应该融入语言教学还是分开教学?要取得长久的效果需要多长时间?这些问题的研究目前仍没有令人满意的结果。然而无论策略研究的结果如何,Ellis(1994)和 Cohen (1998)均认为策略本身无好坏之分,但使用有恰当和不恰当之分,而且受学习者、不同任务、不同方式和不同时间的影响。这些信息对语言教师而言是有用的启发。不可否认学习者都会运用策略来学习语言。而强势学习者和弱势学习者的差别在于强势学习者懂得选择合适的策略完成相对应的任务。不论什么策略如果没有用在适当的任务中,策略使用则无效。因此,策略是否有助于促进语言学习依赖于学习者是否很好运用它们,是否能在合适的任务中运用恰当的策略而不取决于他们会使用多少策略。重要的是策略的选择。所以,策略培训目标应该专注于通过自我发现来决定在什么情形下,什么任务中使用什么策略。在于不仅能保证弱势学习者而且也有助于强势学习者。研究的另一个重要意义是语言教师不应该把外语教学仅仅看作是语言的教授。正如 Wenden(温登,1985)所写,学习者必须学会自己如何去做教师在课堂上所做的一切。教师应该通过对学习者的策略训练使他们了解各种策略从而能够脱离教师而进行自主学习——一种终生受用的学习方式。策略的培训是策略的介绍及使用的训练,它应该融入语言技能训练中去。

五、结束语

二语习得是一个复杂的过程,影响外语学习的既有外部条件因素,如语境、交际需要等,又有内在因素,如母语迁移和学习者个体差异等。在此我们着重讨论了个体差异的4个方面,年龄、学能、动机、学习策略。外语学习的成功是众多因素相互作用的结果。成功的途径也有许多,我们不可能给每个成功的学习者画一个单一的图解。而对个体差异研究这种认识对语言教学的重要意义是,如果教学方式与学习者所偏好的学习方式相吻合,那么不同程度的学习者都会达到同一个成功水平的。因此,对语言教学有益的启示是:(1)重视个体差异,对不同年龄、不同学能学习者进行分级,采用不同教学方式满足不同的学习需求。(2)重视教师对学习者学习动机的影响。通过设计教学语态、教学内容、教学活动及教学环境,运用灵活的教学方法来激发和提高学习者学习动机。(3)帮助学习者培养学习策略。在语言课堂上融入策略的学习和训练,使学生能够全面了解策略,使用策略并最终掌握策略,从而能够脱离教师自主学习——一种学习者终身受益的方法。

参考书目:

[1]戴运财. 语言学能对二语习得的影响[J]. 外语教学与研究,2006(6).

[2]杨连瑞,李绍鹏. 国外二语习得个体差异研究的新进展[J]. 外语学刊,2009(5).

[3]王初明. 外语是怎样学会的[M]. 北京:外语教学与研究出版社,2010.

[4]朱维芳,曹文. 大学新生英语营实践报告——新生入学心理调整及学习技巧强化训练[J]. 外语教学与研究,1999(2).

[5]Cohen, A. *Strategies in Learning and Using a Second Language*[M]. London: Addison Wesley Longman Limited, 1998.

[6]Cook, V. *Second Language Learning and Language Teaching*[M]. London: Arnold, 1996.

[7]Krashen, S., M. Long, R. Scarcella. *Age, Rate and Eventual Attainment in Second Language Acquisition*[J]. TESOL Quarterly13: 573 – 82. 1979.

[8]Johnson, L. and E. Newport. *Critical Period Effects in Second Language Learning: the Influence of Maturational State on the Acquisition of English as a Second Language*[J]. Cognitive Psychology21: 60 – 99, 1989.

[9]Snow, C. and M. Hoefnagel-Hohle. *The Critical Age for Language Acquisition:*

Evidence from Second Language Learning[J]. Child Development49:14 -28. 1978

[10]Domyei,Z. *The Psychology of the Language Learner:Individual Differences in Second Language Acquisition*[M]. MahwahNJ:Lawrence Erlbaum Associates,2005.

[11] Larsen-Freeman, D and Long, M. H. *An Introduction to Second Language Acquisition Research.* [M] Beijing: Foreign Language Teaching and Research Press,1991.

[12] Carroll, J. *Twenty-five Years of Research on Foreign Language Aptitude.* In Diller, K. C. (ed.), *Individual Differences and Universals in Language Learning.* Rowley,M. A:Newbury House,1981.

[13] Gardner, R. C. & Lambert, W. *Attitudes and Motivation in Second Language Learning*[M]. Rowley,Mass:Newbury House Publishers,1972.

[14]O'Malley,J. & Chamot,*A. Learning Strategies in Second Language Acquisition* [M]. Cambridge:Cambridge University Press,1990.

[15]Wenden,A. *Learner strategies*[J]. TESOL Newletter 19:1,4 -5,7. 1985.

[16]Oxford,R. L. *Language Learning Strategies:What Every Teacher Should Know* [M]. Boston:Heinle and Heinle,1990.

[17] Ellis, R. *The Study of Second Language Acquisition* [M]. Oxford: Oxford University Press,1994.

[18]Skehan,P. *Theorizing and Updating Aptitude*[A]. In P. Robinson(ed.),2002.

[19]Crookes,G. & Schmidt,R. W. *Motivation:Reopening the Research Agenda*[J]. Language learning 41 (4),469 -512. 1991.

[20] Bailystok, E. '*Achieeving Proficiency in a Second Language: a Processing Description' in Phillipson etal.* (eds). 1991.

[21] Harley, B. *Age in Second Language Acquisition* [M]. Cleven, Avon: Multilingual Matters,1986.

[22]Carroll,J & Sapon,S. *Modern Language Aptitude Test* (MLAT). New York: Psychological. 1959.

[23] Pimsleur, P. *Pimsleur Language Aptitude Battery* (PLAB). New York: Harcourt Brace Jovanovich,1966.

[24] Singleton, D. *Language Acquisition: The Age Factor* [M]. Cleven, Avon: Multilingual Matters,1989.

培养大学生英语批判性思辨能力的教学模式初探

首都经济贸易大学外国语学院　杨静

摘　要：大学英语教学只是注重学生听说读写语言技能的训练，缺乏对大学生的批判性思维能力的培养。学生在英语课上回答问题和参与问题讨论时都会出现思维僵化、无话可说或回答的内容肤浅、逻辑混乱、条理性差的情况。这要求我们在大学英语教学过程中设计出能够充分调动学生批判性思维能力发展的任务和相应的教学模式。本人结合本校大学英语翻转教学的改革，从提高学生批判性思维能力的角度来尝试一种新的教学模式。

关键词：大学英语；批判性思维；教学模式

Abstract: College English teaching only focus on the training of listening, speaking, reading and writing abilities, and lack of cultivating the ability of critical thinking. In college English class, it is common to see the dry speech, rigid thinking, intellectual shallowness, logical disorder and disorganization circumstances in students' discussion. It's essential to design the teaching tasks and models which can contribute to the development of students' critical thinking. The author attempt to implement a new teaching model to improve college students' critical thinking by combining the school's flipped classroom reform.

Key Words: College English; Critical thinking; Teaching model

目前大学英语教学面临着改革，我国传统的大学英语教学一直存在着重语言能力训练、轻思维能力培养的倾向。在外语技能训练的过程中，只片面强调词汇记忆、机械模仿，而忽视了学生分析问题、创新求异以及独立对问题提出见解等思维能力的培养（何其莘等，1999；文秋芳，2006）。教师权威、学生盲从的传统教学模式束缚了学生思维的主动性和批判意识，阻碍了批判思维能力的发展。大学英语课堂可以通过营造课堂环境、小组讨论、反思性教学、评估活动等方式培养大学生的批判性思维能力（李迎新，2011）。因此教师在设计教学任务时应做到以新颖来激发学生的兴趣，以疑问来调动学生的好奇，以情感来感染学生的兴趣，让现代外语教学充分体现语言、思维、情感的交融。教师应该了解学生的背景和兴趣，引领学生全面地认识事物,进行主动地思考、质疑;而且教师应该创造良好的课堂气氛和教育环境并转变教法(卢丽虹,2007;罗明江,2008)。在设计任务活动的同时,教师必须充分考虑大学生的心理特点和认知需求,合理设计具有现实意义的探索性任务,调动学生积极地去思考,通过各种活动获取对知识的理解和洞察,通过分析、综合、评价等高级思维技能找出解决问题的办法,从而提高学生的批判性思维能力。

一、批判性思维能力培养的必要性和重要性

1991 年,美国国家教育目标制定小组就曾将"思维能力、交际能力和解决问题的能力"列为 21 世纪大学生培养目标。1999 年英国国家课程标准提出了学习者应具备的 5 种思维能力,分别是:信息处理能力、推理能力、质询能力、创造性思考能力和评价能力。中国科学院院长路雨祥院士曾经指出:"一个拥有持续创新能力和大量高素质人力资源的国家,将具备发展知识经济的巨大潜力;一个缺少科学储备和创新能力的国家,将失去知识经济带来的机遇。"创新人才培养的重任,理所当然落在了高等教育的肩上。以中美教育为例,在知识学习方面,中美两国的教育有着极为不同的传统。中国教育注重对知识的积累和灌输,注重培养学生对知识和权威的尊重,注重对知识的掌握和继承以及知识体系的构建。美国教育则注重培养学生运用知识的实际能力,注重培养学生对知识和权威的质疑、批判精神,注重对知识的拓展和创造。这两种教育表达了对待知识的不同态度,中国教育表达的是对知识的静态接受,美国教育表达的是对知识的动态改变。中国学生处在被传授知识的状态,其知识广度、对未知事物的探究力、创造力和学习兴趣不如异国伙伴。由批判性思维获得的知识是学生通过发挥主观能动性,不以书本知识为迷信,不以权威为答案,通过论证过程产生的。批判性思维过程要求学生掌握知识获得的过程。在此过程中,学习知识只是一种手段,学习一种知识是为了了解更多的知识。为此,我国培养创新人才,必须培养学生的批判性思维,使其通过批判性的方式获取知识。学习者面对 21 世纪信息的海洋、世界日益发生的巨变,需要具备终生学习的能力。"学会学习、学会思考"成为本世纪民主和公民教育中的核心要素。

二、批判性思维的构成

批判性思维运动的创始人杜威认为批判性思维是一种反省思维,是一个问题解决的过程,并且把概念、分析、综合、判断、理解、推理、假设、检验作为反省思维的基本要素(杜威,1991)。恩尼斯认为批判性思维指个体对做什么和相信什么做出合理决策的能力(Ennis,1984)。国际公认的批判性思维权威,美国"批判性思维国

家高层理事会”主席、“批判性思维中心”研究主任保罗(Richard W. Paul)博士对批判性思维下的定义是:“简言之,批判性思维就是通过一定的标准评价思维,进而改善思维。批判性思维是积极地、熟练地解析、应用、分析、综合、评估支配信念和行为的那些信息的过程。这些信息通过观察、实验、反省、推理或沟通收集或产生(Paul,2008)。”“特尔斐”项目组还构建了批判性思维能力(思辨能力)的双维结构模型。根据该模型,批判思维包括认知能力和情感特质两个维度。其中认知能力包括:阐明、分析、评价、推理、解释、自我调节;情感维度包括:探究、自信、思想开阔、思维灵活、无偏见、诚实、谨慎、思变等情感特质。该模型强调批判性思维包括具体的思维技能,同时还包括批判的意识、态度,需要开阔的思维、独立思考、审视他人及自身观点的批判精神(Facione,1990)。林崇德(2006)的三菱结构思维能力模型(即思维目的、思维过程、思维材料、思维自我监控、思维品质、思维中的认知与非认知因素)和文秋芳等(2009)的层级思辨能力模型(即第一层元思辨能力和第二层思辨能力)(李莉文,2011)。

很多研究者认为思维能力培养中,除了要培养技能,也要培养人们使用技能的意愿(disposition)。思维能力就像弹钢琴,有弹钢琴的技巧,不等于愿意去弹钢琴;掌握思维技能不等于人会去使用这些技能。一个好的思考者除拥有思维策略和技能外,还应有探索、询问等意愿。罗素在 20 世纪 60 年代就曾提出态度、知识和思维技能是思维能力的基本组成成分(王淑花,2010)。Beyer(拜厄)曾特别指出 thinking(思维)和 thinking skills(思维技能)并非同义词,思维是对感官输入和记忆中的信息进行心理控制,从而发现意义、进行推理、形成思想和判断的复杂心理活动,往往涉及多层面的处理机制,会同时或反复使用很多的技能、知识和信息(Beyer,1991)。思维技能则是些离散的、可以准确描述的心理活动。人们已经发现了很多思维技能,如记忆、相关性判断、分类、预测、判断一个主张可行与否、综合、推断关系、做出结论等。思维技能是有效思维的基石或工具。根据运用思维方式的不同进行划分等级,其中“知识”、“理解”和“应用”属于低级的思维技能,“分析”、“综合”、“评价”则属于高级思维技能。高级思维技能和低级思维技能的主要区别在于:低级思维技能主要是记忆、简单理解和使用被动接受的信息,而高级思维则是包括积极、创造性的处理原有的信息的过程。当前我国学生知识学习主要采用的是低级思维技能,即知识、理解、应用,很少有高级思维技能(刘义,2010)。

三、批判性思维培养的策略

目前在国外批判性思维的教学策略很多,运用教学策略主要是进一步帮助学生学习。教师在课堂教学中适当使用批判性思维教学策略,不仅能够提高教学的有效性,而且能够提高学生的学习效果,从而达成教学目标。下面选择国外常用的批判性思维教学策略加以探讨。

(一)提问式教学(Socratic Questioning)

提问式教学法(Socratic Questioning)是被人熟知的培养思辨能力的教学。这种辩驳是以古希腊哲学家苏格拉底创造的方法为基础的。苏格拉底式提问以受过训练的实践、有意义的对话为依据。苏格拉底,认为受过训练的实践能激发学生通过逻辑的思维来验证观点、肯定他们的正确性。这一技巧要求教师表现出对主题并不知道,通过提问题的方式和学生进行对话。借助于这种"问答交流",学生最大限度地掌握了有关这一话题的知识。苏格拉底式提问技巧是一个探究深层含义的有效方式。它可以被运用于各个层次的学生,也可以运用于课程学习的不同阶段。通过运用苏格拉底式提问,教师可以促进学生独立思考,成为学习的主体。在此期间,高级思维技巧在学生思维过程中被激发,比如:讨论、辩论、评估和分析。保罗归纳了4种培养批判性思维心智特征的教学方法:第一,设立相关情境,让学生自己思考,发现问题。学生思考的过程要充分考虑各种要素,发现信息,活用所拥有的知识和技能。第二,教师提供各种可能,设置不同的思考角度,引出学生的不同观点,充分运用已有的信息,对问题进行理解。引导学生敢于提出与以往不同的观念,借由反方的证据对自我的观点进行修正。要能够接受讨论中的各种观点,因为每种观点都有自己的证据。关键是论据不同,论证的过程不同。第三,引出证据和根据。教师要引导学生就某种主张询问其理由,探索其确凿性。第四,确保探讨课题的时间。批判性思维是一种反思行为,要经历长时间的尝试错误,课题的解决要经过反复的思考。这种方法可以使学生在获得批判性思维技能后,运用这一技能,并进一步获得批判性人格特质。

(二)合作学习(Cooperative Learning)

合作是当今社会的一项重要技能。教学过程中通过合作不仅能够获得多方支持,形成更为客观的知识,同时也会形成合作精神。合作性学习具有很强的社会性,主要是通过一定人数组成的小组共同学习。在小组中,大家目标一致,分工不同,通过努力,共同解决问题。合作学习的好处在于,小组成员之间相互信息交换,彼此提醒弱点,发现各自证据和推理上的不足,积极进行改正。韦尔斯总结出人们在获取知识时所要经历的4个阶段:(1)在个人亲身经历基础上的对知识的认识;(2)与他人的信息交流和理解;(3)与他人共建对知识的理解和认识;(4)达到对知识更深层次的理解。人们在获取知识的努力中可能经历由内及外再由外入内的过程(Wells,1999)。因此在合作学习中,小组成员之间可以通过别人来矫正自己的理解,这样对于批判性思维的建立具有很好的作用。

(三)讨论教学(Discussion Teaching)

讨论教学法是批判性思维教学中比较典型的方法,这种方法相对于演讲式教学法更有助于提高批判性思维能力,著名批判性思维研究专家保罗等学者就认为不断质疑与发问是批判性思维的重要特征。教师与学生在探讨学习内容过程中的对话可以促进学生的认知发展和教师与学生之间的情感沟通;教师与学生交流可以提升学生对社会文化内涵的理解及接受能力。而小组讨论可帮助学生探究不同观点,增加其知识反映速度,让其主动倾听别人的意见,并提升学生与学生之间的社会交往能力和合作能力。讨论式教学中,韦尔斯认为文字表述能够帮助学生把对学习内容的浮浅认识在与人分享的过程中升华为对概念的深层理解,完成从人际心理的互动对话(inter-mental)到内在心理的自我对话(intra-mental),这一过渡是从社会话语 (social speech)到内在话语(inner speech)的转变(Wells,1999)。在课堂上,老师与学生的交流可以调动学生获取知识的兴趣,提高学习能力和对知识的感悟力,向学生传授进入社会交往的模式和方法,增加学生与人交往中的文化感知与生存智慧。通过师生的大量交流,可以促进和活跃学生的思维能力。有效的讨论有如下特点:(1)倾听讨论或辩论中他人观点;(2)回顾反思自己和他人观点的异同;(3)摒弃个人偏见,尝试理解他人观点的支撑论据;(4)总结同一命题的多维观点,做陈述性发言。教师可以采取学习者自述、与同伴互听或班级陈述等方式。该环节给学习者提供反思语言输入的机会、对提高口语表达的丰富性、流利性有很大帮助,使批判性思维成为一种常态。因此,小组讨论为批判性思维教学有效的教学法之一。

(四)运用思维导图(Mind mapping)

思维导图能够使无序的思维变得清晰、有序、高效,并激发创造性思维及批判性思维。思维导图是通过树状结构来呈现思考、将放射性思考具体化、直观化的过程的辅助思维工具(刘敬华 2013)。思维导图又叫心智图,是表达发射性思维的有效的图形思维工具,它简单却又极其有效,是一种革命性的思维工具。思维导图运用图文并重的技巧,把各级主题的关系用相互隶属与相关的层级图表现出来,把主题关键词与图像、颜色等建立记忆链接,思维导图充分运用左右脑的机能,利用记忆、阅读、思维的规律,协助人们在科学与艺术、逻辑与想象之间平衡发展,从而开启人类大脑的无限潜能。思维导图因此具有人类思维的强大功能。绘制思维导图需要从纸的中心画出主题图形(圆形,方形或其他图像),以主题图形为中心,使用曲线向周围发散出去,每条线条上写出一个关键词,根据主题的级别依次发散分支,不同级别的主题用线条粗细来区分。学习者可以根据自己的喜好使用图画、颜色、符号等图文并重的方式创造性地绘制思维导图。对于学生口语表达思维僵化、无话可说的现象,思维导图的分支绘制能够激励、刺激学习者深入地挖掘主题内涵,从不同角度、不同方面进行思考。在小组讨论过程中,思维导图也可以帮助学习者理清思路、理顺逻辑关系,从而不断地提高学生的批判性思维能力。

四、培养批判性思维能力的教学模式

在传统的课堂中,学习内容和课堂活动方式基本全部由教师安排,学生只是坐在教室按照老师的要求被动地参与。教师与学生的关系是“教”与“学”的关系。学生处在一个被动接受知识的位置,成为被改造的对象,教师是课堂的唯一决策者,传递知识和规定所学的内容。这种师生角色关系不利于学生批判性思维的培养与发展。在这种方式的熏陶下,学生将会失去他们应该享有的思维发展空间和对未知世界的兴趣和渴望。这是传统教学模式的一个缺陷。我们应该改变这种教学模式,改变教师的理念,创造出新的教学模式,来培养学生的批判性思维能力。批判性思维是一个提问的过程,在外语教学中提倡多鼓励学生提出问题,从而发展批判性思维(李瑞芳,2002)。在新的课堂环境中,要让学生积极地参与到课程建设中来,充分地发挥学生的主体性和能动性;让学生对自己参与设定的学习内容经过认真思考,提出问题,然后解决问题;让学生以小组为单位组织课堂的教学活动,教师起到参与和督导的作用。在这种过程中,学生通过交流互动不断加深对学习目的的理解和对自身角色的认识,逐渐增加独立思考和独立解决问题的意识,并开始摆脱被动学习的角色,不断地提高学生自主学习的能力。只有让学生的观念和态度发生转变,他们才能摆脱对教师的依赖。在教师的引导和鼓励下,学生能明确自己的观点,表达自己的想法,并主动与他人进行交流,不断地提高和加强批判性思维能力。

以下是以《大学英语全新版综合教程》为教材,运用提问、讨论、合作和绘制脑图等批判性思维的教学策略,设计出的教学模式。

(一)教学任务设计

操作步骤分为课前、课中和课后三个阶段:

课前	1. 全班学生自愿分成8组,明确组员名单,每组学生完成主讲一个单元的任务。
	2. 学生要对所学的单元进行预习,老师提前把教案 PPT 和相关视频都发给学生,供其自学或小组合作学习使用,对所学的单元课文提出 10 个问题,供课上讨论。
	3. 每组学生分别查找与每单元主题相关的文章,提出一至两个问题课上讨论,并提前一周发到公邮。同学们可以提前看到文章和问题,并做讨论准备。

续表

课上	1. 用 Quiz 的形式对学生的预习情况进行检查。主讲小组提出问题,组织全班分组进行讨论,问题结合课文内容,包括相关文章的一到两个问题,教师对课堂讨论进行监控与指导。
	2. 讨论结束后,每小组就所提的问题汇报讨论结果。
	3. 主讲小组把不同观点归类,做汇报总结。
	4. 教师总结点评。
课下	1. 独立完成课后练习,下次课检查讲解。
	2. 通过课下的自学与课上的讨论,学生已对本单元的话题形成了自己的观点,完成一篇与本话题相关的作文。老师对好的作文点评。
	3. 定期让每个学生写出心得体会,提出建议,改善教学。

(二)具体实施细节

1. 全班 38 人,分成 8 组,每组 4 ~5 人。每组主讲一单元的任务,共 8 个单元,以抽签的形式挑选任务。避免无人愿意承担第一组任务。

2. 主讲小组把提出的与课文相关问题和找到的相关文章提前一周交老师把关,通过后提前一周发到公邮,同学们可以提前准备要讨论的问题。有的小组找的文章和问题不合格,由老师提供。

3. 课上讨论时,主讲小组成员分别参与到各个小组中讨论。在讨论的过程中,学生遇到思维僵化的情况,老师引导学生运用思维导图来打开思路。

4. 主讲小组要阐述相关文章的大意和提出一至两个问题,供大家课上讨论。

5. 课上讨论小组是随机形成,每次由不同的人组成一组。主讲小组组织提问,每次由每组不同的学生来回答问题,避免总是一两个积极的学生回答问题,创造每个学生发言的机会。

6. 老师总结点评后,每组同学对主讲小组进行评价打分,老师提供打印好的评分表。

7. 学期末让学生填写问卷调查,收集和分析数据,调整教学策略。

五、总结

本文论述了运用新的教学模式来促进学生批判性思维能力的发展。通过一学期的教学实践,本人发现一些研究成果:学生课前自主学习,预习和查找相关文章,提高了自主学习的能力,改变了其学习观念和态度;课上与同学的热烈的讨论,对所学的内容加以运用,激发了思辨能力;课下通过写作来反思,有利于学生记忆能力、理解能力、应用能力、分析能力、评价能力、创造能力的发展。

在完成新的教学任务过程中,学生们积极地参与到课程建设中来,充分地发挥学生的主体性和能动性。在老师的指导下,学生自己设定内容,提出问题,解决问题。学习的内容是以教材为基础,学生再根据自己的兴趣查找到相关的资料,从而扩大了阅读量,丰富了学习内容。由于小组讨论要提出的问题,是大家集思广益,所以提出的问题比较新颖,角度独特。在解决问题方面,学生通过三轮的思考,即课前准备、课上讨论和课下总结,能找到解决问题的方案。这些教学活动设计都有助于他们批判性思维能力的发展和培养。

本次教学模式实践的局限性:首先,在教学实践中老师的工作量增加了很多,课前要花费大量的时间做准备工作,课后也要做大量的反思工作,不断地改进任务规则。其次,课堂中有很多不可控因素,如果主讲小组准备不充分,组织不好课堂或有些小组没有做好预习,就会影响讨论效果和教学效果,老师需要及时加以调整和引导。最后,在评估方面,老师通过学生完成的各项任务对其打分,再加上学生的互评分,能够督促学生认真地完成任务,促使其思辨能力的发展,但是如何更加客观和有效地测量与评定大学生的批判思维能力?如何能更好地设计出精确测量和评定大学生思辨能力的教学任务?这些方面还需要做进一步的研究。

参考文献:

[1] Beyer B. *Teaching Thinking Skills: A Handbook for Secondary School Teachers* [M]. London: Allyn and Bacon, 1991.

[2] Ennis R. H. *A Logical Basis for Measuring Critical Thinking Skills.* Educational Leadership, 1984.

[3] Facione, P. A. *Critical Thinking: A Statement of Expert Consensus for Purpose of Education Assessment and Introduction* (Executive Summary). "the Delphi Report" [M]. Millbrae, CA: California Academic Press, 1990.

[4] Paul, Richard and Elder, Linda. *The Miniature Guide to Critical Thinking: Concepts and Tools.* [M] Foundation for Critical Thinking Press, 2008.

[5] Gordon Wells. *Dialogic Inquiry Toward a Sociocultural Practice and Theory of Education.* Cambridge University Press, 1999.

[6]李莉文. 英语专业写作评测模式设计:以批判性思维能力培养为导向[J]. 外语与外语教学, 2011.

[7]李瑞芳. 外语教学与学生创造性和批判性思维的培养[J]. 外语教

学,2002.

[8]刘义．大学生批判性思维的研究:概念、历史与实践．华中科技大学博士论文,2010.

[9]刘敬华．口语教学中批判性思维缺失现象及培养模式研究[J]. 湖北第二师范学院学报,2013.

[10]李迎新,孙燕．大学英语教学与批判性思维培养[J]. 河北师范大学学报(教育科学版),2011.

[11]卢丽虹,田夕伟．大学英语教学中批判性思维的培养[J]. 中国成人教育,2007.

[12]罗明江,李旭．论大学英语教学中批判性思维的培养[J]. 黑龙江高教研究,2008.

[13]文秋芳,周燕．评述外语专业学生思维能力的发展[J]. 外语学刊,2006.

[14]文秋芳．口语教学与思维能力的培养[J]. 国外外语教学,1999.

[15]王淑花,吴尚义．国外思维能力培养研究综述[J]. 教育与职业,2010.

[16]约翰·杜威．我们怎样思维·经验与教育[M]. 姜文阂译．北京:人民教育出版社,1991.

Study on the Differences in Business English Writing Evaluating Criteria in Chinese Classrooms and Offices

首都经济贸易大学外国语学院　喻永阳

Abstract: For decades, Chinese universities have devoted considerable efforts to develop college students' English level from many aspects, but there still remain gaps in what students have acquired in classrooms and what business people require in offices. This paper uses a Likert-Scale method to calculate and compare the evaluation scores given by business people and Business English instructors. Result shows that there exist major differences on the evaluation criteria while reviewers are reading sample writings.

Key Words: Business English; Evaluating Crieria; Writing; Likert-Scale

I　Introductions

Since the Ministry of Education (China) approved business English as a formalized new discipline in 2007, Business English (BE) has been highly recognized in the society as one of the most prominent and promised disciplines. Statistics show that the number of Chinese universities that have opened business English major courses exceeds 800, and the schooling levels, majors and degrees are getting more diversified (Zhu, 2011). Scholars in China are working on constructing a sound course discipline by designing curriculum, editing textbooks, setting requirements and offering training course to BE teaching faculty. The understanding of the description or definition of BE may vary among scholars, but with little doubt, they believe that BE language teaching should be tailored to the specific learning and language use needs of identified groups of students (Johns & Price-Machado, 2001). So, as a main aspect of BE discipline, Business English Writing course is also goal-oriented and the objectives, planning, contents, instructions, exercises and even the evaluation criteria should serve the goal, which is to increase students' language skills and professional competence and help them pursue their careers in business settings.

In addition, BE instructors should realize there do exist gaps or differences between classrooms (where BE students receive and acquire knowledge in English language and professional skills) and business settings. This divergence happens because what factors that professors consider as effective writing are not the same as those evaluated by managers.

In order to investigate (1) what effective writing is in business people's eyes, and (2) to determine whether teaching faculty hold the same views as the business people, Seshadri and Theye (2000) make eight hypotheses as the ground stone of their research findings and some of them are supported by results. Seen in Table 1.

Table 1 Seshadri and Theye: hypotheses and results

H1	Business professionals are more lenient than business faculty in the global evaluation of reports.	supported
H2	Business professionals are less critical of violations of rules of business writing style than are business faculty.	not supported
H3	Business professionals evaluate reports on fewer criteria than do business faculty.	supported
H4	Business professionals, on the average, spend less time evaluating a report than do business faculty.	supported
H5	Business professionals are more lenient than business faculty in the global evaluation of reports.	supported
H6	Business faculty emphasize mechanics more than do business professionals	supported
H7	Business professionals give higher grades to reports which are less demanding of their time	not supported
H8	Business faculty give lower grades to reports which require more time to grade	supported

In the research held by Seshadri and Theye, they asked fifty business professionals and fifty business professors in the United States to evaluate three randomly selected business reports (a persuasive message, a strategy of one topic and a brief). And then their eight hypothesis are partly proven. Their findings conclude that business professors emphasize the *process* of writing while business professionals focus more on the *product*. (Seshadri and Theye, 2000: 21).

While in Chinese universities, English is a subject of foreign languages research and study. Business English writing are mainly taught by English language teachers with little or no business experience instead of business faculty, which means the education and training received by business students mainly focus on language itself.

Ⅱ Methodologies

In this paper, sample writing review has been employed. Two types of business writing homework (one e-mail and one business report) written by English major junior students who all passed CET 6 were passed to two groups of reviewers, one is a group of 10 English teachers (all of them are Chinese) and the other is a group of 5 business people (2 are Chinese-Americans and 3 are from English-spoken countries). These reviewers were asked to evaluate the written materials by completing a rating sheet consisting of the following criteria: theme, contents, grammer, lexical use, sentence structure, business manner and communication efficiency. Among these criteria, 3 of them are form language aspect, such as grammer, lexical use, sentence structure and 3 of them are from business aspect, such as theme, business manner and communicative efficiency and the last one (contents) is considered as business and language aspects. The rating sheet was designed as a Likert-type scale from excellent to poor (excellent is scored as 5 and poor as 1) and the reviewers were required to give ratings from the above 7 criteria. The data were collected through e-mails and interviews and the results are listed in Table 2:

Tabel 2: A Likert-type Scale of Business English Writing Evaluation

		Excellent 5	Above Average 4	Fair 3	Below Average 2	Poor 1	Average
Business professionals	Theme		2	1	2		3
	Contents		1	2	1		2.4
	Grammer		2	3			3.4
	Lexical use		2	1	2		3
	Sentence structure		2	2	1		3.2
	Business manner		1	1	2	1	2.4
	Communication efficiency			2	1	2	2

续表

		Excellent 5	Above Average 4	Fair 3	Below Average 2	Poor 1	Average
Academic professors	Theme	1	4	4	1		3. 5
	Contents		5	3	2		3. 5
	Grammer		1	5	3	1	2. 6
	Lexical use		3	6	1		3. 2
	Sentence structure		1	5	3	1	2. 6
	Business manner		5	4	1		3. 4
	Communication efficiency		5	3	2		3. 3

Table 2 shows that business professionals are more concerned about the business manner and communication efficiency and they are less lenient on evaluating the business writing sample than academic professors. From language aspects which include grammer, lexical use and sentence structure, business people reviewers gave higher average scores which respectively are 3. 4 in grammer, 3 in lexical use and 3. 2 in sentence structure, compared with the average scores of 2. 6, 3. 2 and 2. 6 given by BE instructors. Business people care less on the language itself. However, situation becomes greatly different when business people were revising the sample writing from their professional aspects. All business respondents gave a lower evaluation on business aspects and the average scores are 3 in theme, 2. 4 in contents, 2. 4 in business manner and the lowest 2 appeared in communication efficiency. Also, BE instructors gave a relatively higher score for these criteria and the average score from universities were 3. 5, 3. 5, 3. 4 and 3. 3. So, the comparison indicates the following results: (1) Business people place heavy concern on the business factors and they are more strict on evaluating communication efficiency and business manner. Because they believe these two factors not only fulfill the task of communication, but also show the style of working and the efficiency of operating jobs, which are essential in business. (2) University instructors concern more on language skills, such as grammer, lexical use and sentence structure. They measure the level of students' writing skills from the aspect of language itself. This may because most BE instructors in China are lack of not only Business education, but also working experience in business world. They received degrees in

English Language Study or English Literature and change their major to ESP after taking a teaching post. Some of them received further education or training course on business, which will greatly improve their understanding on BE teaching.

Furthermore, even after decades of BE course development, there still is lack of an efficient way to evaluate the quality of BE writing. The examination used in Chinese universities is still unable to evaluate the efficiency of ESP writing, which is the efficiency of information dissemination. The grading guidelines mainly focus on the use of grammar (time tense, spelling, numbers and etc), syntax and sentence structure, Even some writing softwares focus more on some solid standards while the transaction of sentences, the logic and the contents of their writings are paid little attention.

Ⅲ Conclusion

Business English discourse, or BE writing, is an integrated communication skill which required frequent practice and training. As a branch of ESP, BE Writing not only requires English language skills, but also needs the writers' comprehensive understanding on business. BE instructors need to focus on language and business skills, but business skills cannot be learned well just by memorizing business theories or reading business books. BE instructors should focus more on business writing materials which are widely available in business offices or worlds and generate their own understanding about the business aspects and pass this knowledge to their students.

Since just 15 participants offered their suggestions in this study, a greater variety of participants who have more diverse business or English teaching experience could be taken into consideration in future studies. More research methodologies would also be employed in the future, such as questionnaire or interviews. With a larger sample size, the result of Likert-Scale could be more reliable. However, this study has provided some useful information concerning the different criteria used in the classrooms and offices.

The authors would like to express appreciation to the fifteen participants in this study. Their quick response and professional revision made this study possible.

Reference

[1] Wenzhong, Z. & Peng, C. (2011). New Developments of Business English from ESP in China. *Theory and Practice in Language Studies*, Vol. 1, No. 4, pp. 379 – 383,

April 2011.

[2]Francesca, B. C. ,& Catherine, N. (2006). *Business Discourse.* Part II, Applying Business Discourse Research. 77 - 83.

[3] Seshadri, S. , & Theye, L. (2000). *Professionals and Professors: Substance or Style?* Business Communication Quarterly, 63(3), 9 - 23.

[4] http://tiespj. tespa. org. tw/esp-teachers-perceptions-of-business-english-courses/

[5] Johns, A. M. , & Price-Machado, D. (2001). *English for Specific Purposes (ESP): Tailoring Courses to Students' Needs and to the Outside World.* In M. Celce-Murcia (Ed.) Teaching English As a Second or Foreign Language. Boston: Heinle & Heinle.

针对学习者个体差异的大学英语教学模式研究
——多元智能理论视角

首都经济贸易大学外国语学院　赵静

摘　要:本研究以美国发展心理学家加德纳的多元智能理论为基础,借鉴美国多元文化教育理念,在了解学习者个体智能存在差异的同时,进一步分析学习者在英语学习策略和学习习惯上的不同,提出充分利用其智能优势,探索适合具有不同智能偏好的多样化教学模式,提高学习者的学习动机和学习兴趣,培养有效的学习策略。本研究主要从大学公共英语教学和商务英语专业教学入手,对现有教学模式进行分析,探讨多元智能理论在大学英语教学中的应用,并提出教学模式的改进方法和建议。在进一步提高教师课上教学效果的同时,引导学生找到适合自己的学习方法和策略,建立适合自己的学习风格,尤其是探寻可行的多样化的适合每个个体发展的独特教学方法和与之相适应的多样化评估方式,使学生对自己的学习和发展具有更自觉的责任,从而达到培养实用复合型优秀人才的教育目标。

关键词:多元智能理论;美国多元文化教育;学习者个体差异;大学英语教学模式

Abstract:This research is based on Gardner's theory of multi-intelligences and analyzes the differences in English learning strategies and learning habits referring to American multicultural educational idea while trying to understand the individual learners' differences of their intelligence and make full use of their strong points. This research explores suitable and multiple teaching methods for different students with different intelligent preferences to stimulate their learning motivation and develop their effective learning strategies. Mainly from the aspects of college public English teaching and business English teaching, this research explores the application of multi-intelligences theory, feasible and diversified teaching modes, suitable and corresponding assessment, and puts forward the methods and suggestions of how to improve classroom effect and how to guide students to find suitable method and strategy of learning in order to establish their own learning styles, and therefore by exploring diverse, suitable and effective teaching methods for every individual enables students to raise the awareness of responsibility for their learning and development in the future.

Key Words: theory of multi-intelligences; American multicultural education; learners personal differences; teaching modes of college English

一、引言

近年来随着大学扩招,我校来自全国各地包括港澳台地区、偏远农村地区和少数民族地区的学生呈上升趋势。由于各地对英语学习的要求不同,表现在听说读写译方面的英语基础水平亦有差异。学生的英语基础水平参差不齐,对教师教学提出了更高的要求。我校长期采取英语快班和普通班分级教学的方式,这在某种程度上缓解了基础水平差异过大带来的教学问题,但从实际教学效果来看,并不能从根本上解决学生水平个体差异问题,尤其对普通班里基础水平较低的学生来说,直接影响他们继续学习英语的兴趣和信心。那么该如何解决英语基础水平参差不齐带来的诸多教学问题,比如学习焦虑和英语水平较低学生的不自信等问题;如何改变单一的教学模式,采用多样化的教学组织形式和教学方法,探寻更加适合每个个体发展的独特教学模式,最大程度地提高学习兴趣,从而有效地促进学生的全面发展;如何寻求与多元教学相匹配的多样化评估方式,建立促进学习者发展的多元教学评价,以使学生有多种形式来展示自己的才能;如何了解学生的个性差异和智能偏好,以此划分班级,制定符合不同水平学生的教学内容和教学方案,找到相应模式。

20 世纪 60 年代开始,国外教育研究者对如何实施有效教学进行大量研究,研究的重点集中在教师的课堂活动上,而我国对有效教学的大量研究开始于 20 世纪 90 年代后期。教学策略是近 20 多年来随着学习策略研究的加深开始受到越来越多的关注,而根据学习者个体差异的教学模式只是在近些年才开始受到重视,人们对学习者在学习中的心理因素和智力因素进行了大量研究,其中最为著名的理论之一是“多元智能理论”。

二、多元智能理论

(一)多元智能理论的内容

多元智能理论是美国哈佛大学著名发展心理学家霍华德·加德纳(Howard Gardner)于 1983 年在《智力的结构》(Frames of Mind)一书中提出的,他通过对智能的多年研究和探索,认为人类的智能主要是由语言智能、数学逻辑智能、视觉空间智能、身体运动智能、音乐律动智能、人际交往智能、自我认知智能、自然探索智能和存在智能组成,后两种智能是 1995 年之后补充进来的。

语言智能(Verbal-Linguistic Intelligence)是指有效地运用口头语言或文字表达

自己的思想并理解他人,灵活掌握语音、语义、语法,具备用言语思维、用言语表达和欣赏语言深层内涵的能力。

数学逻辑智能(Logical-Mathematical Intelligence)是指有效地计算、测量、推理、归纳、分类,是有效运用数字和推理的智能。

视觉空间智能(Visual-Spatial Intelligence)是指准确感知视觉空间及周围一切事物,并且能把所感觉到的形象以图画的形式表现出来的能力。这项智能要求人对色彩、线条、形状、形式、空间及它们之间关系的敏感性很高,感受、辨别、记忆、改变物体的空间关系并借此表达思想和情感的能力比较强。

身体动觉智能(Bodily-Kinesthetic Intelligence)是指善于运用整个身体来表达想法和感觉,以及灵巧地运用双手制作或操作物体的能力。包括特殊的身体技巧,如平衡、协调、敏捷、力量、弹性和速度以及由触觉所引起的能力。这类人喜欢动手建造东西,喜欢户外活动,与人谈话时常用手势或其他肢体语言。

音乐律动智能(Musical-Rhythmic Intelligence)是指人能够敏锐地感知音调、旋律、节奏、音色等能力。表现为个人对音乐节奏、音调、音色和旋律的敏感。这类人拥有音乐的天赋,具有较高的表演、创作及表达音乐的能力。

人际交往智能(Interpersonal-Social Intelligence)是指能很好地理解别人,特别具有组织能力、协商能力、分析能力和人际交往能力。这项智能善于察觉他人的情绪、情感,体会他人的感觉感受,辨别不同人际关系的暗示以及对这些暗示做出适当反应的能力。

自我认知智能(Intrapersonal-Introspective Intelligence)是指能认识到自己的能力,把握自己的长处和短处并吸收他人的长处,能够把握自己的情绪、意向、动机、欲望,喜欢独立工作和独立思考,能自尊、自律,并具有规划自己生活的能力。

自然探索智能(Naturalist Intelligence)是指善于观察自然界中的各种事物,能认识和辨别植物、动物和自然环境的事物的能力。包括对社会的探索和对自然的探索两个方面。这项智能有着强烈的好奇心和求知欲,有敏锐的观察能力,能了解各种事物的细微差别。

存在智能(Existential Intelligence)是指人们表现出的对生命、死亡和终极现实提出问题并思考这些问题的能力。这种智能有对人生中诸多问题进行深入探索的能力。

加德纳认为,人类的智能是多元化的而非单一的,每个个体都有自己突出而独特的智能,而且每个个体都是独一无二的,都拥有不同的智能优势组合。加德纳打破了一般传统智能理论所依据的两个基本假设,其一是人类的认知是一元化的;其二是单一可量化的智力适用于每个人。他主张采用多种方式呈现教学内容,为学生取得成功提供多种选择。同时他特别强调学校教育的改革必须重视学生个体的差异,因此,在教学过程中必须尊重每个学生的差异,充分发掘每个学生的智能潜力,满足每个学生的学习需要,促进每个学生的发展。

多元智能理论是一种“内在建构性”的学习观,在对教学本质及特点的理解上,与建构主义的学习理论有相同之处,都特别强调每个人都是以自己的方式来理解知识和建构自己对事物的认识。所以,多元智能理论在教学中特别关注学习者个体智能的差异对教学的意义。按照多元智能理论,智能既可以是教学的内容,又可以是教学内容沟通的手段或媒体,这个特点对于教学是很重要的。加德纳强调学校教育的宗旨应该是开发多种智能并帮助学生发现适合其智能特点的职业和业余爱好。他认为学校教育的目标并不只是培养学生的智能或基本学科内容和技巧,而是学生必须对待定的学习主题有深入的理解,有进一步独立思考和解决问题的能力,并且强调教学过程中学生角色的主动性。根据多元智能理论,各种智能是以潜能的形态存于每个个体之中,只要给予适当的鼓励、机会、环境和教育,几乎每个人的所有多元智能均能发展到相当的高度,甚至可以远远超乎我们的预期。

(二)多元智能理论对英语教学改革的启示

加德纳的多元智能理论强调智能的多元性、差异性、实践性、创造性和可开发性。在学习上,各种智能起着同样重要的作用,一般的人都有发展这些智能的潜力,因此,教育应该在全面开发每个人的各种智能上,为学生创造多种多样的展现智能的情景,为所有的学生提供发展的多元途径,给他们多样化的选择,促使学生自发地对自身的强项和优势进行充分开发,挖掘自身的潜能。根据多元智能理论,并非每个人的智能都能够达到最高水平,但有的方面会较为突出,学生可以使用不同的智能方式来学习、理解和应用知识,那么我们就不能用传统的单一的教学方法和评价方式进行教育教学和评价学生的发展。既然智能是多元的,教学也应该是多元的信息传递和多元的评价,即高校教学应通过多种渠道进行教育教学活动并采用不同的评价手段和方法衡量学生的学业情况。只有这样,才可能真正发挥教学和评价的功能,多培养具有创造能力和解决实际问题能力的学生,才能真正促进学生的全面和谐发展。在教学过程中要从充分开发学生的各种智能出发,培养每个人在新的情境下的实践能力和创新能力,这种实践和创新能力的培养也是大学英语教学改革的核心与目标。我们在大学英语教学改革与创新模式上可以借鉴美国多元文化教育理念和方法。

三、针对学习者个体差异的调查

(一)调查步骤及方法

为了了解不同学习者的个体差异,找到适合他们的多样化教学模式,首先需要相关数据的收集,笔者参照 Creswell(克雷斯韦尔,2002)的步骤方法,具体程序如下:

(1)选择 2013 级三个班的学生作为问卷对象进行调查,2013 级英语课没有分快班和普通班,每个班的学生英语水平都参差不齐,有英语基础水平非常高的学生,也有相对较低的,还有根本听不懂英文授课的学生。在这三个班进行问卷调查,基本能反映整个年级的情况。从他们那里采集的数据比较客观,能够为我研究的问题提供有效信息。

(2)在做问卷调查前,给学生解释了此次调查的目的,并征得了他们的同意。因为大多数学生都渴望学好英语,尤其是尽快通过四、六级考试,同时能够提高英语的实际应用能力,他们愿意与我合作完成这一研究,共同寻求更有效的教学模式和方法。

(3)在确定与本研究有关的变量与所需收集的数据后,笔者制作了"针对学习者个体差异的大学英语教学模式研究问卷调查"表,问卷旨在了解学生的个体差异,问卷内容包括性格、民族、爱好、来自地区、英语基础水平和学习动机等方面的情况。

(4)数据的采集。在问卷调查之前我向所有参与者解释说明了此课题的研究内容,希望这次研究对他们的英语学习和教师的教学有益,我还向他们说明回答问卷的方式,时间大约 10 分钟。

(5)在学生的大力配合下,顺利完成了相关数据的采集。本次调查共发放问卷 112 份,收回有效问卷 110 份。

(二)调查结果

通过对问卷的统计与分析,调查结果如下表:

序号	内容	选项(人数/百分比%)
1	性别	男 35/31.8　女 75/68.2
2	民族	汉族 93/84.6　回族 6/5.5　蒙古族 5/4.6　维吾尔族 2/1.8 满族 1/0.9　壮族 1/0.9　土家族 1/0.9　羌族 1/0.9
3	性格	外向性格 19/17.3　内向性格 16/14.6　内外结合型性格 75/68.2
4	地区	城区 62/56.4　郊区 19/17.3　少数民族地区 15/13.6 农村地区 13/11.8　山区 1/0.9

续表

序号	内容	选项(人数/百分比%)
5	个人爱好	音乐 60/54.6　数学 19/17.3　绘画 21/19.1　体育 22/20 舞蹈 5/4.6　计算机 1/0.9　看书 1/0.9　语言学习 1/0.9 英语 1/0.9　足球 1/0.9　台球 1/0.9
6	海外经历	是 10/9.1　否 90/81.8
7	英语基础水平	基础水平好 10/9.1　一般 69/62.7　较低 31/28.2
8	喜欢学英语	是 37/33.6　否 10/9.1　不讨厌也不喜欢 63/57.3
9	喜欢英语启蒙老师	是 56/50.9　否 13/11.8　不讨厌也不喜欢 41/37.3
10	开始学习英语时间	幼儿园 19/17.3　小学 84/76.4　初中 7/6.4
11	接受过英语课外辅导	是 79/71.8　否 31/28.2
12	英语强项	语法 28/25.5　听 21/19.1　说 14/12.7　读 45/40.9　写 21/19.1 译 14/12.7　无强项 12/10.9
13	英语弱项	语法 39/35.5　听 62/56.4　说 60/54.6　读 22/20　写 45/40.9 译 40/36.4
14	学英语的动机	通过四、六级考试 54/49.1　出国深造 21/19.1　实际应用 65/59.1 兴趣 1/0.9　要求学 1/0.9
15	中学英语课授课语言	英语 3/2.7　汉语 16/14.6　英汉结合 91/82.7
16	希望英语课的授课语言	英语 28/25.5　汉语 1/0.9　英汉结合 81/73.6
17	学习英语的方式和习惯	大量背单词,读课文做阅读;一般以听为主,很少写,也很少读出声;听英文歌、看英文电影;学英语只靠课上;好好上课,完成作业;课上紧跟老师教学,课下背单词,读课文,练听力;多读文章,培养语感;多做练习;在户外大声朗读文章;积累句型和词组;课上认真听,课下好好写作业;每天做篇阅读,有时听英语新闻
18	对大学英语的期望	多媒体化;提高听说和写作水平;通过四、六级考试;能用英语与人交流;英语更实用;雅思目标达到 7.0;多听材料,多做翻译;加强听说训练;取得好成绩;全英文授课加外教授课;多训练口语,提高实际运用能力;英语整体水平有较大提高

(三)调查数据分析

从问卷调查结果可以了解受调查者在性格、民族、爱好、来自地区、英语基础水平和学习动机等方面的情况,分析如下:

(1)从"民族"上看,在110名接受问卷调查的学生当中,少数民族学生17人,占到15.5%,这说明少数民族学生在不断增加;从"地区"看,来自郊区的学生为19人,少数民族地区15人,农村13人,山区1人。郊区学生占到17.3%,较偏远的农村、山区和少数民族地区学生占到26.4%,这部分学生与城市学生有一定的文化差异,比如在调查中发现,城市的孩子接触英语较早,基本都是在小学甚至幼儿园就开始学习英语;初中开始学习英语起步较晚的大部分就是来自这些地区的学生,这些地区由于处在偏远地区,所以存在诸多因素,比如地理环境因素、民族和文化因素以及语言环境等因素,这些因素会造成教育体制不太完善、不太重视英语的学习、教师的水平和师资匮乏等问题,应当引起社会各界的注意。笔者在教学过程中注意到这部分学生往往学习比较认真,表现出渴望学好知识的愿望,自己很焦虑。学校应在分级教学上考虑这部分学生,细化分级制度,对程度较好的学生来说,上课内容增加、速度加快并有更高要求;对基础薄弱的学生,加大课时量,从基础知识补起,配备有经验的老师并制定与之相匹配的评估方式。在大学英语课堂,按照多元智能理论和多元文化教育理念,更要尊重每个个体差异,要尊重他们的文化,发掘他们的智能特点,鼓励他们的学习热情,以免由于英语基础问题产生学习焦虑,失去学好英语的信心。

(2)从"英语强项"来看,"读"占的比例最大,是40.9%,其他项的顺序依次是语法、写、听以及说和译,所占比例分别是25.5%、19.1%、19.1%、12.7%、12.7%。从"英语弱项"上看,听和说最高分别占56.4%和54.6%,其次是写40.9%、译36.4%、语法35.5%和读20%。这说明中学的教学更重视英语的读,这与英语教学长期重视阅读理解的应试教育有关。听和说是最大的弱项,而恰恰这两项是将来实际工作和生活中最实用的技能。笔者在与学生的交谈中发现,有些地区特别是边远或少数民族地区,高考没有听力,平时根本没有这方面的训练,刚上大学造成跟不上听不懂的局面。从数字看,他们对英语听说能力的提高又有较迫切的愿望。这就要求教师在平时上课加大这两方面的训练,利用多媒体手段,多提供语言环境,并督促他们课下多练习。

(3)从"英语学习动机"方面看,希望通过四、六级的学生有54人,占49.1%,这部分学生的目的很直接,就是先通过四级考试,拿到与之挂钩的学位证书,将来找工作更顺畅。但可喜的是有更多的学生65人选择"实际应用",人数占到一半以上，这说明相当一部分学生学习英语没有把通过四、六级，拿到学位证作为学习英语的最终目标，他们学习语言更注重对语言的使用，希望提高英语的实际运用能力，对自己将来的工作和生活有益。还有 19.1% 的学生选择的学习动机是“出国深造”，也表达了将来需要实际使用英语语言的愿望。总之，无论学习英语的动机如何，在我们的课堂上，教师都要尊重和利用学生学习的动机，采用多样化教学模式，吸引学生，使其输入最有用的知识。

(4)从受调查者对“英语学习习惯和方式”的描述和“对大学英语的期望”内容上，我们可以看到学生学习英语好的习惯和方法，就是课上认真听讲，课下完成作业，进行大量训练。同时，我们也看到他们存在的问题，大部分学生还是缺乏自主学习的意识和能力，依赖老师课上教学内容的心理过强，这样也许对一时的应试有所帮助，但是教师应该培养他们不过度依赖他人并主动学习的意识和习惯。在对大学英语的期望上，反映了学生渴望提高听说、写作和翻译能力的愿望，说明他们更注重英语的实际运用能力，能与人顺畅地交流，这也应该是大学英语教学的最终目的。

(5)从“个人爱好”上看，喜欢音乐的人数最多有 60 人，占到 54.6%，喜欢体育的有 22 人、绘画 21 人、数学 19 人、舞蹈 5 人，分别是 20%、19.1%、17.3% 和 4.6%，这反映了受调查者的职能偏好的不同，有些学生的爱好不止一个，有的多达三个。那么教师可以在教学上引入多样化的教学模式，比如喜欢音乐的学生最多，在学习词汇时可以使用音乐教学的方式，比如学习词汇 obsess 时，单纯地给出例句不那么形象生动，正好有一首好听的英文歌 *Obsessed*，是由美国著名歌手玛丽亚·凯莉(Mariah Carey)制作和演唱的一首专辑主打歌曲，歌曲由迷人的电音和黑人 POP 以及玛丽亚·凯莉的演唱技巧堆叠而成，歌曲节奏感强烈有趣，广泛受到大家的喜爱。歌词中反复出现这个词，教师可以先让学生听歌写歌词，如果是个新词，反复听到会特别留意，然后教师讲解歌词的意思，特别是“obsess”一词在歌词里的用法和其他的常用形式，这样的学习方式会使学生更感兴趣，学习效果会更好。另外，这种模式也会对 9.1% 学生中不喜欢学英语，但喜欢音乐的学生起到一定的作用，充分发挥他们的潜能，调动他们的学习积极性。只有学习者本身感兴趣，想学好，才能真正达到我们的教学目的。

四、大学英语教学模式的改进措施

多元智能理论的提出，让我们认识到传统的教学方式已无法满足学生多元智能的发展和需要，符合学生个性发展的多样化教学模式亟待开发，借鉴班克斯的多

元教育5个维度,英语课堂教学模式的改进措施如下:

(一)整合教学内容,丰富文化知识,实现教学课程的动态化和多元化

教学内容的整合首先是整合教学教材。一直以来英语课都是统一教材,教材内容虽然在不断改进,但从文化角度来看,还应该增加学生更感兴趣的话题和内容,因为对话题和内容的不熟悉会直接影响他们的学习兴趣,满足不了来自各地区文化存在差异的学生的发展。因此教材的编写内容应涉及多民族、多文化,使学习者开始接触时就产生浓厚的兴趣。这就需要既懂专业知识又有多种文化知识的教研人员进行编写。再者,课上仅学书本上的知识远远不够,还需任课教师对课上内容的补充,多找一些学生感兴趣的话题。

教师可以将原来教材的内容具体化,然后给予学生具体的角色。例如在商务英语课堂上,教师可以把一笔交易拆分成一个个小任务,包括负责电话预约的前台信息收录员,负责接待访客的公关部员工,模拟外商参观工厂的生产流程,助理业务员从事的询盘、报价、下单等基本程序,负责保险、支付等任务的结算部业务员。学生通过完成任务就可以完成一笔交易,既掌握了国际贸易业务知识,又在实际操作中训练了英语语言。在全球性危机发生后,国际金融市场的剧烈波动成为世人关注的焦点。我们在国际商务英语课程中可以结合国际外汇的走势,来分析其中波动的缘由。而来自海外媒体的诸多信息成为主要的参考对象,这些信息几乎都是原版英文,学生可在分析过程中熟悉相关的英语知识,提高自身对相关领域的反应灵敏度,从而实现教学课程的动态化和多元化。

(二)营造语言环境,借助文化接触和探究的好奇心,提高学习兴趣

异国的文化会激发学生的好奇心和跨文化交际动机,心理学的研究表明新颖的东西能激发人的兴趣,吸引人的注意力。现代认知心理学认为认知上的不和谐能够引发好奇心。文化定型是在对文化差异的概括上产生的,通过文化定型交际者自然而然地感知到自身文化与他文化的差异,从而产生趋同确认以形成适应性新文化的心理趋势。语言教学与文化背景知识并举是提高教学水平、多出人才的核心。因此教学上应加入更多的文化元素和信息,激发学生学习语言的兴趣。

充分运用多媒体手段,引入大量的视频教学资源,多提供语言环境。多媒体教学方式引入课堂使得以往那种以老师为核心的"平面小课堂"逐步变成了老师、学生以及众多视频、音频资料共存的"立体大课堂"。英文视频教学资源在我国随处可见,但是有些学生对观看原声电影在英语学习中的策略及作用存在诸多的疑虑。现阶段要解决的关键问题是教师在视频资源与学生之间要构建一条"渠道",在教学过程中随时对可能出现的文化冲突给予及时有效的解释,指导学生正确理解这些新奇观点和内容,从而提高学习动机。

(三)重视知识建构,强化文化意识,注重学习策略的培养

首先,在教学中可以让学习者从自己的民族或角度出发,他们所接受的知识的多少,会受到自己的家庭文化背景和观念的影响。家庭的支持会对学校教育起到配合作用,因此,要不断提升家长对孩子学业的关心和学生学习英语的意识,让家长和学生们用长远的眼光看问题,认识到学习英语的重要性,学习英语不仅是课程标准的要求,更重要的是社会和时代发展的要求。

其次,要注重学生学习策略的培养。Oxford(1989)认为学习策略指的是学习者在语言学习中所采取的具体行为。有些学生自主学习能力差的根本原因是其始终处于学习的被动地位,简单地使用机械记忆方法,练习不少但都属于无声地做题,读与写的功能发挥不完善。元认知策略是培养学习者自主性的关键。这需教师加强指导和针对性地引导。特别是加强他们基础较差的英语听、说方面的实践。下表是学生学习常用策略:

学习常用策略

记忆策略	认知策略	补偿策略	元认知策略	情感策略	社会策略
有计划复习	操练	合理猜测	制定学习重点	克服焦虑	与他人合作学习

除去元认知外,情感策略也不可忽视。情感策略基本上可分为克服英语学习中紧张和焦虑心理;使用英语与他人交流与表达;监控并调整英语学习中的情绪等三部分内容。一些学生常用的情感策略是能在英语学习中克服焦虑心理,最不擅长鼓励自己、监控和调整学习中的情绪。由诸多外界环境影响,基础不好的学生怀有自卑情绪,经常出现情绪心理变化波动,又不能很好控制其心理,更不敢用英语与他人交流和表达,这是影响学生的听说能力最主要的因素。因此正确、有效引导学生应用情感策略应引起教师的高度重视,同时注意培养学生良好的个性心理素质和良好的情感品质。

(四)减少思想意识偏见,采用多样化教学策略,提高个体发展

在教学中和思想意识上应减少偏见。教师上课时首先要了解学生的不同文化背景,对待学生要公平,了解不同的心声,鼓励学生的个性发展,让他们树立信心,勇于表现自己,这样他们主观上不会自暴自弃,将来遇到什么困难都不是障碍,反而会把它当作前进的动力,将来带着自信走出农村、走出大山,带着民族的自豪,很快融入社会,做国家有用的栋梁。还可以让更多的人了解他们自己的文化,以便将自己的地区或本民族的独特文化发扬并传承下去。

多元智能理论所倡导的教学观是一种尊重个体差异、强调个体差异,针对个体差异来进行教育的因材施教观。教师在教学中,必须重视学生智能的差异,要根据每个学生不同的智能特点,采用与之相匹配的教学策略。当前,高校传统的教学模式是缺乏个性、忽略差异的。教师在课堂上,用同样的方法向不同的学生教授相同的内容,这样的教学模式完全忽略学生的个体差异,扼杀了学生的个性和潜能,不利于学生的发展。根据多元智能理论,同一门课程,可以根据学生不同的智能结构特征,采用学生擅长的智能方式来教学。人类是智能多元的,才能也应该被赋予更广泛的含义,成功的定义与路径也是多元的,教育在培养全面发展的人的基础之上,必须重视学生的个性差异。教师应当去探寻更加多样化与适合每个个体发展的独特教学方法,使学生对自己的学习和发展具有更自觉的责任。

(五)加大学校支持力度,强化公平教育,建立多元教学评价体系

公平教育应体现在教育的每个环节。根据加德纳的多元智能理论,每个孩子的智能都是多元的,只是某些智能未被发现,有待开发。有的边远少数民族能歌善舞,有的民族擅长骑马打猎,有的人喜欢合作学习,有的人善于独立思考。教师应了解不同学生的智能优势,因材施教,灵活教法。学校在政策上应给予必要的支持,教师应首先了解学生的文化背景,以便找出存在的问题,让所有学生接受好的教育。

传统的教学评价无论在理念上还是方法上都难以满足促进学生有效发展的需求。传统的教学评价常常与学生的生活和学习情境脱节,将学生的智力片面化,难以反映学生的独特性。既然智力是多元的,成功的定义是多样的,那么与之相应的教学评价也应该是多维度的、多元的和全方位的,使每个个体优势领域和特别才能都能得到充分的展现和认可。应加大形成性评估的力度,以多元的方式评价学生的学业成绩。运用情境化、动态化和多元化多维度的评价方法,真正有效的教学评价应以现实生活中真实的社会角色为参照,在真实而具体的情境中评价学生。这样的评价既能促进学生的发展,也有利于培养现实生活需要的实践能力与创造能力。在对学生的评价时,要尊重个体的差异,设计更加科学合理的评价方式,建立有效的多元教学评价体系。

五、结论

加德纳的多元智能理论为高校教学模式的改革与创新提供了全新的视角,我们要充分认识到每个学习者的智能多元化,其智能偏好各不相同,智力组合形式、学习风格和发展方向也各不相同,因此,我们在教学上应该运用多维度多形式的教学模式，尊重学生的不同特点，善于挖掘，使他们更好地发挥各项学习智能，为他们将来走入社会有更好的发展搭建平台。

我们应该进一步从理论和实践层面对高校教学模式进行改革与探索。设置强调实践能力和创造力培养的教学目标，采用多样化的教学组织形式和教学方法，建立促进学习者发展的多元教学评价体系，构建多样化的、促进学生全面发展的新型教学模式。教学模式的改革离不开教师与学生的共同努力，当双方都有针对性改变和积极参与时，体现的便是教与学相互推长的动态效果。另外，大学英语教学中，教师自身的语言素质和文化修养、教学观念和教学理论水平、教学技能技巧和教师的自主发展能力都是教学模式的改进与提高的关键。

经济全球化趋势给英语教学的发展带来了机遇，也给广大教师带来了挑战。只有在充分利用多媒体技术、改革教学方法、加强实践教学环节、大力培养双师型教师、改革考试制度等方面不断探索的基础上适时适度地调整教学模式，才能取得良好的教学效果，为社会培养更多高素质的英语人才。从上个学期开始，我校部分教师在英语课堂进行“翻转课堂”教学模式的实践，这种模式尊重学习者的多元智能和个体差异，使学生可以按照自己的学习步骤、习惯和风格学习，这在一定程度上满足了学生的个体学习需求，提高学习兴趣，但是要想达到我们的预期效果和目标，还需更长时间的摸索和实践。总之，大学英语教学的改革需要我们社会各界的共同努力和支持，需要学校制度的改革，需要学生家长的积极配合，以及任课教师的不断学习和对改革工作的热情。这不但关乎教育质量的提高，也关乎广大教师的职业发展。

参考文献：

[1] Banks, A. J. *An Introduction to Multicultural Education* (2nd *ed.*) [M]. Boston: Allyn & Bacon, 1999.

[2] Creswell, J. W. *Educational Research: Planning, Conducting, and Evaluating Quantitative and Qualitative Research* (2nd *ed.*) [M]. New Jersey: Pearson Education International, 2002.

[3] Davies, P. & Pearse, E. *Success in English teaching* [M]. Oxford: Oxford University Press, 2000.

[4] Gadner, H. *Frames of Mind, The Theory of Multiple Intelligences* [M]. NewYork, Basic Books, 1983.

[5] Hedge, T. *Teaching and Learning in the Language Classroom* [M]. Oxford:

Oxford University Press,2000.

[6] Kemmis, S. & McTaggart, R. *The Action Research Planner* [M]. Geelong, Victoria: Deakin University Press,1982.

[7] Krashen S. *Principles and Practice in Second Language Acquisition* [M]. Oxford: Pergamon Press,1982.

[8] Nunan, D. *Second Language Teaching and Learning* [M]. Heinle & Heinle/Thomson Learning Asia,1999.

[9] Oxford, R. L. *Language Learning Strategies* [M]. Newbury House,1989.

[10] Robert E. Slavin. 教育心理学:理论与实践(第7版)[M]. 北京:北京大学出版社,2004.

[11] 摆贵勤. 多元智能理论在大学英语教学中的应用[J]. 成都大学学报(社科版),2010(3).

[12] 杜钢. 美国多元文化教育的变革与问题[J]. 教育学术月刊,2011(4).

[13] 沈银珍. 多元文化与当代英语教学[M]. 杭州:浙江大学出版社,2006.

[14] 文秋芳. 英语学习策略论[M]. 上海:上海外语教育出版社,1996.

[15] 王笃勤. 英语教学策略论[M]. 北京:外语教学与研究出版社,2002.

文学与文化研究

民国时期女作家作品在英语世界的译介与传播

首都经济贸易大学外国语学院　郝莉

摘　要：民国时期对外出版的作家作品多以革命大背景下的阶级与民族斗争为主题，而女作家作品的对外出版有其自身特点。部分女作家将革命与女性主义结合，在作品中表现了革命语境中女性的命运，另一些女作家则选择脱离革命背景，在选择翻译的自己作品及撰写的英文自传中表达自己独特的女性主义思想。这些作品为西方社会了解中国近代女性及女性主义思想提供了较为丰富的文本资料。

关键词：民国；女作家；英文出版；女性主义

Abstract: Most modern works published in English in the Republican period took class and national struggle against the revolutionary background as their themes. However, translation and English publication of women writers' works has its own characteristics. Some women writers combined revolution with feminism, and represented women's fortune in the revolutionary context. Others chose to disregard the revolutionary background, and expressed their unique feminist thoughts through the essays and stories chosen and translated by themselves and the autobiographies written and published in English. These works provided fairly rich material for the western society to understand modern Chinese women and feminist thoughts.

Key Words: Republican period; women writers; English publication; feminism

随着20世纪初新文化运动的开展，大量的西方文学作品被译介到中国，对中国的思想变革与发展以及文学写作产生了巨大的影响。新文化运动代表人物胡适便指出，“翻译西洋近代和现代的文学名著”是新文学运动的重要任务之一。与此同时，以美国为首的西方国家出现了最早的一批汉学家，但他们的研究重点大都为中国古典文学与文化，对中国现代作品则极少涉猎。因此，与强劲的西学东渐之风相比，西方媒体对中国现代文学与文化则兴趣不大，中国现代文学的对外出版数量稀少，西方对中国现代文学文化的了解极为匮乏。自20世纪30年代起，为加强中

本文在写作过程中得到澳门大学英文系李德凤教授的指导与帮助，特此表示感谢。

西文化交流,让西方了解现代中国的深刻变化,一批有留学经历、中英文功底深厚的国内作家学者以及在华的西方记者将部分现代作家的作品推介到西方,其中包括了一些谢冰莹与陈衡哲等女作家的作品。

一、民国时期女性作家作品对外出版总体介绍

从20世纪30年代初至新中国成立期间,出版界向西方推介的中国优秀现代文学作品中,大部分均为与当时抗日救国时代背景紧密相关的左翼作家以阶级与民族革命斗争为主题的作品,其中以男性作家作品为主。以创立于1935年8月、旨在推介中国现代文学作品的重要英文杂志《天下月刊》为例,自其创刊至1941年8、9月停刊止,共发行56期,其"译文"栏目重点译介了现代中国作品共38篇,作者包括鲁迅、沈从文、巴金等,仅有5篇来自女性作家,分别为凌叔华、萧红与冰心。在西方出版界,鲁迅是第一位引起关注的现代作家。他的《狂人日记》由敬隐渔译为法文,发表于《欧罗巴》杂志1926年第5－6期上。1929年,敬隐渔继续翻译了一些鲁迅的其他作品如《孔乙己》和《故乡》,以及一些其他作家的短篇小说,并结集为《阿Q正传及其他现代中国短篇小说选集》在法国出版,其中收入了女作家冰心的短篇小说《烦闷》。1930年,米尔斯(E. H. F. Mills)将此书转译为英文在伦敦出版,次年在美国出版。美国驻华记者埃德加·斯诺花费5年时间编译的《活的中国:现代中国短篇小说选》于1936年在美国出版。在序言中,斯诺指出,他翻译出版这部作品的初衷并非迎合西方读者的兴趣,或者为了满足西方对东方的猎奇心理,而是为了介绍中国具有文学价值的作品到西方。[①] 而由于斯诺战地记者的身份,以及他和左翼作家的密切关系,他认为最能代表中国的作品便是以革命为背景的左翼文学作品,而丁玲入选本书的两篇短篇小说也同样是写于20世纪30年代的革命文学作品。

女性作家并未引起过多重视。除上述杂志与作品集中选译的少量短篇作品外,仅有少量女作家作品得以以单行本形式选译出版。其中,谢冰莹的《从军日记》与《一个女兵的自传》被译介为各种文字并在海外产生广泛影响。另外,陈衡哲亲自编译出版了自己的散文集《中国女性及其他四篇散文》(The Chinese Women and Four other Essays),丁玲的短篇小说集《孩子们及其他短篇小说选》(Our Children and Others)与《我在霞村的时候及其他短篇小说选》(When I was in Sha Chuan and Other Stories)也分别于1941年与1945年出版。

---

① 埃德加·斯诺. 活的中国:现代中国短篇小说选. 长沙:湖南人民出版社,1983.

大部分编辑与译者均无明显性别意识。一些女性作家创作的作品得到了译介，主要是因为其作品以革命为题材，而并非作品体现的女性主义意识。在致力于将中国现代文学译介到西方的过程中，也出现了一些女性的译者，如美国的项美丽(Emily Hahn)及女作家杨刚。但遗憾的是，在革命的大背景下，这些译者也未表现出明显的性别意识，未能有意选择女性作品进行翻译。项美丽是美国杂志《纽约客》的记者，1935 年来到中国，在《天下月刊》发表多篇书评，并与邵洵美合译了沈从文的中篇小说《边城》。杨刚不仅协助埃德加·斯诺进行了《活的中国》的编译工作，并且在邵洵美和项美丽的帮助下于 1938 年翻译了毛泽东的《论持久战》。1941 年她翻译了沈从文的《乡城》，发表于《天下月刊》。

然而译介到西方的女性作家作品并未仅仅局限于以战争为背景的革命文学范畴。以谢冰莹为代表的女性作家在作品中将女性主义与革命相结合，表现了中国革命语境中的女性主义思想，一方面树立了"革命女性"的新形象，另一方面表现了革命环境下女性的生存困境。而以陈衡哲为代表的女性作家，大力推介自己的作品，不仅亲自承担起编辑与译者的身份，而且努力与西方媒体建立密切联系，直接用英文写作出版，将自己作品中的女性主义思想传递到西方。

二、革命语境中的女性主义思想：谢冰莹

最早翻译为英文的女性作家作品是谢冰莹的《从军日记》。1926 年 5 月，《中央日报》副刊连载了谢冰莹的这部自传体作品，立刻在文坛引起了轰动。文中谢冰莹记录了自己挣脱传统家庭的束缚，成为一名女战士的传奇经历。著名的作家林语堂随即将其译为英文，发表在该报的英文版上，并于 1930 年结集为《中国女战士的书信与战时随笔集》由上海商业出版社出版。同时，这部作品被译为包括法文、日文、俄文等在内的多国文字出版，谢冰莹也因此在国际范围内名声大噪。虽然包含了早期女性运动的一些元素，如反对缠足、争取教育机会、反对包办婚姻等，但是与其他作品中争取到自由之后仍然迷茫痛苦的"娜拉"们不同，在谢冰莹的自传中，她通过参军，为自己争取了进入公共生活、获得与男性平等地位的机会，成为中国革命女性的典范人物。1930 年 8 月，法国著名报纸《小巴黎人日报》刊登了详细介绍本书内容的评论文章《一位参加中国革命的女孩》，著名作家罗曼·罗兰也致函向她表示敬意，盛赞其为"努力奋斗的新女性"。1936 年，谢冰莹将自己前半生的传奇经历进行整理，写成了《一个女兵的自传》，由上海良友图书出版公司出版。1940 年，纽约出版了这部自传的英译本 *Girl Rebel: The Autobiography of Hsieh Pingying*，由林语堂作序，林的两个女儿林如斯与林太乙翻译。1943 年，由 Tsui Chi

重新翻译并稍有删节的另一版本 *Autobiography of a Chinese Girl* 在伦敦出版。同样,这部作品也引起世界各国的关注,被译为德、日、意、法、葡等多种文字出版,并多次重译再版,甚至被选入美国、日本等国家的中学课本。最新的版本为 2001 年谢冰莹的女儿贾莉莉(Lily Chia Brissman)及女婿翻译的 *A Woman Soldier's Own Story:The Autobiography of Xie Bingying*,也是目前最全的译本。作为唯一一部在国际上产生广泛影响的中国革命女性的自传体作品,谢冰莹的自传无疑是革命时期女性主义作品的代表。"她的作品激励了无数中国年轻女性为实现解放而斗争。在这方面这是一部经典作品。它不仅创立了新的文学体裁,并且代表了一类新的中国女性:不是为了父兄,而是为了危难中的国家与自我解放而穿上军装的现代'木兰'。"①

三、革命之外的女性主义声音:陈衡哲

在作品被译介到西方的女性作家中,陈衡哲与凌淑华两位女作家与众不同,她们兼作家、编辑与译者为一身,均受过良好的西方教育,有很深的英文功底,在用中英文创作的同时,参与选择和翻译自己的作品,并通过与西方的直接交流推介自己具有强烈女性意识的作品。她们翻译及写作的英文作品与革命的大背景并无关联,而是以描写女性生活为中心的散文、小说及自传为主,从不同角度向西方展示了中国女性的鲜明形象。

陈衡哲是中国第一位女硕士,女教授。她于 1914 年考入清华大学,随即被派往美国瓦沙女子学院留学,于 1919 年获得学士学位,1920 年于芝加哥大学获得硕士学位。在美国留学期间,她亲身经历了第一波女权主义运动,这对她的思想和写作产生了很大的影响。回国以后,她仍然与西方学术界保持密切联系,并从 1927 年起连续 4 次参加了两年一届的太平洋国际学术会议。1931 年,会议在上海召开之前,陈衡哲用英文编写了《中国文化论集》一书,其目的是为了给西方读者提供一幅中国文化的生动图景,特别是着重它的变化方面。② 陈衡哲亲自为论集撰写了序言与结论,并选入了另一位女作家曾宝荪的文章《中国妇女的过去与现在》。1934 年,为使西方更多地了解中国的女性生活现状,她选择翻译出版了自己的散文集《中国女性及其他四篇散文》。

① Weili Ye. Review:*A Woman Soldier's Own Story:The Autobiography of Xie Bingying*. The China Journal, No. 49(Jan. ,2003):229.

② Sophia H Chen Zen. Editorial Foreword. *Symposium on Chinese Culture*. Shanghai:China, Institute of Pacific Relations. 1931.

1935年左右，陈衡哲用英文撰写并出版了《一个中国女孩的自传》，书中主要记录了自己17岁之前的生活经历。自传作为此时期女性文学中新的文学体裁，是女性文学的一个重要组成部分，是女性作家主体意识的集中体现。虽然中国古代历史上不乏优秀的女作家，但由于封建礼教的约束，她们的作品不可避免地具有一定的局限性，在很大程度上是主流男性文学的附庸。而真正意义上具有主体意识的女性文学则直到20世纪初期才产生，是西方进步思潮与“五四”新文化运动共同作用的结果。女性的自传书写是几千年来女性写作中的一个重要转折。在中国历史上，自传多为名人志士所作，通常篇幅短小，内容较少记录生平经历，多为记述自己的政治理想与道德情操，目的通常在于启示与教育后人。而女性“主内”的边缘身份造成其缺乏独立人格，因此亦没有撰写自传的资格。20世纪初，越来越多的女性通过接受教育进入社会领域，获得工作机会，打破了传统社会中“内”与“外”的界限，从而使生活的重心从男人与家庭转为自身。而“五四”新文化运动大力推崇的人文精神与个人主义思想也为女性作家提供了一个绝佳契机，使她们得以以独立的形象浮出历史地表。此时期几乎所有的重要女作家均不约而同地书写了自传，记录自己的人生经历与思想变化。与此同时，西方媒体也希冀了解重大社会变革中中国女性的生活现状，而女性作家的自传显然是最为直接与可信的渠道。谢冰莹的《从军日记》与《一个女兵的自传》便是在此背景下被译介到世界各国并产生影响的。陈衡哲亦深知自传的书写有利于树立独立自主的新女性形象、表达女性主义思想，因此用英文撰写并出版了这部自传。

作为少数英文出版的中国女性自传之一，这部作品具有鲜明的女性主义特色，表现了当时众多女性作家作品中女性主义思想的主要内容，表达了女性对权利的主要诉求，即反对缠足、争取教育机会、反对包办婚姻、争取自由独立等。Tieniu Cheng 对这部自传中的女性主义思想进行了深入分析，认为陈衡哲的自传写作颠覆了传统的写作方法，在开始部分使用了寓言故事，而非通常的父辈或祖先的叙述。在故事中，陈衡哲将“长江”比喻为女性主义先驱，使用了一系列积极词汇如“突破”、“征服”等形容女性，而使用了一些消极词汇形容男性。在自传的第二章陈衡哲对自己家庭的母系传统进行了梳理，从曾祖母写起，记录了几代女性所接受的良好教育与沿承的文化传统，以此来取代传统的以父系血统族谱为主的自传写作。另外，陈衡哲还大胆提出女性比男性更聪明、更适合教育的观点。①

① Tieniu Cheng. *Writing Women's Experiences in the Early Twentieth Century China: A Study of Chen Hengzhe's Autobiography*. International Journal of Business, Humanity and Technology, Vol 1, No. 3, November 2011.

四、结语

综上所述,民国时期女作家作品的对外出版有其鲜明特点。首先,虽然从整体上看,在当时的政治背景下,女作家作品在西方出版数量相对较少,并且大多数编辑与译者性别意识较弱,在作品的选择上多以革命题材为标准,但有些女作家在作品中表现出强烈的女性意识,或者将革命与女性主义思想相结合,表现革命环境下女性的命运,或者描写革命语境之外的女性生活。其次,一些女作家不仅在自己的作品中表现出强烈的女性意识与女性主义思想,并且深刻认识到中西交流中的严重不平衡现象,即西方文化文学作品被大力译介到中国,并产生深刻影响,而西方对中国文化的了解非常匮乏。因此她们有意识地通过编辑介绍中国文化的书籍及向西方推介自己的作品,使西方得以了解中国文化的发展及女性生活的现状。她们身兼作家、编辑、译者等身份,选择自己的作品进行英译,并通过与西方媒体的联系出版了自己用英文撰写的自传作品。再次,这些对外出版的作品从多个角度较为全面地描绘了中国女性的生存现状,不仅体现了反对缠足、争取教育机会、反对包办婚姻、追求自由恋爱等近代中国女性主义思想,还表现了女性如何通过参加革命来实现对权利与自由的追求;不仅包括对上层社会女性家庭生活及心理状态的描写,而且对底层妇女的生存困境也进行了生动叙述。这些作品为西方世界了解中国近代女性及女性主义思想提供了较为丰富的文本资料。

Jane Austen et Charles Darwin

首都经济贸易大学外国语学院　苏明鸣

Bien que Jane Austen (1775—1817) ait toujours fait attention aux détails de la vie social, certains lecteurs considèrent qu' elle a écrit des histoires du Cendrillon. Il est intéressant d' explorer les correspondances entre les œuvres d' Austen et les théories anthropologiques de Darwin sur les liens de parenté, l' organisation sociale et la culture. Mes études sur Austen sont liées aux critiques actuelles sur ses œuvres, et notamment sur sa vision de l' ordre social de son époque. Certains la voient comme une conservatrice d' une société traditionnelle, tandis que d' autres la considèrent plutôt comme une réformatrice qui a confiance en Libéralisme. Malheureusement ces arguments se limitent à une certaine radicalité ou conservatisme de la part d' Austen. Mais les œuvres, écrites après les années 1790 (surtout *Persuasion*) sont profondément enracinées dans l' observation d' un monde en mouvement. Il me semble qu' Austen a accepté l' importance de valeurs traditionnelle, tout en faisant une satire de l' autorité patriarcale et de la mobilité social.

Selon Peter Knox-Show, Austen, comme d' autres auteurs des Lumières avant elle, a dilibérément évité toute attache politique, même en sphère privé. Sa nièce Caroline n' a jamais remarque un quelconque parti près chez sa tante, que a soit sur la Révolution Française ou sur d' autres événements de l' époque. ①Par conséquent, je suggère d' étudies le pouvoirs intellectuel de Jane Austen plutôt qu' une appartenance politique à travers ses livres.

Les personnages dans ses livres sont confrontés à une question fondamentale "comment dois je vivre ma vie?", et ses romans tentent d' en donner quelques réponses possibles. Je pense qu' Austen a été flexible sur certains points. Pendant un certain temps, sa contribution pour l' anthropologie n' a pas été reconnue. Il est important de

① Voir Caroline Austen, "My Aunt Jane Austen: A Memoir", in Littlewood, ed., *Critical Assessments*, I, 48 noter que la nature et l' action humaine sont centrales dans ses intrigues concernant les liens de parenté, le mariage, et la profession. Il est fait mention de Jane Austen dans un travail comparatif entre Darwin et d' autres écrivains de l' époque. On évoque les idées de l' évolution en citant Jane Austen. Peter W. Graham, dans son nouveau livre *Jane Austen and Charles Darwin: Naturalists and Novelists*, tente une comparaison grâce à une conversation intellectuelle, montant ainsi que la manière de crées des personnages chez Austen et Darwin peuvent être interchangeables.

Persuasion, le dernier roman d' Austen, publié après sa mort en 1818, semble différent des précédents de par sa suggestion de l' évolution. Ce roman insiste sur la capacité de l' individu à pourvoir s' élever grâce à ses efforts et son mérite plutôt qu' à son rang. Bien que *Persuasion* annonce un monde pré-darwinien, Austen suggère que l' on doit voir clairement et plus loin. Selon Peter Know-Show, Austen a toujours eu des idées progressistes et souhaites modifier sa façon de pensée en fonder des progrès de la société.

Persuasion est surtout une histoire d' amour. On trouve que les romans de Austen se concertent principalement sur la lutte pour l' existence, s' accouplerant et la compétition, les liens familiaux, la relation avec autrui. Par conséquent, Austen a centré l' attention du lecteur sur les règles du la cour et la mariage. Il est intéressant de voir que l' histoire d' amour écrite par Jane Austen anticipe le cas de la sélection sexuelle de Charles Darwin dans *The Descent of Man and Selection in Relation to Sex* (1871). En premier parti, je explore la relation logique entre Austen et Darwin.

Par ailleurs, j' apprécie la satire de Jane Austen concernant l' émiettement d' un vieil ordre social, grâce auquel elle a réclamé une certaine mobilité sociale dans *Persuasion*. En fait, la mobilité sociale est une expression clé au 19ème siècle, qui implique des valeurs telles que la flexibilité, le potentiel, la liberté et le mouvement. Donc, la mobilité est un facteur crucial dans le roman de Jane Austen. Dans le second parti, J' étudie la manière dont Austen a divisé la mobilité en sphère domestique et sociale. Selon Austen, ce qui est donné aux êtres humains dans ou par la nature pouvait être amélioré par les hommes et les femmes en fonction des circonstances.

Par conséquent, je crois qu' explorer le lien intellectuel entre Austen et Darwin à travers l' étude de leurs œuvres fera sens. Ici, je me concentre sur *Persuasion*, ainsi que sur les travaux du Darwin *OnThe Origin of Species* (1859) et *The Descent of Man* (1871). Bien que les questions politiques et religieuses soient continuellement présentes dans les livres, et qu' elles auront une bonne place dans cette étude, je insiste une position plus neutre en examinant les différentes manières de Austen pour l' exprimer. En conclusion, Je fais une étude comparative sur Jane Austen et Charles Darwin, romancière et naturaliste, et puis je trouve les similitudes entre les deux grands auteurs.

The girl Jig in Hemingway's story *Hills Like White Elephants*

首都经济贸易大学外国语学院　高悦伶

Abstract: Ernest Hemingway's *Hills Like White Elephants* was published during the "Roaring Twenties", a time of luxury and new freedom for woman. It is a story about an American man and a pregnant girl and also about power relation between them. The couple's lifestyle, along with the clash of power between them, is a source of conflict throughout the story. The complex relationship between Jig and the American illustrates the reluctance men had to the changing role of women in 1920s. This paper aims to demonstrate how the girl has grown up from a weak and dependent character into a brave and mature individual who rejects the man's authority after the painful struggle in the helpless and hopeless states under the great pressure of the man. Through this short story, Hemingway is declaring that women have the ability to think for themselves.

Key Words: the role of men and women; conflict; authority

Ernest Hemingway wrote a short story titled "Hills Like White Elephants" in 1927 during the "roaring twenties", a time of prosperity, luxury and more importantly, new freedoms for women. The empowerment and the continual push for equal status for women have become widely popular and successful only in recent history. Before the 1920s, women were seen as inferior to men. The role of women in society change with the rise of the Women's Rights Movements and the passing of the 19th Amendment in 1920, which granted women's suffrage. Slowly women were seen more and more as equals to men, but it was not without conflict. The 1920s were also characterized by the lavish lifestyles many people led. It was not uncommon for people to pick up their lives and travel abroad, like the expatriate characters in *Hills Like White Elephants*. The couple's current lifestyle, along with the clash of power between them, is a source of conflict throughout the story. Through the character's development and ability to come to her own decision despite her boyfriend's constant pressure suggests the girl Jig has developed into a mature individual who rejects the man's authority as well as his desire to abort the baby. To follow the girl's development in *Hills like White Elephants*, it is essential to have a clear sense of the setting in which her development takes place. In the setting, Hemingway works out the story's conflict, which revolves around the development of his female character. The personal evolution of the female protagonist, Jig, can be divided into four major steps. (Renner 1). The first revolves around the typical submissive and passive behavior expected of women who is not even knowing her own mind, accustomed to following a masterful male for her direction in life. In the second movement she comes to a realization of her own mind—her own welfare, dreams and values. In movement three she asserts herself for the first time. In the final one we may see the result of her development toward self-realization: the reluctant and still a bit resentful capitulation of her male companion.

Giving a new twist to the majority opinion, I would like to argue and analyze the female character in a quite different perspective. Since I think the published commentary has not looked closely enough at the development of the female character through the story and has greatly underestimated Jig's character.

The true power of the story is the dialogue between the two characters. Through the back and forth banter, the reader recognizes the "clash of the male and female sources of power and authority" (Urgo 36). Jig is first introduced as a girl who seems upbeat and frivolous. She describes the hills off in the distance as "white elephants" to which the man replies "I've never seen one" (Hemingway 211). Jig's response "No, you wouldn't have" is key to understanding the relationship between the two and gives the rise to the first conflict in the story (211). Her response is evidence of rising tension between the two, which has culminated to the point where Jig becomes defiant. Jig displays her manipulative powers by changing the subject to an advertisement written Spanish. She carefully chooses a topic that the man would know about in order to make him feel empowered. In doing this, she reveals how she is actually the dominant one in the relationship. On the other hand, the man feels like he is superior to since he had the ability to translate language, while Jig doesn't. The man's retaliation is also significant. He says "I might have. Just because you say I wouldn't have doesn't prove anything" (Hemingway 211). Urgo points out that the man's cadence is childish, indicating the girl has the power to make him act more like a boy than a man (37). More over, Paul Rankin argues that "what set the man off was Jig's access to knowledge and experience that the man cannot have, the first-hand knowledge of what white elephants look like. (236). The man knows he will never fully understand what is like to be in the girl's position, and that irritates him. His desire for knowledge and therefore power over the girl reveals his naivety since she is in an unpleasant situation.

Jig recognizes her ability to control man and continues to display her discontent through her language and more specifically in her sarcastic and witty response. After the couple receive the drinks, Jig's comments on how it tastes. "everything tastes of liquorice, especially all the things you've waited so long for, like absinthe" (Hemingway 212). In Spain, it is common for people to consume natural liquorice, which is known to have an intense bitter taste (Far Louis). Not only was Jig delicately revealing her knowledge of the drink's composition, she was also implying that she is currently unhappy with her "bitter" lifestyle and wants to change it by settling down and raising a family. Her desire to settle down signifies her maturity while the man, who has the ideals of many Americans during the twenties wants to keep living a life of luxury without having the responsibility of a father. Furthermore, Jig looks across the hills and says, "I wanted to try this new drink. That is what we do, isn't it—look at things and try new drinks?" (Hemingway 212). She discovers that she has been living this superficial meaningless life. Her mentioning of the hills indicating that she is thinking herself of a life with her baby since she compares the color of the hills to the pale skin of a white elephant.

The color white often symbolizes purity and innocence, which evokes an image of a newborn baby. The round hills are also similar to the curves of a woman during the later stages of pregnancy when abortion is no longer an option. Jig is also playing with two beads on the bamboo curtain. The two beads symbolize a new life jig would have with her baby and ultimately the two options Jig has. Jig is tumbling the two options around in her head just as she is physically tumbling the beads in her hand. Through her contemplation it is evident that she is giving a lot of weight to the decision she has to make, proving she is no longer a naive girl, but a mature woman. Jig's body language, tone and rhetorical question indicate that she is daydreaming about a life with her baby and also suggests that she does not want to go through with the "operation".

The American uses his knowledge of the operation to try to convince Jig to go through with it. He oversimplifies the process by saying, "It is really an awfully simple operation... It is not really an operation at all" (Hemingway 212). The man knows the procedure has the risks involved. But he has to oversimplify it in order to convince Jig, He repeatedly brings up the topic by consoling the girl first saying, "if you don't want to, you don't have to," but he always qualifies it with, "I think it is the best thing to do" or "I know it is perfectly simple" (Hemingway 213). The American undoubtedly wants Jig to have the abortion, explicitly stating, "It is the only thing that makes us unhappy," He includes Jig his claim by strategically saying "us", but in all of his other claims he uses "I", as in "I think" and "I know", which reveals his actual self-centered nature. In rectify the man's selfish tendencies and choking authorities are the real causes of Jig's unhappiness, not the prospect of having a child.

Jig is clearly distraught by the man's incessant urges to go through with the operations and blurts out, "Then I'll do it. Because I don't care about me." (Hemingway 213). She lets the man know that he is acting in a selfish manner by implying that he doesn't care about her. Jig walks over to the other side of the train station, which shows the fields of grain and trees along the banks of the Embro, which are symbolic of the fertility of the girl's womb. She then notices the shadow of a cloud moving across the field of grain, representative of the man's looming presence and authority. Jig makes the light of the situation and says, "we could have everything." (213). The man agrees "We can have the whole world", while she contradicts her previous assertion saying, "No, we can't. It isn't anymore." The man is confused and believes she is referring to the whole world, but in reality she is referring to baby. Jig realizes the stark reality that if she goes through with the "operation", she can never take it back, and at the same time, compares the baby to "the whole world" meaning that her baby is worth everything to her. Jig's maturity is finally proved when she finally places the baby before herself.

The hedonistic view of the American is contrasted by the girl's desire to accept responsibility of her child. Jig tries to include the man in her future by saying "we could all get along", implying that the three could live happily together (Hemingway 213). Despite Jig's rational motion, the man says, "I don't want anyone else. And I know it is perfectly simple" (Hemingway 214). Ironically, the girl turns out to be more rational than her knowledgeable, scientific counterpart who finds it hard to defend the abortion without repeating its simplicity. This proves to the last straw for Jig and it draws a sarcastic remark followed by "would you please, please, please, please, please, please, please, stop talking ?" (Hemingway 214). Jig can no longer hide her frustration and she distracts herself from the man. Realizing it would be impossible to change her mind, the man takes the bag to the other side of the train station, the side that the Jig had previously walked over towards and viewed the fertile landscape. Relieved, Jig says no to the man: "All right. Then come back and we'll finish the beer." (Hemingway 214). She is satisfied that the man has conceded to her wishes and forgives him for trying to convince her otherwise. The act of drinking beer together is a way of communication where the two have set aside their differences and put the baby first.

The complex relationship between Jig and the American illustrate the reluctance the man had to changing role of women in the 1920s. Through her sarcasm, maturity and ability to rationalize, Jig embodies the defiance and strength of the Women's Rights Movement. The American represents the collective conservative view that men should control over their families, especially their spouses, which is evident in his constant effort to convince Jig that having an abortion is the best option. Jig's firm stance against the man's endless efforts reveals that she is no longer under the authority of the male figure. Through this short story and the dialogue within, Hemingway is declaring that women have to think for themselves and are as capable as their male counterparts, who are not to acting immature and foolish.

Works Cited

[1] Farlouis, Shnnon. *The Health Benefits of LiQuorice.* Associated Content from Yahoo! . 4 May 2010. Web. 10 Feb. 2011.

[2] Hemingway, Ernest. *Hills like White Elephants.* The Complete Short stories of Ernest Hemingway. New York: Simon and Schuster, 1987.

[3] Rankin, Paul. *Hemingway's Hills Like White Elephants.* Explicator 63. 4 (2005): 234 – 37.

[4] Renner, Stanley. *Moving to the Girl's Side of Hills Like White Elephants.* Hemingway Review 15. 1 (1995): 27 – 42. Ebsco. Literary Reference Center.

CCCCD. 12Apr. 2007 <http://web. ebscohost. com/lrc/detail? vid = 8&hid = 9&sid = f569c01b - 6a25 - 4ef1 - 9340 - 97c95dd120a8%40sessionmgr108 >.

[5] Urgo, Joseph R. *Hemingway's Hills Like White Elephants*. Explicator 46. 3 (1988):35 - 37.

劳伦斯式“福音”
——《虹》的“反圣经”叙事和“拉纳尼姆”情结

中国传媒大学文学院　李贝贝

摘　要:英国20世纪作家D. H.劳伦斯因从小受家庭传统的熏染,而对基督教的神圣文本《圣经》非常熟悉。他的很多作品在备受争议的同时,也都打上了《圣经》的烙印。出版于1915年的《虹》是劳伦斯的代表作品之一,本文拟从宗教视角出发,探讨《虹》与《圣经》的关系。《虹》无论从整体的叙事结构、局部的细节和场景还是直接的话语引用,都采用了“圣经式叙事”手法,劳伦斯借此形式是想打造属于自己的福音书,因此小说又在形式和内容上体现出“反圣经”的特点。笔者将具体分析以上特点在文本中的表现,并进一步阐释《虹》所体现的劳伦斯的宗教观和救世之道。

关键词:《虹》;反圣经;拉纳尼姆;宗教观

Abstract: Affected by family tradition since the childhood, British author D. H. Lawrence was familiar with the Bible which was the sacred text of Christianity. Most of his works were both controversial and biblical, for example, *The Rainbow*, one of Lawrence' s representative works and published in 1915. From the perspective of religion, I aim at elucidating, the relationship between *The Rainbow* and the Bible. From the whole narrative structure, partial details and scenes to the direct quotation of sentences in the Bible, *The Rainbow* employed the biblical narrative pattern by which Lawrence attempted to create his own Gospels, so this novel also presented the characteristics as a counter-Bible. In this paper, I analyzed its manifestations in this novel in detail and elucidated Lawrence' s religious values and the way of salvation.

Key Words: The Rainbow; counter-Bible; Rananim; religious view

《虹》是英国作家劳伦斯在“一战”期间经过多次改写而最终面世的一部作品。厌恶战争的劳伦斯同时又希望它可以根治文化弊病,从而开启一个新的时代。他以为到1915年战争将结束,作品《虹》也将问世,届时报喜的时刻将会到来。然而同年9月《虹》的出版,之后因“有伤风化”而被查禁,不仅使劳伦斯名誉扫地,也使他意识到自己正身处大暴雨的前夕,却过早地将彩虹升到了天空。作品自问世以来,英美评论界对其“漠视社会道德”的“生殖崇拜”和“性欲狂欢”耿耿于怀,而无法正视其价值,直至20世纪50年代,评论家利维斯和哈里·T·穆尔掀起劳伦斯复兴热潮才使其作品逐渐得到重视。然而,走进《虹》使我们同样感到困惑而醒目的除了到处洋溢的力比多激情,还有遍布全书的《圣经》中话语。这一方面容易造成宗教狂热的表象,另一方面神圣性话语和力比多激情的混杂并置很容易被误解为是一种亵渎,为了避免简单化的误读,将《虹》纳入宗教视角的研究便成为必要。

中外学术界关于《虹》与《圣经》关系的研究虽有涉及但成果不多。国内的成果多从原型批评的角度出发,侧重于分析《虹》对《圣经》中意象、人物形象和场景的比附和挪用现象,但缺少对这种叙事方式与小说内涵之间的关系、作者意图以及宗教观的深入分析。对此,笔者考察了中外学术界的已有成果并认为,劳伦斯在《虹》中确实采用了“圣经式”的叙事方式,并同时在内容和形式上又表现出了“反圣经”的特点,然而作者既非宗教狂热亦非亵渎,而是旨在打造一部劳伦斯式的福音书,从而表达他自己的宗教观和“救世之道”,下面笔者将逐一对此进行具体分析。

一、“圣经式”叙事

在《虹》中,无论从整体的叙事结构、局部的情景模仿还是具体到对《圣经》话语的直接引用都为这部小说披上了“圣经式”叙事的外衣。

首先,从整体的叙事结构来看,小说经历了类似于《圣经·创世纪》中的伊甸园、洪水失乐园和以虹立约三个阶段。小说开篇描绘了布朗温家族世代生活在玛斯农庄的场景,他们精神饱满、生活富足、繁衍生息。男人们满足于牛群与土地的活计,而女人们却向往着更多的自由和未知的世界。这俨然一副人间伊甸园场景,男人们正如亚当,女人们则是易受蛇诱惑的夏娃。第九章,大洪水带走了第一代人汤姆·布朗温的生命,而在小说结尾处第三代人厄休拉看到了彩虹。同样的结构和意象也出现在《圣经·创世纪》第九章,耶和华在洪水消灭人间罪恶后与诺亚及其后裔立约,“凡有血肉的,不再被洪水灭绝”,并把虹放在云彩中作为与地立约的记号。这里的洪水与彩虹作为《圣经》中出现的意象同样也具有象征意义。

其次,小说中的很多场景和细节都与《圣经》有关。例如第二代人威尔·布朗温的雕刻——“夏娃诞生图”。“树枝上有一只鸟正展翅欲飞,一条蛇正盘着树向它伸过来。”[①]T. R. Wright(莱特)在《劳伦斯与圣经》(*D. H. Lawrence and the Bible*)中认为这表达了对“人类的堕落”的矛盾情绪,夏娃的动机是追求智慧,正如鸟儿

① [英]D. H. 劳伦斯. 虹[M]. 黑马等译. 上海:上海三联书店,2014:110.

具有向更高处飞翔的欲望,而蛇对鸟的恶的意图却预示着死亡,即不遵从上帝指令的惩罚。此外,对于爱情中的安娜来说,威尔的到来就像"天使加百列向圣母报告耶稣要降生那样",①她只得像服从天使那样服从他。当二人陷入矛盾,怀孕的安娜效仿《圣经》中的大卫在主面前脱去衣服快乐地跳舞,以此宣告她是属于自己的造物主的,而拒绝接受威尔这个男人的统治。显然,类似这样的挪用会触怒一些传统基督徒和不理解劳伦斯的读者,从而被冠以不敬和亵渎的罪名。

除此之外,作者还在小说中借人物之口直接引用《圣经》中的话语。如"在天上没有婚姻",②"上帝的儿子看到人的女儿容貌娇美就选她们为妻",③"在礼拜日世界,人可以在水面行走……随着云柱穿过沙漠,看得见噼啪作响但还没烧尽的灌木丛",④以上分别出自《圣经》的"马太福音"和"创世纪"等章节。

笔者以为,这种"圣经式"叙事,一方面跟劳伦斯的家庭传统有关,正如他自己所说:"我是靠《圣经》长大的,似乎在骨髓里都有《圣经》的成分。"⑤另一方面,劳伦斯模仿《圣经》的形式是为了打造一部表达自己宗教体验和理想的"福音书"。在《论信教》一文中,他表示"上帝是存在的",只不过他"在宇宙中的位置不是固定不变的",⑥他认为《圣经》的原作被懦弱和无趣的所谓基督教正统错误地阐释了,僵化的教义和宗教系统已无法找到变换了位置的上帝,我们必须寻找一条新路,这条路不是唯一的,但必须靠心中的圣灵指引,劳伦斯宣称他已走上了一条不同的路。

二、劳伦斯式"福音":"反圣经"特质

"反圣经"(counter-Bible)一词是 Robert Fraser 所采用过的概念,他是詹姆斯·弗雷泽《金枝》一书的编辑,他认为当一种宗教以文本的形式固定下来,那么就很难再被革新,因为文本的每章每句都会被援引来支持它的守旧性。如果没有固定的文本,宗教将会更容易改变,并会随着文化的发展来调整自身。因此我们需要"反圣经"式的文本,来对抗使宗教系统僵化的神圣文本。《虹》如同《金枝》也具有"反圣经"特质,虽然劳伦斯模仿了《圣经》的外部叙事特征,骨子上却与其传统价值观相悖而行,他试图用新的宗教观给阐释者们强加在《圣经》上的死板教义和奴

① [英]D. H. 劳伦斯. 虹[M]. 黑马等译. 上海:上海三联书店,2014:110.
② [英]D. H. 劳伦斯. 虹[M]. 黑马等译. 上海:上海三联书店,2014:128.
③ [英]D. H. 劳伦斯. 虹[M]. 黑马等译. 上海:上海三联书店,2014:263.
④ [英]D. H. 劳伦斯. 虹[M]. 黑马等译. 上海:上海三联书店,2014:271.
⑤ 冯季庆. 劳伦斯评传[M]. 上海:上海文艺出版社,1995:24.
⑥ [英]D. H. 劳伦斯. 性与可爱——劳伦斯散文选[C]. 姚暨荣译. 广东:花城出版社,1988:373.

性道德松绑。

（一）反圣经内涵：肉体信仰

《虹》的“反圣经”特点首先体现在贬斥基督教的僵化教义和不真实性，而对其所恐惧的肉体、性推崇至极，正如他所说：“我的伟大宗教就是相信血和肉比智力更聪明。”①以第三代人厄休拉为例，她第一次接受福音教义便很反感。《福音书》中提到“富人进入天堂比一头骆驼从针眼中穿过还难”、②“将你所有的一切卖掉，并送给穷人”，③这使她陷入痛苦的抉择，她确实想做正当的事，然而在现实生活中她并不想当穷人。当她违反了基督教教义教训了打她耳光的妹妹，心里却舒畅极了。可见这些不真实的死板教义并不能唤起她的宗教热情，反而让她陷入混乱和痛苦。然而她热爱耶稣，她把耶稣想象为自己的完美情人，“她听取耶稣的精神教诲”，以此“迎合自己肉欲的需要”，④这样的描写大大颠覆了《圣经》中耶稣的神圣形象，在当时的社会环境中难免被打上离经叛道的标签。

除此之外，《虹》的第十章，谈到了耶稣复活的话题，作者在此发问，为什么耶稣不能闪耀着生命之光升天，为什么耶稣升天后死亡的躯体上会有可怕的伤口？作者的理想是，耶稣复活后，肉体和精神都很完美，并在真实的肉体中生活、相爱，最终获得完整，没有伤痕和瑕疵。然而在基督教《新约》中却常常宣扬耶稣受难后，以肉体的牺牲换得精神的重生，来证明耶稣的精神性而排斥肉体性。而劳伦斯在此却同时强调了肉体的复活，作为一个完整的人投身到世间生活的洪流中，“和兄弟一起愉快地吃饭”，“欢乐地吻所爱的人”，“设宴欢庆肉体的婚姻”……⑤劳伦斯在《复活的上帝》中叙述道，耶稣以前是救世主、教诲者，却不是一个完整的人，而复活的耶稣作为一个集灵肉于一身的自由人，注定要生活在地上而非升入天堂，来保护生命的玫瑰不受践踏。查尔斯·罗斯曼认为，“劳伦斯式的‘福音’颠覆了约翰福音对精神的强调，回归到《创世记》开头几章中对肉体的赞颂”。⑥ 劳伦斯如此强调本性无非是对现代社会中越走越远的理性之路、道德重压以及个性丧失现象的回击，并且试图予以匡正的一次尝试。然而他以激烈高呼的姿态宣扬与主流价值观相悖的观点，在当时的语境中难免面临名誉扫地的风险。

---

① ［英］D. H. 劳伦斯. 劳伦斯书信选［C］. 刘宪之等译. 哈尔滨：北方文艺出版社，1999：63.

② 《圣经·约翰福音》，第1章，第14节.

③ 《圣经·路加福音》，第18章，第22节.

④ ［英］D. H. 劳伦斯. 虹［M］. 黑马等译. 上海：上海三联书店，2014：274.

⑤ ［英］D. H. 劳伦斯. 虹［M］. 黑马等译. 上海：上海三联书店，2014：269.

⑥ 熊沐清. 变形的耶稣：《儿子与情人》中的宗教蕴涵［J］. 外国文学研究，2007（1）.

(二)突破权威:多彩之“虹”

《圣经》作为基督教的神圣文本具有权威和不容置疑的性质,一切价值评判以上帝所说为依据,那么《虹》作为“反圣经”文本,其特点还体现在其对绝对真理和权威的突破。

“虹”一意象来源于《圣经·创世纪》,是上帝与人立约的标记,这点在上文中已做过阐释。作为小说中的意象,“虹”一直被认为是新生、希望、两性和谐的象征。T. R. Wright 在《劳伦斯与圣经》中指出,“虹”对于劳伦斯而言还意味着打破单一白光统治的多样性,这一方面是由于虹本身的多彩颜色,另一方面这也是上帝与诺亚之约的另一层含义。他还认为这一点与巴赫金的理论相似,即把小说提升到一种对话式或具有内部劝说性的论述,以此来反抗单一神学式的权威话语。

《虹》表面上嵌套了一个“圣经式”的权威叙事,而劳伦斯又在其内部增加了不稳定的叙事因素。首先,他在小说中设置了几对二元对立的矛盾,例如男性与女性、精神与肉体、一元论与多元论等,这使得相互冲突的观念得以展现,质疑和辩论的声音打破了单一叙事的稳定性。以安娜和威尔为例,二人的观念不仅代表了男性与女性之间的冲突,同时也反映了劳伦斯对宗教的矛盾态度。威尔是笃信宗教并对其充满激情的,而安娜则相信智慧是万能的并痛恨威尔的盲目依恋。对于玻璃窗上的擎着旗子的小羊图案,威尔以为这是耶稣的化身,是纯洁和做出牺牲的象征,他为此着迷;而安娜则抵抗这种象征和神秘体验,并嘲笑这是一只滑稽荒唐的羊。她还蔑视威尔的轻信奇迹,认为《圣经》中所说的“水可以变成酒”只是谎言。二人争论的高潮是林肯大教堂,威尔认为这里就是完整与永恒,是秩序和绝对的代表,大教堂在此也是一元论的代表。然而,与完全陷入狂喜的威尔不同,安娜则认为这里纯粹是限制,她追求的是超越屋顶的自由的权利,吸引她的是石柱上那些不那么和谐的奇特小脸谱,在这里安娜扮演了打破一元论限制、寻求更多自由的角色。在文本最后虽然威尔宗教信仰坍塌,看似以安娜的胜利结束,但是作者字里行间表露出对威尔的同情,又使读者难以下定论。正是这些冲突与争论作为小说的不稳定因素,消解了绝对权威的存在,形成了《虹》的另一个“反圣经”特点。

三、劳伦斯的“拉纳尼姆”:法与爱的和弦

那么,作者在《虹》中要表达的宗教理想到底是什么?他心中的“拉纳尼姆”和厄休拉所追求的彩虹高挂之地又在哪里呢?

“拉纳尼姆”(Rananim)一词的意思是翠绿、新鲜和茂盛,是劳伦斯在其好友所唱的希伯来歌曲中获得的灵感,它就是劳伦斯心中的天堂和圣地。“一战”期间,

劳伦斯曾多次向一些思想家、艺术家发出邀请,想要切实地行动起来去寻找这个理想之地,实现他的乌托邦理想,却均以失败告终。他还在作品中寄寓了他的“拉纳尼姆”理想,即他的新宗教观,具体即指法与爱的和弦。

在《托马斯·哈代研究》一书中,劳伦斯将学说和故事的矛盾称作法与爱的矛盾,二者的矛盾统一形成了艺术形式。他还将此概念应用于其宗教观。他认为“一神论,法,都是属于女性的;男性的伟大宣言是《新约》,《新约》里命令人们要再生,去获得鲜明的自体:爱与多重性侵入了法与犹太人的一元论”。“通常情况下两性总是不平衡的”①,劳伦斯追求法的肉体和爱的精神的结合。他认为人类的历史进程,第一个时代是法的时代,只有当男性女性找到自己的地位,相结合,并报告圣灵的来临才可能进入第三时代。那个时代的艺术将如同圆满婚姻一般,圣灵将爱——男人和法——女人结合为一体并拥有最终的和谐。但目前我们仍处于“结尾性的间歇期”,完结是圣灵支配的时代。显然,劳伦斯为了追求福音书式的神感效应而牺牲了文字的清晰。但是,在他这些零散的哲学思辨中,我们总能听到一个声音,即“两性的和谐,将产生第三种力量,并立于法与爱、女人与男人之间,如同圣灵处于圣父与圣子之间一样”。② 他从三位一体的思想方法中推证出一个相互分离又相互抗争的力量,以此来剖析文化的衰亡与复兴。

劳伦斯所说的法与爱的时代的更替也体现在《虹》所描述的布朗温三代的家族更替中。第一代汤姆·布朗温的时代继承了祖先们与土地、山川河流的亲密的血液相融的关系,尽管这种关系受到了女性渴望超越和获取更多自由的威胁。他们日出而作,日落而息,天地万物丰富的生命创造流入他们的血管中。汤姆和莉迪亚夫妇在此环境中找到了属于自己的和谐。这是属于《旧约》的时代,是法的时代。劳伦斯认为随着基督教的发展,这种古朴的血性热情逐渐消失,人类终于失去了与宇宙的一体,失去了肉体、性、情绪、激情与大地、太阳和星星的一体。第二代安娜与威尔,二人的宗教观念有着根本性分歧,安娜迫使威尔摆脱对宗教的盲目依恋、听天由命的状态,达到不那么舒服、他很不情愿的精神独立,她要他处于未知世界的边缘而不是轴心,然而安娜自己却堕入了做母亲的停滞状态。两人的探索并没有完成。第三代人厄休拉,首先抛弃了死板教义,宗教的虚幻世界与“工作日世界”让她陷入痛苦的混乱,斯克里宾斯基的出现燃起了她情欲的激情,异性的力量一度使她的肉体和灵魂充盈而完满。然而斯克里宾斯基作为一个被现代社会文明规训的人,他与厄休拉并没有达到最终的和谐完满,厄休拉最终大病一场,摆脱了

① [英]弗兰克·克默德.劳伦斯[M].胡缨译.北京:生活·读书·新知三联书店,1986:52.

② [英]弗兰克·克默德.劳伦斯[M].胡缨译.北京:生活·读书·新知三联书店,1986:51.

与他的关系，却看到了大地之上的彩虹。然而彩虹只是过早地升起。厄休拉所处的不过是劳伦斯所说的“结尾性的间歇期”，她的任务就是要走出荒野，到达上帝许诺的乐土。而虹的出现则另一方面表明了劳伦斯的乐观态度，他相信一个新的时代必将开启，他心中的“拉纳尼姆”也终会实现。

综上所述，劳伦斯在《虹》中模仿了《圣经》的权威叙事，并借此框架表现了他具有“反圣经”特点的新宗教观，即对古朴的血性热情地推崇、他的肉体信仰以及法与爱的和弦。随着现代文明的发展，科学和理性主义的思潮占据了统治地位，机器和知识扼杀了古朴的宗教和诗意的想象，生态破坏、信仰的衰落和一系列社会问题的出现使得“人类的生存困境”成为现代社会的主题，对此伯格森、尼采、叔本华等人掀起了以强调内心体验、直觉和无意识的意志为代表的非理性主义思潮来反驳人类“过度发展”的理性。在此语境中的劳伦斯，既受非理性主义的影响，又开辟了自己的一条道路，他曾自豪预言自己将改变世界未来一千年的历史进程，虽然我们无法预知他心中的“拉纳尼姆”是否终会到来，但他的探索至今仍有着不可忽视的现实意义，它启迪着人们不断思考，在理性和非理性的调和中继续摸索前行。

参考文献：

[1][英]D. H. 劳伦斯．虹[M]．黑马等译．上海：上海三联书店，2014.

[2] T. R. Wright. *D. H. Lawrence and the Bible* [M]. Cambridge University Press,2009.

[3]Hugh Steven. *From Genesis to the Ring*: *Richard Wagner and D. H. Lawrence's Rainbow*[J]. Textual Practice,2014,vol28:4.

[4]Gerald Doherty. *Violent Immolations*: *Species Discourse*, *Sacrifice and the Lure of Transcendence in D. H. Lawrence's The Rainbow*[J]. Modern Fiction Studies, 2011, vol57:1.

[5][英]弗兰克·克默德．劳伦斯[M]．胡缨译．北京：生活·读书·新知三联书店，1986.

[6][英]D. H. 劳伦斯．劳伦斯散文[C]．黑马译．北京：人民文学出版社，2008.

[7][英]D. H. 劳伦斯．性与可爱——劳伦斯散文选[C]．姚暨荣译．广东：花城出版社，1988.

[8][英]D. H. 劳伦斯．劳伦斯书信选[C]．刘宪之等译．哈尔滨：北方文艺

出版社,1999.

[9]田俊武. 从变形耶稣到血性意识——劳伦斯宗教观嬗变历程[J]. 国外文学,2010(2).

A Study on Beijing Han People's Current Communication with Chinese Ethnic Minority

首都经济贸易大学外国语学院　刘丽

Abstract: China has 55 ethnic minorities all together and all of them can be found in Beijing. However, the Han is still the largest ethnic group in Beijing in regard of its population and distribution. For the sake of social stability of this city and China, it is very vital to understand the situation of Beijing Han people's communication with Chinese ethnic minority people. In addition, China has been concerning its ethnic relations since its establishment, and in view of this point, the present study is of very importance. This paper is mainly based on a survey. The data show that the first seven ethnic minorities Beijing Han people are most familiar with are the Hui, the Uygur, the Miao, the Mongolian, the Man, the Zang and the Zhuang. In contrast, some other Chinese ethnic minorities are not well known by Beijing Han people, such as the Achang, the Deang, and the She. Furthermore, Beijing Han People know more about the lifestyle, holidays and religion believes of a few ethnic minorities in China; however, they don't know well about most ethnic minorities in China. Most Beijing Han people know about these ethnic minorities chiefly by TV and movies. Besides, Beijing Han people are willing to communicate with ethnic minority people, whereas their attitudes toward living, working and marrying with ethnic minority people are not very positive.

Key Words: interethnic communication; Beijing Han people; Chinese ethnic minority people

According toBeijing Sixth National Census in 2010 main data bulletin, the number of Han population is 18,811,000 and accounts for 95.5% of the total resident people in Beijing; meanwhile, the number of ethnic minority population is 801,000 and accounts for 4.1% of the total resident people in Beijing (2011). Compared with the data of 2000, Han population in Beijing has increased 5, 827, 000 and ethnic minority population in Beijing has increased 216, 000 (Beijing Statistics Bureau, 2011). In addition, there are over 30 ethnic minorities on average living in each district of Beijing city. Compared with the data of 2000, the number has also increased. How well do such a large number of Beijing Han people communicate with these ethnic minority people? Up to now, no relevant researches have discussed it. Nevertheless, because the communication situation between Han people and ethnic minority people in Beijing involves the stability and development of this city and even the whole country, it becomes very vital to study this topic. In addition, China has been valuing its ethnic relations since its establishment, and in view of this point, the present study is of very importance. Therefore, the purpose of this paper is to delve into the current communication of Beijing Han people with ethnic minority people from the angle of Beijing Han people. In order to achieve this goal, a survey has been conducted to find out the results.

The present survey employs a questionnaire with an open question and 21 close questions. Likert's five-point scale is applied to the closed questions. The whole survey is undertaken to answer the following three types of questions concerned. First, to which ethnic minorities are Beijing Han people familiar most. Second, to which extent do Beijing Han people know about Chinese ethnic minority people and the channels. Third, to which extent are Beijing Han people willing to communicate with Chinese ethnic minority people, focusing on living, working and marriage. The first two types of questions are closely connected to the third type of questions. Based on the results of the first two types of questions, we can better understand the results of the third type of questions.

Participants

A total of 234 Beijing Han people participate in this study. They are mainly college students, college teachers, employees in some private and state-owned companies, employees in some government organizations, workers in some markets, students under college, and persons staying at home. They are all selected at random. Among of them, the answers of 201 participants are effective (139 women and 62 men). The age of all participants ranges from ten years old to seventy years old (see Figure 2). However, the ages of participants chiefly concentrate on the range from eighteen years old to forty years old. Their education backgrounds focus on Bachelor Degree, Master Degree and Middle School Degree (see Figure 3).

Procedure and Data Collection

One questionnaire is designed for the current study (see Appendices), including basic information about participants, one open question and twenty-one closed questions. The basic information about participants contains three aspects: sex, age and education background. The open question in the questionnaire aims to examine which ethnic minorities Beijing Han people are most familiar with. The participants can write down as many Chinese ethnic minorities as they can in an order of familiarity. Question 1 to Question 12 attempt to examine the extent to which Beijing Han people know about Beijing ethnic minority people and the channels. Finally, Question 13 to Question 21 are designed to find out the extent to which Beijing Han people are willing to communicate with Beijing ethnic minority people. Questionnaires are handed out at random by investigators to Beijing Han people who are willing to participate in the present study. When the investigators hand out questionnaires to participants on site, participants are required to answer the questions at once. It takes the participants three or five minutes to finish the questionnaire and then the questionnaires are collected after finished. When the investigators hand out questionnaires to participants by email, participants are required to email their finished questionnaires back to the investigators as soon as possible. Participants are told the purposes of the study before they begin to answer their questionnaires for the reason of protecting their rights to know.

Results and Discussions

Considering the ethnic minorities with which Beijing Han people are familiar most, 177 participants write down the names of these ethnic minorities and one participant names as many as 18 Chinese ethnic minorities. The first seven ethnic minorities they know most are as follows: the Hui, the Uygur, the Miao, the Mongolian, the Man, the Zang and the Zhuang. One important reason is that these five Chinese ethnic minorities possess more population than the other Chinese ethnic minorities and may accordingly exert more influence so that they are known by Beijing Han people. Based on Beijing Sixth National Census in 2010 main data bulletin, the Man, the Hui and the Mongolian appear in the top three positions in the list of the Chinese ethnic minority population in Beijing, with the Man accounting for 41.9%, the Hui accounting for 31.1% and the Mongolian accounting for 9.6% (Beijing Statistics Bureau, 2011). Moreover, the rank does not change compared with ten years ago. In contrast, some other Chinese ethnic minorities are not well known by Beijing Han people, such as the Achang, the Deang, and the She. These are also relatively smaller ethnic minorities in China in view of their population. However, some other ethnic minorities are obscured by Beijing Han people. For instance, the Moso is not one of Chinese ethnic minorities, but one of branches of the Naxi inYunnan Province (Shi, 2008). Similarly, the Amei is not one of Chinese ethnic minorities, either, but one of branches of the Gaoshan (Song and Chen, 2001). The Hakka is not considered a Chinese ethnic minority as well because it is one of the most important branches of the Han that moved from the Yellow River Drainage Area to southern part of China in history due to wars and famines (Yang, Lin, Li, Fu and Fan, 2009). There are two so-called ethnic minorities that do not exist in 55 Chinese ethnic minorities list and they are the Hayi and the Sani. It is likely that participants confuse the two with another two ethnic minorities: the Hani and the Sala (see Figure 1).

As for the extent to which Beijing Han people know about Beijing ethnic minority people, six aspects within twelve questions are investigated as follows: lift style, holidays, culture and art, religion believes, values, and history. Based on Likert's five point scale, five response levels are used to obtain the extent of knowing (see Figure 4). Figure 5 shows that most Beijing Han people just know about Beijing ethnic minority people a little or do not know well. If the five response levels, from the strongly positive one to the strongly negative one, are graded as five points, four points, three points, two points and one point, each item will get its following corresponding mean score as shown in Figure 5. It can be inferred that Beijing Han People know more about the life style, holidays and religion believes of a few ethnic minorities in China. However, they don't know well about those aspects of most ethnic minorities in China.

For the purpose of exploring whether there exist differences between male participants and female participants about the extent to which they know about ethnic minorities in China, this study makes a hypothesis testing on two independent samples. This hypothesis supposes no differences exist on the above extents between male participants and female participants.

Among twelve questions, the differences only can be found in Question 1 and

Question 7,and furthermore the mean values of male participants are smaller than those of female participants in both cases. This displays that the extent to which male Beijing Han people know about the life style and religion believes of a few ethnic minorities in China is lower than female Beijing Han people. In contrast, obvious differences due to different ages and educational background are not found on the extent to which Beijing Han people know about ethnic minorities.

Regarding how Beijing Han people know about Chinese ethnic minorities, it is shown in Figure 6. According to this figure, a majority of participants choose TV and movies as their major channels to know about ethnic minorities, totally accounting for 79. 1%. Books rank the second with a percentage of 59. 7% and the third main channel is the press with a percentage of 44. 28% . However, they seldom know about those ethnic minorities by face-to-face communication and this communication channel only accounts for 3. 98% . It is obvious that Beijing Han people do not frequently communicate with ethnic minority people. Nevertheless, Chinese ethnic minorities are always reported in media and introduced in books and magazines.

The final analysis focuses on the communication of Beijing Han people with Chinese ethnic minority people. Figure 7 shows 83. 5% participants answer that there are ethnic minority people among people they know, while Figure 8 demonstrates that 43. 71% participants respond they do not always communicate with ethnic minority people and 36. 53% participants respond the chance of their communication with ethnic minority people is neutral. It can be found that the communication between Beijing Han people and ethnic minority people is not so frequent. However, as is shown in Figure 9,80. 24% participants who know ethnic minority people claim that there are no communication obstacles between them and ethnic minority people. One of the most important reasons owes to the Chinesization of many ethnic minority people when they live together with the Han people and differences are narrowed therefore. Another important reason is that the chance of most Beijing Han people communication with ethnic minorities is not so frequent as discussed above, though most of them claim that they know ethnic minority people. Among 19. 16% participants who claim the existence of communication obstacles between them and ethnic minority people, most of them hold that different life styles may explain the communication obstacles with a percentage of 62. 5% . The second big obstacle is due to language with a percentage of 50% and the third big obstacle is due to religion belief with a percentage of 46.88% (see Figure 10).

The study reports that no participants refuse to communicate with ethnic minority people although the extent of refusal is different (see Figure 11). 46% of participants claim they do not refuse to communicate with ethnic minority people at all. 41% of participants express that they do not too much refuse to communicate with ethnic minority people. This also can be reflected again in Figure 12. Most participants adopt neutral attitudes. The attitudes of participants toward living, working and marrying with ethnic minority people are mainly neutral. Furthermore, it can be inferred although Beijing Han people do not refuse to live, work and marry with ethnic minority people, they do not show very positive attitudes toward close communication with ethnic minority people. After all, there still exist differences between them that affect their communication. For instance, during the process of survey, some participants say that it is not easy for them to adapt themselves to some strange lifestyles of ethnic minorities.

According to the above studies, it can be concluded that most Beijing Han people do not know about ethnic minority people well and they are willing to communicate with ethnic minority people. Moreover, there are no obvious obstacles when most of them communicate with ethnic minority people. Nevertheless, the chance that Beijing Han people communicate with ethnic minority people is not so frequent. Therefore, the communication of Beijing Han people with ethnic minority people should be enhanced in future for more harmonious relationship between the Han and Chinese ethnic minorities. Especially, Beijing Municipal Government concerned should take effective actions to improve this important communication. Some relevant organizations or societies in Beijing can also hold some activities to make Beijing Han people know more about those ethnic minority people who live and work around them. Although this paper has obtained some meaning information about Beijing Han people's current communication with Chinese ethnic minority people, some problems are still worth noticing in future studies. First, the number of participants in the present study is not large enough because of the difficulty of getting more help and further studies should involve more participants. Second, more detailed questions can be complemented into questionnaire to make the survey more complete.

References

[1] Beijing Statistics Bureau. (2011). *Beijing Sixth National Census in* 2010 *Main*

Data Bulletin. Beijing: Author. Retrieved from http://www.bjstats.gov.cn/rkpc_6/pcdt/tztg/201105/t20110504_201366.htm

[2] Beijing Statistics Bureau. (2011). *Beijing Sixth National Census in* 2010 *Main Data Bulletin*. Beijing: Author. Retrieved from http://www.bjstats.gov.cn/rkpc_6/pcsj/201105/t20110530_203335.htm

[3] Shi C. G. *The Yongning Moso*[M]. Kunming: Yunan University Press, 2008.

[4] Song S. H., Chen K. J. *A Brief Introduction to Chinese Ethnic Groups* [M]. Beijing: Minzu University of China Press, 2001.

[5] Yang L. L., Lin Y. L., Li Y., Fu Y. & Fan L. J. *Historical migrations of China* [M]. Beijing: China Modern Economy Press, 2009.

Appendices

1. Questionnaire

Instructions:

Thank you very much for your participating in this survey. The purpose of the survey is not to ask about personal matters. It simply aims to study how you know about the culture of Chinese ethnic minority people and your communication and acceptance with them. Your answer will not be made public.

Part I. Please fill in the following information.

Sex:__________ A. male B. Female

Age:__________ A. 10 ~ 20 B. 21 ~ 30 C. 31 ~ 40

D. 41 ~ 50 E. 51 ~ 60 F. above 60

Education Background:__________

A. Elementary B. Middle C. Polytechnic

D. Junior College E. Bachelor F. Master G. Doctor

Part II. Please write down the ethnic minorities in an order of your familiarity.

____

____

____

Part Ⅲ. Please read the questions and write down your choices in brackets.

1. The extent to which you know about the life style of a few ethnic minorities in China. (   )

A. know well B. know fairly C. know something D. know little E. know nothing

2. The extent to which you know about the life style of most ethnic minorities in China. (   )

A. know well B. know fairly C. know something D. know little E. know nothing

3. The extent to which you know about the holidays of a few ethnic minorities in China. (   )

A. know well B. know fairly C. know something D. know little E. know nothing

4. The extent to which you know about the holidays of most ethnic minorities in China. (   )

A. know well B. know fairly C. know something D. know little E. know nothing

5. The extent to which you know about the culture and art of a few ethnic minorities in China. (   )

A. know well B. know fairly C. know something D. know little E. know nothing

6. The extent to which you know about the culture and art of most ethnic minorities

in China. (　　)

A. know well　　B. know fairly　　C. know something　　D. know little

E. know nothing

7. The extent to which you know about the religion believes of a few ethnic minorities in China. (　　)

A. know well　　B. know fairly　　C. know something　　D. know little

E. know nothing

8. The extent to which you know about the religion believes of most ethnic minorities in China. (　　)

A. know well　　B. know fairly　　C. know something　　D. know little

E. know nothing

9. The extent to which you know about the values of a few ethnic minorities in China. (　　)

A. know well　　B. know fairly　　C. know something　　D. know little

E. know nothing

10. The extent to which you know about the values of most ethnic minorities in China. (　　)

A. know well　　B. know fairly　　C. know something　　D. know little

E. know nothing

11. The extent to which you know about the history of a few ethnic minorities in China. (　　)

A. know well　　B. know fairly　　C. know something　　D. know little

E. know nothing

12. The extent to which you know about the history believes of most ethnic minorities in China. (　　)

A. know well　　B. know fairly　　C. know something　　D. know little

E. know nothing

13. The Channels of your knowing about Chinese ethnic minorities (Your choices should be no more than three. If you choose I, please write down your choice in the blank.):(　　)

A. TV&Movies　　B. Books　　C. Press　　D. Broadcast

E. Websites　　F. Classes

G. Direct communication　H. Introduction from other people　I. ____________

14. Are there ethnic minority people among those you know? (If you answer no, please skip Question 15,16 and 17 and answer Question 18 to Question 21). (　　)

A. Yes　B. No

15. The chance of your communication with ethnic minority people. (　　)

A. a great many　B. always　C. neutral

D. not too many　E. never

16. Are there obstacles when you communicate with ethnic minority people? (　　)

A. Yes　B. No

17. The reasons that you think there exist communicationing obstacles between you and ethnic minority people. (Your choices should be no more than three. If you choose F,please write down your choice in the blank.) (　　)

A. language　B. lifestyle　C. thought pattern

D. religion belief　E. Value　F. ____________

18. Do you refuse to communicate with ethnic minority people? (　　)

A. not at all　B. not too much　C. neutral　D. a little

E. very much

19. Are you willing to live together with ethnic minority people? (　　)

A. strongly agree　B. agree　C. neutral　D. disagree

E. strongly disagree

20. Are you willing to work together with ethnic minority people? (　　)

A. strongly agree　B. agree　C. neutral　D. disagree

E. strongly disagree

21. Are you willing to marry with one person from ethnic minorities? (　　)

A. strongly agree　B. agree　C. neutral　D. disagree

E. strongly disagree

Thank you very much!

2. Figures:

Figure 1 Familiarity Degree of Beijing Han People with Chinese Ethnic Minority

Ethnic Minority	Hui	Uygur	Miao	Mongolian	Man	Zang	Zhuang	Dai	Chaoxian	Bai
Sample Size	147	110	102	97	94	87	83	78	72	65
Percentage(%)	73.13	54.73	50.75	48.26	46.77	43.28	41.29	38.81	35.82	32.34
Ethnic Minority	Tujia	Yi	Gaoshan	Kazak	Buyi	Dong	Qiang	Hani	Yao	Oroqen
Sample Size	56	42	32	29	23	21	19	17	13	11
Percentage(%)	27.86	20.90	15.92	14.43	11.44	10.45	9.45	8.46	6.47	5.47
Ethnic Minority	Baoan	Naxi	Hezhe	Shui	Pumi	Russian	Jing	Jingpo	* Mosou	Tajik
Sample Size	10	10	9	7	4	3	3	3	3	3
Percentage(%)	4.98	4.98	4.48	3.48	1.99	1.49	1.49	1.49	1.49	1.49
Ethnic Minority	Tu	Xibo	* Amei	Pulang	Dulong	Ewenki	Lahu	Li	Sala	Gelo
Sample Size	3	3	2	2	2	2	2	2	2	2
Percentage(%)	1.49	1.49	1.00	1.00	1.00	1.00	1.00	1.00	1.00	1.00
Ethnic Minority	Yugu	Achang	Deang	* Hayi	Jino	* Hakka	Mulao	* Sani	She	
Sample Size	2	1	1	1	1	1	1	1	1	
Percentage(%)	1.00	0.50	0.50	0.50	0.50	0.50	0.50	0.50	0.50	

Figure 2 Age Distribution

Age	Below 18	18 ~ 30	31 ~ 40	41 ~ 50	51 ~ 60	Above 60
Sample size	8	118	58	11	2	4
Percentage(%)	3.98	58.71	28.86	5.47	1.00	1.99

Figure 3 Education Background Distribution

Education Background	Elementary	Middle	Polytechnic	Junior College	Bachelor	Master	Doctor
Sample size	2	34	8	17	77	48	14
Percentage(%)	1.00	16.92	3.98	8.46	38.31	23.88	6.97

Figure 4 The Extent to Which Beijing Han People Know about Beijing Ethnic Minorities People

Num	Item	Percentage(%)						
		Know well	Know fairly	Know somehow	Know little	Know nothing	Missing Value	Total
1	the extent to which you know about the life style of a few ethnic minorities in China	0	4. 48	29. 35	61. 19	4. 98	0	100
2	the extent to which you know about the life style of most ethnic minorities in China	0	6. 47	42. 79	45. 77	3. 48	1. 49	100
3	the extent to which you know about the holidays of a few ethnic minorities in China	0. 50	8. 96	33. 33	51. 24	5. 97	0	100
4	the extent to which you know about the holidays of most ethnic minorities in China	1. 00	3. 48	25. 87	61. 19	7. 46	1. 00	100
5	the extent to which you know about the culture and art of a few ethnic minorities in China	1. 00	6. 47	34. 83	48. 26	8. 46	1. 00	100
6	the extent to which you know about the culture and art of most ethnic minorities in China	0	3. 98	29. 35	55. 22	10. 45	1. 00	100
7	the extent to which you know about the religion believes of a few ethnic minorities in China	1. 00	5. 97	37. 31	48. 76	6. 47	0. 50	100
8	the extent to which you know about the religion believes of most ethnic minorities in China	0. 50	6. 97	34. 33	50. 75	7. 46	0	100
9	the extent to which you know about the values of a few ethnic minorities in China	1. 00	10. 95	25. 37	50. 25	12. 44	0	100

续表

Num	Item	Percentage(%)						
		Know well	Know fairly	Know somehow	Know little	Know nothing	Missing Value	Total
10	the extent to which you know about the values of most ethnic minorities in China	0.50	6.97	22.39	55.22	14.43	0.50	100
11	the extent to which you know about the history of a few ethnic minorities in China	1.49	12.44	26.37	47.26	11.94	0.50	100
12	the extent to which you know about the history believes of most ethnic minorities in China	2.49	5.47	23.88	58.21	8.96	1.00	100

Note: The number of participants who chooses one item divided by the total sample number equals the percentage of this item.

Figure 5 Mean Score of the Extent to Which Beijing Han people Know about Beijing Ethnic Minority People

Num	Item	Mean score
1	the extent to which you know about the life style of a few ethnic minorities in China	2.53
2	the extent to which you know about the life style of most ethnic minorities in China	2.33
3	the extent to which you know about the holidays of a few ethnic minorities in China	2.47
4	the extent to which you know about the holidays of most ethnic minorities in China	2.29
5	the extent to which you know about the culture and art of a few ethnic minorities in China	2.43
Note: Each effective answer scoring total divided by the number of participants who gives effective answer to each item is equal to the mean score of each item.		
6	the extent to which you know about the culture and art of most ethnic minorities in China	2.27
7	the extent to which you know about the religion believes of a few ethnic minorities in China	2.46
8	the extent to which you know about the religion believes of most ethnic minorities in China	2.42

续表

Num	Item	Mean score
9	the extent to which you know about the values of a few ethnic minorities in China	2. 38
10	the extent to which you know about the values of most ethnic minorities in China	2. 24
11	the extent to which you know about the history of a few ethnic minorities in China	2. 44
12	the extent to which you know about the history believes of most ethnic minorities in China	2. 34

Figure 6 Channels of Beijing Han people Knowing about Chinese Ethnic Minorities

Channel	Sample Number	Percentage(%)
TV&Movies	159	79. 10
Books	120	59. 70
Press	89	44. 28
Broadcast	60	29. 85
Websites	32	15. 92
Classes	22	10. 95
Direct communication	8	3. 98

Figure 7 Are There Ethnic Minority People among Those You Know

	Yes	No	Missing Value
Sample Size	167	29	5
Percentage(%)	83. 08	14. 43	2. 49

Figure 8 The Chance of Your Communication with Ethnic Minority People

	A great many	Always	Neutral	Not too many	Never	Missing Value
Sample Size	8	22	61	73	2	1
Percentage(%)	4. 79	13. 17	36. 53	43. 71	1. 20	0. 60

Figure 9 Are There Obstacles When You Communicate with Ethnic Minority People

	Yes	No	Missing Value
Sample Size	32	134	1
Percentage(%)	19. 16	80. 24	0. 60

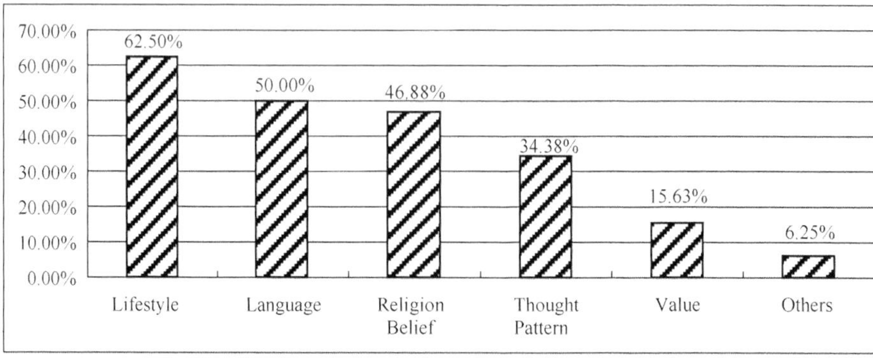

Figure 10 The Percentage of Communication Obstacles between Beijing Han People and Ethnic Minority People

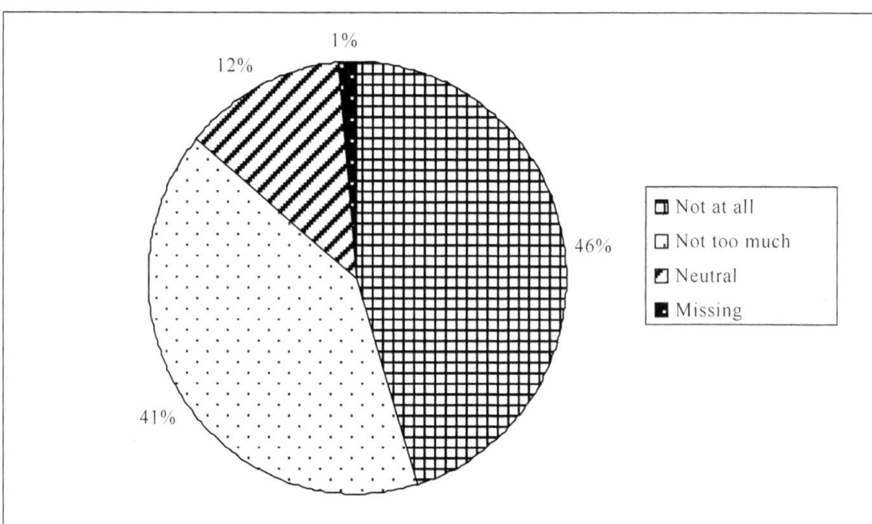

Figure 11 The Extent to which Beijing Han People Refuse to Communicate with Ethnic Minority People

Figure 12 The Extent of Willingness to Communicate with Ethnic Minority People

Num	Question	Number of Chooser						
		Strongly agree	Agree	Neutral	Disagree	Strongly disagree	Missing Value	Total
19	Whether are you willing to live together with ethnic minority people	30	32	119	20	0	0	201
20	Whether are you willing to work together with ethnic minority people	37	29	124	11	0	0	201
21	Whether are you willing to marry a person from a ethnic minority	29	25	91	46	8	2	201

中国跨国公司差异化管理和文化融合研究
——基于生态管理研究视角

首都经济贸易大学外国语学院　刘重霄

摘　要:对于跨国企业文化,传统的研究路径为:文化差异必然产生文化冲突,冲突具有零和博弈的性质,水火不相容。为了减轻文化冲突对企业文化造成的负面冲击,需要采取一定的策略,促进文化的融合,最终形成一种新的文化。本研究的观点认为,不同文化之间存在差异,这些差异既可能造成文化冲突,也可能形成文化互补。在某种程度上,冲突可以通过管理手段化为互补,形成非零和博弈。中国跨国公司文化以"合和"文化和H基因为基础,通过基因、环境和偶然事件三个要素的整合形成C型组织文化,成为解决差异化管理的策略。

关键词:中国跨国公司;C型组织文化;生态视角

Abstract: The traditional research of multinational corporate culture always follows such way: the cultural differences will inevitably produce cultural conflict, which is featured with the nature of the zero-sum game, just as fire and water are incompatible. In order to alleviate the negative impact caused by cultural conflict to the corporate culture, it is necessary to take certain strategy to promote the fusion of culture and form a kind of new culture. The present study holds the view that the differences between different cultures may, on one hand, cause cultural conflicts, but, on the other hand, can also form cultural complement to each other. To some extent, the conflict may turned into complement through an effective means of management, forming a non-zero-sum game. Take Harmony culture and H gene as its foundation, Chinese multinational corporate culture, with the integration of the three elements gene, environment and chance event, form a special organizational culture "C", serving as the diversified management strategy.

Key Words: Chinese multinational corporations; "C" organizational culture; ecological perspective

在跨国公司跨文化研究中,往往注重不同文化之间的差异性对企业、员工以及管理者产生的不同影响。差异性容易产生文化冲突,而冲突具有零和博弈的性质,冲突双方水火不相容,大多产生负面影响。而主流跨文化研究的任务和目的就是采取一定的策略,减少甚至消除这种差异性,减轻差异冲突对企业文化和管理造成的负面冲击,最终促进文化融合,形成一种较为单一的全新文化。

但现实的情况是,不同文化之间存在的差异(这里的文化是一种泛指文化,大到国家文化,小到个人文化)既可能造成文化冲突,也可能形成文化互补。在某种程度上,冲突可以通过管理手段化为互补,形成非零和博弈。正如水火关系一样,尽管水火不相容,但水与火之间可以通过金属容器这个媒介相容并存,并合为一体,转换成水的一种新的形态,开水或水蒸气。而这里的媒介即为管理手段。互补性保证了差异性文化的共生,形成了文化的多样性。多样性文化需要差异性管理,差异性管理符合生态性管理的自然规律。一般来讲,差异会导致矛盾,但任何事物都有两面性,矛盾并不一定都是坏事,矛盾可能会阻碍发展,但矛盾也是形成创新机制的一个因素。但目前学界从差异中探索跨文化管理创新机制的研究实践和成果却很少。

管理包括对人的管理和人自身的管理。不容否认,不同文化之间的"人"的确存在很多差异性,但人作为一个整体,他们之间也肯定存在一些共性,如马斯洛的需求理论中,人人都会有生存需求、生理需求、社会需求、自我价值实现需求等,只不过是在需求的程度和需求的先后顺序上存在一些差别。但在跨文化管理研究中,对人类共性文化管理所涉及的研究很少。但突破常规思维,在跨管理研究和实践中,到底更应该关注共性还是差异性呢?差异一定需要管理吗?我们设想一下在人类出现之前或完全原生态的森林或海洋中,各种物种之间的差异性大于共性,世界五彩缤纷。在一个简单的生物链中,老虎吃狼,狼吃兔子,兔子吃草,草吸收土里的各种营养成分。大家各有所需,各有各的生存环境和生存空间以及生存方式,这是最自然的一种生态管理,而这种生态管理的核心因素就是差异性。在跨文化管理中是否可能存在一种生态管理呢?依据传统的企业文化,西方人绩效考核的标准是数量,日本人绩效考核的标准是质量;日本人晋升的条件是工作年限,中国人晋升多依据与领导的关系。而在一家跨国公司中,肯定存在不同的岗位,这些岗位有着不同的规范和要求,也就是说,不同的岗位适合不同文化背景的人,这是一个跨国公司这一社会实体应该具有的一种自然属性。假如仅有共性呢?一个餐桌上既有肯德基这样的美式快餐,又有比萨这样的意大利传统美食,还有中国特色的烤鸭,以及日本和韩国青睐的寿司。相对于一个具有不同文化背景的跨国人力资源团体来讲,大家可以各享其爱。但对于相同文化背景的团队,比如都是具有中国文化背景,大家可能会争抢烤鸭,这样便会出现两种情况,一种是人人都吃不饱(也可能会产生有人能吃饱、有人会挨饿的情况);第二种情况就是生产更多的烤鸭。

但无论怎样,烤鸭终究是一种短缺资源,总会引起员工之间的竞争。以此看来,差异造就共存,共存产生量的积累;共性导致竞争,竞争导致质的发展(文化的同一性会导致同质人群之间的竞争,根据生物性的优胜生存原则,竞争促进原有企业文化的发展,形成创新力)。

以自然生态系统为例,依次性的食物链形成纵向管理链,虎,狼,兔,草;而同类物种形成横向管理链,如虎具有不同地域、不同性别和不同年龄之分。纵向管理链具有互补性,横向管理链具有互补与竞争两种特征,但其中互补性占主要成分,竞争为次要成分,因为只有几乎完全同质的事物之间才会形成竞争,但这种概率相对于互补性概率来说非常小。也就是说,我们能够在同一性中发现其互补性。纵向管理链(食物链型)为差异性管理,重在识别差异;横向管理为差异化管理(又称精细管理),重在同一性中识别互补性,进行策略应用。纵向管理需要硬性指标,如教育背景、专业方向、社会经历等;横向管理强调软性指标,如素质与能力、智性、情商等。生物链是以食物需求为基础的单纯生存性需求的生物性管理,遵守的契约文化为自然法则;企业管理是以社会效益为基础的多层性需求的社会性管理,遵守的契约文化为社会法则。进行差异化管理,首先要识别差异,然后确定差异性(互补性),最后实施差异化(策略应用)。

在人与文化的博弈中,常规思维认为人是弱势方,只能适应文化,文化可以改变人,可以塑造人,可人本身就是一个非常具有革命性的因素,人可以适应文化,同时人也可以改变文化,甚至创造新文化。在跨文化管理中,人不一定要适应某一种固定的文化,跨文化本身就是一种文化。它是一种多元文化融合而成的文化,是一种独立的文化,其中有冲突的因素,也有和谐的因素;有积极的因素,也有落后的因素。作为一种独立的文化,跨文化中的人力资源便不再是一种相互冲突、不可协调的个体,而是相互联系、彼此相交的部分,我们不能再以一种解决矛盾的思路去处理它们之间的关系,而应从一个整体的角度,去看待整体的各部分之间的相互关系。所以,跨文化不是几种文化的混合,而是与其他几种文化并列的一种世界文化大家庭中的文化。

中国跨国公司同样是一种融合文化,但该融合文化的核心和本质仍然摆脱不了中国文化的本质,这种本质是进行差异化管理的基础。

威廉·大内Z理论的提出,虽然从侧面说明了曾以美国企业制度为楷模的日本模式可以超越美国模式,但中国企业文化不同于日本,中国企业文化的自创性少于对发达国家的模仿性,还未形成国家层面抽象化的组织模式。针对中国的特殊状况,有的专家研究了中国企业无形资源优势转移问题;有的专家分析了中国儒家文化的特殊性;也有专家基于中西传统文化差异和我国传统体制对企业文化造成的不利影响方面,论述了中国跨国公司文化形成的障碍;还有专家从中、日、美文化的区别,尝试性提出了中国式管理以及中国企业文化的核心要素。由于中国跨国公司形成历史短,可供选择的案例不多,尽管以上研究从不同角度打开了中国跨国公司研究的大门,但没有抓住中国企业文化的核心思想和研究主线,没有对空泛的现象进行概括化和抽象化,研究成果不能代表中国企业文化跨国整合的基本模式,也没有从事物发展的角度进行深化研究,没有回答中国跨国公司企业文化形成过程以及新型企业文化的本质特征。但随着我国企业跨国并购速度的加快和规模的扩大,这方面的研究需要进一步深化。

中国跨国公司“传承母体优秀文化基因、融合西方先进文化基因”的形成模式,使参与融合的两种不同的企业文化之间将呈现出独特的博弈模型和发展路径。中国跨国公司的发展现状与20世纪80年代日本企业在美国发展的情形具有相似之处,日本曾以美国企业制度为楷模但最终形成了自己的企业管理模式并超越了美国,虽中国的企业在理论上还未形成一个像日本J型企业一样的C型(Chinese)组织模式,但中国经济的成功从侧面反映了中国企业管理的成功。中国企业能走向世界成为跨国公司,其组织模式与组织文化的核心要素是什么呢?威廉·大内的Z理论启发了我们,以企业文化跨国整合为契机探索C型组织的核心因素。假设企业文化具有生命体的基因、环境和偶然事件三个要素,“合和”文化是中国文化和中国企业文化的核心,“H(harmony 和谐思想)”基因是中国企业文化抽象出的核心母体基因。依据生物演化理论,基因具有的先天遗传、后天获得以及变异特征,中国企业文化必然要传承其优秀的H文化基因,但面对变化的环境(西方文化的核心是“分合”文化,“自我”是它的核心母体基因),又不得不进行基因变异与再造。基因变异意味着不同优秀基因的融合与创新,基因变异与再造过程就是新企业文化形成的过程。在基因、环境、偶然事件(人的因素)三个因素中,企业文化基因就是母国与东道国企业文化基因的融合体,环境是指企业移植前后的具体的生存环境,偶然事件(人的因素)是指移植前后企业员工所接受的领导风格以及员工素质等。中国跨国公司文化将面临如何融合一个完全不同的文化基因,如何适应一个完全异样的生存发展环境,如何融入并接受一个异质性的群体。而这一过程将是C型组织核心要素形成的过程。

生物学的基因理论在跨国公司企业文化形成中重新释义,试图在企业文化形成模式上有所突破。从纵向演化角度研究跨国企业文化,明晰中国企业文化本体跨国移植前后的三个决定要素,即企业文化基因(“合和文化”和“和谐”思想与东道国国家文化基因或企业文化基因)、环境(母国企业生存与发展环境与东道国生存与发展环境)和偶然事件(同质性人群与异质性人群),并运用企业文化契约观和资源观理论,形成了中国跨国公司文化差异化管理和融合策略:跨国公司文化就是母国企业原有心理契约的继承和修改过程,中国企业文化跨国整合后的 H 基因再造模式与采用融合战略所形成的全新文化,可以最大限度地减少文化差异所造成的文化冲突。

参考文献:

[1] David. H. Holt, Karen. W. Wigginton. 跨国管理[M]. 北京:清华大学出版社. 2005:17.

[2] Fons Trompenaars, Charles Hampton-Turne. 在文化的波涛中冲浪:理解工商管理中的文化多样性[M]. 关世杰译. 北京:华夏出版社,2003.

[3] Heenan, D. A. and Perlamutter, H. V. *Multinational Organizational Development* [M]. Reading MA: Addison-Wesley, 1979.

[4] 威廉·大内. Z 理论——美国企业如何迎接日本的挑战[M]. 北京:中国对外翻译出版社,1984.

《苹果酒屋的规则》的成长主题研究

首都经济贸易大学外国语学院　马丹

摘　要:长篇小说《苹果酒屋的规则》是美国小说家约翰·欧文的代表作,讲述了年轻人荷马的成长历程。本文试从小说内容和结构上来分析该小说的成长主题。

关键词:成长主题;规则

Abstract:The novel *The Cider House Rules* is the representative work of the American novelist John Irving. It depicts the growth experience of the youth Homer. This paper analyzes the initiation theme in terms of structure and content of the novel.

Key Words:Initiation theme;Rules

约翰·欧文(1942—　)是当代美国最知名的小说家之一。他的作品呈现出高超的叙述技巧、独特的原创性和优美的文学性。《苹果酒屋的规则》是欧文的代表作,讲述了年轻人荷马的成长历程。

成长是人生的必经阶段,也是人类个体生命的重要体验,因此也成为文学的永恒主题之一。在美国文学史上,青少年成长小说历来占有突出地位。因为作为移民国家来说,“美国作家没有悠久的文学传统作依凭,他们的创作总是从头开始。他们的创作体验与青少年的成长体验有许多相似之处。因此,他们喜欢选择年轻人作为小说的主人公”。

成长小说“是以叙述人物成长过程为主题的小说,是讲述人物成长经历的小说。它通过对一个人或几个人成长经历的叙事,反映出人物的思想和心理从幼稚走向成熟的变化过程”。成长小说的叙述结构相当模式化:天真——诱惑——出走——迷惘——考验——失去天真——顿悟——认识人生和自我这个基本模式或在此基础上的变异。不同的时代背景会赋予作品截然不同的时代经验。美国成长小说与社会文化的变迁息息相关,同时也反映了美国文化。《苹果酒屋的规则》所叙述的故事发生于20世纪初至60年代,主要围绕堕胎这个敏感问题而展开(在当时的美国,堕胎还没有合法化),同时也反映了黑人种族歧视、“二战”、同性恋等历史事件及社会现象。故事同时也围绕着主人公荷马的成长而展开。

荷马·威尔士是圣克劳兹孤儿院出生的一名孤儿(出生于一九二几年)。他多次被领养,却始终没有成功,因此成为孤儿院的特殊“问题”。孤儿院的创始人兼院长韦尔伯·拉奇是一个独身的产科医生。出于对一段往事的极度愧疚和对那些想要堕胎却求助无门的孕妇的深切同情,他在孤儿院的附属医院里按照孕妇本人的意愿秘密帮她们堕胎。出于父亲对儿子般的深爱,他一方面有意识地培养荷马的信心与责任感,一方面一点一滴地向荷马传授妇科知识。在尚不满 20 岁时,荷马已经完全可以胜任一名资深助产士兼合格堕胎师的职位。然而,在对待堕胎的问题上,荷马却有他自己的信仰。“他并不怪拉奇医生,他认为这里面并不简单存在谁对谁错的问题。这不是拉奇的过错,他只是依据自己的信念行事。”但是“一想到 8 个月的胚胎有了表情,荷马便感觉到了别人所说的灵魂的存在。”因此荷马向拉奇医生宣布他决定绝不替人堕胎。

对于在孤儿院长大的孩子们来说,社会对于他们来说充满了诱惑。荷马也不例外。在他为孤儿院的孩子们朗读《大卫·科波菲尔》和《简·爱》时,他常常会与小说中的主人公产生共鸣,能深切体会小说主人公的感受。尤其是当他步入青春期后,他常常感觉到内心的焦灼不安、对于千篇一律生活的厌倦和对自由的渴望。他对于自己的未来产生了迷茫感,并渐渐滋生出不可遏止的出走的念头。在拉奇医生的默许下,他抓住了一次偶然的机会,与来到孤儿院进行堕胎手术的同龄人华力和坎蒂一起来到位于海边的观海果园,从而踏上了发现自我的心路历程。

拉奇医生曾经写道:“在别的地方,都存在着所谓的‘社会’,可圣克劳兹却没有‘社会’,也不存在社会常见的各种选择……这里的一切都比较单纯……”因而对于荷马来说,一旦接触到孤儿院以外的世界,这对于他就意味着一个更为复杂的环境和社会。很多事物将会超越或挑战他已有的认知。正如拉奇医生所言,观海果园的生活与圣克劳兹有着天壤之别。在这里荷马见识了大海的别样风情,领略了现代文明的新鲜神奇,他努力地学习新的生存技能,例如游泳、驾驶汽车,以及其他一些与生活或果园劳作有关的机器操作等。更令他心醉的是他充分体会到了自由,与华力建立了深厚且唯一的友谊,并感受到了坎蒂带给他的爱情的美好。与此同时复杂的社会也带给他许多的震撼和迷惘。他目睹了歧视、家暴、斗殴、乱伦、邪恶行径等等的丑陋现实,同时也在经历成长的困惑之后,慢慢地学着去把握生活的规则,并最终确立自己人生的方向。

来到观海果园后让他最为惊诧的就是无处不在的“规则”。生活中似乎充满着人们从不言明的行为准则。然而你却不得不小心揣摩体会并不得不接受这一连串的规则行事。在与临时工(黑人)工头亚瑟·罗斯的接触中,荷马对规则有了深刻的体悟。罗斯先生在被一个白人小伙言语挑衅后用精湛的刀法挑开了年轻人衬衫上所有的纽扣却没有对他的身体造成丝毫的伤害。后来罗斯告诉荷马,在与白人相处时,他们黑人有自己的规则可循。每逢收获季节,在苹果酒屋厨房的电灯开关旁,总是贴着一张规则单,对工人的行为进行具体的规定。然而,无论荷马以何种笔调、口吻和措辞来写这个规则,它似乎只是一种被视若无睹的虚空权威。当荷马和罗斯先生谈起此事时,罗斯先生告诉他,黑人临时工们谁都不把这些规则放在心上,因为黑人有他们自己的规则。15 年后荷马无意间得知,事实上除了工头以外这些临时工根本就目不识丁,而且他们有的人从未意识到贴在开关旁的是规则,有的以为那只是开关的使用说明。荷马意识到罗斯先生的规则才是苹果酒屋的真正规则。这件事促使他开始思考他身边的其他人都奉行着怎样的规则。而华力和坎蒂也都表达出在一定的前提下他们都会尊重罗斯先生的规则的观点。最终荷马认识到人们真正遵守的是潜藏在自己内心的规则。

在得知拉奇医生去世的消息后,荷马迫不得已克服自己的不适,违背自己绝不替人堕胎的原则,替罗丝做了手术。而这次事件促使荷马顿悟了。他突然意识到他不能扮演最坏的上帝。他决定将根据她们的意愿为她们提供服务,接生或堕胎都行。这件事情也最终促使荷马决定回到圣克劳兹,按照拉奇医生的设计和希望,以富兹·史东医生的身份接掌孤儿院。

小说中的许多人物的名字本身就带有象征意义。例如拉奇医生的名字(Larch)是一种落叶松的名字,它象征着一种坚韧、常青的品质。而荷马的新身份史东(Stone)更是代表着坚忍不拔、脚踏实地和值得信赖的品质,这也表明荷马是拉奇医生最理想的接班人。当荷马欣然接受这个新名字而决定让荷马·威尔士成为过去时,也就意味着他在精神上和文化上获得了新生,意味着他从天真状态过渡到了成年的经验状态。15 年的出走,荷马作为一个孤儿他始终没有找到一种真正的归宿感、一个让他安心的精神家园,而回归圣克劳兹则是他做出的审慎的心灵选择。

参考文献:

[1]陈湘柳主编. 美国成长小说的伦理价值研究论文集[M]. 北京:北京第二外国语学院旅游教育出版社,2014.

[2]侯金萍. 华裔美国小说成长主题研究[M]. 广州:暨南大学出版社,2014.

[3]徐丹. 倾空的器皿——成年仪式与欧美文学中的成长主题[M]. 上海:上海三联书店,2008.

[4][美]约翰·欧文. 苹果酒屋的规则[M]. 刘国枝译. 上海:上海译文出版社,2002.

西方“吸血鬼”电影中“他者”身份的困惑

首都经济贸易大学外国语学院　任菊秀①

摘　要:通过对《惊情四百年》、《夜访吸血鬼》及《暮光之城》等经典“吸血鬼”系列电影进行分析,探讨了西方古老母题的“吸血鬼”电影所经历的由纯粹恐怖到丰富人性探索的历程;剖析了“吸血鬼”身份形象由完全对立于人类的“他者”逐渐转变为人类的“同质异形体”的异化变迁;阐释了西方文化中“吸血鬼”这一身份的建构与其文化困惑,以及电影所映射出的更深层次的文化寻根特质内涵。通过剖析“吸血鬼”电影所反映的“他者”式的边缘身份叙事,解读了现代“吸血鬼”电影所映射的西方现实世界中边缘群体的“他者”式边缘身份特质。

关键词:吸血鬼;他者;边缘群体;文化寻根

Abstract:In this paper,with an analysis on the movie stories of “*Dracula*”,“*Interview with the Vampire*:*The Vampire Chronicles*” and “*Twilight*”,a discussion has been made on the course from terror to humanity in the theme of vampire movies of old motif. The building of the vampires’ identity images in western culture and their cultural perplexity as well as the profound cultural connotaion of their root-seeking have been probed by way of illustrating the development of vorious vampires’ “other” identity images from being completely opposite to those of human beings to forming men’s paramorphs. On the basis of an exploration to the way of narration of “other” with the marginal status reflected in the vampire movies, an interpretation has been derived to the “other” identity of the marginalised social groups in the real western society.

Key Words:vampires;“other”;marginalized social groups;cultural root-seeking

近年来,谱写出普罗大众集体催眠效应的哥特式舞曲“吸血鬼”电影的再次兴起,给业界带来了更为强劲的冲击。哥特式恐怖电影,向来只是满足特定受众群体的一类影视作品。与以往不同的是,《暮光之城》系列“吸血鬼”电影,从纸媒世界的一炮而红,到众多小说迷对电影改编的热力追捧,再到暮光男女主角自带新闻的

---

① 作者简介:任菊秀(1983—　),女,山东高密人,博士,首都经济贸易大学外国语学院讲师。主要研究领域为英美文学。

各式宣传,将“吸血鬼”电影热推向了一个从未有过的高度。美国系列电视剧《吸血鬼日记》的热播又掀起了“吸血鬼”影视的另一个新的高潮,就连没有吸血鬼文化背景或渊源的许多亚洲国家竟然也在其影响下拍出了具有东方韵味的“吸血鬼”电影。

一、身份建构与文化焦虑

“吸血鬼”电影,就其类型而言,可归类于恐怖电影的一个亚系列,这是因为“吸血鬼”电影的主题思想的各类延伸无论怎样也无法摆脱掉其哥特式恐怖电影特有的嗜血元特征。尽管“吸血鬼”迷们对“吸血鬼”与“吸血鬼”类型的考证层出不穷,五花八门,却依然拿不出真正确凿的证据证明“吸血鬼”的真实性,但作为不朽的“人类”化身,银幕上的“吸血鬼”们却在不间断地向观众们一遍又一遍诉说着其独特的杂交身份及其身份困惑。电影界不厌其烦地演绎着“吸血鬼”的故事并乐此不疲地助推着其银幕身份形象的变迁,这与业界对“吸血鬼”特殊假定身份所映射信息的关注是分不开的,也就是说,“吸血鬼”这种超自然的杂交物种,其身份具有明显的“他者”潜在因素。银幕上“吸血鬼”身份的构建,是与电影所映射出的人们对现代社会人身份建构的思索密不可分的。

从1922年电影《吸血鬼诺斯费拉杜》[①]发行至今,“吸血鬼”电影随着时代的变迁,其类型也呈现出不同的历史阶段性变化。银幕上的“吸血鬼”形象从最初的纯粹恐怖血腥的嗜血怪物形象,到颇受争议的具有社会黑暗组织的社会隐形存在,变成了如今深受女性追捧爱慕的英雄骑士类形象。从嗜血怪物到英雄骑士的身份特征变化所映射出来的不仅仅是“吸血鬼”电影的主题思想,而且是其更深层次的文化内涵和身份认知的建构。

就其文化内涵来讲,“吸血鬼”母题具有典型的西方性和西方宗教特质。第一部“吸血鬼”小说《德拉库拉》诞生于19世纪和20世纪之交,正值西方逐渐过渡到工业社会的时期,人的物质化产生了对传统体制、伦理、宗教的怀疑和颠覆,吸血鬼正是这一精神倾向的代言。[②] 而“吸血鬼”题材以电影形式呈现,其较为经典的要

---

① 《吸血鬼诺斯费拉杜》是1922年由德国导演茂瑙拍摄的“吸血鬼”默片,是人类电影史上第一部里程碑式的哥特电影。

② 邵小晗,《绝不是一场简单的血腥饕餮——从吸血鬼文化的精神内核看吸血鬼电影的类型美学》,《电影评介》,2010年第20期,第21页。

算《惊情四百年》①、《夜访吸血鬼》②等。

在《惊情四百年》中,主人公"吸血鬼"以德古拉伯爵为原型,其形象带有典型的中世纪"吸血鬼"的原型特征。400 年前的产物,丑陋的魔鬼面容,狰狞狡诈的面部表情和眼神,外加阴森恐怖的生存环境和出场声效。正如德古拉伯爵在影片中所言:"我什么也不是,没有生命,没有灵魂,别人憎恨我厌恶我,对世人来说,我死了,我是人人得而诛之的魔鬼,我是——德古拉。"这些妖魔化的特质无不彰显着电影对"吸血鬼""他者"身份的界定。

在故事内容上,《惊情四百年》套用了一个极为俗气的浪漫殉情的爱情故事,而在宗教伦理上,爱情的感化使得选择了魔鬼的德古拉伯爵再次投入到上帝的怀抱。在阴森恐怖的情景设计之外,德古拉伯爵的故事是通过他 400 多年的爱情寻觅来展现自己"吸血鬼"身份的建构和解构的。在妻子去世之时,德古拉伯爵放弃了自己的上帝子民身份而投身到魔鬼阵营中,这其实契合了 20 世纪后半叶西方民众走出战争、回归家园后的迷茫状态。在妻子之死的浅层表象之下,电影表现的不是主人公对爱情的忠贞,而是对自我价值的认知和对自我身份的鉴定与解构,是对人类存在意义和奋斗价值的另类思考。而主人公在其后对妻子的魂是现代人米娜的引诱过程,是对其身份的解构和重新建构的过程。这一过程可以看作是当代西方人士所面对的多元文化的现代性冲击过程和自身身份的否定式修正的过程。然而,故事最终依旧回到了正义战胜邪恶的俗套式结局上,完成了西方传统文化和现代文明最终战胜了另类的古老传统的使命,虽然留下了巨大的创伤,但依旧皈依到以宗教为基础的西方文明的深层根基中来。古老的"他者"被以爱情为依托的西方文明,以爱情的名义将其处死的方式,宣布了对"他者"身份的解构式的救赎。

二、身份困惑和文化寻根

如果说《惊情四百年》是对"吸血鬼"德古拉伯爵阴森恐怖、狰狞邪恶形象的魔鬼化刻画,那么演员阵容最强、艺术成就最大的《夜访吸血鬼》则是对"吸血鬼"内心世界最为深刻的揭示。《夜访吸血鬼》这部电影,虽然引入了布拉德・皮特和汤姆・克鲁斯两位殿堂级白马王子式的好莱坞帅哥出演,但却摈弃了《惊情四百年》中人类爱上"吸血鬼"的陈俗的罗曼蒂克式的爱情故事情节。该影片另辟蹊径,试

① 《惊情四百年》是 1992 年首映的好莱坞"吸血鬼"电影,由加里・奥德曼、基努・李维斯主演。是由布拉姆・斯托克的经典吸血鬼小说《德古拉》(Dracula)改编而成。

② 《夜访吸血鬼》,由尼尔・乔丹执导,布拉德・皮特、汤姆・克鲁斯、斯蒂芬・瑞等人主演的吸血鬼电影,是由安妮・赖斯小说《吸血鬼编年史》的第一部《夜访吸血鬼》改编而成。

图在深层次上揭示“吸血鬼”这个人类社会幻想中的“他者”的生存状况和存在困惑，进而使人们更加关注主流社会下的“他者”的存在困境。

在所有的“吸血鬼”电影中，“吸血鬼”的变形要依赖于另一个“吸血鬼”将其血液进行杂交混合，从而使其不生不死。《夜访吸血鬼》中的“吸血鬼”也不例外，布拉德·皮特饰演的路易，在遇到了由汤姆·克鲁斯所扮演的“吸血鬼”莱斯特后，完成了被同化的过程。以这种方式产生的“吸血鬼”其身份完全有别于人类的“他者”，这不但剔除掉了欧洲正统信仰中关于上帝的造物说，也有悖于自然科学中的遗传学说。从“吸血鬼”产生的角度看，“吸血鬼”与人类是同体异质或同源异型的。它既是自身身份的创造者，也是这种身份的制造产物，它同时位于生产线的起点和终点。正是这种身份的尴尬特质导致了“吸血鬼”的文化焦虑和寻根意识，又由于其“他者”的边缘身份，而使“吸血鬼”在跻身于人类的正统世界时又失去了属于自己身份的话语权。

在电影《夜访吸血鬼》中，路易试图寻找自己的“吸血鬼”身份根源。在作为人类话语承载者的图书馆里查寻吸血鬼渊源的资料时，路易面对的是五花八门的记录，而银幕展现给观众的则是各式各样被人类扭曲变形了的“怪物”，它们成了讴歌人类美好善良的“他者”。图书馆作为人类特有资料的收藏所在地，所记录的自然是人类这一中心的话语记载。当他们在图书馆里查寻吸血鬼渊源的资料时，注定是查不出有价值的线索的。人类凝视“吸血鬼”的目光中充满的是人类的道德价值观和文化传统观。以此目光审视出来的“吸血鬼”的历史是被扭曲了的历史、被整形了的历史。然而，“吸血鬼”则是被视为不同于人类的“他者”，是臆想出来的产物，是人类至善至美的参照物。当然，《夜访吸血鬼》的作者赖斯，并没有简单地继续停留在“吸血鬼”乃是人类的美好的“他者”这一点上，而是将对立的社会属性进行了进一步的置换。“吸血鬼”是魔鬼之子，正如《夜访吸血鬼》中的台词那样，“魔鬼的所有才能都来自上帝，而魔鬼是上帝创造的，我们也就是上帝的孩子。”

《夜访吸血鬼》除却“吸血鬼”自身身份的正名外，其作品本身也具有某种文化寻根特质。“吸血鬼”形象作为当代文化的幻影，试图对现代文化的深渊进行显形式构建。后冷战时期的“吸血鬼”文学的再叙述，反映出某种代表主流大众文化的美国社会的内在文化困惑。正如戴锦华在《无影之影——吸血鬼流行文化的分析》中所讲，“吸血鬼成为美国大众文化的核心，而美国大众文化使用此形象的功能之一是处理美国的欧洲想象。这个准原型形象在某种意义上说是个有效的切入口,带出来一个 19 到 20 世纪的重要大众谱系。”[①]在《夜访吸血鬼》影片的开始和结尾出现的记者马洛伊就属于美国现代文化的典型代表。马洛伊在听完路易讲述的“吸血鬼”故事之后,对“吸血鬼”身份充满憧憬,力图劝说路易将其变成“吸血鬼”从而得以永生。这个片段颇为有趣,寓意颇深,隐含着“吸血鬼”电影开始从最早的欧洲文学作品中的“吸血鬼”的邪恶阴影中走出。美国文化将“吸血鬼”文化视为与之相对应的具有神秘特质的欧洲传统文化的现代延续。在美国现代价值观的重述中,欧洲具有了文化意义上的长生不老。从某种角度上讲,缺乏传统文化根基的美国在面对欧洲传统文化的舶来品时,往往会缔造出对欧洲神秘化了的幻想。“吸血鬼”是在大众社会想象中所缔造出来并拥有悠久历史的皇室或贵族的孤独幽灵。在《夜访吸血鬼》中,“吸血鬼”莱斯特身为法国大革命前的贵族,而路易也是庄园主出身。各式各样的“吸血鬼们”宛如“《圣经》中的天使”[②],身着华服,或出席各种中世纪的舞会,或在欧洲各地游历。在克劳迪娅和路易的“吸血鬼”寻根历程中,他们去的目的地便是巴黎。在那里他们找到了阿曼德和其他一些“吸血鬼”,找到了旧世界的“吸血鬼”总部,而这个总部就坐落在象征欧洲鼎盛时期文化的剧院之中。《夜访吸血鬼》中美国文化的寻根此刻到达了终点,与欧洲文化具有“主体同质性”的美国文化更多地掺杂了现代主义价值观。影片中,当阿曼德试图将路易作为其接班人时,新旧文化的冲突突显出来。背离欧洲文化太久的美国文化,在无限憧憬欧洲文化具有整体脉络性的同时也已经形成了具有自身特点的文化价值体系。寻根的终点显然不是结局,现代文化背后的传统缺失是自身存在的尴尬所在,它既没有办法延续传统文化,也没有办法另辟蹊径发现自身独有的文化身份。

如再加引申则不难发现,这种身份特质犹如处于后殖民社会中的西化群体,最为典型的有如人们通常所说的“香蕉人”等。同样,西化群体在西方现代社会的话语结构中,并没有完成其自身的寻根诉求。在追询“我是谁”这个存在本体论的问题时,无法在第一世界或者第三世界任何一种文化中找到“命名”。这种介于第一世界和第三世界之间的杂交身份是现代社会的时代产物,并且随着世界化进程的深入,其群体也在不断地壮大。一方面,他们长期受到第一世界的经济政治文化渗透;另一方面,他们又有第三世界的血缘关系和受到来自祖先传统思想的影响。在东西方文化的冲突中,他们长期处于失语或无根状态。显然,身份困惑和寻根历程

① 戴锦华,《无影之影——吸血鬼流行文化的分析》,《文艺争鸣》2010 年第 10 期。

② Wright, Dudley, *Vampires and Vampirism: Legends from Around the World*, Lethe Press; Reissue edition (June 2001) p. 167.

受挫自然要衍生出文化焦虑的问题。作为西化人士，他们既不能容忍西方世界对“东方”的神秘化和妖魔化，也不认同东方世界对“西方”的神圣化和丑化，同时又不赞同对自己“东方”身份的过度强调。如同被边缘化了的嗜血怪物“吸血鬼”，虽然没有话语权，但当跻身在所谓的人类正统世界时，却又无法抑制自身嗜血的本能。

《暮光之城》系列电影中“吸血鬼”的身份形象显然与之前的“吸血鬼”形象相差甚远。俊美的少年，青春阳光，具有典型校园浪漫喜剧中的男主人公特征，满足了少女对白马王子的无尽想象。然而，这种形象仅仅可以称为切合了当代的审美需求和流行趋势，而该影片却并非真正意义上的校园偶像剧，其脚本的刻画实质依旧要置于“吸血鬼”文化的框架中。这依然是一个讲述“他者”寻找身份、寻找认同以及多元文化在西方社会的重新建构过程。在《暮光之城》系列电影中，“吸血鬼”所处的环境不再是孤独的。他们拥有自己的社会团体，住进了现代化设备的房子里，拥有和青年学生一样的社会交际和体育活动。然而，因其特殊的功能体征，“他者”的异化成分依旧存在，只是变得美好和令人向往。

《暮光之城》中的“吸血鬼”，其身份在从最初欧洲资产阶级文明困惑中“他者”的文化影响表征中跳脱出来后，试图获得主流身份的认同。他们的身份和文化处境也从《夜访吸血鬼》中的男妓，变成了典型的中产阶级家庭成员。他们面容姣好，拥有多种特异功能，又拥有如现代科技一般的高效和速度，并打着和平的旗号，在正义诉求的道路上杀伐征战。这些都完美地呼应了西方保守主义的核心价值观。“吸血鬼”爱德华一跃从“他者”的嗜血怪物演变为体现西方核心价值观的主流意识形态代言人。而电影中的“他者”称号自然而然地转化给了具有狼人身份的印第安人群体。跻身于被西方文化宣扬和美化最大化的美国文化之中，印第安文化却在其本土失去了原本主人公应拥有的话语权地位，沦为了外来文化的参照物，成了自己故土上的“他者”。在欧洲文明向往的道路上，贝拉自然会无情地摒弃这片土地的保护者狼人——印第安伙伴——的追求。然而，书写出狼人宿命般地爱恋上了贝拉和爱德华的女儿，就显然凸显了作者一厢情愿的美国种族大团圆的和解意义。“因此，《暮光之城》是美国社会中保守主义新主流的有效大众文化实践，表明新主流叙述如何重新成为可能，一种最保守主义的价值观如何找到一个有效的实践，在突破了所有的经过 60 年代的洗礼、后 60 年代所可能有的心理抗拒之后，使人们重新接受和由衷拥戴一套新的合法性话语。”①

① 戴锦华，《无影之影——吸血鬼流行文化的分析》，《文艺争鸣》，2010 年第 10 期，第 39 页。

三、同性恋和边缘身份

“吸血鬼”电影所反映的身份困惑，除了文化焦虑和“他者”身份的异化以及寻根之旅外，还有明显的“他者”式的边缘身份叙事。赖斯在《夜访吸血鬼》中通过对“吸血鬼”生存现状和内心情感的细腻刻画，赋予了“吸血鬼”新的象征身份，即现实世界中受排挤的弱势或曰边缘群体。同性恋自古以来就被视为人类文明社会中反家庭和反伦理道德的非正常行径。现实社会对同性恋的恐惧，使得同性恋者在现实社会中无法企及认同感而带有典型的“他者”式边缘身份标识。于是，在绝望中他们对现实社会投以同等的冷漠和厌恶，从而导致了同性恋群体孤寂的存在状态。而在这部影片中，莱斯特和路易以及克劳迪娅组成了某种意义上的同性家庭。莱斯特是美国文化中男同性恋者的“攻”，他主动选择伙伴，在嗜血中得到了等同于性交的狂热体验。同化路易的咬颈过程如同亲吻，充斥着色情，带有明显的性交象征。莱斯特在谈论他的受害者时说：“吸吮他们的生命、他们的死亡，我爱他们。”同时，在《夜访吸血鬼》中，布拉德·皮特饰演的路易则扮演着男同性恋者中的“受”角。他在走向“吸血鬼”道路时是有选择的，莱斯特的到来只不过是这一过程的直接诱因罢了。在寻根的同时，作为同性恋形象的代表，其自身则带有一定的自毁欲望。在变成“吸血鬼”最后的时刻，路易全身颤抖，处于一种激情的狂喜之中，接着影片具有象征意义地让莱斯特和路易飞升到空中完成了他们血液的融合，达到了同性恋式的性交高潮。

在《夜访吸血鬼》中，路易的身份得不到社会普遍价值观的认同，他一方面无法摆脱其固有的同性恋身份，另一方面又试图回归大众社会，重新做一个有普通社会道德观念的人。社会上存在一种普遍的看法，认为同性恋不是先天的，而是后天被引诱的。世界上最古老的吸血鬼阿德曼邀请路易为自己的同伴时，路易开始是同意的。然而，当他看到在这个同性恋社会中，女人俨然成了祭品时，尤其是在最珍爱自己的克劳迪娅化为灰烬之后，路易压抑着自己的同性恋情感，以道德的名义将这个古老同性恋阵营摧毁。在影片的结尾，路易试图阻止同性恋的延续。他虽然拒绝了同性记者马洛伊的同化要求，但马洛伊最终还是被莱斯特同化。用影片中的“吸血鬼”身份隐喻现实社会中的同性恋者现象是不可阻止的，这显然是在血腥杀戮背后，影片营造的一种对现实主流社会道德价值威胁的最大恐怖效果。

随着艾滋病在全球的爆发和蔓延，人类对艾滋病的恐慌与日俱增，特别是在二十世纪七八十年代，有关艾滋病的宣传铺天盖地。然而，艾滋病的染病和传播与生活的放荡不无关系，大多数患者的染病与毒品静脉注射及男性同性恋有关。艾滋病也像“吸血鬼”一样被视为魔鬼的孩子。“吸血鬼”身份的幻影，显然也符合这种人类未知的通过血液传播的瘟疫形象和其同性恋载体。“《夜访吸血鬼》是艾滋病最新近在艺术领域产生的反响，而它是一部最能赢得大众成为其观众的影片。尽管小心翼翼地徘徊在明确表现同性恋的边缘上，它还是塑造了不断打破一个个禁忌的英俊年轻人，而这些年轻人同时也在畅饮彼此血液这种受禁物，但他们最终却可以逃脱惩罚。”①在“吸血鬼”的世界里，虽然以血液为媒介的传播并没有像艾滋病那样对生命的存在构成威胁，但却在另一个层面上宣告了“吸血鬼”人类身份的结束。对“吸血鬼”的惩罚正在于此，同它所映射的同性恋形象相同，“吸血鬼”无法被主流社会接受，而成为社会主流的“他者”；其身份也无法融入社会的主流文化，无法被主流社会价值观认同，而徘徊于社会道德价值观的边缘。

参考书目：

[1]Wright, Dudley. *Vampires and Vampirism: Legends from Around the World*[M]. Lethe Press, Reissue edition, 2001.

[2]A. Rice. *Interview with the Vampire*[M]. Headline Publishing Group, 1976.

[3]安妮·赖斯. 夜访吸血鬼[M]. 顾炜译. 译林出版社，2007.

[4]布·斯托克. 德拉库拉[M]. 刘思远译. 上海外语教育出版社，2003.

[5]戴维·斯尔卡. 魔鬼秀：恐怖电影的文化史[M]. 吴杰译. 上海：上海人民出版社，2005.

[6]戴锦华. 无影之影——吸血鬼流行文化的分析[J]. 文艺争鸣，2010(10).

[7]刘立刿. 英语恐怖片背后的文化缩影和心理危机[J]. 电影评介，2008(24).

[8]麦永雄，付飞亮.《夜访吸血鬼》中的同性恋[J]. 电影评介，2007.

[9]邵小晗. 绝不是一场简单的血腥饕餮——从吸血鬼文化的精神内核看吸血鬼电影的类型美学[J]. 电影评介，2010(20).

[10]斯蒂芬妮·梅尔. 暮光之城：暮色[M]. 覃学岚，孙郁根，李寅译. 接力出版社，2008.

[11]斯蒂芬妮·梅尔. 暮光之城：新月[M]. 龚萍，张雅琳，李俐译. 接力出

① [美]戴维·斯尔卡著，吴杰译，《魔鬼秀：恐怖电影的文化史》，上海人民出版社，2005，第373页.

版社,2008.

[12]斯蒂芬妮・梅尔．暮光之城：月食[M]．龚萍译．接力出版社,2008.

[13]斯蒂芬妮・梅尔．暮光之城：破晓[M]．张雅琳,龚萍译．接力出版社,2008.

[14]苑野．吸血鬼传说在西方文学中的流传和演变．硕士论文,2006.

[15]周淑茹．关于《夜访吸血鬼》的几种读法[J]．鄂州大学学报,2010.

爱德华·艾比的深层生态思想

首都经济贸易大学外国语学院　石海毓

摘　要:美国生态文学作家爱德华·艾比以描写美国西南部沙漠的宁静与壮美而闻名。他深受深层生态思想的影响,他的作品中随处可见所有生命生来平等、多样性与共生性以及土地伦理等思想。

关键词:生态文学;爱德华·艾比;深层生态思想

Abstract: Edward Abbey, American environmental literature writer, is famous for his description of the tranquility and sublime of the desert in the southwest America. He was influenced by the deep ecology, as a result, his works are full of deep ecological thoughts such asequality of all lives, diversity and co - existence, land ethic and so on.

Key Words: environmental literature; Edward Abbey; deep ecology

美国生态文学作家爱德华·艾比以描写美国西南部沙漠的宁静与壮美而闻名。艾比的代表作《大漠孤行》(Desert Solitaire)出版于1968年,以其有关自然与人类和谐共处的新论、独特的文学魅力,成为自然文学的经典之作。在艾比的作品中随处可见深层生态思想的印记,在深层生态学的生物学概念进入主流之前的几年,艾比就提出:所有生物拥有平等权利,如果多样性能够得到保护,那么,以人类为中心的秩序必将会变得更加以生物为中心。①

一、所有生命生来平等

奈斯指出:"深层生态学的一个基本准则就是,原则上每一种生命形式都拥有生存和发展的权利。"深层生态学把平等的范围扩大到整个生物圈,是生态中心意义上的平等。生态中心主义平等,是指生物圈中的一切存在物都有生存、繁衍和充分体现个体自身以及在"自我实现"中实现自我的权利。即,在生态系统中,一切生命体都具有内在目的性,都具有内在价值,都处于平等的地位,没有等级差别,人类不过是众多物种中的一种,在自然的整体生态关系中,既不比其他物种高贵,也

① James Bishop Jr. , *Epitaph for a Desert Anarchist, the Life and Legacy of Edward Abbey*, p. 152.

不比其他物种更坏。[①] 深层生态主义者认为生物圈中的一切都具有内在价值,“既然我们认为我们拥有内在价值,而我们自身的存在又与其他存在物密不可分,那么,那些存在物也应当拥有内在价值。因此,生态中心主义平等的基本思想是生物圈中的所有生物即实体,作为与整体相关的部分,都具有平等的内在价值。”[②]

艾比指出,地球上的一切生命都是神圣的,都有其继续存在的权利,同时也拥有平等享有地球所提供的一切生存资料和适宜的生存环境的权利,因此,人类应该怀着敬畏之情对待其他生命。人类并不是地球的主宰,每一种生命,甚至是每一个个体生命都具有其与众不同的个性。艾比强调沙漠生态系统的和谐与平衡,在《大漠孤行》第三篇“天堂中的撒旦”中艾比讲述了自己与一条牛蛇(gopher snake)和谐相处的经过。艾比身体力行,他向我们展示了应该如何对待人类以外的生命,“所有的生物都情同手足”,因此,爱护、尊敬其他生命就等于爱护我们自己。

“我喜欢各种形式的生命,甚至包括细菌、小虫、昆虫、蝎子。”艾比并不认为人类能做任何事来消灭地球上的所有生命。事实上,生命本身是好的。如果人类愚蠢到要毁灭自己的生命,不必剥夺其他可以存活的生命的利益。即使地球上没有了人类,它也仍然会是一个宜居之地。“我确实不知道狗、野生动物或是小鸟有着怎样的意识,但我的印象是它们都很享受自己的存在,我认为这是值得的。”生命,无须理由,自自然然地存在就是自然赋予生命的权利,人类无权干扰其他生命的存在。所有生命生来平等,是因为“在大多数人看来,生命本身是有内在价值的,不管它是哪种形式的生命”。[③]

二、多样性和共生性

多样性和共生性原则是奈斯归纳的深层生态学的特点之一。生态系统中物种的多样性与丰富性,是生态系统稳定和健康发展的基础,因此,一切存在物对生态系统来说都是重要的、有价值的。

利奥波德在《荒野》一文中指出荒野是人类从中锤炼出那种被称为文明成品的原材料。荒野不是一种具有同样来源和构造的原材料,它是极其多样的,因而,荒野的多样性决定了它所产生的被理解为文化的最后成品是多种多样的。反过来,世界文化的丰富多样反映了产生它们的荒野的相应多样性。[④] 每一块荒野、荒

---

① 胡志红:《西方生态批评研究》,第 41 页。

② 雷毅:《深层生态学思想研究》,第 50 页。

③ 戴斯·贾丁斯:《环境伦理学》,第 151 页。

④ 奥尔多·利奥波德:《沙乡年鉴》,第 178 页。

野的每一个点上都是独特的,都具有独特的价值。即使是人迹罕至的沙漠,也自有其存在的意义和价值。艾比向人们展示了沙漠的独特:“我像个饿汉般贪婪地注视、凝望掠过眼前那片饱受烈日炙烤的、险峻的不毛之地,铁轨旁的电线杆一一闪过,反光的电线若隐若现,忽明忽暗。但在这些线条、道路和邻近的山脊之外,远方台地和孤峰奇异的轮廓却几乎纹丝不动,只是在遥不可及的距离外来回缓缓移动,形状呈奇特之直角的玫瑰色岬角仍在视线范围内,在我缓缓改变的视野内一次停留一两个小时。那里的一切,就在那里,既无敌意也不友善,却满溢着力量和神秘的希望。”①在艾比看来,沙漠充满了力量和神秘的希望,这就是它存在的价值。

三、大地伦理

对于荒野,梭罗首次提出:“我们所说的荒野是除了我们之外的一种文明。”在日记中,这位瓦尔登诗人写道:我所行走于其上的地球不是一个死的没有自动力的物体,它是一个实体,有精神,是有机的,并且会对其精神受到的影响做出反应的。而被称为“美国新环境理论的创始者”的奥尔多·利奥波德则倡导一种开放的“大地伦理”,呼吁人们以谦恭和善良的姿态对待土地,他提出“一件事只有当它趋向于保护整个生物圈的完整性、稳定性和美丽,才是正确的,如果相反则是错误的。”②利奥波德的这一关于生态良心的基本原则成为艾比的灵感来源之一。

在艾比看来,“荒野(wilderness)这个词本身就是音乐。”为何这个词有如此的魅力?艾比设想荒野能够唤起人们对往事的怀想——“一种合理的不只是感情用事的对我们已失去的而我们的祖先所知的美国的怀念。这个词暗示着过去和未知,暗示着孕育了我们的大地。它意味着失去的事物以及仍展现的事物,意味着遥远同时又亲密的东西,意味着存在于我们的血液及神经中的东西,意味着超越了我们且没有极限的东西。”③荒野存在于过去的积淀和对未来的预示中,在艾比看来,荒野是家之所在,是精神的慰藉之处,是自由的源泉。

在《大漠孤行》中,艾比写道“对荒野的热爱不仅仅是对不可及的事物的渴望,对荒野的热爱是一种对土地忠诚的表达。”④

艾比将这些环境伦理融入写作,他的作品成为人与自然之间象征性戏剧的再现。

---

① 爱德华·艾比:《旷野旅人》,第 11 页。

② Ibid. ,p. 221.

③ Edward Abbey, *Desert Solitaire: A Season in the Wilderness*, p. 189.

④ Edward Abbey, *Desert Solitaire: A Season in the Wilderness*, p. 190.

中国现代知识分子史研究：青年郭沫若(1914—1924年)

【斯洛伐克】马里安·高利克著

中国传媒大学文学院　王晓燕译

这是一项关于中国现代作家、学者郭沫若先生(1892—1978)在1914年至1924年青年时期思想和学识发展的研究，指出了他从传统纲领到泛神论再到马克思信念的转变。

在中国现代学者中，郭沫若被认为是第二位最能代表中国现代文化特征的重要人物，仅排在鲁迅(1881—1936)之后。郭沫若和鲁迅的青年时期、命运在某些方面极为相似，不过因为学识和艺术类型的分别，他们还是有相当大的区别。

实际上，在郭先生学识和思想发展的最重要的十年里，我们希望更为详细地告诉读者的是，这个发展主要发生在日本，仅仅有一部分在中国本土。他生命中很重要的一个日子是1914年1月14日。坐落于中国内地四川省西南部的美丽的峨眉山，是中国名山之一，也是他的"长征"的出发点。途经他小学和中学就读的城市嘉定，后经过成都、天津、北京、中国东北各大城市，历朝鲜，最后抵达日本。[①] 他发现自己来到一个新天地，这里与他过去度过了21年光阴的世界完全不同。那个远东强国，一度自豪地称自己为"中华"，自诩为世界中心，自认为是"中国中心论"世界秩序的载体，这种观念(可能一度盛行)在那时的日本和中国本土都已经失去了它的光环。[②] 这种思想观点上的变化在日本有着更久远的历史。回溯到德川时代(1603—1867)，具体说是17世纪中叶，这种观念就开始褪色，最后完全颠覆。

甚至那时已经出现这样的观点：认为在对智慧、人性和英勇等诸类公民品德的遵守和践行方面，"日本都大大超越了中国，毋庸置疑远远比中国更配得上'中央

---

① D. T. 罗伊：《早年郭沫若》，剑桥(麻省.)，哈佛大学出版社，1971年，第7～56页。

② J. K. 菲尔班克《原初秩序》见其编著《中国之世界秩序》，剑桥(麻省)，哈佛大学出版社，1968年，第1～14页。

王国’的美名。”[1]后来，在 19 世纪的前 10 年里，平田笃胤（1776—1843）声称，文明世界的真正源头不是中国，而是日本。[2] 且不说所有不必要的、当时没有可靠证明的自夸，我们看到的“中华与夷狄”的对立具有完全不同的意义。至少在一个时期里，日本人把“中国中心世界秩序”变成了相反的“日本中心世界秩序”。它不再是中国人眼中日本人野蛮的问题，而是恰恰相反。然而，在这种思想背叛中，日本人不是故意遗忘就是有意篡改了一些东西。例如，起初常常是中国人在很大程度上促进日本人西化，特别是在外贸、制造业和其他方面。但随后日本人开始在各方面赶上了他们的导师，尤其是在技术、工业生产、商业、战争甚至文化等领域，通过自己的诸多努力超越了师傅。

中日甲午战争期间（1894—1895），“倭寇”日本人打败了古代传说中华尧舜大帝的后裔。中国人透过自己的“中国中心论”世界观的扭曲棱镜看世界的时间太长了，甚至在他们已经意识到欧洲的“远洋魔鬼”何其强大、所向披靡之后仍然如此。两年的中日战争打开了很多中国知识分子的眼界。他们中很多人的妄自尊大幻觉让位于本身软弱无力的羞耻感受。他们试图进行必要的改革——然而，这些改革从来没有得以强力执行，1898 年被称为“百日维新”的运动成为 20 世纪初中国发生巨大变化的前兆而载入史册。很多知识分子惊叹于日本人的成功。那时的岛上帝国开始表现出同情中国改革家或革命者的迹象，支持他们与来自中原以外的满族做斗争，乐意帮助中国人进行广泛的专业学科教育，包括政治、经济、军事、科学和文化，但同时也表现了野蛮的侵略行为，比如肆无忌惮地开采、政治暴力、残忍兽行等。

1900 年到 1937 年期间，中国在日本求学的留学生数量比在其他欧美发达国家的多得多。基于十分完全的数据和概略的评估，Y. C. 王给出的数字是超过 34000 人。[3] 中国留学生选择日本出于多种原因。一个重要的选择因素是地理位置毗邻，留学费用比其他国家的要低，两国象形文字（不过并非语言上的）相关，还有就是政治避难。郭沫若一直渴望走出自己狭隘的、保守的地方圈子，进入更广阔的天地，所以毫不犹豫地抓住了这个最初的机遇。是他哥哥郭开文的老同学、同事张次瑜在一次偶然的机会带他到日本的。郭开文仅仅能够支持半年的资费，郭沫若必

---

① H. D. 哈路图尼《德川家康时期思想之中国功能》，见入江昭《中国与日本：政治与文化互动随笔》，普林斯顿，新泽西，普林斯顿大学出版社，1980 年版，第 14 页。

② H. D. 哈路图尼《德川家康时期思想之中国功能》，见入江昭《中国与日本：政治与文化互动随笔》，普林斯顿，新泽西，普林斯顿大学出版社，1980 年版，第 26 页。

③ Y. C. 王：《中国知识分子与西方：1872—1949》，教堂山，北加利福尼亚大学出版社，1966 年，第 119 页。

须在那短短的时间里准备好通过必修语言考试,这种考试通常需要两年的学习才能通过。①

天赋超群的郭沫若在1914年6月成功地通过了东京一所中学的入学考试。② 如果说那是史无前例的,那么他可能为他的成就而感到自豪,不过他早在中国就经过了一定的语言学习;他早在1908年就在嘉定的中学学习过日语。③ 郭沫若报名语言考试的学校是第一高级中学,在那里他参加了一年的特别班学习,为的是能够跟上日本学生的中学课程。④

恰好在1914至1915学年期间,第一次世界大战在遥远的欧洲爆发,日本政府向袁世凯(1859—1916)总统为首的中国政府提出令中国丧权辱国的"二十一条",一旦中国接受,就意味着中国满洲、内蒙古、山东、中国东南海岸、长江流域沦为日本人的殖民地,日本人将获得整个中国版图的经济、政治控制权。当时,郭沫若正在参加佛家学者桂馨谷讲授"大乘起信论"的讲座,大乘起信论是"唯识"的根本教义之一,不同于达摩、瑜伽行派或法相宗的特点——法相。⑤

在先前关于这段时期的一个研究中,我们讨论了唯识对瞿秋白(1899—1935)学识上发展影响的问题,我们也试图介绍这种学说的扼要特征。⑥ 在此,要达到我们的目的,也许需要注意到这种十分复杂的纯理论哲学来自以下论点的推论,"客观世界只不过是我们意识的产物,客观世界是并不存在的,内在的思维能力(即意识)表现的状态仿佛就是一个外部世界。因此整个外部世界都是幻觉。"⑦

郭沫若明确称赞这种学说,但他也不是十分相信,这对他的无政府主义主张毫无阻碍。在那个生死存亡的年代,确切地说在1915年5月7日他写下一首诗,表示随时准备为自己的祖国而战斗甚至捐躯。⑧ 他与几个朋友一起回到上海,但是那里没有打仗,因为当时的袁世凯已经部分接受了日本人的要求,三天后,郭沫若又回转东京。⑨

---

① Y. C. 王:《中国知识分子与西方:1872－1949》,教堂山,北加利福尼亚大学出版社,1966年,第116页。

② D. T. 罗伊:《早年郭沫若》,剑桥(麻省.),哈佛大学出版社,1971年,第56页。

③ D. T. 罗伊:《早年郭沫若》,剑桥(麻省.),哈佛大学出版社,1971年,第56页。

④ D. T. 罗伊:《早年郭沫若》,剑桥(麻省.),哈佛大学出版社,1971年,第57页。

⑤ D. T. 罗伊:《早年郭沫若》,剑桥(麻省.),哈佛大学出版社,1971年,第58页。

⑥ M. 高利克:《中国知识分子史研究 II:青年瞿秋白(1915—1922)》,《亚非研究》第十二卷,1976年版,第92～95页,第102～103页。

⑦ K. 陈:《中国佛教历史研究》,普林斯顿,普林斯顿大学出版社,1964年版,第321页。

⑧ 谷辅林:《郭沫若世界观中的泛神论问题》,《文学评论丛刊》第8期,1981年版,第9页。

⑨ D. T. 罗伊:《早年郭沫若》,剑桥(麻省.),哈佛大学出版社,1971年,第59页。

蒋百里（1882—1938）是 1920 年文学研究会的创始人之一，也是梁启超（1873—1929）的亲密伙伴，在他的著作《欧洲文艺复兴时代史》中写下了以下的句子，似乎在 20 世纪 20 年代下半叶是千真万确的："现代欧洲史的曙光来自两次伟大的浪潮：第一，希腊思想复兴，就是'文艺复兴'；第二，原始基督教的复苏，这带来'改革'。我们国家今后的新转折点也应该从两个方向发展而来：第一，情感，（包括）新文学和新艺术；第二，理性，（包括）新佛教。"①后来的演化取向各异，而这两个源头代表了马克思主义和儒家学说，尽管无数人竭力说明后者涉及一些不同的东西。郭沫若那时对佛教的兴趣在某种程度上可能是偶然的，但的确与他的内心需要一致。

作为一个嘉定少年（那时才 14 岁），郭沫若打碎了"支配观念和生产力的神灵"②塑像，在碎片上撒尿来表达自己的藐视。自然，佛教的迷信形式与唯识学说之间的差异是巨大的。作为主观唯心主义的一种现象，它在世界哲学中属于最复杂的系统（在纯理论思考的意义上）。

对唯识研究的兴趣当然起源于 1915 年之前很久。来自清朝末年的许多新学学者，例如康有为（1858—1927）和梁启超以及他们的追随者们，已经在研究佛教了，在此之前，还有伟大学者龚自珍（1792—1841）和魏源（1794—1856）。③

郭沫若对佛教感兴趣不只是为了赶时髦，也不是因为其源自印度哲学的教义已被中国所接受。唯识体现了一种在本质上外来的印度学说与本土道教教义密切联系的特色，我们可以从哲学家庄子（公元前 3 世纪）的著作中总结得出道教的教义，至少部分上如此。这有关梦境是哲学范畴，而梦幻（或者梦境一般的）是人类、自然和宇宙存在的形式。唯识哲学的核心体现在印度婆薮盘豆（公元 4 世纪或 5 世纪）的简要准则中，被中国人称为"一切唯识"，④意思是"一切都只不过是意识"。意识（但这个术语往往也解释为"思维能力"）不是最正确的词。它也构成某种"无意识"形式，不过不同于 S. 弗洛伊德在心理玄学中发现的无意识。在原文中，它被称为阿赖耶识，并由此"演化出我们看到的外部现象"。⑤ 在此，意识是持续产生外部现象的所有现象的"种子"。

① 梁启超：《清代知识分子走向》（第 2 次印刷），剑桥（麻省.），哈佛大学出版社，1970 年版，第 117 页。

② D. T. 罗伊：《早年郭沫若》，剑桥（麻省.），哈佛大学出版社，1971 年，第 24 页。

③ 梁启超：《清代知识分子走向》，剑桥（麻省.），哈佛大学出版社，1970 年版，第 115 ~ 118 页。

④ 《成唯识论》，香港，成唯识论出版委员会，1973 年，第 cxxx 页。

⑤ 冯友兰：《中国哲学史》第二卷，普林斯顿，普林斯顿大学出版社，1953 年，第 304 页。

我们已提到了庄子和唯识学派的基本相似点。① 但他们之间存在更多的东西,就我们意识到的来说,迄今为止没有人进行过有助于更详细解释他们的对比研究。我们至少应该关注他们其中之一。在著作的第二章里,庄子谈到一则简短的逸事,包含了深刻的哲学信息:“昔者,庄周梦为蝴蝶,栩栩然蝴蝶也,自喻适志与。不知周也。俄然觉,则蘧蘧然周也。不知周之梦为蝴蝶与,蝴蝶之梦为周与? 周与蝴蝶,则必有分矣。此之谓物化。”②

唯识学派的哲学家没有如此诗意的情形,但也力图证明他们的主张。这个学派的主要著作《成唯识论》的注解之一在以下段落中尤其强调:“……例如,当梦见两个人之间发生交媾时,尽管(这个梦的)对象不是真实的,然而他们(做梦的人)依然有所体现,男人遗精,女人来潮。”③

在第一个案例中,“梦幻”有助于中国道学家解释这样的论点,“尽管在一般的状态下,事物之间存在差异,但是在幻想或者梦境中,一个事物也可以成为另一个。”事物之间的转化“证明事物之间的差异不是绝对的”。④ 在第二种情况下,“梦幻”有相当不同的目的。它在此声称的不是事物的相关性、价值或观点,而是十分严格的、教条式的“尽管不存在除意识以外的真实对象,然而虚构事物起作用(例如遗精)的因素是成立的。”⑤

我们无法得知唯识学说是否给郭沫若留下印象,或者留下的印象达到什么程度。如果确有印象,那还要归功于他在 1912 年阅读了《庄子》,并对其产生了浓厚的兴趣。我们有必要提到他用于说明那个时期(与原配夫人结婚)的唯一引文来自文章的开头,就是那个关于蝴蝶的典故。南郭子綦的话在某种程度上印证了郭沫若的自我认知,我们在以下论述中可以发现这一点,也许是在中国本土哲学和文学提出的观点中有史以来最值得注意的。

“可乎可,不可乎不可。道行之而成,物谓之而然。……恶乎然? 然于然。恶乎不然? 不然于不然。物固有所然,物固有所可。无物不然,无物不可。故为是举,莛与楹,厉与西施,恢恑憰怪,道通为一。”⑥西施是古代一位著名的美女,而郭

① 高利克:《中国知识分子史研究 II:青年瞿秋白(1915—1922)》,《亚非研究》第十二卷,1976 年版,第 92 ~95 页,第 102 页。

② 《庄子全集》B. 华生译,哥伦比亚大学出版社,1968 年版,第 49 页。《庄子引得》,北京,1974 年版,第 7 页。

③ 冯友兰:《中国哲学史》第二卷,普林斯顿,普林斯顿大学出版社,1953 年,第 323 页。

④ 冯友兰:《中国哲学史》第二卷,普林斯顿,普林斯顿大学出版社,1953 年,第 64 页。

⑤ 冯友兰:《中国哲学史》第二卷,普林斯顿,普林斯顿大学出版社,1953 年,第 323 页。

⑥ 《庄子全集》B. 华生译,哥伦比亚大学出版社,1968 年版,第 40 ~41 页.《庄子引得》,北京,1974 年版,第 4 页。

先生的未婚妻、年轻的太太丑陋、未受过教育、思想落后,他把她叫作“黑猫”,也许从不“了解”她。① 令人惊讶的是,他并没有违背自己婚姻的父母之命,而他的默许自然是基于对庄子著作的阅读。

仔细分析唯识理论最根本的诗意哲学“诗篇”将揭示出这样的论点,认为“一切都只不过是意识”来自于以下三行诗句:

诸般意识泾渭分明:认知与认知之对象。
因此,灵魂和律法都不存在
因此,一切都只不过是感觉。②

在此,灵魂代表“我”,律法代表“法”,即自我以外的外部事物。郭沫若是中国现代个人主义最重要的代表人物之一,可能根本没有认识到二者的关系,因为否定了它们的客观存在,即“我法非别实有”。③ 如果在那之后不久,1915 年夏末,他想皈依佛教,这还有其他的原因。一年半的勤奋学习,使他患上严重的神经衰弱症。他的心理压力还伴随着失眠、噩梦、头痛和眩晕。④ 他没有求助于唯识理论,也没有诉诸精神治疗的任何其他佛家学说,而是深入自己的记忆。他 1906 年在嘉定的一位老师易曙辉,外号“猛虎”,是王阳明(1472—1529)学说的信徒。⑤ 1915 年 9 月中旬,在冈山考入第六高级中学之后,郭沫若买了部《王文成公全书》。这部著作是谢廷杰于 1572 年编撰的,包括王阳明的散文作品、信札、诗歌和杂记等,是对王阳明及其哲学进行研究的基础资料。⑤

他每天读十数页书,练习两次静坐,每次半小时,琢磨书中的内容,试图平复自己纷乱的思绪。⑥

如果婆薮盘豆的泛神论学说不能满足郭沫若的要求,那么王阳明以其泛实体主义哲学,不但成为郭沫若心仪的哲学家,成为他连接古老的中国和印度哲学价值观的桥梁,而且引导他开始认识欧洲学说,尤其是现代思想:他更进一步了解了庄子、老子(公元前 4 世纪)和孔子(公元前 551—公元前 479)的思想,并开始接触乌

---

① D. T. 罗伊:《早年郭沫若》,剑桥(麻省.),哈佛大学出版社,1971 年,第 44 ~ 45 页。

② Cf:《成唯识论》,香港,成唯识论出版委员会,1973 年,第 cxxx ~ cxxxiii 页。

③ Cf:《成唯识论》,香港,成唯识论出版委员会,1973 年,第 502 ~ 503 页。

④ D. T. 罗伊:《早年郭沫若》,剑桥(麻省.),哈佛大学出版社,1971 年,第 59 ~ 60 页。

⑤ D. T. 罗伊:《早年郭沫若》,剑桥(麻省.),哈佛大学出版社,1971 年,第 23 页。

⑥ 郭沫若:《儒教精神之复活者王阳明》,见郭沫若《唯识论集》,《文艺研究》第四版,上海,1929 年版,第 79 ~ 80 页。

帕尼沙德、B. 斯宾诺沙和 J. W. 歌德。[①]

1924 年 6 月,在“王阳明——儒家精神复兴者”的论文中,郭沫若回想起他赞赏这位卓越哲学家和政治人物观点和事迹的时代。文章的开头是自己的主要社会伦理主张,即人格的自由发展,他在王阳明身上看到了自己的楷模。依照他的解说,王阳明一生的意义不在于无常的观念,即生命现象、生命存在、变化过程和生命终止,从来没有稍息片刻,也没有受苦受难,他看到的是与疾病和死亡“抗争”的一生。[②] 他的反抗精神不是满足于逃避现实的道教学说,也不是悲观的佛教教义,而是人本主义的儒家思想,尤其是他关于“天堂、俗世和一切事物唯一本质”的根本假说,[③]据说是儒家奠基人宣扬的思想,信仰由此而来,是一种“自我扩充”。[④] 但孔子的教义两者都不是。至于王阳明,他的教义是关于前者而非后者。确实,孔子与他的学生曾子对话时说,他的学说中存在“唯一”;然而,在科学上我们可能证明“唯一”的无穷性。[⑤] 在王阳明的学说中,“合而为一”或者“万物一体”[⑥]的观点是他世界观的真正基础,而他的其他观点“心即理”[⑦]仅仅是这种关系更加本质形象化的例子,尤其是关于人和宇宙之间的关系。

然而,王阳明不是郭沫若认为的利已主义者。理由之一是,这是一个中国古时鲜为人知的概念,尽管他的一些信徒亦步亦趋;[⑧]在中国古时,那几乎是不可能的,它是主体儒家思想的绝对异端。个人主义的每一个主要权衡尺度都有瓦解关于思想与一切事物的本质统一假说的趋势,妨碍所谓的“天理”构架和消除(思想的)私

① 郭沫若:《儒教精神之复活者王阳明》,见郭沫若《唯识论集》,《文艺研究》第四版,上海,1929 年版,第 80 ~ 81 页。此外,见郭沫若《创造十年》,具体参见《郭沫若文集》第七卷,北京,1958 年版,第 58 页。

② 郭沫若:《儒教精神之复活者王阳明》,见郭沫若《唯识论集》,《文艺研究》第四版,上海,1929 年版,第 85 页。

③ 郭沫若:《儒教精神之复活者王阳明》,见郭沫若《唯识论集》,《文艺研究》第四版,上海,1929 年版,第 86 页。

④ 郭沫若:《儒教精神之复活者王阳明》,见郭沫若《唯识论集》,《文艺研究》第四版,上海,1929 年版,第 86 ~ 87 页。

⑤ 《论语》,《中国经典》第一卷,台北,1969 年版,第 169 页。

⑥ 郭沫若:《儒教精神之复活者王阳明》,见郭沫若《唯识论集》,《文艺研究》第四版,上海,1929 年版,第 89 ~ 92 页。J. 秦:《赢取智慧:王阳明之道》,纽约 - 伦敦,哥伦比亚大学出版社,1976 年版,第 126 ~ 128 页。

⑦ 郭沫若:《儒教精神之复活者王阳明》,见郭沫若《唯识论集》,《文艺研究》第四版,上海,1929 年版。J. 秦:《赢取智慧:王阳明之道》,纽约 - 伦敦. 哥伦比亚大学出版社,1976 年版,第 57 ~ 61 页。

⑧ Wm. de. 百利:《明代思想中的个人主义与人道主义》见其《明代思想中的自我与社会》,纽约 - 伦敦. 哥伦比亚大学出版社,1970 年版,第 145 ~ 247 页。

欲(人欲)。[1] 此外,它对社会秩序有着深远的影响,甚至危及它的存在。在"思想和事物本质相同"的假说中,郭沫若尤其强调"同一性",认为它是宇宙区别于"天"、"道"和"本体"的根本原因,因为有些东西的存在是运动着的;一切事物都是存在的表现,是它的过程实体化(动态)。[2]

郭沫若认为,通过王阳明,他理解了中国古代庄子和老子的哲学。[3] 至于他对于前者哲学的领悟并没有在所研究的论文中有所体现。至于后者,他声称其导致了"利己主义"。郭沫若对王阳明社会激进主义的赞赏导致了他对老子清静无为社会理想的批评态度。他并没有对老子的学说进行科学客观的研究,而仅仅根据老子的一些陈述做出推断,并且主观地进行补充。老子的确不属于那些毕生将利己主义奉为圭臬的人。老子宣扬的其实是大公无私的精神,在他著名的作品中写到人与人之间的关系,认为人本应相互善待,理应正视知识、欲念,以及人应该拥有什么样的品质:"少私寡欲。"[4]

根据早些时候对1923年5月命名为"中国文化之传统精神"进行的研究来判断,郭沫若对老子和他的反宗教学说有了更加正确的见解——对于三代(夏、商、周)之前的时期,他表示了更多的同情:"雄鸡啼晓。"他在诗中写道,"革命思想家老子像太阳一样升起。他完全消灭了对三个王朝的偏见,诅咒其他学说的道德哲学,从它们当中摘出人和神的概念,并代之以'道'。他说:'道'者,先天地生,视之不见,听之不闻,无极,无名,恍恍惚惚,为万物之母。'道'为宇宙之本质。"[5]在老子的学说中和那个时代,郭沫若从文字中看到了"中国哲学史的复兴",冲击了过去由于对"解放个性"和回归夏商周三朝之前所谓的民族精神和自由思想的需求产生的他律伦理观和宗教偏见。[6] 当然,他没有明确说出他自己在这方面的想法。事实上,即使基于现在的知识,我们对于那个时代的思想特征,也毫无所知,无法判断。郭先生关于老子的高见尽管常常被错误地公式化,引导他也转向这位哲学家来解决自己世界观中的一些基本问题。老子的态度坚定了他的无神论和生活实事求是的观点(存在是现实的表现)以及所有人类行为的结果显然也是目标(或者至

① Ubelhor, M.: DaskosmischeOrdnungsprinzip (t' ien-li) und die personlicheWiinsche (jenyii). Oriens Extremus, 27, 1980, 1, pp. 25 ~ 32.

② 郭沫若:《儒教精神之复活者王阳明》,见郭沫若《唯识论集》,《文艺研究》第四版,上海,1929年版,第89 ~ 90页。

③ 郭沫若:《儒教精神之复活者王阳明》,见郭沫若《唯识论集》,《文艺研究》第四版,上海,1929年版,第85页。

④ 威利:《道与力》,伦敦,乔治·艾伦与昂温有限公司,1934年版,第46页。

⑤ 郭沫若《中国文化之传统精神》见《文艺研究》第四版,上海,1929年版,第4页。

⑥ 郭沫若《中国文化之传统精神》见《文艺研究》第四版,上海,1929年版,第5页。

少是其一)"自我完成"的信念。[①]

根据郭沫若的观点,老子世界观中最后这两种特征也适用于孔子,他在孔子的学说中发现了泛神论,而非无神论。1919 年的五四运动之前,以及之后的几年里,他并没有加入到将《论语》视为唯一真理的孔子信徒的行列。他也许对古代的欧阳修、崔述等人一无所知,甚至对那些当今大部分学者都知道的人也并无了解。[②]他也许是出于由新学流派著作而引发的感动,出于某些原因,他不把孔子单纯看作是公元前 6 世纪和公元前 5 世纪的一个重要历史人物,相反,他认为孔子属于中国历史所有时代的伟大哲学家,甚至是全世界的圣人和导师。[③]

郭沫若参照老子和《易经》阐释了孔子学说的主要观点,《易经》补遗被称为《十翼》,通常认为是孔子所作,但也有说法认为是西汉前期孔子的后学所著。[④] 这种说法本身不足为奇。补遗的作者应当对老子哲学十分熟悉。在研究中国文化传统精神的论文中,郭沫若引用了《易经》的一段内容,其中"孔子"[⑤]和老子之间的共性尤其明显。在此,我们再现了他的言外之意,以助于加深读者的理解。

"一阴一阳之谓道,继之者善也,成之者性也。仁者见之谓之仁,知者见之谓之知,百姓日用而不知,故君子之道鲜矣。显诸仁,藏诸用,鼓万物而不与圣人同忧,盛德大业至矣哉! 富有之谓大业,日新之谓盛德。"[⑥]

结合"阴阳"的要素,"道"使人想起老子的传统主张,《道德经》第 42 章中说:"道生一,一生二,二生三,三生万物。万物负阴而抱阳。"[⑦]

郭沫若在阅读这两段引文时,也许发现了物质统一的观点,两段话都用了"道"这个词,都与"阴"和"阳"有关系,另一方面孔子称之为"易",表现出相对无限的存在周期连续(时间上的)或相邻(空间上的)变化的特性:"易再现了生命现象本身无法用阴和阳揣摩的东西叫作'神'。"[⑧]

与"易"一样,如前所述,在此"神"也表现为存在的一部分,但是无法通过理性

---

① 郭沫若《中国文化之传统精神》见《文艺研究》第四版,上海,1929 年版,第 13 页。

② 冯友兰:《中国哲学史》第二卷,普林斯顿,普林斯顿大学出版社,1952 年,第 381 页。

③ 卡姆·路易:《当代中国孔子思想评论》香港,香港中文大学出版社,1980 年出版,第 3 ~ 4 页。从 20 世纪 20 年代到 30 年代,对孔子生平和作品研究构成了中国学术研究的基点,这在 H. G. 克里尔的著作《孔子:人与神话》中得到了较好的描述和分析,纽约,1969 年版,第 23 ~ 25 页。

④ 冯友兰:《中国哲学史》第一卷,1952 年版,第 379 ~ 381 页。

⑤ 郭沫若《中国文化之传统精神》见《文艺研究》第四版,上海,1929 年版,第 7 页。"孔子"形象是从他从来没有写作过或编撰过的文本中被广泛建构起来的。

⑥ 冯友兰:《中国哲学史》第一卷,1952 年版,第 384 页。

⑦ 冯友兰:《中国哲学史》第一卷,1952 年版,第 383 ~ 384 页。原文参见老子《道德经:下篇》,台北,1966 年版,第 5A 页。

⑧ 引自郭沫若《中国文化之传统精神》见《文艺研究》第四版,上海,1929 年版,第 7 页。

或情感的认知来理解。郭沫若认为,尽管无法用理性或情感去阐明,这种“神”在基督教或者穆斯林泛神论中是上帝的外延,是法则制定者,是宇宙独特物质的表现。据说“孔子”知道和了解与“神”一样的物质。物质在“善”的意义上得以发展,尽管它不是“神”的有意识的发展;这是由物质固有属性所决定的。①

在此,对“神”的理解来自于与中国哲学或者宗教中通常意味不同的意义,在中国哲学和宗教中这种意义包括死者的灵魂和神仙。② 在这方面,“神”表达了“超越所有变化的深奥力量”,③也许就是“道”本身意味着的“一”。根据郭沫若的观点,“道”和“易”是对等的概念,是两个拥有相同本质的同义词。④ 刚才根据《易经》解释的“神”的概念在一定意义上也拥有相同的关系。郭沫若只不过是“推论”出他的“孔子”学说,把他归因于“本质即神”的观察⑤,不仅仅根据世界观的观点局限性来解释,而且也参考了哲学史,他写道:“在孔子的学说中,我们能看到泛神论的观点。”⑥

尽管郭沫若明显认为庄子是最伟大的人物,或者至少是中国泛神论者中最卓越的代表,对此他在文章中却很少提及。仅仅在他研究《惠施的性格及其思想》中才不时提到这位哲学家。与惠施的第十个矛盾论点有关:“热爱万物;天地一体。”⑦尽管诠释庄子文献的知名大家之间也许没有人以这种方式提出这种论点,而郭沫若认为它表达了显著的泛神论观点,而且这也是庄子哲学体系的核心。他至少在这个问题上投入的精力与其余九个论点上的一样多。

于他看来,是庄子的道教世界观的基础,尽管它属于一个不同学派哲学家的思想。在我们前面已经引用的庄子著作第二章中还提到:“夫天下莫大于秋毫之末,而泰山为小;莫寿乎殇子,而彭祖为夭。天地与我并生,而万物与我为一。”⑧郭沫若对结尾最后一句的阐释与 B. 沃森截然不同。在引文之后他又补充说:“当然,也就是相当于说天地和万物归于一体。”⑨这种本质恰恰是“道”,他还补充了《庄子》

① 引自郭沫若《中国文化之传统精神》见《文艺研究》第四版,上海,1929 年版,第 7 页。

② Wing-tsit Chan 编译,《中国哲学》,普林斯顿,新泽西,普林斯顿大学出版社,1963 年,第 789 ~ 790 页。

③ Wing-tsit Chan 编译,《中国哲学》,普林斯顿,新泽西,普林斯顿大学出版社,1963 年,第 266 页。

④ 郭沫若《中国文化之传统精神》,见《文艺研究》第四版,上海,1929 年,第 6 页。

⑤ 郭沫若《中国文化之传统精神》,见《文艺研究》第四版,上海,1929 年,第 6 页。

⑥ 郭沫若《中国文化之传统精神》,见《文艺研究》第四版,上海,1929 年,第 7 ~ 8 页。

⑦ 郭沫若《文艺研究》,第 71 ~ 74 页。1938 年后,他在《创造十年续篇》写作了有关于庄子研究的几段话。见《郭沫若选集》第 7 卷,第 186 页。

⑧ 《庄子全集》B. 华生译,哥伦比亚大学出版社,1968 年版,第 43 页。《庄子引得》北京,1974 年版,第 5 页。

⑨ 郭沫若《惠施的气质与哲学》,《文艺研究》第四版,上海,1929 年版,第 72 页。

第六章的段落："夫道有情有信，无为无形；可传而不可受，可得而不可见；自本自根，未有天地，自古以固存；神鬼神帝，生天生地；在太极之先而不为高，在六极之下而不为深，先天地生而不为久，长于上古而不为老。"①

由所有这些说法看来，郭沫若将"道"理解为所有存在的本质，所有存在都是"道"时间上的、空间上的表现，"道"凌驾于所有这些方面，就涉及的形式而言，倾向于庄子，然而，在内容方面，则倾向于泛神论的言论，构成那时世界观的广泛基础："万物是道的表相。本质和现象是一体的，我就是道本身——本质。本质不会消灭，我也不会；本质是无穷无尽的，因此，我也是永远存在的。因此，从时间的角度看，我可以说：我与天地同时出生。从空间的角度看，我可以说：万物和我一同构成本质。"②

以上句子与《少年维特之烦恼》序引中的说法一样——"我就是上帝（神），整个自然都是我的表现"，③都是泛神论者关于世界令人十分震惊的声言。

在郭沫若所有的哲学信念中，这些观点酝酿已久，并且他们并非仅仅与庄子和B. 斯宾诺沙有直接联系。郭沫若在古希腊哲学、印度哲学当然还有现代欧洲哲学中寻找它们的根源。他早在泰勒斯和他的圣水、赫拉克利特和他的神火以及德谟克利特和他的原子中看到这一点；也在《圣传》的神水、乌帕尼沙德的婆罗门和瓦伊斯学派的哲学原子论中找到了根源。④

至于外国起源的哲学学说，他最初（1915 至 1916 年左右）感兴趣的是印度卡比尔（1440—1518）⑤的泛神论，然后是乌帕尼沙德（公元前 1000—公元前 300）。⑥他也许读过拉宾德拉纳·泰戈尔翻译的《卡比尔诗百首》，还有那长长的《引言》。⑦他更倾向于认为卡比尔是一位诗人（我们可能从他将卡比尔列为自己最尊敬的三大世界泛神论者之一的事实而猜到这一点），⑧而并非一位哲学家，因为他不赞同卡比尔的过度宗教神秘主义，也不同意婆罗门与灵魂关系的观点，这种关系假定上

---

① 《庄子全集》B. 华生译，哥伦比亚大学出版社，1968 年版，第 81 页。《庄子引得》北京，1974 年版，第 16 页。

② 郭沫若《惠施的气质与哲学》，第 73 页。

③ 郭沫若《少年维特之烦恼序引》，《文艺研究》第四版，上海，1929 年版，第 341 页。

④ 郭沫若《文艺研究》第四版，上海，1929 年版，第 2 页和第 71 ~ 72 页。

⑤ D. T. 罗伊：《早年郭沫若》，剑桥（麻省.），哈佛大学出版社，1971 年，第 66 ~ 67 页。

⑥ D. T. 罗伊：《早年郭沫若》，剑桥（麻省.），哈佛大学出版社，1971 年，第 66 ~ 67 页。

⑦ E. 昂德山《翻译与写作导论》，参见《卡比尔诗百首》，伦敦，麦克米伦出版公司，1954 年重版，第 v ~ xliv 页。

⑧ 郭沫若《三泛神论者》，《女神》第八次印刷，上海，1928 年版，第 103 ~ 104 页。本选本最初出版于 1921 年。

帝或者绝对事物与自我之间存在差异但没有实质性的条件一致。[①] 随后郭沫若探及究竟或研究乌帕尼沙德时,他深深为自我的观念所动,强调自我在整个乌帕尼沙德思想中的重要性,作为一种哲学和宇宙的范畴,也作为普遍的主体,同时也是一种对象:"我实际上就是这整个宇宙,[②]而且深信灵魂是自我和非我的前提。"[③]婆罗门作为宇宙和对象的因素也许仅仅是他兴趣中的一个从属对象;然而他对婆罗门和灵魂一致的问题却深深着迷。

这种关于我们内心的个别本质与普遍的本性及其现象(当然还有中国道学家)的知识和认识是郭先生关注和赞赏自然、宇宙、太阳、满天星斗的苍穹、个体的生命现象和人类伟大著作的根源。[④] 乌帕尼沙德中的"那是你"[⑤]概念遍及他周围的宇宙和万物,正如盐溶入海洋。在某个时期,尤其是五四运动期间,可以在他许多乐观的语调和颂扬文体作品中清楚观察到欣喜、极乐或者积极的快乐(阿南达),乌帕尼沙德哲学中的人类和宇宙现实的状态与对婆罗门和灵魂之间关系的认识相联系。[⑥] 此外,我们已经看到他如何构建自己新世界的模型,是他全新的太阳系宇宙,咏赞新宇宙的能量、光芒、热力和生命。[⑦] 当然,在建模的过程中,他没有完全依附乌帕尼沙德的学说;他的灵感源泉有很多,来自于中国、小亚细亚、埃及、犹太和希腊的观念、神话、文学,上至 W. 惠特曼和对天文学和物理学的认识,可以追溯到 1920 年左右。他统一了他们的泛神论世界观,形成看世界的恰当、独特无神泛神论方式,区别于他接触的所有其他"万有神教"。

那时候对郭沫若的世界观和创作或者翻译工作有着十分有利影响的是 J. W. 歌德的诗歌、散文、戏剧、理论和论文著作。他早在 1917 ~ 1918 年在冈山第六高级中学的时候就读到了《诗与真》,歌德的作品被规定为必读研究内容。[⑧] 关于歌德的创造性著作,最重要的是《浮士德》和《少年维特之烦恼》。

也许在此用只言片语介绍这些著作的背景没有什么不合适的。写作《少年维

---

① E. 昂德山《翻译与写作导论》,参见《卡比尔诗百首》,伦敦,麦克米伦出版公司,1954 年重版,第 xiv ~ xv 页,第 xx ~ xxi 页,特别是第 xxviii ~ xxix 页。

② S. 宾德拉纳:《印度哲学》第一卷,纽约,麦克米伦出版公司,1951 年,第 158 页。

③ S. 宾德拉纳:《印度哲学》第一卷,纽约,麦克米伦出版公司,1951 年,第 159 页。

④ 郭沫若诗二卷《女神》与《星空》,后者最初发表于 1923 年。

⑤ S. 宾德拉纳:《印度哲学》第一卷,纽约,麦克米伦出版公司,1951 年,第 170 页。

⑥ 郭沫若《女神》,其部分诗歌被 J. 李斯特翻译为英文,部分诗歌被 A. C. 巴尼斯选编为《女神诗选》,北京,1958 年版。

⑦ 见笔者专著《中西文学碰撞里程碑:1898—1979》三章,布拉蒂斯拉娃 - 威斯巴登,斯洛伐克科学院出版社,1986 年。

⑧ D. T. 罗伊:《早年郭沫若》,剑桥(麻省.),哈佛大学出版社,1971 年,第 68 ~ 69 页。

特之烦恼》(1774)和《浮士德》之前,歌德在哲学领域中经历了一段相对漫长的发展道路。他的前辈包括(我们将不会一一提到所有的名字)M. 勒舍、赫拉克利特、阿那克萨哥拉、恩培多克勒、普罗提诺、罗赫尔和弗朗西斯·培根,这些都是欧洲中古神秘主义者,还有霍布斯、笛卡尔以及尤其重要的斯宾诺莎。[①]

在秘密准备写作《少年维特之烦恼》的时候,歌德特别关注斯宾诺莎的哲学,但是他仅仅是间接地知道这些知识,因为大部分内容都是基于来自约翰·科莱鲁斯收集的单方面的、错误的见解。[②] 根据科莱鲁斯的观点,斯宾诺莎是一个骗子,[③] 当歌德在1773年春天开始阅读原作时,斯宾诺莎在歌德(还有黑格尔和恩格斯)[④] 这里变成了伟大的哲学家。因此,他笔下的维特直接有斯宾诺莎的影子。他回忆起斯宾诺莎,还有《诗与真》。他赞叹歌德为自己的激情提供了一处宁静的避风港。[⑤] 这最后一句话仅仅是部分正确的。歌德笔下的《狂飙运动》显然饱含激情,需要某种约束,但是在斯宾诺莎的"平静世界"中,人类和个人的自我沉浸于"个人无限"[⑥]之中,在维特的信札中我们可以清楚感受到歌德的躁动不安和压力。他感到困惑,在斯宾诺莎的体系中,"人在上帝和善面前的个体性"[⑦]消失无踪。但那时以及后来他在夏绿蒂·冯·施泰因的陪伴下一块愉快地读到斯宾诺莎的时候,歌德赞成斯宾诺莎学说的基本假说,上帝就是本质,世上仅仅存在唯一的本质,就是上帝或者自然,而个体事物(包括人类在内)仅仅是神明的一部分,等等。

郭沫若读到《诗与真》时就已经对斯宾诺莎有所了解,正如他后来在回忆中证实的那样,显然他对歌德的评价很感兴趣。[⑧] 他直接和间接地阅读了斯宾诺莎的著作。他在斯宾诺莎作品上倾注的精力完全有可能远不如对于歌德那么专注与持久,也许是因为斯宾诺莎跟他有更远的距离吧。他清楚回忆起自己对斯宾诺莎的《伦理学》、《神学政治论》和《逻辑哲学论》的兴趣。[⑨] 至于歌德,他不仅阅读,而且翻译了《浮士德》和《少年维特之烦恼》;这两部著作代表了他那时候工作的激情。在《少年维特之烦恼》的序言中,他写下了自己对泛神论最全面、最有影响力的评论:泛神便是无神。一切的自然只是神的表现,自我也只是神的表现。我即是神,

---

① M. 李奥斯彻《歌德的精神世界》,斯图加特,S. 希瑟尔出版社,1948年,第19~57页。

② H. 图克《歌德与浮士德》,莱比锡,威廉格雷伯出版社,1921版,第102~103页。

③ H. 图克《歌德与浮士德》,莱比锡,威廉格雷伯出版社,1921版,第103页。

④ 卡尔. 马克思、恩格斯《马克思恩格斯全集》第20卷,柏林,迪茨出版社,1962年版,第315页。

⑤ J. W. 歌德《歌德全集》第21卷,斯图加特,第164页。

⑥ M. 李奥斯彻《歌德的精神世界》,斯图加特,S. 希瑟尔出版社,1948年,第51页。

⑦ M. 李奥斯彻《歌德的精神世界》,斯图加特,S. 希瑟尔出版社,1948年,第52页。

⑧ 郭沫若《三叶集》第六次印刷,上海,1929年,第17页,最初写于1920年1月18日。

⑨ 郭沫若《创造十年》,第58页。

一切自然都是自我的表现。人到无我的时候,与神合体,超绝时空,而等齐生死。

人到一有我见的时候,只看见宇宙万汇和自我之外相,变灭无常而有生死存亡的悲感。万物必生必死,生不能自持,死亦不能自阻,所以只见得“天与地与在他们周围运动着的力,除是一个永远贪婪、永远反刍的怪物而外,不见有别的。”此力即是创生万汇的本源,即宇宙意志,即物自体。能与此力弥合时,则只见其生不见其死,只见其常而不见其变。体之周遭,随处都是乐园,随时都是天国,永恒之乐,溢满灵台。“在‘无限’之前,在永恒的拥抱之中,我与你永在。”人之究竟,唯求此永恒之乐耳。欲求此永恒之乐,则先在忘我。忘我之方,歌德不求之于静,而求之于动。以狮子搏兔之力,以全身全灵以谋刹那之充实、自我之扩张,以全部精神以倾倒于一切!维特自从与绿蒂姑娘相识后,他说,“自从那时起,日月星辰尽管静悄悄地走它们的道儿,我也不知道昼,也不知道夜,全盘的世界在我周围消去了。”如此以全部的精神爱人!以全部的精神陶醉!以全部的精神烦恼!以全部的精神哀毁!一切彻底!一切究竟!所以他对于疯狂患者也表示极端的同情,对于自杀行为也绝不认为罪过反而加以赞美。完成自我的自杀,正是至高道德——这绝不是中庸微温者所能体验的道理。[①]

我们需要对这段长长的引文进行更加详细的分析。认为泛神论定义为无神论的最初说法来自郭沫若对神或者上帝(中国人现在将二者都归纳为“神”的概念)的判读以及表达本质的各种说法。这种说法体现了郭先生言辞的根本核心。其余部分构成本质的更加详细引申,一切都是存在的,是永恒的、不可磨灭的、无穷无尽的,一直以来总是存在的,也将永远存在,过去、现在、将来的一切都是如此,仅仅存在时间和空间的变化而已。郭沫若对自我和上帝的判读也构成他的个性,不是自己神化或他人奉若神明的表现,而是宇宙统一的体现,与自然和万物归一,与一切存在的目的一体。

在接下来的论述中,郭沫若似乎回到了1915到1922年他刚开始熟悉泛神论的那段时间,简要地回忆了一下他探索和开始接纳这种观念的各个阶段(或者至少在他的思想中昙花一现)。第一个阶段是十分正统的佛家思想,要求无我的存在,表现出浮屠原始学说方面的特性,正如哲学家纳佳鲁那(公元2世纪左右)写道:“如来佛(十浮屠之一)不时教导我们,灵魂是存在的,在另一些场合中他又说灵魂是不存在的……那么,这两个观点哪一个代表着真理?无疑是关于否定灵魂的教义。这种教义是如此晦涩难懂,浮屠本来就不是打算讲给那些愚钝的人听的,也不

---

① 郭沫若《少年维特之烦恼序引》,第341~342页。

是说给那些缺乏善根的人听。"[1]想必,郭沫若从来没有赞成无我的概念,尽管他对此深思过,并努力接纳这种思想。

引文中还有更多内容在否定唯识理论的传道方面。自我信仰是关于被称为"末那"的七八种人类意识或者思考意识的苦难(烦恼)的四个根本源头之一。接下来的是:我痴、我慢和我爱。[2] 郭沫若无偏见地依照自然规律把我信统一到对世界的非传统自由认识。他所做的,正如青年时代的歌德那样,把自己对自然现象的把握当成自然神明的表现(神明和自然之间没有任何差异),即使自然神明的行为就像"怪兽"一样,时而毁灭一切,时而创造万物。然而,这种观点也与斯宾诺莎的见解一致,根据这种观点,各种现象都是可以创造或者消灭的,都不是本质的东西。[3] 斯宾诺莎的确曾经命名过郭先生的"力"神,"不仅仅是事物存在的实际原因,而且是事物的本质。"[4]歌德也承认同样的自然规律。郭先生参照中国古代某个时期关于"神"道的实现、印度哲学中的婆罗门和阿南达,得出关于本质的狂热言语,认为它是与伊甸园和上帝天国统一的。郭沫若读到维特将"在万能的上帝永恒拥抱的光辉中"与绿蒂相伴时,感到"永恒的快乐"。[5]

自我扩张之于郭沫若意味着实现泛神论的自我实现。这是一种自我表现的形式——创造社会员的第一口号,创造社有着重要的浮士德式特性。自我扩张是一个过程的抽象概念,是这位伟大的传统人道主义者以浮士德的口吻诉说时提到的:"Und so mein eigen Selbst zu Ihren Selbst erweitern/Und, wie sie selbst, am End auchichzer scheitern"。[6] 郭沫若在上升到社会和人类"及时行乐"的精神——活动与休息、喜悦与悲伤、陶醉与清醒——到之后一个相应的伦理支架时,他承认浮士德式和维特式神的存在。在他的观念中,自我扩张完全等于或者十分类似于先前写到的自我完善。他在孔子、老子、康德和歌德的身上看到了显著的自我完善榜样。[7]

在某些方面,郭沫若走得比歌德更远,甚至比斯宾诺莎更进一步。他对人和神(或者自我和上帝)的辨别十分严肃,至于维特感到困惑的问题:"是什么人,这种

① S. 拉达克里希南,第389页。

② 冯友兰:《中国哲学史》第2卷,1952年版,第312~313页。

③ B. 斯宾诺莎《伦理学》,伦敦,牛津大学出版社,1927年版,第18页。

④ B. 斯宾诺莎《伦理学》,伦敦,牛津大学出版社,1927年版,第27页。

⑤ 郭沫若《少年维特之烦恼》,第10次印刷,上海,1932年版,第179页。

⑥ J. W 歌德《浮士德》,莱比锡,菲利浦出版社,1974年版,第57页。

⑦ 郭沫若《中国文化之传统精神》,见《文艺研究》第四版,上海,1929年版,第5~14页。

高尚的半神?”[①]或者浮士德的疑问:“我是上帝吗?”[②]于他来说是毫无干系的,至少在相当长的一段时间里、在理论领域中如此。与歌德相比,赫德更吸引青年时代的郭沫若,18 岁的少年歌德写道:“什么? 我是神? 我就是神,我就是上帝! ……上帝,你给了我什么! 你的整个世界我都要自己重新创造。”[③]郭沫若也许并不了解赫德,他们或许只是因为拥有对上帝和人类的近似的观点才偶然地联系在一起。

感觉或情感的前提是使歌德与郭沫若更加紧密联系在一起的又一个纽带。这种多样化变异的概念在中国文学批评中拥有悠久的历史,可在中国的创造性惯例中清楚看到。在欧洲,关于哲学、文学和艺术中感受的问题紧随启蒙运动的结束和浪漫主义时代到来。正如我们在别处已经看到的,中国对情的痴迷持续了近三个世纪(16 世纪到 18 世纪),然后传播到英国和德国,最终扩展到其他欧洲国家,这个过程持续了一个世纪左右(18 世纪到 19 世纪)。在中国对“情”的兴趣总是因为其对立方面“性”、“景”的强调而得以平衡,[④]然而,欧洲的“情”在文学和艺术史中起着巨大的作用;它们是后来两千多年中传统理想主张的由来之一,也是文学和艺术运动的浪漫主义重要因素之一。

在《少年维特之烦恼》的序言中我们可以读到:“他说,‘人总是人,尽管这样不是全无道理,到了热情横溢,冲破人性的界限时,人们总是不能断定这到底是不是有点价值’。我们大都用这样的事实说服过自己,我们可以说,是一种无须证明的事理。侯爵重视维特的理智与才能而忽视其内心时,他说‘我这颗心才是我唯一的至宝,只有它才是一切的源泉,一切力量、一切福佑、一切悲苦的源泉’。他还说,他智所能知,什么人都可以知道,只有他的心才是他自己所独有。他对于宇宙万汇,不是用理智去分析,去宰割,而是用他的心去综合,去创造。他的心渴望在他的身之周围随处创造出一个乐园;他躺在有不易察觉的、不知名的昆虫出没的草地上,不间断地感受着‘全能者的存在’,‘兼爱无私者的徘徊’。一个没有爱情的世界,便没有光亮的神灯。他的心便是这神灯中的光亮,在白壁上立地可以生出种种画图,在死灭中立地可以生出有情的宇宙。”[⑤]

当研究歌德的主情主义时,尽管他对最先引用的句子和最后引文(单引号中的内容)的翻译(确切地说是解释)不同于原文中的意义,郭沫若仅仅从欧洲浪漫主

① 郭沫若把这句话翻译为:“就是这种人,传说中的超人?”
② J. W 歌德《浮士德》,莱比锡,菲利浦出版社,1974 年版,第 19 页。
③ 转引自 W. 冯 · 德 · 斯蒂恩《歌德的时代》,1949 年版,第 138 页。
④ M. 高利克《中国抒情概念:英德文学批评》,1983 年版,第 123 ~ 130 页。
⑤ 郭沫若《少年维特之烦恼译序》,第 339 ~ 340 页.

义开始着手。[①] 他这样做也许是要使他的当代读者们更容易理解这些句子。在此,人是一切事物的尺度,理性及其能力被认为具有普遍性,而心灵仅仅属于个体拥有。然而,人类个体的心灵不仅仅是为自己服务,而且有助于个体与世界的联系或者对世界的创造。郭沫若在前言中称之为爱的,欧洲浪漫主义者和浪漫主义历史学家称之为同情心。[②] 这两者是完全一样的东西,都涉及人内心的和谐、认知和统一,甚至包括人与周围外部自然之间的统一。

歌德把神灯与艺术中模仿过程和人类内心的同情心联系起来。维特曾经写道:"……如果没有爱,生命还有什么价值呢? 神灯没有了光芒。你必须做的是点亮光芒,然后它就能在一面白墙上投下最美丽的五彩画面。哦! 如果这些瞬息万变的仅仅是幻影而已,它也总是给我们带来快乐,我们站在它面前,像天真的孩子一样,对那些神奇的景象感到入迷。"[③]

在神灯作为模仿过程记录仪的概念中,神灯同时又是同样现象的投影仪,歌德和郭沫若对艺术本质的观点彼此非常接近。然而,歌德主要坚持模仿的原则,而郭沫若显然强调创造的因素,相反强调心灵作为栩栩如生宇宙生灭毫无价值的造物主的角色。郭沫若对心灵的强调并不是始终如一的,或者他在"心灵"表达广泛意义的情况下:它一定等同于"本质"、上帝和人类的"大我"。这一想法在诗歌《创造者》中有力地表达出来,那是他 1922 年春发表在"创造社"的创刊号《创造季刊》上的作品,他是创造社的发起人之一。这首诗是他最有表达力的一件作品,郭沫若向他那个时代的年轻读者们展示了自己对神话宇宙论的理解。其中他极少联系中国传统,即使有些许联系,也是关乎他本来所属的中国南方少数民族苗和瑶祖先的传统。[④] 这是盘古的身躯化为世界开天辟地的一种创世版本。郭沫若把他叫作"人神",根据中国文学流传下来的神话观念(尽管与那些根据自己的需要往往改变原始材料的现代神话作者是不一致的),对他的描述是具有"创造精神",独自"创造了光明的世界",眼睛化为太阳和月亮,头颅化为丘陵和高山,头发化为树木和草地,血液化为河流和海洋。

---

① 原文见于歌德:"Man mochterasendwerden, Wilhelm, daBes Menschen geben soil ohne Sinn und Gefiihlan den Wenigen, was auf Erdennocheinen Wert hat"(15. September), und "dasWehen des All-liebenden, deruns in ewigerWonneschwebendtragt und erhalt"(10. Mai). 有趣的是,最后一个例子翻译的与在中国的小说文本有所不同,见第 6 页。这对于第一句同样有效,具体见第 117 页。如此,小说的翻译显得更加准确。

② W. J. 贝特《从古典走向浪漫》,纽约,1961 年,第 129 ~ 159 页。

③ 见胡特尔翻文,第 51 ~ 52 页,歌德原文,第 42 ~ 43 页。

④ W. 芒克《中国古典神话》,斯图加特,恩斯特出版社,1976 年版,第 254 ~ 255 页。E. M. 颜石娜《中国古代神话形成与发展》,莫斯科,1984 年版,第 127 ~ 130 页。

传说中的盘古诞生于混沌，身高九万里，孕育了整整八万年才破茧而出，这种观念对于郭沫若来说意味着混沌，可以产生一个全新的天堂和世界，由此诞生全新的人类。

准备与朋友一起发行第一期《创造季刊》以及翻译《少年维特之烦恼》时，他遵循着同样的观点：从当代的混沌世界中创造一个全新的世界，呈现先前提到的积极快乐、无私的个人主义、自我表现和自我扩张。神灯仅仅可以提供想要实现的不完全映象。在他看来，"大我"就是具体体现"本质"的知识解放的"自我"，是客观现实在所有形式的内心所有方面的具体化，是自我发展的保障，而发展至少包括那些在自然、社会、文学和艺术的各种知识形式领域中对他产生影响的现象。郭沫若本身就是自己宇宙的"造物主"：

> 我唤起周代的雅伯，
> 我唤起出国的骚豪，
> 我唤起唐世的诗宗，
> 我唤起元室的词曹，
> 作《吠陀》的印度古诗人哟！
> 作《神曲》的但丁哟！
> 作《失乐园》的米尔顿哟！
> 作《浮士德》悲剧的歌德哟！
> 你们知道创造者的孤高，
> 你们知道创造者的苦恼，
> 你们知道创造者的狂欢，
> 你们知道创造者的光耀。①

郭沫若指出歌德泛神论的第三个特点，反映在《少年维特之烦恼》中，就是对本性赞赏。在前言中，他继承了维特关于这个话题的声言，引用了符合自己关于人与本性关系的观点。实际上，他略过了维特某个不符合自己看法的声言。整个段落内容如下："我今后只皈依自然。只有自然是无穷地丰富的，只有自然能造就伟大的艺术家。为便于条条框框起见，有很多要说的，几乎同样的东西可以说成赞扬中产阶级的话——坚持这些规则而决不会产生任何糟糕的或低级趣味的东西，正

① 郭沫若《创造者》，《郭沫若选集》第1卷，重印，第286～287页。

如让自己遵循法律、秩序和繁荣的规范一样,决不会成为无法容忍的邻居或者无恶不作的恶棍。另一方面,人可以说自己喜欢的一切,一切的规矩准绳,足以破坏人们对于自然的感受和表现的能力!”①

此外,歌德原文第20~21页我们可以看到郭沫若在他引用的片段中略过了第二句和第三句的开头。② 在小说本身这些句子的翻译中,他也稍微有些扭曲了歌德表达的信息。歌德明确地表达了“为便于条条框框起见,有很多要说的”,他的引用是“有些人坚持维护规则”,这与歌德的说法十分不一致。他翻译的措辞也与歌德十分不同:“赞扬中产阶级时几乎可以说同样的话”,也就是“或者他们同意非常有学问但低浅的理解”。显然是因为郭沫若讨厌条条框框,正如我们在别处指出的,他鄙视那个时代的“中产阶级”。歌德站在他的社会一边,社会秩序良好,坚持公认的社会、伦理和道德准则,而郭沫若倾向于不表达、不翻译歌德的观点,而是只做了一个评注阐述他个人的观点。

最后,郭沫若进一步得出关于维特式泛神论的两个其他特点:对原始生活方式(往往保持简单的本性,不受文明世界的影响)的向往和尊重孩子。对后一个特点的思考促使他得出一个相当广泛的评论,指向古代东方哲学或宗教的类似问题。一个特定的诱因是他的孩子们和他的日本同居爱人佐藤美子。从他的诗中显然可以看到,他至少对孩子们投入了相当多的关注。③ 即使并非所有传统的标准都与孩子们有着青年歌德幻想的维特文艺塑造那样的联系,郭先生的论证仍然是值得一提的。郭沫若引用了老子的话,认为人在聚气的时候应该力求像婴儿一样柔软(专气致柔,能如婴儿乎)。④ 他其实是对自己的记忆力过于自信,结果引用错误。至于哲学家孟子(公元前374至公元前289年),除了存在一个语法上不改变原意的细微之处以外,他的引文是精确的。根据他的观点:“伟大的人总是能保持一颗如新生儿般的心灵。”⑤他也谈到来自《旧约》的先知以赛亚的帮助和对未来社会的憧憬:“豺狼必与绵羊羔同居,豹子与山羊羔同卧。少壮狮子,与牛犊,并肥畜同群。小孩子要牵引他们。”⑥希伯来作者想到的是一个乌托邦社会,以诗歌的形式确定下来,而歌德看到孩子们成为成人的“楷模”。

---

① Cf. 胡特尔翻文,第30页。

② 郭沫若《少年维特之烦恼译序》第342~343页,见郭沫若小说译文第45页。

③ 郭沫若《三叶草》第40~42页,第47~48页,《女神》第129~135页和第208~209页。

④ 《少年维特之烦恼译序》第153页;《道德经》,台北,1966年,第5B页。

⑤ 《孟子》D. C. 罗. 哈蒙德 · 华斯译介,米德尔塞. 企鹅图书集团,1970年版,第130页。见《孟子赵注》台北,1970年版,第4A页。

⑥ 《以赛亚》,11章6节。

然而,郭沫若使这个概念更加具体化,因为孩子们"一天中没有片刻不是专心投入造物、表达和快乐中。孩子的生活就是天才的缩微,是生命自我实现的缩影。"①

1921年6月上旬,郭沫若见到了他在冈山的老同学李闪亭(死于1927年)。那是在京都帝国大学经济学系。李闪亭在那追随日本著名的马克思主义传播者河上肇(1879—1946)教授处学习。李闪亭推荐郭沫若去读河上肇的杂志《社会问题研究》,但是郭沫若在相当长的一段时间里没有读河上肇的作品,也没有读到李闪亭关于"工人阶级专政"的解释,他毫不相信"资本主义制度必然被推翻"的观念。②

郭沫若在1923年10月拉宾德拉纳·泰戈尔访问中国的时候写下的文章或多或少简要地表现了他先前的研究。③ 鉴于邓中夏(1897—1933)、恽代英(1895—1931)及其他闻名的青年共产主义者风靡一时出现的新形势,郭沫若开始认真研究社会主义概念和马克思哲学,并开始传播有关文学的需要,④显然,他也受到日本发生事件的影响,日本的革命文学和无产阶级文学已经开始,发行了《种时人》杂志。⑤ 那时,他的文学批评研究和1921年到1924年之间获得的经历和知识正处于一个积极的表现派作家时代,逐渐把他引向马列主义。在他对泰戈尔的"谴责"中,我们可以读到:"我相信,唯物主义者关于历史的解释提供了对世界形势解决方法的唯一思路。直到世界的经济制度发生转变,像婆罗门现实、个人的尊严和爱的福音这种的东西只能是有产阶级和有闲阶级的吗啡或者可卡因,而工人阶级们只能沉浸在自己的汗水和鲜血中。"⑥

哲学复兴的过程是循序前进的,因为恰好在1923年到1924年期间,他写下了关于泛神论相关问题理论方面的大量文字。1923年5月,在他关于泰戈尔的文章发表之前6个月,他在给朋友宗白华(1897—1986)的一封信中声称,资本主义制度是引发第一次世界大战的唯一原因,这已经被富有远见的哲学家们预言过了,伟人而富于行动力的人们揭竿而起,要求铲除其发源的罪恶根本。他明确提到K. 马克思和V. I. 列宁是那个时代年轻人仰慕的英雄。⑦

---

① 郭沫若《少年维特之烦恼译序》第345页。

② 郭沫若《创造十年》第95~96页。

③ 郭沫若《泰戈尔来华的我见》,《文艺研究》第289~301页。

④ M. 高利克《现代中国文学批评之创世纪1917—1930》,布拉蒂斯拉娃,斯洛伐克科学院出版社,1980年版,第129~141页。

⑤ G.,T谢伊:《日本左翼文学》,东京,政法大学出版社,1964年版,第69~126页。

⑥ D. T. 罗伊:《早年郭沫若》,剑桥(麻省.),哈佛大学出版社,1971年,第155页,最初见于郭沫若《泰戈尔来华的我见》第299页。

⑦ 郭沫若《论中德文化书》,《文艺研究》,第22页。

郭沫若的学识上发展形成了一种奇怪的状况,尤其是在1923年的下半年和1924年最初的几个月,当时,他自己仍然在努力表达泛神论的观点,同时开始对马列主义表示明显的兴趣,他的世界观变得更丰富,社会、阶级、经济及其他观念随后引导他的哲学方向发生彻底的变化,走向辩证历史唯物主义。

那是一个很复杂的过程,常常充满着互相矛盾的转变、阻力、对没有能力控制自己和周围世界(无论是现在还是遥远的过去)的人的间歇探索。在他关于泰戈尔的文章发表之后一个星期,正如我们刚刚看到的,他站在历史唯物主义的观点一边(由此也站在马克思思想一边),正值日本无政府主义者大杉荣(1885—1923)被暗杀之际,又发表了一篇文章,文字中至少部分表达了无政府主义。大杉荣是个人主义的支持者,宣扬"人的盲目行动——人类精神的爆发"。[①] 在郭沫若的文章《国家的与超国家的》中,他对牢笼般的国家提出抗议,认为人民像鸟儿一样被禁锢着,呼吁国家联合为"超国家"联盟,"四海同胞",据说这也是中国古代哲学家宣扬的。[②] 这种世界主义假定超国家框架的存在,在郭沫若时代是一个乌托邦的希望。[③]

我们也可以在郭先生20年代初的文学发展中发现类似的矛盾对立趋势。激进的乐观主义时代为悲观的寂静主义甚至失败主义所取代。很多其他人可以不费吹灰之力引用在此提到的恰当例子。

1922年7月12日,他完成了一部作品,其中有关于长江和黄河的戏剧性的对话,在结论中他呼吁中国人民为自由而战,就像美国人已经在1775年到1783年完成了推翻英国统治的伟业,法国人完成了法国大革命,俄国人取得了伟大的十月社会主义革命胜利。[④] 他在另外的短篇剧本《孤竹君之二子》中传达的是一种截然不同的精神,同样是同年11月末在日本完成的。[⑤] 在这篇剧本中,他描写了孤竹的两个儿子伯夷和叔齐,遇到经历过殷商朝最腐败国王周辛(史记于公元前1154—1122年在位)的渔夫和村民。这兄弟俩决定不和他斗,也不以任何方式谴责他,因为那与统治王朝的忠诚道义悖逆,而是"隐于首阳山,采薇而食之。"[⑥]

---

① 华宇,达夫《自由的陷落:一个现代日本的个人肖像》,剑桥(麻省). 哈佛大学出版社,1969年版,第62页。

② 郭沫若《文艺研究》第414页。

③ 郭沫若《文艺研究》,第414～415页。

④ 《郭沫若选集》第1卷,第300页。

⑤ 《郭沫若选集》第1卷,第195～213页。

⑥ 《郭沫若选集》第1卷,第213页。

V. I. 列宁于 1924 年 1 月去世,[①]得知爱人和三个孩子在日本受罪(甚至他的爱人打算杀婴和自杀)时,他"感到自卑、不足、内疚、消沉、不满和多疑",[②]这对他最后决定投身于哲学领域、世界观或空想方向或多或少有一定影响。1924 年 1 月,第 39 期《创造早报》杂志刊登了郭先生翻译尼采的《查拉图斯特拉如是说》的最后部分。著作《论祭司》第四章第二段有郭沫若表达的深刻、细腻思想,如下:"而你们,我的兄弟,如果想要获得自由,一定要得到比任何救赎者更伟大人物的赎救!"[③]有一样是可以确定的:紧接着以上引文,他又翻译了两个来自尼采的句子,仅此而已。

对尼采的翻译尚未完成,郭沫若于 1924 年 4 月又开始翻译河上肇的著作《社会组织与社会革命》。

该书原本在李闪亭 1921 年建议郭沫若阅读的杂志中出现过,[④]那时他在 1924 年 4 月 18 日拜伦之死 100 周年之际的一封信中接纳了合作者、朋友成仿吾。他没有致力于自己承诺为《创造季刊》写作有关拜伦的文章,而是投入到河上肇著作的翻译中。[⑤] 在后来 1924 年 8 月 9 日寄给成仿吾的一封信中,郭沫若表达了自己深信建立科学社会主义是可能的,人们生活在"人尽其能,各取所需"的原则下,将成为"个人自由发展以社会自由发展为条件的社会组织形式"。他认为迈向这个社会的道路是所有受奴役人民必须踏上的"唯一道路"。他宣布自己已经成为"马克思主义的坚定追随者",我们在一定程度上应该对此持保留意见,因为那时的"庸俗社会学派"要素,尤其是与马克思主义的势不两立,在他的世界观中是相当根深蒂固。[⑥] 除了其他原因,那也是由于他的苦难。缺乏财资意味着在《社会组织和社会革命》的翻译版本介绍到中国之后他被迫继续翻译新的版本。[⑦]

河上肇著作的翻译工作成为郭沫若未来发展道路上最重要的转折点。该书把他从"酣睡"中唤醒,"为他展示了走出暗中摸索的出路",还将他从"死亡的黑影"中解救出来。[⑧]

至此,他的无神泛神论成为历史。

---

① D. T. 罗伊:《早年郭沫若》,剑桥(麻省.),哈佛大学出版社,1971 年,第 156 页。

② D. T. 罗伊:《早年郭沫若》,剑桥(麻省.),哈佛大学出版社,1971 年,第 156 页。

③ 尼采,《查拉图斯特拉如是说》,R. J. 赫林达勒,哈蒙德·华斯等译介,企鹅出版集团,1967 年,第 117 页。

④ 郭沫若《创造十年续篇》,第 182 页。

⑤ 张君编《现代名人书信》,上海,1937 年,第 168 ~ 172 页。

⑥ 郭沫若《孤鸿》,见《郭沫若选集》第 10 卷,北京,1959 年,第 286 ~ 301 页。

⑦ 郭沫若《孤鸿》,见《郭沫若选集》第 10 卷,北京,1959 年,第 292 页。

⑧ 郭沫若《孤鸿》,见《郭沫若选集》第 10 卷,北京,1959 年,第 292 页。

参考文献:

[1]D. T. 罗伊. 早年郭沫若[M]. 剑桥(麻省):哈佛大学出版社,1971.

[2]J. K. 菲尔班克. 原初秩序.//中国之世界秩序. 剑桥(麻省):哈佛大学出版社,1968.

[3]H. D. 哈路图尼. 德川家康时期思想之中国功能.//入江昭. 中国与日本:政治与文化互动随笔. 普林斯顿:普林斯顿大学出版社,1980.

[4]Y. C. 王. 中国知识分子与西方:1872—1949[M]. 教堂山,北加利福尼亚大学出版社,1966.

[5]M. 高利克. 中国知识分子史研究 II:青年瞿秋白(1915—1922)[M]. 亚非研究(第十二卷),1976.

[6]K. 陈. 中国佛教历史研究[M]. 普林斯顿:普林斯顿大学出版社,1964.

[7]谷辅林. 郭沫若世界观中的泛神论问题[J]. 文学评论丛刊(第8期),1981.

[8]梁启超. 清代知识分子走向(第2次印刷)[M]. 剑桥(麻省.):哈佛大学出版社,1970.

[9]Cf. 成唯识论. 香港:成唯识论出版委员会,1973.

[10]冯友兰. 中国哲学史(第二卷)[M]. 普林斯顿:普林斯顿大学出版社,1953.

[11]B. 华生译·庄子全集[M]. 纽约:哥伦比亚大学出版社,1968:49.

[12]郭沫若. 儒教精神之复活者王阳明.//郭沫若. 唯识论集. 文艺研究第四版. 上海,1929.

[13]论语. 中国经典第一卷. 台北:1969.

[14]Wm. de. 百利. 明代思想中的个人主义与人道主义.//明代思想中的自我与社会. 纽约－伦敦:哥伦比亚大学出版社,1970.

[15]Ubelhor, M. Daskosmische Ordnungsprinzip(t' ien-li) und die personliche Wiinsche(jenyii). Oriens Extremus,27,1980,1

[16]威利. 道与力[M]. 伦敦:乔治·艾伦与昂温有限公司,1934.

[17]卡姆·路易. 当代中国孔子思想评论[M]. 香港:香港中文大学出版社,1980.

[18]冯友兰. 中国哲学史[M]. 北京:商务印书馆,2011.

[19]Wing-tsit Chan 编译. 中国哲学[M]. 普林斯顿:普林斯顿大学出版

社,1963.

[20]E. M. 颜石娜．中国古代神话形成与发展．莫斯科:1984.

[21]尼采．查拉图斯特拉如是说[M]. R. J. 赫林达勒,哈蒙德华斯等译介．企鹅出版集团,1967.

[22]E. 昂德山．翻译与写作导论．//卡比尔诗百首．伦敦,麦克米伦出版公司,1954.

[23]郭沫若．三泛神论者．//女神(第八次印刷). 上海:1928.

[24]S. 宾德拉纳．印度哲学(第一卷)[M]. 纽约:麦克米伦出版公司,1951.

[25]M. 李奥斯彻．歌德的精神世界[M]. 斯图加特:S. 希瑟尔出版社,1948.

[26]H. 图克．歌德与浮士德[M]. 莱比锡:威廉格雷伯出版社,1921.

[27]马克思,恩格斯．马克思恩格斯全集(第 20 卷)[M]. 柏林:迪茨出版社,1962.

[28]W. 歌德．歌德全集(第 21 卷)[M]. 斯图加特:S. 希瑟尔出版社．

[29]郭沫若．三叶集(第六次印刷)[M]. 上海:1929.

[30]B. 斯宾诺莎．伦理学[M]. 伦敦:牛津大学出版社,1927.

[31]J. W 歌德．浮士德[M]. 莱比锡:菲利浦出版社,1974.

[32]M. 高利克．中国抒情概念:英德文学批评[M]. 1983.

[33]W. J. 贝特．从古典走向浪漫[M]. 纽约:1961.

[34]W. 芒克．中国古典神话[M]. 斯图加特:恩斯特出版社,1976.

[35]孟子．D. C. 罗．哈蒙德华斯译介[M]. 米德尔塞:企鹅图书集团,1970.

[36]M. 高利克．现代中国文学批评之创世纪 1917—1930[M]. 布拉蒂斯拉娃,斯洛伐克科学院出版社．

[37]G. ,T 谢伊．日本左翼文学[M]. 东京:政法大学出版社,1964.

A. S. 拜厄特《巴别塔》中的自由主题探究

首都经济贸易大学外国语学院　姚成贺

摘　要:个人的自由是A. S. 拜厄特《巴别塔》的主题之一。小说围绕主人公裘德·梅森的寓言式虚构作品《乱语塔》与社会现实生活展开,以这部分文本的内容及其出版后的遭遇表达了绝对自由的不可行性,塑造了在追求知识与分享思考的过程中获得自由空间的知识分子尤其是知识女性形象,并通过语言教育委员会内部阵营之间的论辩展现教育管理者关于霸权与自由的理念与策略。拜厄特在小说中通过描写《乱语塔》中绝对自由理想的破灭、知识分子的自由渴求、关于教育理念及其反馈的讨论勾勒了一幅当代的自由谱系图。

关键词:拜厄特;《巴别塔》;自由;虚构;现实

Abstract: Individual freedom is defined as one of the major themes in A. S. Byatt's *Babel Tower*. The novel reveals the failure of absolute freedom by focusing on *Babbletower*, written by Jude Mason, and its publication case. It also portrays intellectuals acquiring free space in the course of knowledge pursuit and share, as well as strategies of hegemony and freedom presented in the discussion of the Education Committee. Byatt provides an outline of contemporary conception of freedom through the description of the utopian illusion for freedom in *Babbletower*, desire for freedom of the intellectuals, as well as educational concepts and their feedbacks.

Key Words: A. S. Byatt; *Babel Tower*; freedom; fiction; reality

《巴别塔》(*Babel Tower*, 1996)是英国当代作家拜厄特(A. S. Byatt)四部曲中的第三部。沃海德(Celia Wallhead)曾探讨《巴别塔》中不同话语的描写以及语言与真实的关系,认为"《巴别塔》关注的是语言的力量、篡改不同话语的能力、个人的自由及其对集体社会生活的影响"(133),将个体自由定义为这部小说的主题之一。拜厄特对自由问题一直颇为关注,她曾经专门研究默多克(Iris Murdoch)小说中的自由问题,认为默多克的所有作品都可视为"对个体自由程度的研究"(Byatt, 1965:6)。默多克认为真正的、难以预测的个体生活在具有自由程度的世界里,"自由、独立与丰富多彩、复杂多变的世界相联系"(同上)。通常人们认为可以畅所欲言便是一个自由国度的标志，默多克在《形而上学与伦理学》（Metaphysics and Ethics）中论及“自由”时对此持反对意见：“我们的自由不只是进行不同选择、做出不同行动的自由，也是在思考和信仰方面有所差异的自由，能够以不同的方式观察世界，并以不同的词语描述这些不同的结构”（72～73）。她强调的个体自由是拥有独立思考空间、独特观察视角、语言表达能力的自由。

以智性书写著称文坛的拜厄特对此颇为赞同，并在作品中塑造了一系列追求这种个体自由的人物形象。《巴别塔》围绕虚构的内文本与现实生活展开，表现当代人陷入樊笼、追求自由的不同方式，并以主人公裘德·梅森的寓言式作品《乱语塔》表达绝对自由的不可行性，由此探讨英国60年代社会对于自由的认识。自由一般分为三个层次，即自在的自由、自为的自由、自在自为的自由（邓晓芒，69）。拜厄特在小说中通过描写《乱语塔》中绝对自由理想的破灭、知识分子的自由渴求、关于教育理念及其反馈的讨论勾勒了一幅当代的自由谱系图。

一、《乱语塔》：绝对自由的失败

自在自为的自由是最高层次的自由，也是人类理想的自由王国。正如康德提出的“目的国”（康德，441），在这个理想的王国中，人人都是目的，人人都拥有自由。镶嵌在《巴别塔》中、由主人公裘德·梅森创作的寓言式作品《乱语塔》，讲述了一个自由乌托邦的创建与幻灭。裘德在作品中描绘了不堪忍受现实压迫的一队人马深夜出逃。他们穿越邻山，进入隐蔽的山谷，到达领导人卡尔·沃特一处隐蔽的房产，目的是“以真正自由的形式建立他们自己的小社会，而不是言辞中、狂迷的或恐怖意义上的自由”（12）。①

《乱语塔》中关于自由的实验是一种广义上的自由，包括教育、政府机构、劳动力、精神生活、激情生活，以及艺术、衣着、食品、房屋装饰、植物种植等看似次要的事务。卡尔沃特等人以建立理想的自由王国为目标，追求的是法治社会的制度保障下的自由。裘德在法国游学期间逐渐对法国文学产生兴趣，钻研了傅里叶、尼采的著作与思想。他在《乱语塔》中主要探讨了自由的问题，尤其是法国大革命后傅立叶和萨德侯爵的自由观念。傅立叶宣扬天才创造历史，他把来自“人的本性”的“情欲引力”看作社会发展的动力，认为人的一切自然欲望都可归入新的天堂、新的耶路撒冷，人类可以通过激情与欲望的放纵获得社会的和谐。萨德侯爵认为自然激情都应得到国家的允许和认可，他以嘲讽的笔调再现了颂扬人类理性与自由

① 拜厄特小说原文均引自 A. S. Byatt, *Babel Tower.* (New York: Vintage, 1996)，以下仅标注书名缩写与页码。

意志的启蒙思想：如果人人追求自由激情，那么谁来阻止我伤害他人的欲望？正如这样的理想在法国大革命时期的失败，《乱语塔》中绝对自由的理想国度最终也走向灭亡。

与强烈追求自由、人们可以在自由的名义下为所欲为的法国相比，当时的英国是一个相对保守的国家，时刻担忧过度自由带来的不利后果。《乱语塔》出版之后的遭遇验证了这一点。作品的内容与风格超出了部分知识分子在英国传统文化范围之内的阅读期待，因而遭到起诉。《乱语塔》的自由主题在法庭庭审过程中激起了来自不同学科知识背景的学者与专业人士的讨论。大学教授玛丽－弗朗斯·史密斯在其中读到了法国思想，特别是法国大革命后关于自由与限制的争论，因而强调了作品的文学性与历史性内涵。与之相反，律师奥古斯丁将其中的自由解读为“性表现的完全自由，无论那将是多么令人恶心或变态的性表现”（*BT* 529），这样的自由堕落为残酷、疯狂与破坏。在陈述自己的观点时奥古斯丁将《乱语塔》案与《查泰莱夫人的情人》一案对照考察，认为《查》案中受审的并非小说作者，而是背叛和放荡的查泰莱夫人。《乱语塔》一案则是被告裘德因为他的想象力、他创造的世界、他的思想倾向而受审。与无罪的《查》关于爱情、婚姻与语言的问题不同，《乱语塔》引发的问题是一个残暴与邪恶的问题。他还提醒法官刚刚结束审判的荒原谋杀案①，指出主犯或多或少都受到了虚构文学作品的影响，“不要认为那只不过是一本书，人人都为书所感动，生活可以因为这些虚构的作品而丰富、而改变或毁灭”（*BT* 530）。这番说辞并非凭空捏造。1959 年英国颁布《淫秽出版物法案》（*Obscene Publication Act*），第二年，《查泰莱夫人的情人》（*Lady Chatterley's Lover*，1928）一书于劳伦斯去世 30 年后在英国受到审判，所有劳伦斯专家、英国文学专家、道德伦理学者、教区神父等聚集于法庭之上，进行咄咄逼人的庭审追问，辅之以难以招架的诱供技巧，共同评说这部小说的价值，尤其是其对于世道人心的拯救作用。原告为将《查》判为“淫秽书籍”禁止出版，当庭朗诵该书中的性描写段落，并询问证人们的感受。为劳伦斯进行辩护的证人们则耐心执着地将他们的研究心得以最简明却最有说服力的方式道出。双方的措辞都典雅而富有文采，使整个事件

---

① 伊安·布兰迪（Ian Brandy）与迈拉·亨德雷（Myra Hindley）是一对无情的荒野杀手。他们绑架了曼彻斯特地区 5 名儿童和少年，在对其进行性虐待与非人折磨后，杀害了他们，1966 年被捕入狱。此案特别恐怖之处在于，凶手仅仅为了获得谋杀的快感而行凶。经搜查，布兰迪确实在图书室藏有萨德的著作，并且曾经鼓励亨德雷阅读这类书籍。如今，受害者被埋葬在荒原，两位凶犯仍在监狱服刑。荒原谋杀案与《查泰莱夫人的情人》出版商审判案都是这一时期道德环境形成过程中的重要公众事件，对 60 年代后期英国文化的发展趋势产生重要影响。拜厄特在《巴别塔》开篇对此案作注，参见 A. S. Byatt, *Babel Tower.* （New York：Vintage，1996），x.

的描写饶有趣味和张力(《译海》编辑部)。这一历史案件也成为衡量《乱语塔》社会道德危害性的对照砝码。

裘德对于自由有着自己的理解,直接与犀利地表现在他对服饰威胁个体身份的见解中。他在《乱语塔》中塑造了参孙·俄利根这一角色,借他之口就服装问题阐发自己关于真实自我的观点。参孙一针见血地指出,穿着制服的人与被绳索束缚的人并无二致,它们不是真正的人,而是“一个符号,一种职责,一个游走的概念”(264),制服为此人代言,掩盖了他的真实身份和意图。裘德不仅在作品中畅谈思想,还在现实生活中身体力行。到弗莱德丽卡的文学班上听课时,他常常穿着一身“脏兮兮的蓝色带下摆的天鹅绒外套和一件看上去像警察穿的斗篷,铁灰色的一簇头发披在肩上,油乎乎、亮闪闪”(334)。在解释自己不修边幅的外表时他说:“我必须这样做,这样才符合我的天性,这代表我的身份和真正的本性……我无法戴着面具生活”(334)。《乱语塔》遭到起诉后,出版社组织了由代理律师和辩方证人参加的讨论公审的策划会议,众人一致要求裘德修整外貌和衣着,使外表常规化。弗莱德丽卡作为他的同事劝说道:“上帝啊,这只是张面具……你的角色是一位白衣骑士,你必须看起来像个受人尊敬的社会成员,因为法庭只相信一个拥有常规外表的人(524)。”为了参加这场庭审游戏为自己的书写辩护,裘德无奈妥协,听从大家的意见放弃了自己一直坚持的“天性外表”,穿上炭灰色的法兰绒西装、白衬衫,还干净利落地打了一条绯红色领带。但是改头换面之后的他却形容憔悴、仿佛气数已尽,像是“刚刚结束监禁,或再次入狱的囚犯,或刚刚结束反思现实世界的僧侣”(204)。合身的衣服看起来像是悬挂在衣架上一般死气沉沉,与稻草人无异。对裘德这个无法“戴着面具”生活、坚定追求自我个性的人来说,这种常规化的外表无异于一把锋利的匕首,扼杀了他仅存的一线生气,剥夺了他所珍视的自由。法庭是他最不愿意出现的场合,法官就是那个他在作品中称之为穿着制服的人,那个游走的符号。裘德在心底里鄙视他们,却对他们高高在上决定自己和作品的命运这一事实无可奈何。在他看来,既然上帝已死,那么法律应该保证个人自由行事的权力(9)。但事实并非如此简单,裘德在法庭审判机制、社会道德舆论、出版社社会名誉等多重压力之下不得不做出妥协。

二、思考与写作:知识分子的自由渴求

对于任何真正渴求自由的人来说,需要“最迫切的莫过于知识,以及获得它的手段——也就是说,让他最能够从事于知识工作的持久条件”(艾伦,145)。当代是一个知识与权力相联结的时代,身处其中的知识分子不得不面对知识本身的进

步以及知识与权力的联结带来的主体危机，并以适应时代的形式踏上主体性建构之途。此时的知识是“一个特定空间，主体在其中可以采取某个立场并谈论他在话语中要处理的对象”（Foucault，1989：182～183）。作为知识话语的言说主体，面对后现代主体危机的当代知识分子在这个特定空间内做出重建主体性的尝试。福柯并未自始至终遵循一种统一确凿的权力理论，相反，他在权力面前反复权衡，纠结于知识、权力、主体复杂关系的考量。初期，他将权力视作否定、压制、紧闭性的，权力剥夺了主体人的自由。而后，福柯借鉴了尼采的权力观，他不再将权力视作消极的、否定的，而是将权力确定为积极的、生产的，权力锻造和铸就了它的对象。最终，福柯的权力表现为一个开放的场域。由“考古学”研究到“谱系学”研究，福柯认为话语构型和知识谱系的分析更依据权力战术和策略，“知识以一个压迫式的暴君转化为知识和权力的战略性联结”，现代社会中的权力和知识之间是相互渗透、相互建构的关系。

在《巴别塔》中，知识与权力的联结集中体现在知识分子身上，他们作为知识的言说者在求知的过程中认识自我、发现自我、反思自我，也由此走上权力之途。对于知识分子而言，保持自身自主性的自由是弥足珍贵的，但他们懂得自由的真正含义，因而会选择更为理性与智性的方式寻求自由。他人眼中不修边幅的尼采主义者裘德坚称，自我实现首先以摆脱欲望的羁绊为基础，其次应力求展现真我。相对于年轻艺术家们的革命热情，裘德认为写作是一种“更为安全”、使人达到永恒的反抗形式（229）。他创作《乱语塔》以抒发自己的思想与对人性的看法，实际是一种反抗现实的手段。正如克里斯蒂娃所言，与图像文化相比，“词语文化、小说叙述以及它为沉思保留的位置……乃是进行最低限度反抗的一种变体形式”（6）。作家有权利在自己的作品中以自由的形式、语言表达个人对社会、对人性的思考。因为“唯有文学论述，才能巧妙地将自身权利意愿、思想表达及策略灵活运用等各项因素，生动地结合并展现出来，才能为自身的思想自由，提供最灵活的可能性场域”（高宣扬，2005：20）。以文字和书写作为中介，可以使自身及其生活历程通过反思和曲折回归的方式，向充满可塑性和伸缩性的自由王国无限延伸（高宣扬，2005：21）。

裘德所追求的自由是自为的自由，是具有自我意识的能动自由。他所反对的学生暴动实际上是停留在幼儿阶段层次较低的自由，那仅仅是自由意识的萌芽。裘德本人选择了写作的反抗形式，但这种获取自由的方式也并非完美，因为作者选择的自由与作品出版、作品描写内容是两类不同的自由。即选择是自由的，但可供选择的可能性并不是自由决定的，作者也只能选择现实已有的可能性，选择符合出版制度与读者阅读期待的写作内容。裘德尽管具有相当的智慧与天赋,却以危险重重的方式写作,最终被诉诸法庭接受审讯。事实是他的看似安全的反抗形式同样遭到了围追堵截,更为隐晦的反抗因其更为厚重的思想背景而遭到严厉的处置。

同时,拜厄特的女作家身份让她对知识分子的性别差异问题格外关注。她笔下的女主人公弗莱德丽卡成功摆脱了父亲的权威到剑桥学习英国文学,原本钟情于大学里满腹经纶、才华横溢的才子,却因姐姐斯黛芬妮的意外死亡而身陷与富家子弟奈杰尔的婚姻泥沼。结婚之后,弗莱德丽卡逐渐意识到自己与童话中灰姑娘的相似之处:丈夫奈杰尔的父亲是船业富豪,他们居住的乡间别墅意指城堡,儿子雷奥的降生是童话的结局。不同的是,她所面对的不是残忍的继母,而是有暴力倾向、剥夺妻子自由的丈夫。在看到婚姻对自己的囚禁之后,她携儿子雷奥逃出了那栋剥夺其身体与精神双重自由的房子。与男性知识分子相比,女性更倾向于与他人分享自己获得的任何信息。这种知识分享的欲望让教学成为许多女性知识分子实现自我、获得自由的途径。对她们而言,教学不仅是知识的分享,也是自由思考的空间。弗莱德丽卡曾在课堂上引导学生们讨论福斯特与劳伦斯作品中的爱与婚姻,尤其强调"联结"的重要性。他们不喜欢机械化的生活、城市、碎片与瓦解,福斯特的苏塞克斯与劳伦斯的诺丁汉郡都带有失去的乐园的色彩。弗莱德丽卡将这一点与他们笔下智慧女性的激情与欲望联系起来,称那是"为了自由与征服,为了思想与本能"(329)。在伦敦,弗莱德丽卡以在塞缪尔·帕默艺术学院教授英国文学课程和给出版社新书写书评谋生。初为人师,她面对的是学习成人教育课程的学生。与大学生不同,这些学生渴望思考并且来自各种各样"现实"的世界:工作、婚姻、生育、死亡、成功、失败,他们生活的世界恰是年轻学生们希望在书本间寻找答案的生活经历(222)。在教学活动中,弗莱德丽卡不仅享受了知识分享的乐趣,更获得了自己所钟爱的文学阅读与思考的自由天地。四部曲中的其他女性人物形象如弗莱德丽卡的剑桥高才生姐姐斯黛芬妮、完成了以蜗牛为研究对象的博士论文的杰奎琳、在学生课程改革运动中开设有关占星学讲座的艾娃·维基诺贝尔都试图以思考获得自由。在作者笔下,她们被塑造成苦于找不到自我实现途径、不甘躲在男性光环之下生活的向往独立自由的女性形象。

三、爱与自由:教育理念及其反馈

20 世纪 60 年代西方社会面临的众多问题给青年人反抗体制提供了许多具体对象。他们的反抗都以自由的名义进行,包括破坏与杀戮等激进行为。在《巴别塔》之后四部曲的第四部小说《吹口哨的女人》(*A Whistling Woman*,2002)中,学生们成立了“反大学”组织,高举“打破人为限制,为自我表现创建一方自由天地”的旗号。他们要求校方改变大学课程设置,将一切知识纳入课程范围:无论是抽象的宇宙哲学、所谓的疯癫、资本主义制度的灭亡,还是制作柑橘果酱、蔬菜烹饪、种植香豌豆等实践活动。因为“世界是五彩斑斓的,反大学亦应如是”(85~86)。学生运动组织者之一格莱格·陶德对系主任、哲学家文森特·霍奇基斯直言:权力机构总是在谈论自由言论。自由言论是一个物化概念,是一个神秘化了的绝对价值。他们以此来压制质疑,让所有的信仰变得如出一辙、了然无趣、枯燥乏味。“自由意味着改变,改变意味着行动,而非喋喋不休、只说不做。”(298)这番见解道出了学生们对于“自由”的狭隘认识。正如《巴别塔》中裘德对于艺术学院学生革命的评价所言:他们以自己的方式践行原创的理想,不愿同枯燥复杂的过去有任何瓜葛,这种行为是在打破固有的链条(421)。

围绕教育展开的思考与论辩是《巴别塔》的重要内容之一。教育体系内部人物身份具有流动性特征,知识分子需要学习以获得知识,而成为知识分子的他们又将对受训主体与知识话语实施控制与规训,继而不可避免地遭遇知识对象打着“自由”旗号的反抗行为。小说中北约克郡大学副校长维基诺贝尔指出将政治与社会中的规则与语言结构的形式相类比毫无意义,语言结构在任何社会都适用。他认为学校应该讲授语言的形式,因为“如果不知道如何描绘我们思想的结构,我们就无法分析它们的本质与局限”(186)。这让读者了解他提倡的教育理念与强调语法重要性的原因,也由此理解高举自由大旗的学生将反抗的矛头指向他的原因。学校教育体制在促成知识传承、培养知识分子的同时也成为知识分子施展权力的空间。它对受训主体行使知识霸权,控制知识的合法性。正是这种“霸权”与“控制”令作为教育主体的学生产生自由被剥夺的压迫之感,采取了激进的反抗形式。

究竟是遵循“规训与权威”还是崇尚“爱与自由”?《巴别塔》中的斯蒂尔福思语言教育委员会就这一问题进行了激烈的讨论。委员们从语言习得理论与认知心理学理论的高度研究儿童的语言习得规律,并以此制定学习计划与方针政策,监管学校的语言教学情况。委员会将对中小学英语语言的教学问题提出建议,包括一些具体问题:如阅读教学运用声音还是视觉,语法教学具有哪些优缺点,针对修正与规则如何进行自由表达。斯蒂尔福斯教学委员会为讨论语言教学与儿童语言习得提供了平台,专家们将教学问题提升到哲学问题的高度。如他们回顾了哲学家、教育家布伯(Martin Buber)教师拥有从其文化背景继承的无上权威的观点。这种体系随着文化权力的瓦解逐渐加强,显露出“权力意志”的弊端。与之相对的极端是过分强调“爱”，权力退化为理想的相互依存与慈爱模式，从专业的教学关系退化为单纯的个人关系。这种关系并不能在教师与学生之间长久地持续，因为它依靠的是诚信与耐力，然而事实上，并非所有的教师都对学生怀有真诚的喜爱（188～189）。

儿童时期的自由属于自在的自由，这种自由自在只有在失去的时候才能够为人所知，在拥有的时候则是完全意识不到的。因此，这种自由常常带有怀旧的感伤主义色彩（邓晓芒 69）。《巴别塔》中的教育委员会成员们追溯自己孩提时代的学校学习经历来发表各自见解，并分裂为遵循“规训与权威”和崇尚“爱与自由”的两大阵营。布伯对教与学主体关系的论述延伸至教学氛围及语法规则的认识中，认为学生必须学习语法。这与维基诺贝尔的观点不谋而合。崇尚爱与自由一方则认为语法是一个陷阱，一种压迫。学生应该在自由宽松的环境中顺其自然地学习语言，“一旦明白儿童在造句方面的天赋，我们就不必急于强迫训练”（143）。学生们不需要读懂弥尔顿、多恩，他们只需要学会如何写求职信和读政府报告，学习的目的从“占有”知识发展为“运用”知识。此处的悖论是，儿童，包括童年时代的这些委员们，是完全意识不到自己的自由状态的。“爱与自由”是来自成年世界的词汇，是“规训与权威”的新的形式外衣。

《巴别塔》中关于教育制度的讨论与思考所表达的教育目标，就是要培养具有健全人格的现代知识分子，他们不仅具有专业的知识技能，也将有能力承担社会责任、影响社会风气。严厉的纪律是现代学校的主要特征，在这里不存在不受规范约束的地方，不存在不受规范约束的行为。未来教育的权威形象——校长和教师——首先被看作是监视并以强制手段维持纪律的专家（鲍曼 95）。青年学生的反抗行为不得不面对两方面的现实，首先，他们拒绝接受机构的规训，以或激进、或保守的方式为自由铤而走险，这对个人的成长道路会产生人们难以忽略的消极影响；其次，知识对象追求的自由行为是相对的自由，是体制内的自由，若非如此，反抗、革命最终只能归于失败。学生运动的组织者之一图菲尔多年以后成为布莱尔首相的内阁大臣，仍然时常从梦中惊醒，回想起当年组织学生运动、闯入学校举办的研讨会现场作乱的那一时刻。是副校长维基诺贝尔对外隐瞒了他的错误才使得他的仕途顺畅，图菲尔年纪渐长，对副校长逐渐由憎恶转为充满爱戴，并发现自己走在与他相似的道路上（Byatt 2003：373）。自由独立并不意味着把自己从环境中孤立出来，更不是与环境格格不入，而是具有不为环境吞噬的自持，自持的程度随个体内在力量变化会有不同的表现。

四、结语

鲍曼（Zygmunt Bauman）对畅所欲言就是自由提出批评意见，他分析了这句话可能的含义："'自由国度'并不能保证我们所做的一切能够达到目的，或者我们所说的一切能够被接受。……因此这句话也告诉我们生活在一个自由的国度里意味着基于个人责任行事。"自由在鲍曼看来不是一件财产，不是属于或者不属于个人的一种品质，而"仅仅作为社会关系而存在：只有作为过去或现在其他条件的对立面之时才有意义"。鲍曼对于自由的悲观论调与福柯的权力概念不无关系。正如不存在自由与强迫，同样不存在统治与被统治，那些掌握权力并为维持权力而斗争的人与那些被剥夺权力并梦想得到权力的人实际并无太大差异。自由是一种关系，不是被拥有的财产，而是像权力一样，仅仅存在于个体之间。拜厄特对于自由与反抗的态度与此类似，她在《巴别塔》中描写不同人物进行以自由为目的的反抗行动，却没有赋予它们以希望。自由与意志密不可分，正如知识与权力的联盟关系坚不可摧。

参考文献：

[1]Bauman, Zygmunt. *Freedom*[M]. London: Open University Press, 1998.

[2] Byatt, A. S. *Passions of the Mind: Selected Writings*[M]. London: Vintage, 1993.

[3] Byatt, A. S. *Degree of Freedom: Early Novels of Iris Murdoch*[M]. London: Vintage, 1994.

[4]Byatt, A. S. *Babel Tower*[M]. New York: Vintage, 1996.

[5]Byatt, A. S. *A Whistling Woman*[M]. London: Vintage, 2003.

[6]Foucault, Michel. *The History of Sexuality. An Introduction. Vol.* 1. New York: Vintage Books, 1978.

[7]Foucault, Miche. *Archaeology of Knowledge*[M]. London: Routledge, 1989.

[8]Murdoch, Iris. "Metaphysics and Ethics". *Existentialists and Mystics: Writings on Philosophy and Literature.* New York: Penguin Books, 1999: 59 ~ 75.

[9]Wallhead, Celia. "The Un-utopian Babelic Fallenness of Language: A. S. Byatt's Babel Tower". *Dreams and Realities: Versions of Utopia in English Fiction from Dickens to Byatt*, eds. A. Gomis and M. Martinez. Almeria: University of Almeria Press, 1997.

[10]巴里·艾伦．知识与文明[M]．刘梁剑译．杭州：浙江大学出版

社,2010.

[11]鲍曼. 立法者与阐释者——论现代性、后现代性与知识分子[M]. 洪涛译. 上海:上海人民出版社,2000.

[12]邓晓芒. 什么是自由?[J]. 哲学研究. 2012(7):64 ~71.

[13]高宣扬. 福柯的生存美学[M]. 北京:中国人民大学出版社,2005.

[14]康德. 康德著作全集(第4卷)[M]. 李秋零译. 北京:中国人民大学出版社,2005.

[15]克里斯蒂娃. 反抗的未来[M]. 黄晞耘译. 桂林:广西师范大学出版社,2007.

[16]林剑. 人的自由的哲学探索[M]. 北京:中国人民大学出版社,1996.

[17]《译海》编辑部. 审判《查泰莱夫人的情人》[M]. 广州:花城出版社,1996.

The Responses to Thoreau's Rational

首都经济贸易大学外国语学院　高悦伶

Abstract: Through a description of a trial in the court with six jurors who are all famous authors in America, people got a clear idea of those jurors responses to Thoreau's rational for individuality. Among them, Cooper, Longstreet show their sympathy for Thoreau who believed in glorifying individuality and denied a government based on majority rule. However, Hawthorne, Emerson, Melville and Douglass countered Thoreau's argument and hold some quite different views towards Thoreau's rational of individuality.

Key Words: rational; individualism; self-trust; American Government

The temperature in the court had risen considerably in the previous half hour. The only escape for the six jurors came from the courtroom windows, which allowed the onlooker a magnificent view of the Massachusetts coastline. Finally, Henry David Thoreau entered through the double doors of the courthouse and proceeded down the nave of the courtroom to his reserved chair. As in any criminal case, this one began with the detailed prosecution of the charged. This particular prosecution arose from the actions of Henry David Thoreau, who had not only discussed his transgressions in this essay, "Resistance to Civil Government," but also published treatises on numerous occasions. Among the six jurors in this trial. James Fenimore Cooper, a native New Yorker and esteemed author, agreed to recite Thoreau's charges. Cooper first discussed Thoreau's charges of American bastardization, in which Thoreau demonized many American tenets including democracy, expansion and taxation. Cooper continued by asking Thoreau if he had vehemently alienated himself from the American identity by glorifying and obeying his individualism rather than his native country's laws. Thoreau also suggested through his works that those serving in the military should not be viewed as patriots, but as brainwashed machines owned by the American government (Thoreau 53). At the end of Cooper's statement, jurors were asked to decide Thoreau's verdict in a side jury room of the courthouse. I was honored to sit in this meeting with them, after receiving special permission from the judge. After closing the door, Cooper moved to begin the debate over Thoreau's verdict and was given permission by his colleagues. The jurors and I would soon discovered Cooper's sympathy for Thoreau.

Thoreau theorized that a government based on majority rule couldn't be in accord with justice (Thoreau 189). Cooper insisted that the majority could often display incompetence on a number of levels. He then alluded to his novel, *The Pioneers*, in which the majority not only exhibited ineptitude towards their tasks at hand, but chastised the astute minority. *In The Pioneers*, Cooper told of a hunting party whose lack of skill in harvesting their prey was palpable to the reader. One individual, however, a frontiersman named Natty Bumppo, displayed respect towards his prey and carried out the hunt with precision and conservation (Cooper 350). Cooper then asked his fellow jurors if legislation implemented by the government was analogous to the ineptitude shown by these hunters. Should Thoreau's attitude to democracy truly subject him to prosecution?

Augustus Longstreet interjected by agreeing with Cooper's statements. Using southwestern humor got in his short story, "The Horse Swap," Longstreet shone light on the incompetency of what he called, "the Jacksonian masses" (Longstreet 21). Speaking to his fellow jurors, Longstreet described his narrative of the Southern lower Class. A horse trader named "Yellow Blossom" proclaimed that "he was perhaps a leetle, jist a leetle of the man of horse swap that ever stole cracklins out of his mommy's fat gourd" (Longstreet 24). The horse trader's confidence coupled with his stupidity led him to purchase a blind horse. Longstreet then asked his audience how a nation could call itself "just" when it allows the uneducated and impoverished to cultivate its policies. After a brief moment of silence, Nathaniel Hawthorne rose and countered Longstreet's assumptions.

He argued that one cannot categorize the upper and lower classes as "superior" and "inferior", especially when it comes to political activism. Citing his short story, "My Kinsman, Major Molineux," the native of Massachusetts spoke of the upper echelon as corrupt and unfit to govern the community. Robin, a country boy, entered a colonial town in search of wealth from his relative, Major Molineux, a governor of the Royal Crown (Melville12). After searching for an entire night, he would learn that the community had seen too much of the corruption of his office. The unified community effectively protested, thereby ending Molineux's exploitation. Hawthorne then asked Longstreet how the lower class could be capable of such accomplishments. Without waiting for a reply, he concluded an uneducated Southerner such as Robin mirrored many qualities of Jasper in Longstreet's story. He claimed that the value of community would enslave Robin, and many like him, to prosper as an individual because the opportunity presented itself within the town (Hawthorne 115). It was the many who ousted the few who obstructed the community's full capabilities. Having said this, Hawthorne took his seat, promoting Ralph Waldo Emerson to share his thought on the matter.

Emerson would begin by digressing to Thoreau's original prosecution. He believed that the core argument was not whether the majority was fit to rule, but whether the idea of trust could be seen as a deterrent for accepting the United States legislature as a governing body. He stated that "Resistance to Civil Government" defined the conscience as the primary moral compass of each individual, and that the American government divides the individuality by "extracting the diabolical from the divine" (Thoreau 197). Thoreau, according to Emerson, believed that this division from the divine created a meek and conformist community. According to Thoreau's treatise, "Men generally under such a government like this, think they ought to wait until they have persuaded the majority to alter (unjust laws). They think that if they should resist, the remedy would be worse than the evil" (Thoreau 197). Emerson then asked if the soldier's fighting for American expansion fell into this classification of subservient men. After Thoreau agreed, Emerson continued by alluding to his own work, Nature.

Emerson believed that the widespread suffocation of individualism in the United States stemmed from the clinging of old traditions and notions of property, expansion, taxation, and civil duty. These aloof individuals Emerson viewed, have failed to tap into their innate knowledge and understanding of the natural world (Emerson, Nature 8). Only the unification of all natural sensations in the universe can lead us to true knowledge and firm individual trust, superior to any artificial government (Emerson, Nature 8). Although every human has this unique gift, one of the American traditions advocates a matrix in which functionality to society takes priority over the understanding of nature. Before Emerson could continue, Frederick Douglass intervened, beginning with a brief appraisal of Emerson's comments.

As expected, his opening comments pertained to his slavery day's. He first agreed with Emerson that many lack the moral compass that they might derive from self-trust. The institution of slavery, which thrived in the South, had been spreading by those soldiers Thoreau referred to in his essay. He then directly quoted a passage from Thoreau on his thoughts about government oppression: "For my own part, I should not like to think that I ever rely on the protection of the state. But, if I deny the authority of the State when it presents its tax bill, it will soon take and waste all my property, and so harass me and my children without end" (Douglass 897). Douglass compared Thoreau's experience to his early life with "Master" Thomas Auld and Mr. Covey. In the perilous six months, he spent with the slave-maker, Douglass had described himself as a broken man. Mr. Covey had "broken my body, soul and spirit" (Douglass 895). The African American author abhorred the fact that the United States had deployed its military to conquer new lands so that slavery could spread. He continued by commenting on Emerson's theory of nature. As a former slave, Douglass's experience with nature is accordance with self-trust had been mixed. On one hand, it was a dangerous place that slave catchers lurked. It also was the place where slaves like Douglass would work tirelessly from sunrise to sunset under the crack of the whip (Douglass 888). Despite this negative perception of the natural world, Douglass could relate Emerson's theory. As recorded in his autobiography, Douglass described the northern flowing Chesapeake Bay spawning his transformation from his suicidal depression after a terrible confrontation with Mr. Covey to that of intrepidity. This sources of inspiration improved his spirits, empowering him to envision "the better day coming" (Douglass 897).

Having listened to the trial thus far, Herman Melville interrupted Douglass by questioning his comments on self-trust. If Douglass agreed with Emerson's theory of nature, to what extent did he credit ability to read in his escape to freedom? Having been well versed in Emerson's weariness with book-reading, Douglass replied that his encounter with the Chesapeake Bay that instilled a self-trust that would eventually lead him to becoming a successful author (Emerson 62d1). He then concluded by saying Thoreau's assertion that one's self-trust should remain superior to that of man-made laws was indeed noteworthy.

Melville replied with skepticism. The stories of nature and self-empowerment had been coming from either famous individuals or fictional characters. If the root of Thoreau's view of civil disobedience did indeed derive from self-trust, it was essential to review real accounts of the effectiveness of self-trust as a governing agents. In his short story, "Benito Cereno," Melville recounts the naïveté of ship captital Amass Delano off the shores of Chile. Throughout his experience in an unidentifiable vessel, *San Dominich*, Captain Delano's—the reader can sense that something is awry (Melville 356). Melville stated that his reason for giving subtle clues about Captain Cereno's state of peril was to illustrate how Delano is lack of awareness. If Thoreau's motto, "Know Thyself" became a primary directive of American infrastructure, the nation would not last among other powerful nations (Thoreau 201). Melville continued by rejecting Thoreau's comments on the military. He believed that within any population, an army was crucial for protecting its government and people. Although Captain Delano rumination on his dangerous surrounding was minimal, he still held the high rank of Captain, and when danger struck, his crew would come to his aid (Melville 635). Melville asked his audience what they would have thought if they were being held captive on the San Dominich, and then turned to Thoreau deeming him an ungrateful optimist.

Chaos among the jurors ensued, but soon it was clear that the arguing was among distinct groups. Hawthorne, Cooper, and Melville seemed to have directed most of their attention to Emerson and Douglass. It was too loud to comprehend the verbal diatribes, but it may be assumed they pertained to Thoreau's fate. Longstreet sat silently shaking his head as if he were asking himself why he came to such a trial in the first place. After a few minutes the tension made it seem linger than a few minutes. Cooper asked for order. Cooper asked all the jurors to write on a sheet of paper "yea" if they found Thoreau to be a rational thinker and "nay" if they believe him to be irrational. I could not real all the ballots because of my placement in the room. Emerson, as expected, scribbled yea. Longstreet wrote yea as well. Although I could tell which side Cooper was on, most surprised by Douglass's decision. After supporting Emerson's theory of nature, even after criticism, I would have sworn he would have voted yea, but alas, I had thought wrong. My only reasonable explanation was that he still remained hopeful for a government that slavery was not thought of as an integral component of the society. After the ballots had been cast, the jurors rose from their seats and walked back into the courtroom. Thoreau sat silently grinning as we entered, as if his self-confidence surpassed his fear of condemnation.

Works Cited:

[1] Emerson, Ralph W. Boston, Thruston, Torry, 1849.

[2] Hawthorne, Nathanial "My Kinsman, Major Molineux" The Token. Boston, MA: Grey And Bowen, 1851. 90 - 116.

[3] Longstreet, Augustus Baldwin. The Horse Swap. Maymester 2014 English 252 Class NC state Raleigh Michael Grimwood, prof. 23 - 31.

[4] Melville, Herman. Benito Cereno. Putman's Magazine Oct. -Dec. Moodle Site Maymester 2014 English 252 Class NC State U Raleigh NC. Michael Grimwood, prof. 23 - 31.

[5] Thoreau, Henry David. Resistance to Civil Government. Aesthetic Papers ED. Elizabeth Peabody. FL: Scholars Facsimiles & Reprints, 1957. 189 - 211.

[6] Cooper, James Fenimore. The Pioneers. The American Tradition in Literature. Ed. George Perkins and Barbara Perkins New York: McGraw Hill, 2009.

[7] Cooper, James Fenimore. The Prairie. The American Tradition in Literature Ed. George Perkins and Barbara Perkins New York: McGraw Hill, 2009.

[8] Frederick Douglass. Narrative of the Life of Frederick Douglass. The American Tradition in Literature Ed. George Perkins and Barbara Perkins New York: McGraw Hill, 2009.

中国文化视角下的跨文化交际效果评估

首都经济贸易大学外国语学院　张慧宇

摘　要:交际效果是一切交际活动的最终落脚点,也是评判某项交际活动成败得失的客观依据。本文旨在从中国文化的视角看待跨文化交际效果的评估标准问题,综合借鉴前人研究等成果,提出了"有利有节"简单4字方针,这个方针整合了目标和手段,能够从一个交际的互动过程出发,考虑自身的交际目标,同时注意交际手段,实现双赢的局面。按照这个维度,可以进一步把跨文化交际效果分为4种:①既无利亦无节;②无利却有节;③有利却无节;④既有利又有节。日常的有效或无效的跨文化交际效果案例,证明了这是一个简单又比较有概括力和解释力的效果评估标准。当然最佳的标准还是有利有节,这个评价标准比较符合中国人处事的法则和注重长远的价值取向。

关键词:跨文化交际能力;标准;有利;有节;中庸之道

Abstract: This paper attempts to discuss the evaluation criteria of intercultural communication activities from the perspective of Chinese culture. The author ventures to summarize the criteria into two dimension: "being beneficial" and "being proper", resulting in four outcomes: beneficial and proper; beneficial but not proper; proper but not beneficial; neither beneficial nor proper. The ideal one is to achieve mutual benefits through elegant and considerate communicative tactics, which echoes Chinese values such as the Golden rules and Long-term Orientation.

Key Words: Intercultural communication competence (ICC); criteria; being beneficial; being proper; the Doctrine of the Mean

一、跨文化交际二要素:心理机制、素养

影响跨文化交际效果的要素有很多,有分为五要素的,比如动机(motivation)、知识(knowledge)、态度(attitude)、行为(behavior)和技能(skill)。也有分为三要素的,比如知识、动机和技能。综合起来,影响跨文化效果的要素可以概括为两个:心理机制、个人综合素养。

（一）心理机制：包括交往的驱动力、个人心智、正确归因等心理方面的要素

对于从事跨文化研究的人而言，很难想象会有许多人不愿意进行跨文化交际，他们对于交际的愿望是很低的，任何民族和国家中都会存在这样一些人，不管是位高权重的人，还是普通的黎民百姓，你都会遇到一些对某种文化比较有抵触心理的人。也许是因为文化中心主义，不屑进行交流；也有人不愿意进行跨文化交流，是害怕跨越所谓的“交流舒适区间”（communication comfort zone）；也有人是不自信，想要进行跨文化交际，却不敢实践。寻找到那些比较有进行跨文化交际动力的人，是进行跨文化工作的一个不错的起点。如果是由于个人原因，比如求学、工作的需求，个体比较容易采取主动态度，积极适应所在异文化。有些文化比较自大，不愿意跟其他文化主动接触，也会阻碍来自这些文化的人了解其他文化的主动性。尽管跨文化交际学发源于美国，但是美国人常常被批评为孤傲的、无知的人。有一则笑话，是老师让学生们用自己的话谈谈非洲粮食短缺的问题，美国学生不知道非洲在哪里，英国学生不知道短缺是什么意思，非洲学生不知道食物是什么意思，中国学生不知道用自己的话是什么意思。尽管是一个笑话，但是讽刺意义还是比较深刻的。政治和历史的原因也会促进或阻碍人们的跨文化交际的愿望，冷战时期，社会主义阵营和资本主义阵营内部交往较多，而相互之间却仇视，互相敌对隔离，交往者彼此怀有较深的敌意，不能够友好开展交往；以色列人和巴勒斯坦人之间长期的交战和领土纷争，势必造成双方的敌视态度。因此，个体也受其所在的宏观群体的制约。

（二）个人素养：包括语言文化储备、个人跨文化敏感性培养等要素

瓦兹拉威克等（Walzlawick、Beavin 和 Jackson，1967）认为，所有的语言活动都包含一个内容成分和一个关系成分，特别是在人际交往的时候，言语所表达的是具体的内容，比如争执，可能涉及一个方案，也可能涉及一件事、一种看法、某种利益；但是在言语内容的最后，还是要产生言语者双方的关系，在选择语言策略的时候，也要考虑到对人际关系的影响，是会促进两者的关系，还是会恶化？是消除了误解，还是加深了敌意？因此，在交际的过程中，时刻注意到语言的两个主要功能，信息传递功能和社会关系维护功能。

知识（knowledge）是指对跨文化交际中所需要的必要信息的把握，对自身文化和自我的认知，对交际对象的文化的了解，这些综合一起，有助于交际者在交际过程中确定策略，对情形有一个基本的判断、调整和把控能力，从而很好地实现有效沟通。

对于跨文化交际者来说，首要的，也往往被认为是最重要的知识是语言知识。

我们常听到人们抱怨自己的语言能力不行,影响到了跨文化交际效果。的确,不学习另一种语言,很难深入了解其所在的文化,没有语言作为媒介,可表达的内容甚微。因此,我们针对要进行跨文化工作的外派人员、留学生、访问学者,外派人员最基础的培训还是语言培训。由于短期的语言培训受到时间的约束,在效果方面还存在很大问题。结合我国的外语教学历史,可能在跨文化语言培训中还是要多考虑语言的实用性、日常语言的培训。许多书本上学到的语言知识,在实际使用过程中,会有很大差异。比如书本上说第一次见到陌生人,打招呼要用"How do you do?"作答也用"How do you do?"但是在很多美国人那里,他们可能直接问"How are you?"我们原来的教程中一直说回答这个问题要用"I' m fine, thank you. And you?"这样的回答当然也是对的,但是更多的美国人直接回答"How are you?"到商店购物,店员也很少问你"What can I help you?"或"What can I do for you?"而是一个长长的句子"Do you find everything is fine today?"如果不清楚,就会一时语塞,不知道如何回答。跨文化语言培训应该以实际生活中存在的问题为导向,比如去美国超市一趟,你就会发现超市里有一大批你所不认识的单词,差异巨大的计量单位,除了千克(kilogram),他们可能更多地使用 Oz、pack、liter、dozen;还有一大堆的水果蔬菜的英文;如果再去点个菜,菜单就能绕晕无数人,更不用说来自意大利语、法语的词汇了。总而言之,以交际为目的的语言培训应该紧扣"实用"二字,现在社会变迁快,语言变迁也快,在教学语言的时候,也要及时跟进,语言要跟得上时代的进步。

说到语言知识,除了有声的语言(verbal language)以外,还有一个非常重要的构成部分,就是无声语言知识(non-verbal language)。美国学者爱德华·霍尔(Edward Hall)的《无声的语言》(The Silent Language)可谓是跨文化研究的开山之作。其中,他提出了非语言这种无声语言的力量。霍尔尤其注重时间和空间的理论,他专门设立章节,讨论时间的声音和空间的语言。他说:"时间会说话,而且说得比言词更加明白。由于它不大受人有意的操控,所以它不像有声语言那样受到歪曲。在词语撒谎的地方,它能高声宣示真相。"

无声言语的提出,极大地补充和丰富了沟通过程中对言语(verbal language)的关注,使得参与沟通者更加关注到语言之外的涵义。很多人甚至认为,语言的实质是为了掩盖真相,只有非语言才能揭示真相。在整个沟通过程中,此时无声胜有声的确会频频出现。只有敏感、细腻的沟通者,才能抓住对方的非语言讯息,并且按照其在所属文化的解释方式,进行价值判断,才能有效提高沟通效果,用霍尔的话说,是"鼓励无意识文化(微观文化)的研究",因为人类的未来在于维护无意识文化的多样性,并且将其转化为有利条件。

二、如何判断跨文化交际能力的高低

Spitzberge 为有效沟通所下的定义是:“有效沟通是一种互动,可以见到有效地实现了某些有利的目标,并且所采用的方式在互动发生的情境下是合适的、得体的。”(Competent communication is interaction that is perceived as effective in fulfilling certain rewarding objectives in a way that is also appropriate to the context in which the interaction occurs)。但是如何评价某项交际活动的“效果”才比较客观呢? 交际者一方的判断是否有失公允? 个体特性能否代表群体特征? 以某个跨文化交际的个例来判断更大的“文化”是否会造成刻板印象? 文化模式是如何有意识无意识地介入个人交流中的? “能力”是一个很主观的概念,到底如何判断一个交际者的能力是高还是低呢? 学者们常常用两个形容词来概括一项跨文化交际活动:“有效的”(effective) 和 “得体的”(appropriate)。

何为有效呢? 通俗地讲,有效就是能力转化为效果的过程,因为沟通能力不等于效果,只有实现了以下三个主要的目标,才可以判断沟通是有效的:第一,任务的达成;第二,适应新文化的能力;第三,建立良好的人际关系的能力。(task performance, ability to adapt to the new culture, and the ability to establish healthy interpersonal relationships)检查沟通是不是有效,最直接就是看有没有实现个人所期待的目标,这个目标可以是个人的私人目标,比如成功地说服投资人投资你的项目,也可以是一个公益问题,比如成功地说服某个基金会投资某项公益事业、传教士传递福音。目标的实现需要沟通者首先明确自己的目标是什么? 可以利用的资源是什么? 沟通对象的可能的反应是什么? 采取什么样的策略等。最终检验交际效果需要从以上三个目标来衡量。

何为“得体”? 得体是行事的方式,指参与沟通的人是否采用了交际发生者之间都认可的沟通方式,比如语言和非语言姿势、态度和立场的表达、实现目标的道德考虑等。特别需要注意的是,由于文化差异,在跨文化交际中特别要注意到对方文化的习惯、基本的价值观点、最基本的信仰的忌讳,同时,成功的跨文化交际还需要体现自身的文化特征,这是一个持续平衡的过程。

按照“有效”“得体”两个维度来判断,交际效果可以分为四种:①既无利亦无节;②无利却有节;③有利却无节;④既有利又有节。当然最后一种是最理想的,第一种是最不理想的,等于宣告交际活动的彻底失败。第二种是说交际遵循了交际环境下的要求,方式是得体的,但是没有实现交际目标。这个虽然不是很理想,但是如果是以长久为取向的文化中,可能会对目标中的第三条,即融洽的人际关系的发展有帮助,比如跨文化商务谈判,尽管可能没有实现谈判的目标,但是只要沟通过程愉快,彼此的印象良好,也可能建立起私人关系,培育潜在的合作。第三种交际效果尤其要特别在意,虽然暂时实现了单次的目标,但由于沟通中所采用方式欠妥,比如有欺诈、威胁以及损人利己等不道德的行为,长期下去,就会影响到良好人际关系的建立,进而还会损害到群体的利益。

近些年,越来越多的人走出国门,工作、学习、移民定居、旅游。但随之而来的,是媒体(包括国内媒体和国际媒体)对中国人不当行为的报道。这样的报道可谓屡见不鲜。

2009 年 3 月 27 日,中国台湾北海岸野柳地质公园岩壁上被刻下“中国常州赵根大”字样。当地媒体将此事报道后,赵根大公开道歉。

2012 年伦敦奥运会期间,央视主持人白岩松爬了 528 个台阶,到达圣保罗大教堂金色回廊,看到了“国安是冠军”的涂鸦。

2013 年 5 月网友晒出埃及卢克索神庙有着 3 000 多年历史的浮雕上,刻画着汉字“丁××到此一游”。神庙与汉字,两大文明竟以如此方式相遇。

2012 年 9 月奥地利《航空先驱报》报道,由于两名中国乘客 2 日在从苏黎世飞往北京的航班上打架斗殴,飞机被迫返航。机上载有大约 200 名乘客,在空中飞行 6 个多小时后,于 2 日傍晚在苏黎世降落。

……

以上这些游客还不是严格意义上的跨文化交际,他们只是在异文化中以不当的方式采取行动,实现自己“不恰当”的个人目的,但是这样的群体对于中国人整体形象有损。在跨文化交际中,某些人的“小精明”“小把戏”可能暂时有助于他们实现短期的目标,但是长期下去一定会损害他们的长期利益。中国在改革开放的 30 年间,经济取得了长足的进步,但随着经济的发展,转型期的社会传统道德滑坡严重,唯利是图、不择手段、坑蒙拐骗甚至成为一些人走向“成功”的捷径和窍门了,骄横奢靡成为一部分人的不良生活方式,而正是这一部分比较成功的人,才更可能有更多的机会出国去旅游,去定居,或送子女去国外上学。这些人在与外国人的交往中,如果把在国内所依赖的不正当(甚至可以说不道德)的方式用来和外国人沟通的话,尽管如同在国内一样,也许他们能够实现他们暂时的沟通目的,但长远下去,不是行不通,就是丧失信用。在西方社会中,一个人如果失去了信用,就很难在一个崇尚信用的社会立足。从一定程度上讲,这种沟通效果是伤害最大的一种沟通方式。

三、结论

绝对客观公正地判断一次交际活动的效果到底如何，往往有一定的难度。有些效果是滞后的，有些效果还是溢价的；效果的判断还取决于评判者的立场，还会涉及道德伦理的问题。儒家思想的"中庸"之道，也是判断跨文化交际活动和交际能力的一个非常实用的准则。"中庸"的概念，"中"是适合，它不是一个量上的绝对平均值，而是意味着合适，既不过度，也非不及。"庸"是按照适宜的方式做事。而按照适宜的方式做事就可以长久，就是"善"。这和儒家思想中的"己所不欲，勿施于人"是一脉相承的，也是符合西方交际法则中的"黄金法则"的。"中庸精神"就是适度把握，按照适中方式做事，并力求保持在一个合情合理的范围之内，这是一个综合了方法方式和结果的检验标准，在这个原则指导下的跨文化交际活动，就会综合考虑方式的"适宜性"、"恰当性"、道义上的"合理性"，同时考虑到交际的效果。

参考书目：

[1]Edward Hall. 无声的语言[M]. 何道宽译. 北京：北京大学出版社，2010.

[2]肖群忠. 中国道德智慧十五讲[M]. 北京：北京大学出版社，2008.

[3]弥尔顿·贝内特编著. 跨文化交流的建构与实践[M]. 关世杰，何惺译. 北京：北京大学出版社，2012.

[4]Mitchell R. Hammer, "*Intercultural Communication Competence*" in *Handbook of International and Intercultural Communication*(ed), Molefi Kete Asante and William B. Gundykunst (Newbury Park, Calif. : Sage, 1989).

中国近现代英语教育的发展及其对汉语国际推广的启示
——文化和国际关系的视角

首都经济贸易大学外国语学院　赵海燕

摘　要：纵观英语教育在中国的兴衰沉浮，其受中国与英、美国家关系影响的背后更深层次的机理是中华文化与英美文化的作用关系，通过由此角度进行的分阶段探讨，在基本动力、战略目标、处理异文化间关系方面对汉语国际推广提出建议。

关键词：中国与英美关系；英语教育；汉语国际推广

Abstract: More than one hundred years' ups and downs of English education in China indicates that it is influenced by both the diplomatic and cultural relationship of China and western countries. Research done from this perspective gives the international extension of Chinese inspiration in regard to the basic stimulation, strategic target, and coping with the issues between different cultures.

Key Words: the diplomatic relationship between China, UK and America; English education; Internationale extension of Chinese

文化是语言的灵魂，外语教育因为涉及异文化的传播和影响往往与国际关系内在相关。从中华文化与英美关系的角度梳理我国英语教育的发展亦折射出中华文化对英美文化的"应激性"反应历程，本文分三个阶段进行探讨，以期对汉语国际推广有所启示。

一、鸦片战争前至北伐战争结束

鸦片战争前，工业文明在英、美先后兴起，其经贸自由扩张的本性与清政府"天

本文系北京市教委社科项目"文化触变与中国英语教育变迁研究"（项目编号：SM201510038013）阶段性研究成果。

作者简介：赵海燕（1972—　），女，山东单县人，首都经济贸易大学外国语学院副教授，硕士生导师，从事英语教育与文化触变、英语教育政策研究。

朝上国"的故步自封暂且在接触中相安,与之相随的基督教传教活动却在中国开始了早期的英语教育。1807 年,伦敦会传教士马礼逊来华,开始了基督教新教在我国的传播。进而 1836 年"马礼逊教育会"成立,1839 年马礼逊学校在澳门开办,是为侨民团体有组织地创办的在华第一所较大规模的教会学校。1830 年美国传教士禅治文在广州创办的贝满学校,则是在华开办的最早的教会学校,学校也开设英语课程。我国的英语教育发端于英国传教士在我国的传教活动。

鸦片战争始,西方工业文明的巨大冲击力震动了古老的中华传统文化,一向被视为"奇技淫巧"的坚船利炮、工业器物使清政府认识到差距和落后,在学习科技中促进了英语教育的发展。清政府在文化的器物、技术层面上兴起"洋务运动"以自强。1861 年,京师同文馆成立,这是我国学校正规英语教学的正式开端。19 世纪 60 至 70 年代,洋务派先后兴办了一批外语、军事和科技学校。甲午战后,清政府开始从文化的制度层面借鉴"西学"。1898 年,光绪帝除旧布新:兴办学堂,提倡西学,设立京师大学堂。1903 年颁布《奏定学堂章程》,要求中学堂以上各学堂均开设外语课。一般说来,我国大中学校普遍开设外语课开始于 1903 年。英语教育就此进入我国正规教育体制。1904 年,"癸卯学制"在全国实施,这是我国实施的第一个近代学制,标志着封建教育体制的解体,学堂英语教育从此进入全面发展时期。甲午战后,东效日本、整顿书院、改革学制、将英语教育纳入正规教育体制,是中国从制度层面图强所做出的努力。

这一时期,英、美相继作为世界第一强国对中国的思想文化(意识形态)保持强大的影响,传教活动逐步组织化,教会学校客观上大大推动了中国英语教育发展。19 世纪末 20 世纪初,中国教育存在三种形式的学校:传统的科举制书院和私塾、清政府官办的各种学堂、外国传教士创办的教会学校。其中,发展最快、影响最大和教学效果最好的可能是教会学校。教会在发展英语教育上发挥着主要作用,但其真正目的并不是为了促进中国英语教育的发展,而是出于使中国彻底基督化的需要。

甲午战后,美国逐渐取代英国成为英美对华关系中的主导力量。美国人认为自己的国家是最民主、最自由、最进步的,把自己的社会制度传播到其他国家是不可推卸的责任。这种从文化中延伸出的实力外交和十字军情怀对未来的中美关系亦产生了深远影响。对本国民主制度近乎宗教情结的信仰,使其把"教育"作为改变中国的战略性手段,20 世纪初"退款兴学"计划的实施使美国对中国的思想影响迅速扩大,使中国教育学制和教学"远日近美",扩大了英语教育对日语教育的优势。1922 年民国政府实行"新学制",从模仿日本为主变为模仿英美为主。1927

年,国民党在南京建立的全国性政权确立了英美在中国的“榜样”性影响。

保持和扩大在华“自由贸易”的权益,是英、美19世纪对华关系的主轴,有力地带动了英美特别是美国在思想文化、政治文化方面对华影响力的增强和深入。英语教育也因此确立了对其他外语语种教育的在华优势地位。

二、南京国民党政府成立至新中国与苏联交恶

南京国民党政府成立后全面发展与美英的关系,一方面借以遏制日本的侵略,并消除共产主义在中国的影响,另一方面试图以美国为蓝本在中国建立一个资产阶级民主共和国。

1941年太平洋战争爆发,这一时期美国对华外交政策基点就是“扶蒋、容共、抗日”。反对共同的敌人,维护各自国家、民族的利益,维护世界和平,成为“二战”时期中美关系的主要特点。

当时中国对英语课是很重视的,这从一般中学的英语教学课时就可以反映出来。1936年颁布的《中学英语课程标准》规定,初中每周有英语4课时,高中有5课时,6年合计972课时。浓厚的半殖民地氛围成为社会时尚,学生接触英美文化的机会很多,学校里的数理化等学科很多采用英美原版教材,英文报刊很多。因此,相当一部分学生在中学阶段即完成了听说能力的培养,上大学后主要提高阅读和翻译能力。至于高等学校,英语专业主要是学习英国文学。另外,教会大学都采用直接法进行英语教学。

1949年新中国成立后抗美援朝,中美开始长期直接对抗,中国采取向苏联“一边倒”的政策。中国英语教育受到深刻影响。当时国家的外语政策是推进俄语教育,至1954年,俄语几乎成为学校唯一的外国语。外语教育上的“一边倒”形成了。

20世纪60年代,中苏交恶。1956年7月,教育部下达《关于中学外国语科的通知》,扭转了新中国成立以来忽视英语教育的偏向,这个通知在我国解放后的外语教育中占有重要的地位,是建国以来英语教育的转折点。英语教育在国家建设的需求下受到普遍重视。1962年,英语被正式列为高考科目。

这是一个拿来主义的时期,美式民主共和、苏式共产主义的思想文化(意识形态)先后在“虔诚”的中国确立统治地位,中美关系也从“蜜月”转折至“冰冻”,相应地英语教育在中国亦经历了天壤之别的两种境遇。但是,即便在新中国“一边倒”的时期,英语教育也实现了显著的复苏,这是因为参与国际交往以发展本国的基本需求起到了原动力性质的作用。历史证明,对外来思想文化(意识形态)“虔诚”地采取拿来主义以复制社会制度是行不通的,在文化、教育等领域还往往由于主观绝

对化导致偏颇和损害。英语教育去“意识形态化”势在必行。

三、新中国与苏联交恶至今

中苏关系破裂后,中国在一定程度上对西方国家实行开放政策,英语得到重视。1963 年,周总理几次出访亚洲,提升了中国的国际地位,也进一步加速了英语的教学规模。1964 年 10 月,教育部颁布《外语教育七年规划纲要》,“在学校教育中确定提出:英语为第一外语,学习英语的人数要大量增加。”至此,英语教育在全国“复兴”。

1966 年至 1976 年“文革”期间,英语教育严重滑坡。由于 1971 年中国恢复联合国合法席位及国内政治形势的暂时好转,1972 年和 1975 年外语曾一度受到重视,不少地区编写了一些英语教材。这一时期的英语教材虽不少,但总体上课文题材偏重于政治内容。

1972 年尼克松访华,中美关系开始正常化。1979 年 1 月 1 日,中美正式建交。期间,1972 年 3 月,中英正式建交。这都是对世界战略格局和中国未来发展具有深远影响的重大战略决策。中美建交后,中美合作取得实质性进展。期间,国内“民族虚无主义”“全盘西化”思潮泛起,加之以国际条件,形成“八九风波”,中美关系迅速恶化。此后 20 余年,几经周折较量,在反复、严峻的考验下,中美关系逐渐恢复和改善,且随着中国综合国力的不断跃升,中美合作有所加强。但由于美国的民主原教旨主义情结,中美始终处于战略对抗状态。

1977 年我国恢复高考制度,1978 年,全国外语教育座谈会在北京召开,提出英语教育从小学开始的“一条龙”计划。英语教育进入国家的战略视野,英语成为我国国民教育体系中覆盖面最广、历时最长的一门学科。1983 年,英语完全计入高考总分,中学英语教育由复苏转入正规。1985 年 5 月《中共中央关于教育体制改革的决定》中将外语学科定为中学阶段 3 门主要基础学科之一。大学英语从 1987 年 9 月开始第一次四级考试,1989 年开始第一次六级考试,这项全国统一的英语测试极大地推动了英语教育在我国的快速深入发展。英语水平与升学、毕业、就业、晋升等之间日益紧密的联系家喻户晓。英语社会培训成长为一个巨大的产业。一定意义上,中国进入“全民学英语”时代。正是在这样的背景下,我国成为世界首屈一指的贸易大国。

这一时期,中国开始独立探索社会主义建设道路与规律,逐步开启、发展与以美国为首的西方国家的关系。在经历了“文化大革命”的历史性“试错”之后,中国走上了改革开放的发展道路,逐步建立和完善社会主义市场经济体制,经济和科技实力迅速增长,综合国力大幅度提升,形成中国特色社会主义理论体系。英语教育在“文革”期间严重滑坡主要是因为当时教育领域是受“文革”影响的重灾区,意识形态因素并不是主要的,而“八九风波”后中美之间的再次严重对抗并没有对中国英语教育的深入快速发展造成任何影响,说明中国英语教育彻底摆脱了意识形态的羁绊,进入了完全以国家发展需要为引导的成熟、稳定的发展阶段。这也从一个侧面体现了中国对自己的社会制度、发展道路、思想文化日益增强的自信心,以及“中国模式”的日臻成形。

四、对汉语国际推广的启示

英语教育在中国的兴衰沉浮受中国与英美国家关系影响的背后更深层次的机理是中华文化与英美文化的作用关系。近代以来,在西方率先工业化、现代化的冲击下,我国传统文化遭受了质疑甚至是否定,成为被蔑视、被批判、被革命的对象。特别是建国后的强势反帝反封,不但敌视英美文化,也推动了对被认为是“封建糟粕”的传统文化的彻底清算,使系统的传统文化教育在国民教育中几乎销声匿迹。

然而,中华文化毕竟具有作为世界主要原生文明延绵发展的历史和思想底蕴。经过一百多年的探索和实践,我国已经找到符合中国国情的现代化道路并取得了重大进展,发展模式逐渐成熟和稳定,民族自信心极大增强;“国学热”随之兴起,中国现代社会和传统文化之间的血肉联系被“自然地”梳理和修复,古老的中华文化经过痛苦的涅槃再获新生,其在世界上的影响力将不断增强,成为与英美文化对等交流、平等发展的世界主要文化。

2011 年 10 月 18 日《中共中央关于深化文化体制改革推动社会主义文化大发展大繁荣若干重大问题的决定》指出:要“增强中华文化在世界上的感召力和影响力”“加强海外中国文化中心和孔子学院建设”。汉语国际推广作为传播中华文化的核心平台具有重大的战略意义。纵观英语在中国近 200 年的“国际推广”,其对新兴的汉语国际推广有如下启示。

(一)汉语国际推广的基本动力是国际贸易需求

长期以来,英、美对华关系的基本政策是创造、保持和扩大在华“自由贸易”利益,而伴随贸易扩张主义的则是殖民主义、文化帝国主义的意识和行为。英语教育在我国的发展证明,只有国际贸易需求才最稳定、持久,因而是最基本的动力。我国经济、科技实力持续稳定增强,已成为国际贸易增长的主要引擎,增强国际贸易话语权,是汉语国际推广最深厚的力量源泉。相应地,汉语作为一种“外语资源”,其经济价值得以不断提升。

（二）汉语国际推广的战略目标是实现汉语教育目的国“本土化”

历史上，英、美特别是美国在中国推行各种形式的英语教育是在战略层面上进行的，而英语教育在中国的最终生根、兴旺却是在英语教育举国规模的本土化形成之时，具有讽刺意味的是，同时也是中国抵制美国民主原教旨主义，成功实践“中国模式”之时。汉语国际推广的活力和生命力在于汉语教育逐步在目的国“本土化”。应避免意识形态色彩，在满足目的国民众对汉语教育的现实市场需求的基础上，引导、开发进一步的需求以扩大相应的供应，并在这个过程中实现教材编制、师资力量的本地化。“本土化”的最终目标是使汉语教育纳入目的国的国家教育体制。

（三）汉语国际推广应注重处理好异文化间的关系问题

英美文化霸权像幽灵一样或隐或现地游荡于我国英语教育发展之中。“己所不欲，勿施于人。”汉语国际推广必然伴随着异文化间的碰撞与交流，如何尊重和研究目的国及其汉语学习者的文化背景，深入体察其文化心理，实践中华文化的“和合”理念，化碰撞为交流，对汉语国际推广者的素质要求是很高的，因而，对其的培养和选拔应秉持“宁缺毋滥”，力戒“鱼龙混杂”。更为重要的是，随着汉语国际推广深入实施，汉语客观上所承载的价值观念、思维方式和文化传统将如何参与重构世界新秩序，我们现在就应该做好理论与政策的准备。

参考文献：

[1]李良佑等．中国英语教学史[M]．上海：上海外语教育出版社，2004.

[2]顾卫星．晚清传教士关于教会学校英语教学的争论[J]．解放军外国语学院学报，2002(01).

[3]王晓德．梦想与现实[M]．北京：中国社会科学出版社，1995.

[4]陶文钊，杨奎松，王建朗．抗日战争时期中国对外关系[M]．北京：中共党史出版社，1995.

[5]熊寅谷．我国外语教学今昔谈[J]．贵州大学学报(社会科学版)，1986(06).

[6]胡文仲．我国外语教育规划的得与失[J]．外语教学与研究，2001(04).

语言学与翻译研究

一源论与多源论

——语系亲缘关系研究的跨学科发展

首都经济贸易大学外国语学院　陈媛媛

摘　要:语言起源的问题一直是语言学领域的一个热门问题。关于人类语言的起源是否具有共同的渊源,人们一直争议不断。无论是一源论还是多源论,究其根本都是人类各语系之间是否具有亲缘关系之争。语言学家就这一方面已经进行了长久的努力和探讨,并提供了纯语言的物质材料作为解答该问题的证据。随着语言学之外的各学科不断发展,他们各自的研究结果也为语言起源的问题提供了其他的直接或间接的证据。这些证据在受到质疑的同时,也为语言学进一步解答语言起源之争提供了更多更有价值的视角和思路,也提供了语言学学科本身所缺乏的技术手段。本文通过对语言起源问题多学科研究进行梳理,旨在说明解决语言起源的一源论还是多源论论证需要超越单一语言学学科界限,借助其他学科研究最新成果互相印证才能得出更令人信服的结论。

关键词:语言起源;一源论;多源论;研究方法;跨学科

Abstract: Origin of language has always been a hot issue in the field of linguistics. Scholars have constantly argued about whether there is a common origin or several different origins of human languages throughout the world. The fundamental point of either single-origin theory or multi-origin theory is actually about the kinship between language families. Linguists have long been studying and discussing this issue, and have provided purely linguistic materials as evidence for their opinions. With the development of the subjects outside linguistics, their research results also provide direct or indirect evidence for the origin of languages. Even some evidence may have been brought into question; it certainly has provided more perspectives and technological means for the issue of the origin of languages. This paper reviews the interdisciplinary studies on this issue and concludes that more convincing claim can only be made when the study goes beyond the subject of linguistics and corroboratesits results with the latest research results of other subjects.

Key Words: origin of languages; one-origin theory; multi-origin theory; research method; interdiscipline

一、语言起源之争:论题的学科化

语言起源的问题一直是语言学领域的一个热门论题。早在1772年,德国赫尔德曾因发表《论语言学的起源》获得柏林科学院的奖励。尽管1986年巴黎语言学会成立时明文规定了不接受关于语言的起源方面研究,使之成为语言学研究的一个禁区,但是,1972年召开了第一届语言起源和发展北美会议,并于1983年在加拿大专门成立了国际语言起源和进化学会(Language Origins Society)。由此,语言起源问题的研究成为包括语言学、人类学、考古学、心理学、生物学等诸多学科共同研究的话题,并取得一系列的研究成果。人类语言的起源是否具有共同的渊源,人们一直争议不断。长久以来,人们对于人类语言的起源就一直有一源论和多源论之争。尽管语言起源研究已经从早期的假设臆想阶段发展到实证研究阶段,但就目前的研究阶段以及各学说提出的证据来看,无论是一源论还是多源论的结论都仍属于假说,需要提出更有力的证据,并进行实证研究。一源论认为,人类语言出于同一来源,只是随着人类社会的不断变迁才发生出各种差异,导致今天我们看到的各种语言呈现出纷繁多样的特点。比如20世纪初,意大利语言学家Trombetti(特龙贝蒂)发表的《论语言来源的统一性》通过词根证明世界语言的一源。Swadesh(斯沃德什)也提出了一源论主张,认为不同语言存在亲缘关系。Ruhlen(鲁伦)也支持一元论观点,他通过比较不同语族的同源词,认为世界上语言有一个共同始祖语。而多源论则认为,世界上的各语系之间并无亲缘关系,他们各出自不同渊源的始祖语。早期的语言学家尤其是欧洲的语言学家大多支持多源论观点。尽管这两种说法看似完全对立,但究其研究思路和方法,本质上还是按照各语系之间的亲缘关系为依据,只是结论不同而已。

二、传统语言学的研究方法:历史比较语言学

按照历史比较语言学的研究,从20世纪50年代开始,语系之间的亲缘关系开始成为研究的热点问题。该学科以语系之间的亲缘关系为基础,建立起语言的语系分类。后又提出证据证明各语系之间存在着遥远的亲缘关系,从而又提出了各种超语系假说,将许多语系又包含在这些更大的超语系之中。从20世纪初开始,语言学家开始对语系亲缘关系的研究成果进行总结。20世纪50年代出现了诺斯特拉超语系,该语系被认为是印欧、亚非、卡尔特维、乌拉尔、阿尔泰、达罗毗荼语共同的始祖语。该超级语系的首创者是丹麦语言学家H. Petersen(皮特森),他于1903年提出,到了50年代末,由苏联语言学家Illich-Svitych(斯维图切)发扬光大。

到了80年代,美国语言学家Greenberg(格林伯格)又提出了欧亚超语系说。而诺斯特拉超语系应该是包含欧亚超语系的更大的语系。后来,又有学者提出高加索—汉藏—纳德奈超语系说,他们认为分布在东亚、东南亚、南亚的汉藏语系和欧洲东南的北高加索语系,以及美国和加拿大的纳德奈语系之间可能有亲缘关系。此后,又有学者陆陆续续地提出证据,证明印第安各语系之间、撒哈拉以南非洲的土著语言之间、澳洲土著语言之间,都存在着亲缘关系,可以各自成为一种超语系。

如此种种的语系间亲缘关系,遵循的都是传统的语言学研究方法,主要的考察依据是不同的语言内部是否存在相同或同源的语言物质材料。这些语言物质材料可以积累各语言同源的证据,如果证据充分有力,我们就可以假定人类语言出于同源,反之则不然。Ruhlen就曾列举过一些语言材料的例子,来证明这些语系间的亲缘关系。他的例证大致可以划分为几个类别:第一类可以总结为相同词根,意义相近。比如,为原始澳大利亚语构拟的词根bungu,表示膝盖。在现代的澳大利亚语言中,均可见到由此词根引申出的词汇,用来表示可以弯曲的事物。第二类可以总结为语音相近,意义相同。比如,表示数量“二”的词义,在东南亚所有主要的语言中发音基本相同。第三类可以总结为疑问词相似。比如,为原始澳大利亚语构拟的疑问词“什么”为minnha,在现代澳大利亚语言中均发现类似的词汇,如第而巴语中的“什么”为minya,皮塔—皮塔语种的“什么”则为minha,不一而足。此外,还有一类证据是语言类型学的证据。语言类型学证据主要考察的特征包括语音(有无某些元音等)、句子语序、代词含义差异等。根据Ruhlen的调查发现,以上几类语言材料都可以为语系的亲缘关系提供证据。

关于语言起源的研究,根据Aitchison(艾奇逊)的划分,目前有三种研究方法:亲属比较法、地区比较法、相似点比较法。其中,亲属比较法主要的研究依据是同源词。例如,上文提到的始于丹麦语言学家H. Petersen、盛于苏联语言学家Illich-Svitych的诺斯特拉超语系,就是根据印欧语、乌拉尔语、阿尔泰语、亚非语、达罗毗荼等语中的同源词,确定这些语系同属于一种始祖语,即诺斯特拉超语系。地区比较法主要的研究依据是相同的语言特点在不同地区的分布呈现出渐变的趋势。相似点比较法的研究依据是找出在词形词义上具有相似性的词,并由此建立语言之间的亲缘关系。根据Greenberg的划分,世界上所有5 000多种语言大致可归为12个远古语族。Ruhlen则根据Greenberg划分的这12种语族,分析了其中的同源词。他发现,这些语族中至少有几十个相似的词根,这也为世界语言一源论提供了一定的证据。

但是,坚持世界语言多源论的语言学家,以欧洲的历史比较语言学家为主,认为印欧语并无亲缘语言,因此不可能与其他语言有共同的始祖语。坚持世界语言一源论的语言学家,则认为多源论观点存在很大问题。

三、非语言学证据:分子生物学方法

语言学领域之外的学科不断发展,也为人类语言起源的问题提供了间接的证据。人类学等学科认为,民族与语言不可分割,民族与语言具有相互印证、相互识别的作用。因此,可以通过探讨人类起源的一源性与多源性来论证世界上不同语言之间的关系以及来源问题。

20 世纪开始,人类一直在寻求人类起源问题的科学答案并形成了众多理论(古人类学、考古学、宗教学等)。80 年代以来,随着现代分子生物学 DNA(基因)技术的发展,研究者提出了一个新的现代人类起源理论即“夏娃”理论。“夏娃”理论是分子生物学 DNA 技术发展的产物。20 世纪,人们发现了细胞中的线粒体。1963 年,线粒体 DNA 被发现在许多方面不同于细胞核 DNA。最重要的是,线粒体 DNA 的遗传方式十分独特,即严格的母系遗传。子代的线粒体 DNA 只来自母方,父方的线粒体 DNA 不会遗传给子代。

80 年代,美国加州大学伯克莱分校的威尔逊遗传小组研究了世界不同种族居民的线粒体 DNA,他们发现全人类的线粒体 DNA 基本相同,差异很少。因此,从逻辑上说,现代世界各民族的线粒体 DNA 最终都是从一个共同的女性祖先那儿遗传下来的。威尔逊小组通过追溯不同种族线粒体 DNA 的原型,确定了现代人类线粒体 DNA 的发展谱系。他们得出现代人类的线粒体 DNA 均来自非洲的一位女性,她是人类各种族的共同祖先。威尔逊等人说,“可以将这位幸运的女性称为夏娃,她的世系一直延续至今。”这一理论被称为“夏娃”理论。同时,研究也通过人群中的线粒体 DNA 的差异即线粒体 DNA 中所积累的突变方式证明非洲人是最早出现的现代人类。威尔逊等人认为,当时的非洲其他同“夏娃”同时代女性并没有留下女性后裔,其线粒体 DNA 谱系就断了,只有“夏娃”的女性后裔代代繁衍,成为现代人类的祖先。威尔逊小组根据线粒体 DNA 核苷酸替换率推算,这位人类的共同祖先“夏娃”应当生活在 14 万至 19 万年之前,大概在 9 万至 18 万年之前,她的一些后代离开非洲迁徙到世界各地,并没有与当地土著的古人类混合交融,而是“完全取代了”他们,最终发展为现代世界各地居民。夏娃理论也遭到很多学科的挑战。1984 年,中科院院士吴新智和美国密歇根大学的沃尔波夫、澳大利亚国立大学的索恩共同撰文,提出“多地区进化说”,通过各地的化石等考古学材料来证明现代人类是在 4 个地区出现并连续进化,而且在各个地区之间都有基因交流。以华盛顿大学的坦普列顿为代表的一些分子生物学家也指出夏娃理论在计算机程序及计算方法上的错误。这场讨论至今尚在热烈进行中。但无论结果如何,多学科讨论将有助于更进一步认识人类的起源问题。

因此,如果现代人类共同起源于非洲,那么人类的语言也应该拥有共同的起源,这就为人类语言一源论提供了有力的佐证。20 世纪 80 年代以来,越来越多的学者开始接受一源论的主张。然而,根据考古学等学科的发现,现在很难明确走出非洲的早期智人是否已经具备相应的语言能力,因此,很难证明人类出走非洲之时是否就有语言并保持语言的连贯性(一源论)还是早期智人在走出非洲后再形成不同语言的(多源论)。

四、“奠基者效应”:综合实证研究方法

2011 年 4 月 15 日第 332 期的《科学》杂志上,刊登了一篇《语音多样性支持语言从非洲扩张的系列奠基者效应》的文章。该文章的作者是 Quentin D. Atkinson(阿特金森),就职于奥克兰大学心理学系以及牛津大学认知与进化人类学中心。生物学上的奠基者效应指的是,随着人类的迁移,人类活动范围向外扩张,人类遗传的多样性就会慢慢衰减。奠基者效应被用来证明现代人类起源于非洲的这一理论。Atkinson 认为,类似的奠基者效应理论还可以用来研究人类文明和语言的起源。为此,他采用世界 504 种语言作为样本,对所有这些语言中的音素(phonemes)进行分析,发现这些语言的音素也呈现出和世界人类基因类似的渐变群分布。因此,Atkinson 得出结论,奠基者效应也可以用来证明现代人类语言的起源在非洲。

Atkinson 的研究方法大致如下:他按照《世界语言结构地图集》(World Atlas of Language Structures),根据其地理位置的不同,以及语言分布、语言分类和人口统计学,研究了世界 504 种语言在原音、辅音、音调三个方面的差异。他使用概率统计的方法,证明语言距离非洲越远,语言的音素多样性就越低。按照地理位置的差异,音素多样性由多至少的地区分别是:非洲、亚洲、欧洲、北美、南美、大洋洲。这样一来,人类语言音素多样性的渐变图就和人类基因多样性表现出一致性。尽管人类社会在发展过程中会发生各种影响语言的社会语言学的事件,但该研究得出的数据模式有力地反映了人类语言几千年来的稳固发展,也反映出人类从非洲大迁移的时间梯度。

值得一提的是,复旦大学现代人类学教育部重点实验室的王传超等人,对 Atkinson 的文章提出了质疑,并在 2012 年 2 月 10 日第 335 期《科学》杂志上发表名为《反驳“语音多样性支持语言从非洲扩张的系列奠基者效应”》一文。在本文中,王传超通过对 95 个语系中 579 种语言的语音进行分析,认为语音的多样性分布反映的并不是现代人类的起源,而是人类第二次大扩张,其扩张的中心在亚洲中南部

的里海南岸。根据遗传学的分析,人类第二次大扩张可能发生于两万至四万年以前,涉及世界各个地区,并形成了现代种族的格局。随着人类的不断迁徙,人类的语言也会不断发生变化,主要体现在语法、语音和词汇等方面。其中语音(包括元音、辅音、音调)的变化最有规律。根据语音多样性的分布差异,王传超认为现代语言最近的扩散中心就在里海。

尽管王传超对 Atkinson 的文章进行了反驳,但需要注意的是,他选择的研究方法与 Atkinson 并无大异。他们都是利用生物统计学和生物信息学的方法分析语言材料,同时也都支持语言起源一源性。这种将生物学与语言学结合的综合性实证研究方法将开启一个全新的领域,为语言学跨学科提供新机遇。

由于《科学》杂志上刊登的关于人类语言的文章多以计算机统计的方法为研究基础,所以多引发语言学家的批评。因此,Atkinson 的文章出版之后,也旋即引发了一系列的讨论和批评。以挪威卑尔根大学外国语言学院的 Aleksandrs Berdicevskis 和俄罗斯国立莫斯科大学 Alexander Ch. Piperski 为代表的语言学家针对 Atkinson 的文章提出了批评(发表于 2011 年 12 月 8 日的《科学》杂志)。他们认为,Atkinson 把一种语言中音素的数量和它与非洲的距离做了不当的关联,由此得出音素多样性可适用奠基者效应、人类语言起源于非洲的结论也是不当的。首先,他们认为 Atkinson 所做的语言音素的变化适用生物学的奠基者效应这一假设过于鲁莽。Atkinson 所提供的证据或是难以验证,或是过分依赖推测。其中唯一可行的关联就是现代语言人口数量以及该语言中音素数量的关系。但即使是这两者之间也没有必然的因果联系,特别是当该语言的人口数量如果有大的变动的话,音素的数量是否会发生相应的变化尚不得而知。他们还认为,当奠基者人口从母体人口脱离出来的时候,如果语言中的音素有所丢失,Atkinson 并没有为这些丢失的音素提供任何可信服的解释。小语种应该比大语种更复杂这一假说也与奠基者效应的假设有所冲突。第二点,语言学家担心 Atkinson 的数据和研究方法存在偏见。就数据而言,不同语言学领域的学者,其语法描述的传统和特点也各有不同。就研究方法而言,语言学家则质疑 Atkinson 对于音素多样性(辅音、元音、音调)各部分研究的比重是否恰当。

五、总结

总体而言,语言起源这一问题已经不仅仅局限于语言学这一领域了。仅仅依靠语言学家对语言本身做纯语言物质的分析,已不足以解答人类长久以来关于语言起源的好奇与疑惑。目前,关于语言起源的研究已经呈现出多学科交叉的特点。

人类学、语言学、民族学、遗传学、分子生物学、考古学、解剖学、文化学、认知科学、神经生理学等多学科相互合作,为解答人类语言这一终极问题提供了多方面的视角。各学科提供各自的证据,可以相互验证,也可以为彼此提供有益的思路。此外,语言学作为人文学科,也可以借鉴自然科学等学科的技术手段,弥补自身有限的观察力。因为没有计算机的协助,传统语言学很难在浩如烟海的原始语言材料中归纳总结出蕴含其中的语言规律和模式。因此,现代语言研究的跨学科研究表现出广阔的前景,新一代研究者需要扩大视野和思路,善于借鉴不同学科的研究方法,为语言学的跨学科发展做出贡献。

参考文献:

[1]Quentin D. Atkinson. *Phonemic Diversity Supports a Serial Founder Effect Model of Language Expansion from Africa*[J]. Science vol. 332,2011.

[2]Wang-Chuan Chao, Qi-Liang Ding, Huan Tao, Hui Li. *Comment on "Phonemic Diversity Supports a Serial Founder Effect Model of Language Expansion from Africa"*[J]. Science vol. 335,2012.

[3]Aitchison J. *The Seeds of Speech: Language Origin and Evolution*[M]. Beijing: Foreign Language Teaching and Research Press,2002.

[4]Greenberg Joseph H. *The Languages of Africa*[M]. Bloomington: Indiana University Press,1963.

[5]Greenberg Joseph H. *Languages in the Americas*[M]. Stanford, CA: Stanford University Press,1987.

[6]Ruhlen Merritt. *A Guide to the World's Languages*. V. 1: Classification. CA: Stanford University Press,1987.

[7]Ruhlen Merritt. *The Origin of Language: Tracing the Evolution of the Mother Tongue*[M]. New York: John Wiley & Sons,1994.

[8]Cann, R. L., Stoneking, M. & Wilson, A. C. *Mitochondrial DNA and human evolution*[J]. Nature 325,1987.

[9]袁眉. 语言起源研究综述[J]. 重庆交通大学学报(社科版),2009(10).

[10]王钢. 语言起源的一源论[J]. 外语教学与研究,1994(2).

[11]周流溪."语言起源的一源论"书后[J]. 外语教学与研究,1994(2).

[12]陈保亚. 人类起源于非洲? 从语言起源看非洲假说[J]. 科学中国人,2002(5).

从范畴类型逻辑看蒙太格语法的被动转换规则

首都经济贸易大学外国语学院　崔佳悦

摘　要:蒙太格语法是对范畴语法的继承,其句法规则采纳的是"毗连运算"这种遵循范畴语法函项应用原则的操作。但是在蒙太格语法中体现转换操作的扩展规则那里似乎看不到范畴语法的作用,扩展的转换规则是否遵循范畴语法的规律?本文针对这个问题,以蒙太格语法对英语被动句——"结构被动句"的分析为例,从范畴语法的现代版本——范畴类型逻辑的视角来审视蒙太格语法的转换过程,获得的结论是:范畴类型逻辑提供的工具可以证明被动句转换的合理性,蒙太格语法扩展的转换规则同样遵循了范畴语法的规律。

关键词:蒙太格语法;转换规则;范畴语法;范畴类型逻辑

Abstract: Montague grammar (MG) is the inheritance of categorial grammar (CG), its syntactic rules adopted "concatenation" which strictly follows functor applying rule of CG. But CG seems played no role in extension rule of MG which embodied transformation. Whether extended transformational rule keep to rules of CG is a problem. This paper make analysis of structural passive sentences in English by using MG as examples to interpret transformational process of MG in the perspective of categorial type logic (CTL)—modern stage of development of CG. Actually, the tool provided by CTL can be used to prove the rationality from active sentences to passive sentences, the extended transformational rule of MG also follows law of CG.

Key Words: Montague Grammar; Transformational Rule; Categorial Grammar (CG); Categorial Type Logic (CTL)

转换生成语法(Transformational Generative Grammar,简称 TG)由美国著名语言学家乔姆斯基(N. Chomsky)在 20 世纪 50 年代创立。半个多世纪以来,TG 成为国内外语言学领域中最有影响的语言学理论之一,TG 的提出被誉为语言学界的"哥白尼似的革命"。TG 的主要不足是缺乏关于自然语言语义的系统理论,而蒙太格

本文写作受助于国家社科基金重大课题"自然语言信息处理的逻辑语义学研究"(10&ZD073)。
本文为语言与逻辑的跨学科研究,发表于《湖北大学学报(社科版)》。

语法(Montague Grammar,简称 MG)为弥补这个欠缺,给自然语言的句法生成配置了语义的描写。MG 句法规则的基本操作“毗连运算”来源于范畴语法(Categorical Grammar,简称 CG)的函项应用原则,但 MG 对 TG 转换规则的描述似乎从中看不到 CG 的作用。因此 MG 是否完全遵循 CG 的规律是令人质疑的。本文针对这一问题,通过被动句转换的具体实例,用范畴类型逻辑(Categorical Type Logics,简称 CTL)①所提供的工具证明:MG 刻画转换的扩展规则同样遵循了 CG 的规律,而 CG 是适合于计算的语法理论,本文的工作是从计算机信息处理角度审视 MG 转换规则的研究结果。

一、相关背景

(一) 蒙太格语法

蒙太格语法 MG 是美国逻辑学家理查德·蒙太格(Richard Montague)用数理逻辑方法研究自然语言的形式语义学理论。MG 的研究提供了将句法的生成与语义的组合相对应的模式,受到越来越多的语言学和哲学家的关注,与 MG 及形式语义学相关的学术著作和学术论文不断出版和发表。托马森(Thomason)的 *Formal Philosophy*(1974)和帕蒂(Partee)主编的 *Montague grammar*(1976)等著述对蒙太格语法的早期推广起到了非常重要的作用。道蒂(David R. Dowty)的 *Word meaning and Montague grammar*(1979)和道蒂、华尔、皮特斯(Stanley Peters)合著的 *Introduction to Montague Semantics*(1981),以 Gamut 命名的荷兰学者合著的 *Logic, Language, and Meaning*(1991),卡恩(Cann)的 *Formal Semantics: An Introduction*(1993)等著述在学术界都负有盛名。近年在由荷兰著名学者范·本瑟姆(Benthem)和穆伦(Meulen)主编的鸿篇巨制 *Handbook of Logic and Language*(2011)中,MG 作为首篇被系统深入地阐释。

蒙太格语法来源于乔姆斯基的转换生成语法,基于转换生成语法确立了蒙太格语法的句法部分。在著名的 PTQ 英语部分语句系统中蒙太格共制定了 17 条句法规则 S_{1-17},其中有基本规则($S_1 \sim S_3$)、函项应用规则($S_4 \sim S_{10}$)、合取与析取规则($S_{11} \sim S_{13}$)、量化规则($S_{14} \sim S_{16}$),最后一类是时态与记号规则(S_{17})。②

然而蒙太格语法句法规则中的句法操作却遵循了范畴语法的原则。我们以语句系统中第二类函项运用的规则 S_4和 S_5为例:

S_4. 若 $\alpha \in P_T$且 $\beta \in P_{IV}$,则 $F_4(\alpha,\beta) \in P_t$。而 $F_4(\alpha,\beta) = \alpha\beta'$,并且 β'是把 β 中

---

① 范畴类型逻辑是范畴语法发展的最新阶段,扩大了范畴语法的表达力。

② 邹崇理(2000):《自然语言逻辑研究》,北京大学出版社。

的第一个动词置换成它的现在时第三人称单数而得到的结果。

S_5. 若 $\alpha \in P_{TV}$ 且 $\beta \in P_T$,则 $F_5(\alpha,\beta) \in P_{IV}$。这里若 $\beta \neq he_n$,$F_5(\alpha,\beta) = \alpha\beta$;若 $\beta = he_n$,$F_5(\alpha,\beta) = \alpha him_n$。

上述两条规则中的句法操作 F_4 和 F_5 体现了范畴语法的思想。这里句法操作的作用是把两个表达式毗连在一起,被毗连的两个表达式其中一个属于函子范畴,而另一个属于主目范畴。如"$F_4(\alpha,\beta) = \alpha\beta'$"中 α 可以是专名"John",所属的函子范畴是 $S/(NP\backslash S)$,β 可以是动词"walk",所属的主目范畴是 $NP\backslash S$,$\alpha\beta'$ 就是句子"John walks",所属的结果范畴是 S。S_4 告诉我们:由 α 和 β 进行毗连得 $\alpha\beta'$,其背后隐藏着函子范畴 S/(NP\S)对主目范畴 NP\S 向前运算得到结果范畴 S 的过程,这里的句法操作体现出范畴语法最基本的运算规律——函项应用原则。

蒙太格语法是转换生成语法的延续继承。针对 PTQ 系统的句法规则只能产生 TG 转换生成语法所谓的核心句(基本句式)这个局限,Partee 等学者做了大量的、多方面的工作,扩展了 MG 的表达力,使 MG 能够进一步生成 TG 转换部分获得的非核心句(如被动句)。Partee 对 MG 的修正有:将蒙太格句法规则使用的语符串(strings)表述方式改为加标括号(labeled bracket)式的表述;更重要的是创立了 6 条扩展规则来描述 TG 的转换内容,据此获得自然语言的被动、施事主语省略、宾语提升和主语提升等一系列转换句式①。而 Partee 的学生 Bennett 则充分拓宽了 MG 的句法规则,分为:基本规则(3 条),函项应用规则(18 条),被动转换规则(6 条),合取析取规则(1 条),否定规则(4 条),量化规则(3 条),共 35 条。其中的被动规则对被动句的主语施事和宾语受事的位置调换这一现象缺乏描述,整个转换过程的刻画不够完整。

蒙太格语法在自然语言的句法分析方面较转换生成语法更严谨、逻辑性更强。乔姆斯基的转换生成语法是蒙太格语法的来源理论,后者胜过前者的原因除了有在句法基础上添加了语义描述外,还在于后者的句法分析建立在与自然语言信息处理密切相关的范畴语法基础上,其句法规则所体现的"毗连运算"操作是范畴语法的核心——函项应用原则。然而,MG 描述转换思想的扩展规则跟范畴语法的关系尚不明朗,是否也是建立在范畴语法的基础上,或者说,转换规则刻画的过程是否同样遵循范畴语法的规律尚需论证。

(二)范畴语法和范畴类型逻辑

范畴语法是适合于计算的语法理论,其思想最初源于弗雷格(A. Frege),其完

① Barbara H. Partee (1976) Montague Grammar. Academic Press: New York.

整的表述归功于20世纪30年代的波兰逻辑学家列斯尼夫斯基(Lesniewski)和爱裘凯维茨(Ajduciewcz)①,50年代初美国计算语言学家希勒尔(B. Hillel)出于机器翻译的需要发展了范畴语法。50年代末数学家兰贝克(J. Lambek)提出范畴语法的演算系统。

在范畴语法看来,自然语言分为两个基本范畴:名称范畴NP和句子范畴S,由这两个基本范畴派生出其他范畴;自然语言由小到大的生成可以通过其构成部分所属范畴的逐级运算来实现。范畴运算的规则有:

(1)若α是属于范畴B/A的表达式并且β是属于范畴A的表达式,则$\alpha\beta$是属于范畴B的表达式。

(2)若α是属于范畴A的表达式并且β是属于范畴$A\backslash B$的表达式,则$\alpha\beta$是属于范畴B的表达式②。

比如说:表达式"love"属于范畴(NP\S)/NP,表达式"Mary"属于范畴NP,两个表达式的毗连"love Mary"按照规则(1)就属于范畴NP\S。表达式"John"属于范畴NP,它跟属于范畴NP\S的表达式"Love Mary"毗连,按照规则(2)就获得属于范畴S的表达式"John loves Mary"。上述规则的运用由英语词条生成英语句,其"毗连运算"的操作体现出函项应用的原则,这也是蒙太格语法句法规则的基本思想。

20世纪80年代中期到90年代末范畴语法逐渐走向繁荣。在这一时期,Steedman等人提出组合范畴语法CCG,Capenter等人发展了类型逻辑语义学。21世纪以来,Morrill和Moortgat的工作从范畴运算的算子和毗连的结构规则两方面丰富了Lambek演算,提出范畴语法的非连续系统和混合的多模态系统,这些是范畴语法的范畴类型逻辑发展方向。③

范畴类型逻辑CTL将语言学研究和数学逻辑运算更紧密地结合在一起,CTL的研究对自然语言的计算机分析显示出应用价值。CTL的基本原则是:语言认知就是数学计算,语法分析就是逻辑推演。CTL不仅可以抽象地研究自然语言句法范畴的运行规律,还能够通过引入简单类型λ-演算的工具来展现句法和语义的接口(interface)④。

范畴类型逻辑在传统范畴语法描述"毗连运算"的函项原则基础上,增加了

---

① Bar Hillel, Yehoshua, Gaifman, C. and Shamir, E. (1960). On categorical and phrase structure grammars. Bulletin of the Research Council of Israel. F(9):1-16.

② 邹崇理《自然语言逻辑的多元化发展及对信息科学的影响》,《哲学研究》(2001,1).

③ Kosta Došen, Peter Schroeder-Heister (1994). *Substructural Logics* (*Studies in Logic and Computation*). Oxford University Press:USA.

④ 邹崇理,《范畴类型逻辑》,北京:中国社会科学出版社,2008.

"交换"、"结合"、"添加"和"缩减"等一系列结构规则。CTL 有 Gentzen 风格的矢列表述,用于讨论判定性问题;还有树模式表述,用于直观展示句法生成和语义组合的并行推演;还有公理表述伴随可能世界的框架语义解释,据此讨论系统的可靠性和完全性。所有这些使得范畴类型逻辑作为研究自然语言的工具,其精准性远远强于传统意义上的范畴语法。因此,对自然语言的转换所涉及的"成分变动"和"成分增减"等现象都能够给予充分的解读。

为解答蒙太格语法中的转换规则是否具有范畴语法依据这样的问题,我们列出所需要的 CTL 的 LP 系统如下:

公理:(共三条)

$A1$　$A \rightarrow A$　(等同公理)

$A2$　$(A \cdot B) \cdot C \leftrightarrow A \cdot (B \cdot C)$　(结合公理)

$A3$　$A \cdot B \leftrightarrow B \cdot A$　(交换公理)

规则:(共五条)

$R1$　如果 $A \cdot B \rightarrow C$ 则 $A \rightarrow C/B$

$R2$　如果 $A \cdot B \rightarrow C$ 则 $B \rightarrow A \backslash C$

$R3$　如果 $A \rightarrow C/B$ 则 $A \cdot B \rightarrow C$

$R4$　如果 $B \rightarrow A \backslash C$ 则 $A \cdot B \rightarrow C$

$R5$　如果 $A \rightarrow B$ 并且 $B \rightarrow C$ 则 $A \rightarrow C$

本文第二部分针对英语被动句,采用蒙太格语法的转换规则推演出不同类型的被动句,通过范畴类型逻辑的 LP 系统所提供的工具,证明有关转换过程的合理性。从而论证 MG 的转换规则同样具有范畴语法的依据。

二、用 CTL 分析 MG 的被动转换规则

章振邦先生认为在语用学框架下划分被动结构的方式由"标记理论"支撑。这一理论认为,英语被动结构可以划分为"无标记结构"和"有标记结构","无标记结构"指的是"意义被动","有标记结构"称作"结构被动",如[①]:

(1) The scientific equipment sells well.(这台科学仪器很畅销。)

(2) Friction can be reduced and the life of the machine prolonged by lubrication.(润滑能减少摩擦,延长机器寿命。)

以上(1)是"意义被动",以主动语态表达被动含义,而(2)是典型的结构被动,

① 章振邦,《新编英语语法教程》,上海外语教育出版社,1992.

因为它含有一种形态标记"be/get + 过去分词"。[①] 美国哥伦比亚大学语言学者肯尼斯认为:结构被动语态是一个由连接动词的语法标记(系动词),其后紧跟着动词的过去分词。下面我们讨论结构被动句法的情况,意义被动句的转换留待今后。

在本文第一部分我们看到,蒙太格语法的句法规则分为两大类:一类规则的任务是生成转换语法所谓的核心句。如 S_4:若 $\delta \in P_{NP}$ 且 $\xi \in P_{VP}$,则 $F_4(\delta,\xi) = \delta\xi'$ 且 $F_4(\delta,\xi) \in P_S$。这类规则中的句法操作大都遵循范畴语法的函项运用原则,这些规则主要通过"毗连运算"进行操作,而"毗连运算"体现了范畴语法所谓由函子范畴对主目范畴进行计算的思想。如句法操作"$F_4(\delta,\xi) = \delta\xi'$"表明由 δ 的范畴 S/(S/NP)对 ξ 的范畴 S/NP 进行函项应用获得 $\delta\xi'$ 的范畴 s。F_4 意味着输入的两个表达式的范畴之间进行一次运算得到其输出表达式的范畴,这就是 F_4 体现的范畴语法原则,也是句法规则 S_4 的范畴语法依据。

蒙太格语法另一类句法规则是扩展的转换规则,这类规则获得包括被动句在内转换结果。如 Partee 提出的结构被动句转换规则:

如果 $\varphi \in P_S$,且 φ 形如两种模式之一:

(a)严格模式:$_S[_T[\alpha]_{IV}[_{TV}[\beta]_T[him_i]]]$

(b)非严格模式:$_S[_T[\alpha]_{IV}[_{TV}[\beta]_T[\delta]\gamma]]$

则 $F_{101}(\varphi) \in P_S$,其中 $F_{101}(\varphi)$ 为 $_S[_T[\left\{\begin{matrix}(a)he_i\\(b)\delta\end{matrix}\right\}]_{IV}[\text{is } EN_{TV}[\beta][\text{by}_T[\alpha]]]]$

例子:F_{101}(Mary loves John) = John is loved by Mary。

就句法操作 F_{101} 而言,输入的 φ 其范畴是 S,输出的结果 $F_{101}(\varphi)$ 其范畴也是 S,这个过程似乎没有显示范畴之间的运算。显然,转换规则中的句法操作 F_{101} 不像前面生成核心句的句法规则中的 F_4 那样,关注输入的两个表达式所属范畴之间的运算是否获得输出表达式所属的范畴。可见,考察 *MG* 的转换规则是否具有范畴语法的合理依据应该采取另外的视角。F_{101} 针对的是一个由几个表达式构成的主动句整体,经 F_{101} 的运算使这个语句内部的成分发生一些变化:有些成分位置移动变换(主语名词和宾语名词),有些成分形态发生变化(动词),还增添了一些原来没有的新成分(或减少一些成分)。F_{101} 忽略了这些变化背后是否具有范畴语法的合理依据、是否隐藏着范畴类型逻辑潜在的运作机制,即并不关心形态改变后的动词其范畴跟动词原型的范畴是否相同?增添的成分指派什么样的范畴?F_{101} 强调的只是:输出的被动句其范畴也是 S,但怎样得来并不关注。

---

① 吴平(2009),《汉语特殊句式的事件语义分析与计算》。

范畴语法却在意这些问题，范畴语法近 20 年发展迅猛的新分支——组合范畴语法 CCG 尝试解决 MG 转换规则带来的上述问题。CCG 改变 TG 和 MG 把语言分为深层结构和表层结构的做法，认为自然语言是单层结构，不需要由深层结构转换到表层结构。F_{101} 输入的主动句其内部成分被指派适当的范畴后，经过一次或多次运算获得范畴 S。而 F_{101} 输出的被动句其内部成分也需要指派合适的范畴（指派的范畴未必和主动句的相同），最终目的使得被动句内部成分的范畴运算也能得到 S。依照 CCG，主动句的范畴指派及其运算为：

Mary　　loves　　John

np_1　　$(np_1\backslash s)/np_2$　　np_2

$np_1\backslash s$

s

被动句的范畴指派及其运算可能是：①

John　　is　　loved　　by　　Mary

np_2　　$(np_2\backslash(s/np_1)/(np_2\backslash(s/np_2))$　　$np_2\backslash(s/np_1)$　　np_1/np_1　　np_1

$np_2\backslash(s/np_1)$　　np_1

s/np_1

s

毋庸置疑的是，CCG 是孤立看待主动句和被动句各自的范畴指派及其运算的，主动句是合语法的句子，给它的成分指派适当的范畴，经过逐级运算可得 S，被动句也是合语法的句子，也能够运算得 S。F_{101} 输入的主动句如何进行范畴运算得 S 跟 F_{101} 输出的被动句怎样运算得 S 是没有关联的，换句话说，给 φ 内部各成分指派的范畴系列的毗连是否能够推出给 $F_{101}(\varphi)$ 内部各成分指派的范畴系列的毗连？如果能够推出，依据什么样的范畴类型逻辑工具？甚至给被动句中的动词变体指

① 对于这里的被动句，考虑到系动词“is”和介词“by”在语义上是虚无所指的，故处理成恒等函项对应的范畴。当然 CCG 对被动句中成分范畴的指派还可能做另外的选择，如把“loved”的范畴同动词原型一样指派成“$(np_1\backslash s)/np_2$”，给系动词“is”指派的范畴做相应调整，最终结果要使被动句各成分的逐级运算也获得范畴 S。另选什么方案并不影响我们要说明的观点：CCG 并不关心主动句各成分的范畴指派与被动句各成分的范畴指派有什么关联。

派的范畴为什么不同于给主动句中的动词原型指派的范畴？两者是否有关联？从逻辑的视角看，这些都是有意义的问题，是值得探究的工作。

通常认为，MG 的扩展的转换规则中的句法操作并不直接符合函项运用的范畴语法要求，这些规则中有添加的操作，添加系动词“be”和介词“by”；位置变动的操作，如施事名词和受事名词的位置变换；词条形态改变的操作，如动词原型在被动句中变成了动词的过去分词。我们的看法是：仅仅根据范畴语法最简单的函项运用原则，MG 被动转换规则中句法操作的合理性得不到说明。但是依靠范畴语法最新版本——范畴类型逻辑所提供的工具，综合调动其中的结合、交换等结构规则和单调律等手段，可以在 CCG 停顿的地方继续前进，从新的视角考察被动转换规则的句法操作的范畴语法合理性，即从给主动句各成分指派的范畴系列推出给被动句各成分指派的范畴系列，从而证明 MG 扩展的转换规则同样具有范畴语法的可计算依据。

Partee 系统转换规则的句法操作 F_{101} 可从主动句“Mary loves John”计算得到被动句“John is loved by Mary”。主动句“Mary loves John”的范畴指派如上述，给其词条指派的范畴排列为：$np_1 \cdot (np_1 \backslash s)/np_2 \cdot np_2$。而经 F_{101} 运算后获得的被动句，给其中的词条指派的范畴系列是：这些范畴的逐级运算最后获得的也应是范畴 s。例如被动句“John is loved by Mary”的情况：

$np_2 \cdot (np_2 \backslash (s/np_1))/(np_2 \backslash (s/np_1)) \cdot np_2 \backslash (s/np_1) \cdot np_1/np_1 \cdot np_1$。我们的任务是从主动句的范畴指派系列推出被动句的范畴指派系列，即证明：

(1) $np_1 \cdot (np_1 \backslash s)/np_2 \cdot np_2 \rightarrow np_2 \cdot (np_2 \backslash (s/np_1))/(np_2 \backslash (s/np_1)) \cdot np_2 \backslash (s/np_1) \cdot np_1/np_1 \cdot np_1$

简言之，就是证明：

(2) $np_1 \cdot (np_1 \backslash s)/np_2 \cdot np_2 \rightarrow np_2 \cdot np_2 (s/np_1) \cdot np_1$

是否是范畴类型逻辑中可推出的定理。① 概括来说，就是证明形如 $A \cdot (A \backslash B)/C \cdot C \rightarrow C \cdot C \backslash (B/A) \cdot A$ 的公式是否是 CTL 的 LP 系统的定理。

证明：

(1) $(A \backslash B)/C \rightarrow (A \backslash B)/C$　　(A1 等同公理)

(2) $((A \backslash B)/C) \cdot C \rightarrow (A \backslash B)$　　(由(1)依据 R3 规则)

(3) $A \cdot (((A \backslash B)/C) \cdot C) \rightarrow B$　　(由(2)依据 R4 规则)

(4) $(C \cdot ((A \backslash B)/C)) \cdot A \rightarrow B$　　(由(2)反复交叉使用 A2 和 A3)

① 证明了(2)，根据 $X/X \cdot X$ 跟 X 的互换，就证明了(1)。

(5) $C\cdot((A\backslash B)/C)\rightarrow B/A$ （由(4)依据 R1）

(6) $(A\backslash B)/C\rightarrow C\backslash(B/A)$ （由(5)依据 R2）

(7) $A\cdot(A\backslash B)/C\cdot C\rightarrow A\cdot C\backslash(B/A)\cdot C$ （两次运用单调律）

(8) $A\cdot(A\backslash B)/C\cdot C\rightarrow C\cdot C\backslash(B/A)\cdot A$ （对后件反复交叉使用 A2 和 A3）

可见,$A\cdot(A\backslash B)/C\cdot C\rightarrow C\cdot C\backslash(B/A)\cdot A$ 是范畴类型逻辑 LP 系统的定理,即(2)乃至(1)成立,表明蒙太格语法的被动转换规则符合范畴语法的规律,具有范畴语法的依据。

三、结语

本文通过 Partee 关于结构被动句的转换规则的考察,分析了蒙太格语法的转换思想。从新的视角探讨 MG 扩展的转换规则中的句法操作的范畴语法依据。这个工作采用了范畴语法的最新版本——范畴类型逻辑 CTL 所提供的工具,如交换的结构规则、结合的结构规则以及单调等规则。最终得出结论:MG 是 CG 的发展阶段,不仅生成核心句的句法规则遵循范畴语法的函项应用原则,刻画转换思想的扩展规则也具有范畴语法的可计算依据,MG 的两大类句法规则都可以作为自然语言信息处理的指导理论。

从归化法角度看英文影视作品字幕翻译策略
——以美剧《斯巴达克斯》人人影视字幕为例

首都经济贸易大学外国语学院　方俊青

摘　要:影视作品的字幕翻译作为一种独特的翻译类型,越来越受到关注。本文试图以人人影视发布的美剧“斯巴达克斯”字幕为例,从“归化法”角度解读该策略在字幕翻译中的应用。

关键词:归化法;字幕翻译;《斯巴达克斯》

Abstract: Film subtitling translation has gained more and more attention as a new field of translation. This article attempts to explore the application of Domestication Strategy in the subtitle translation of the American drama “Spartacus: Blood and Sand” by YYeTs.

Key Words: domestication; Film subtitling translation; *Spartacus*

一、研究背景

电影(Movie)、剧集(TV Series)等影视剧作为一种特殊的文化传播方式,人们可通过其蕴含的思想、宗教、历史、民俗等包罗万象的信息窥见异国他乡的风土人情。随着信息化、全球化的高度发展,现如今,影视剧已经成为民间了解其他国家文化的最重要途径之一。字幕作为理解影视作品的核心信息,构成了影视作品的重要内容,与其相伴而生的影视剧字幕翻译,也随之成为一个越来越重要的研究领域,同时成为我国学界瞩目的热点之一。

近年来,随着大量影视作品引进国内及国内观众英语水平的普遍提高,越来越多的人群更倾向于通过网络观看配有双语字幕的原声作品。2010 年,美国 Starz 电视台推出剧集《斯巴达克斯》(Spartacus),同时,我国民间一家非营利性个人团体组织——人人影视字幕组大胆地采用文言文对该剧字幕进行了翻译,一时间引发了字幕翻译与本土化结合的讨论。

二、研究意义

采用适宜的翻译策略,不仅利于观众迅速理解影片的内容,而且利于观众融入影片塑造的文化环境。随着国外影视作品通过更多正规渠道引入国内,以及观众的文化素养和需求的同步提高,以往轻率的翻译会招来铺天盖地的耻笑,而精益求精的字斟句酌也不能适应供给市场的现实情况。优秀字幕翻译的需求日益成为中国电影市场面临的重要课题,而翻译策略中的归化法和异化法的选取也总是成为学界探讨的热点。因此,本文尝试以美剧《斯巴达克斯》为例,从归化法角度探讨汉译字幕翻译策略,以期促进字幕翻译研究发展。

三、理论基础

翻译作为文化沟通的桥梁,难以避免地同时承受着来自两种文化的干预与影响,影视作品字幕翻译也是如此。如何更好地让处于一种文化熏陶下的人顺利理解源语作者的表达意图,从而理解另一种文化,始终是学者们思考的重要课题。1813 年,西方阐释主义学派的创始人、德国古典语言学家、翻译理论家弗里德里希·施莱尔马赫(Friedrich Schleiermacher)在《论翻译的方法》(On the Different Methods of Translation:A History of Translation)中提出:"译者要么尽量不打扰作者而让读者靠近作者,要么尽量不打扰读者而让作者靠近读者。"(Either the translator leaves the author in peace,as much as possible,and moves the reader towards him;or he leaves the reader in peace,as much as possible,and moves the author towards him.)1995 年,美籍意大利学者劳伦斯·韦努蒂(Lawrence Venuti)在其著作《译者的隐身》(The Translator's Invisibility)中把这一理念吸收归纳,将前者称之为"异化"(foreignization),后者称之为"归化"(domestication)。

(一)归化法

归化法(domestication),韦努蒂的定义是:遵守目标语语言文化和当前的主流价值观,对源语言采用保守的同化手段,使其迎合本土的典律、出版潮流和政治潮流。虽然韦努蒂本人不提倡采用这一方法,但美国语言学家、翻译家、翻译理论家尤金·A·奈达(Eugene A. Nida)更倾向于认同归化法的翻译策略,他认为,译文的表达方式应是完全自然的,并尽可能地把源语行为模式纳入译文读者的文化范畴。归化法的目的,是着重向读者或观众展示和传递原作的精神和语义内容,不拘泥于源语的形式。因此,归化法的优点是译文更易于迅速为读者或观众所接受,并不因对文化背景的生疏而产生理解障碍,而这一特点更符合影视作品字幕翻译的特性与实际需要。

(二)影视作品字幕翻译及特点

影视作品字幕翻译属于文学翻译,同时受限于影视作品的视听表现形式,具备自己独特的特性。结合钱绍昌教授提出的影视语言的“聆听性、综合性、瞬时性、通俗性和无注性”来看,笔者认为影视作品字幕翻译应具备以下 4 个特点:综合性、瞬时性、通俗性、无注性。

1. 综合性

影视作品字幕翻译不能脱离其载体,应重视影视作品中人物的动作、表情、语境以及影片所处的时代背景等。

2. 瞬时性

影视作品的画面是动态的,而且影视作品的线性展示方式也难以容许观众回顾,所以字幕翻译传递信息的时间往往随着画面的切换转瞬即逝。

3. 通俗性

影视作品的受众很广泛,文化层次高低不同,因此字幕翻译必须要通俗易懂,易于为观众所理解接受。

4. 无注性

影视作品字幕翻译受限于其瞬时性和通俗性,很难有时间和画面空间容许译者在翻译的同时加注解释说明的文字。

综合来看,影视作品字幕翻译与其他文学翻译一样受源语文化和译语文化两种不同文化语境的制约,同时更受自身特性的种种制约。

四、字幕翻译的制约因素

影视作品是一种以视听表现形式为主的文学样式,而当观众不能听懂或理解源语时,译语字幕就成为最重要的因素之一,结合其特点来看,主要会受到以下三个方面的制约。

(一)观众文化的因素

影视作品受众的文化程度是字幕翻译的综合性和通俗性的体现,是字幕翻译中首要考虑的重中之重。美剧《斯巴达克斯》在美国的分级制度中属于 TV-MA (Mature Audience Only),而译者在翻译时也会受到该剧在中国的受众群体文化程度的制约。一般而言,中国观众对异域的文化背景、人物关系、宗教神话往往会感到陌生,尤其是翻译美剧《斯巴达克斯》这样以西方古代罗马历史为背景的影视作品字幕,需要面对更多的文化交流障碍,译者必须尽可能地使字幕译文既通俗易懂,也要雅俗共赏。

(二)时间因素

字幕翻译的瞬时性使其天然地受到时间因素的制约。不论观众的文化程度、阅读速度如何,字幕翻译者必须要保证观众在人物角色念完台词的时间内,迅速地理解源语言台词的表层意思以及深层含义,有时甚至需要表现出源语言的修辞手法,且必须要与台词时间同步完成。美剧《斯巴达克斯》中的源语言台词为表现时代特征和人物特性,往往台词简短、语句简练,这也意味着时间短暂。该剧的字幕文本显示,绝大多数台词都是在 1 ~6 秒以内完成的,这也是观众接受全部信息的时长。

(三)空间因素

字幕译文不能喧宾夺主,占据大量画面空间,其无注性决定了字幕会受到来自屏幕的空间限制,一般认为,字幕最多不要超过两行,否则会给观众的视觉享受造成一定障碍。而人人影视在加载美剧《斯巴达克斯》的字幕时,采用了双语模式,更加大了空间因素在这一作品中的制约性。

从各个版本的翻译作品最终效果来看,笔者认为当译者更倾向于采用归化法作为翻译策略时,字幕译文往往更能克服前述种种制约,也更能满足观众的需求。而将归化法使用得最淋漓尽致的,当属人人影视字幕组。

五、归化法翻译策略的体现

美剧《斯巴达克斯》全剧共 4 季,由 Grady Hall 执导,于 2010 年 1 月 22 日在美国 Starz 电视台首播,剧集创作改编自意大利作家拉法埃洛·乔万尼奥里的历史小说《斯巴达克斯》,主要讲述了角斗士斯巴达克斯为向罗马复仇,集结其他角斗士奴隶揭竿起义为自由而奋战的传奇故事。剧集背景是公元前 73 年古罗马时代,人人影视字幕组的译者别出心裁地采用了近似于文言文的古汉语语言习惯进行翻译,几乎在第一时间就将观众带回影片所展现的古罗马时代。

例一:You speak as Jupiter hurling bolts from the heavens. (Spartacus:Gods of the Arena. S00E04)

[画面情景:一代传奇角斗士 Gannicus(咖尼卡斯)赞扬好友兼新任教练 Oenomaus(奥诺茂斯)的严厉]

人人影视字幕译文:你言如天神,如万剑从天而降。这句台词属于凯尔特人传奇角斗士 Gannicus,他在剧中是一个张扬不羁而阳光开朗的人,充满了人格魅力,而且与其他大多数出身社会最底层的角斗士的台词不同,他的台词中常常使用古罗马神祇做比喻。Jupiter,即希腊神话中的第三代众神之王宙斯 Zeus,手持闪电掌管宇宙。虽然译文将 Jupiter 概括为“天神”、将 bolt 译为“万剑”,与源语言寓意载体不同,但依托于中国传统神话的用词,两者的喻义是等值的,更好地实现了字幕翻译的目的。

例二：The man could turn day to night with disapproving frown.（Spartacus：Gods of the Arena. S00E01）

［画面情景：罗马贵妇盖娅评价野心勃勃的角斗士训练者巴蒂亚图斯］

人人影视字幕译文：一个能够翻手为云覆手为雨的男人。这句台词的剧情背景是：角斗士训练者——同时也是角斗士们的奴隶主——一次被迫兵行险招之后取得事业进步，满怀意外之喜地离家赴约时，在他家做客的贵妇兼情妇 Gaia 对他的妻子说了这句恭维的话。Gaia 和前文提到的 Gannicus 有些相像，开朗爱笑、放诞精明，时时刻刻感染着周边的各色人等。属于她的台词往往语速很快，例句出现在 00:43:36,200 至 00:43:39,700，从音轨显示信息看，字幕仅允许有 3 秒钟的显示时间。人人影视字幕组的译文此处采用了与源语言一致的修辞方式——夸张。尽管如果直译为："这男人一皱眉都能使白昼变成黑夜"，同样是 15 个汉字，能体现出源语言台词想表达的 Gaia 与 Batiatus 一家的亲近以及 Gaia 张扬的个性，但译者此处使用了中国观众更为熟悉的、典出杜甫诗句的俗语，与直译相比，能更快地、更通俗易懂地让中国观众理解接受。

例三：The lands from which you hail matters no longer. The only thing that does is the sound of my voice and the sand beneath your feet.（Spartacus：Blood and Sand S01E03）

［画面情景：教练 Oenomaus 向新招入的 Spartacus 等角斗士们训话］

人人影视字幕译文：汝自何方来，不足为意，唯吾之号令、履下之地，重若泰山。结合影片剧情，严厉方正的教练 Oenomaus 此句是对桀骜不驯的 Spartacus 的训诫，同时也是在一众新人前立威。译者采用了更偏向书面语体色彩的文言文形式，来表现角斗士教练说这句话时有别于日常闲谈的郑重，使不通英语的观众在字幕入眼的第一时间就能感受到源语言台词传递的精神色彩。译文中"重若泰山"虽然与源语言台词语言形式截然不同，但此处化用简洁的四字成语并改变语序将其后置，便于观众理解源语言台词契合剧情的严肃意味，更有助于领会台词塑造这一人物性格的效果。更重要的是，译文用仅仅 22 个汉字便达成了前述所有效果，节约了画面空间。

作为对比，例句台词在另一版字幕中的译文是：你来自哪里无关紧要，唯一重要的是我说的话和你们脚下的沙。尽管第二种译法清晰直接地表述了台词的文字意义，甚至巧用汉语中韵脚同为 ɑ 的"话"和"沙"来表现 the sound and the sand 的头韵，但与人人影视字幕译文相比，既失去了源语言台词的精神内涵，也因汉字字数多出了约23%,使字幕排版稍显局促。

六、结语

中西方文化的巨大差异鸿沟,使两个同样体量庞大、文化深厚程度不相上下的群体交流充满艰难险阻。翻译作为两个文化交流的桥梁,“归化与异化”在很久以前、甚至早于被学者研究总结定名之日,其优劣就长期处于争论的漩涡中,影视作品的字幕翻译也是这一争论的“战场”之一。笔者以美剧《斯巴达克斯》为例分析该剧字幕翻译的特点,展现归化法这一翻译策略的实际应用,通过简短的对比,体现归化法在影视作品字幕翻译的优势。尽管本剧字幕翻译在个别台词的翻译中也出现了“过度归化”的现象,但瑕不掩瑜,选用归化法作为影视作品的翻译策略不失为一种有效的手段。

参考文献:

[1]杨定婷. 关联翻译理论下看美国情景喜剧字幕翻译中的归化和异化——以美剧《老爸老妈的浪漫史》为例[J]. 海外英语,2014(16).

[2]秦小红. 尤金·奈达翻译理论简介[J]. 海外英语,2014(4).

[3]于涛. 论斯坦纳阐释翻译观下字幕翻译中的译者主体性——以美剧《斯巴达克斯》字幕翻译为例[J]. 科技信息,2013(25).

[4]殷燕. 试析电影字幕翻译策略[J]. 电影文学,2013(12).

[5]余梦瑶. 浅析字幕翻译中的制约因素[J]. 金田,2013(10).

[6]徐亚丽. 电影字幕翻译要不要本土化[J]. 电影文学,2013(10).

[7]韦运会. 论英文电影字幕翻译的基本要素与方法[J]. 电影文学,2012(12).

[8]孙沁沁,顾飞荣. 目的论下的美剧字幕翻译策略——以《生活大爆炸》为例[J]. 内蒙古农业大学学报(社会科学版),2011(6).

[9]胡磊. 影视字幕翻译的现状和发展趋势[J]. 电影文学,2012(3).

[10]伍蓉蓉. 网络美剧字幕翻译中的另类意译[J]. 电影文学,2011(5).

[11]高杨.《功夫》英文字幕翻译中的归化和异化[J]. 疯狂英语(教师版),2007(6).

语篇衔接对同声传译的启示

首都经济贸易大学外国语学院　葛卫红

摘　要:衔接是构造篇章的重要手段之一,由于汉英分属不同的语系,衔接手段也有各自特点。同声传译虽是一种口译形式,其翻译形式的特殊性和听众对最终译文质量的要求决定了语篇衔接的重要性。本文对语篇衔接进行了分析,解释了同传中出现的困难和应对办法,最后阐述了篇章衔接对同声传译的重要性。

关键词:语篇衔接;同声传译;逻辑

Abstract:Cohesive devices are one of the important elements of discourse. As Chinese and English belong to two different language families, the use of cohesive devices is also of different features. Though simultaneous interpretation (SI) is oral, its specialty in interpretation means and the demand of audience on interpretation quality determines the importance of cohesive devices. This paper analyzed cohesive words, explained the difficulties of SI and their countermeasures and elaborated the importance of cohesive devices to SI.

Key Words:cohesive;simultaneous interpretation;logic

一、引言

衔接是语篇理解的基础,使语篇语言简练、信息突出、逻辑连贯。同声传译虽然是一种口译形式,其翻译形式的特殊性和听众对最终译文质量的要求决定了语篇衔接的重要性。本文从篇章语言学的角度,首先对语篇衔接进行了分析,介绍了同声传译这一特殊的翻译形式,解释了同传中出现的困难和应对办法,并阐述了篇章衔接对同声传译的重要性。

二、语篇衔接

衔接是构造篇章的重要手段之一。较早注意到篇章衔接问题的美国描写语言学大师哈里斯(Z. harris)。1985 年在其《话语分析》(Discourse Analysis)一文中,他指出“语言实体往往不是以零散的单词和句子的形式而是以相关联的语句出现的”。韩礼德和哈桑（Halliday & Hasan）认为“衔接产生于语篇中某个语项的解释要依赖（或参照）其中的另一语项之时”（1976：4）。他们认为衔接是一个语义概念，是语义上的一种联系，如果篇章中的某一部分对另一部分的理解起着关键作用，这两部分之间就存在着衔接关系。1976 年，在《英语的衔接》一书中，他们集中探讨了英语的 5 种衔接手段（cohesive devises）：指称（reference）、替代（substitution）、省略（ellipsis）、连接（conjunction）、词汇衔接（lexical cohesion）。1985 年，在《语言、语境、语篇》一书中又把替代和省略合并成一类，将衔接成分分为 4 种（刘辰诞，1999：17）：

A. 照应：语篇中两种成分之间在指代意义上相互解释。指用代词等语法关系表示语义关系，指的是语篇中的一个成分做另一个成分的参照点。

B. 替代和省略：替代指为避免重复，用一种语言成分替代另一种语言成分；省略指篇章中句子或小句中一些基本结构成分的缺省，以避免重复，突出信息。二者十分相似，省略也被称为零位替代。

C. 连接：是一种只能通过参照篇章其他部分才能完全理解篇章的关系，通过连接词、一些副词或词组实现。

D. 词汇衔接：指通过词汇选择在篇章中建立一个贯穿篇章的链条，建立篇章的连续性，是构成衔接的最高级方式。

“语篇指任何不完全受句子语法约束的在一定语境下表示完整语义的自然语言。”（胡壮麟，1994：1）。韩礼德和哈桑在《英语的衔接》一书中认为语篇指任何长度的在语义上完整的口语和书面语的段落。它与句子或小句的关系不在于篇幅的长短，而在于衔接。他们认为语篇具有语篇结构和语言结构，语篇之所以成为语篇在于其“语篇组织”。语篇组织是结合各个衔接手段的抽象概念，每一个衔接点被称为衔接节（cohesive tie）（胡壮麟，1994：13）。

衔接使语篇内部各个成分意义上相互关联，形成信息流动，实现意义上的连贯，共同发挥交际功能。衔接使篇章在修辞上言简意赅，结构上更加紧凑（朱永生，2001：15）。从信息单元、句群、次篇章到整个篇章。

三、同声传译概述

同声传译是一种与笔译截然不同的翻译形式。指的是通过一种语言把另一种语言所表达的思想和情感，以与讲话人几乎同步的速度，用口头形式重新表述出来的一种翻译实践（张维为，1999：6）。同声传译是一种高难度的翻译活动，在翻译过程中，译员必须运用各种相关知识和能力对语言进行精密处理，如理解记忆、分析综合、整合转换,直至发出话语,实现帮助异语双方达到信息交流的目的。源语既是译员进行意义传达、进行交际的根据,同时也会对译员的分析理解、译语的产出造成制约。译语既反映了译员对源语内容的理解和对译语的表达水平,也显示出语言文化及交际等各种因素对意义传达的干扰。

(一)同声传译的独特性

与其他形式的翻译相比,同声传译最大的不同和困难在于译员在只听到不完全信息的情况下,必须在很短的时间内做出快速反应,以最快的速度,最大限度地追求翻译效果的等值,实现交际的目的。这是一项要求非常高的翻译活动,需要译员从始至终都高度集中精力。这其中的过程非常复杂,涉及各方面能力的协调,包括听取源语信息、短期记忆、分析整合、译语表达等。因此,一个好的译员不仅需要扎实的语言功底、丰厚的知识底蕴、良好的口头表达能力,还要有良好的心理素质和快速的反应能力(张维为,1999:13)。著名的口译理论学家 Daniel Gile 将口译活动比喻成“走钢丝”,他指出口译员的注意力在工作中始终处在接近饱和的状态,译员要同时完成的同声传译认知负荷模型(effort model)中不同的任务。

(二)Daniel Gile 的同声传译认知负荷模型

基于对口译过程的实际观察和认知心理学基础研究成果,Daniel Gile 开发出了同声传译认知负荷模型,解释同传中出现的困难,以便开发合适的口译策略和技巧。他认为在同传过程中,有三种精力是最主要的,即听解分析(listening and analysis)、言语生成(speech production)和短期记忆(short-term memory)。同声传译中,译员几乎要同时完成包括这三种精力在内的多个任务,要对源语进行听辩、提取、记忆和分析信息、组织表达译语,每个任务都需要大脑付出一定的精力和劳动,任何小的差错和额外的精力支出就可能引发精力分配失衡,造成翻译任务的失败。对每种精力的具体处理能力根据不同的翻译任务有不同的要求,译员要根据源语及同传情况的变化协调分配其在各个方面所花的精力,即要进行协调作业(coordination effort),将其有限的能量分配给不同的任务。只有不断协调各种作业任务,对每一项任务的精力分配高于其所需,或译员的精力分配总量高于各种任务所要求的总量,译员才能很好地完成口译任务,否则可能会出现信息遗漏或者表达的错误,导致口译出现问题。

因此,Daniel Gile 把同声传译认知负荷模型归纳为:$SI = L + P + M + C$,即同声传译 = 听解分析(L) + 言语生成(P) + 短期记忆(M) + 协调作业(C)。这 4 个组成部分,缺一不可,相互交织。同声传译的过程就如同一个产品的生产过程,在一个生产车间内,几名工人在有限的时间内,共同生产一种产品,每个工人负责产品的一部分,而译员则如同车间管理人员,进行任务分配,协调不同工人之间的工作。几名工人需各司其职,若哪一个工人的工作出现了问题,遇到了特别困难,管理人员就要进行协调,让工作难度小的工人在可能的情况下拿出一定的精力给予帮助,这样才能在规定时间内以较高的质量完成产品的生产,否则或者不能在规定时间内生产出产品,或者只能生产出劣质产品。

丹尼尔(Daniel Gile)还讨论了在同传过程中的问题触发因素(problem triggers),如源语表达速度快、信息密集大、源语噪音大、不熟悉的名称、数字及译员短期记忆饱和等。在以上所提到的构成同传认知负荷模型的4个组成部分中,这些问题触发因素每一个都可能触发问题的产生,导致口译任务失败。

四、语篇衔接与同声传译

奈达在论述翻译时说过:"在传统的翻译法中,译者把注意力集中于词的翻译。后来,人们认识到把词当作翻译的单位不够大,于是基点落在了句子上。接着,翻译家和语言学家指出,把单个句子作为基本单位也不够大。他们认为基点应当是段落,并在某种程度上是整个话语……在翻译段落每一个部分时,都必须从考虑整个段落的高度出发,因为所译的每一部分都必须和其他部分融合在一起,构成一个整体。"由此可见,翻译活动应重视语篇,尤其是各种衔接手段,因为它们是构成语篇语义连贯的重要成分之一,理应受到译员的关注。

不同的语言具有不同的衔接手段,因此译员应逐一从词语、句子和语篇的层面,研究源语和译语各自的照应手段及其之间的差异,从而探索适当的转换途径。由于不同语言的衔接手段各有异同,对原文和译文相应内容的了解和认识,有助于更透彻理解源语语篇信息,把握作者意图,使译语内容更加连贯,结构更加紧凑,表达更加准确和流畅。因此译员应注意源语与译语在衔接成分上的差异,尊重和顺应译语语篇规范,将源语语篇以译语接受的方式恰到好处地表达出来。这里引用一个李运兴在《语篇翻译引论》里的例子,它很清楚地说明了认清照应成分在篇章中的重要性。

(1) No matter how bad the world may become, no matter how much the mass man of the future may lose such of the virtues as he still has, one fact remains. If ***one person*** also refuses to go along with him, if one person alone asserts ***his*** individual and inner right to believe in and be loyal to what ***his*** fellow man seem to have given up, then at least ***he*** will still retain what is perhaps the most important part of humanity.

(Joseph Wood Krutch: *The New Immorality*)

译文：不管世界会堕落到什么地步，不管未来的大众人们丧失多少他们至今还保留的美德，有一个事实依然不变：只要有一个人不肯随波逐流，只要有一个人还会坚持自己植根于心灵深处的权利，信守他的同胞似乎已经放弃的美德，那他至少还会保留着也许是人性中最宝贵的东西。（孙致礼译）

在本段文字中有两条共指链，两种照应关系，一条为划线部分所示：the mass man—he—him；另一条为斜黑体部分所示：one person—his—his—he。两条指代链相互交错很容易让人们产生混淆。译者清楚地区分了这两条指代链，将第一条译为复数，将第二条译为单数，处理得当，译文明白清晰。

翻译活动是译员在源语与目标语之间进行交流和沟通的活动，是一个动态的过程，需要较强的创造性和言语意义的提取能力。在整个翻译活动中，译员是一个传递信息的桥梁，他需要将原文中的信息以尽可能小的损失反应在译文中，而抓住原文中的构造篇章大厦的衔接手段，无疑会使这一过程变得相对简单。在同声传译这一高难度的翻译形式里，译员要在听到部分信息后就开始翻译，在非常短的时间内完成对源语的理解、目标语的组织以及译语的准确流畅的表达等多个任务，这是它的困难所在，也是问题产生的原因之一。因此在同传中，译员更不能局限于词汇和句子的层面上，要从前后文中，从总体的语篇层面上理解源语信息，注意整体译文的衔接，从而保证整体语篇的连续性，体现源语讲话的逻辑层次，增强译语的连贯性、准确度和清晰度。

五、结语

同声传译是一种较为特殊的翻译形式，其特殊困境决定了其语篇整体表达的重要性，译者应重视语篇的衔接的问题，而不是仅仅局限于单独词汇或句子，较好地实现英汉两种语言间衔接手段和方式的转换，从而达到译语质量的最大优化。

参考文献：

[1] Halliday, M. A. K & Hasan, R. *Cohesion in English* [M]. London: Longman, 1976.

[2] Daniel Gile. *Basic Concepts and Models for Interpreter and Translator Training* [M]. John Benjamins Publishing Company, 1995.

[3] Eugene A. Nida & Charles R. Taber. *The Theory and Practice of Translation* [M]. Shanghai: Shanghai Foreign Lanugage Education Press, 2004.

[4]胡壮麟．语篇的衔接与连贯[M]．上海：上海外语教育出版社，1994.

[5]李运兴．语篇翻译引论[M]．北京：中国对外翻译出版公司，2001.

[6]李运兴．英汉语篇翻译[M]．北京：清华大学出版社，1998.

[7]朱永生．英汉语篇衔接手段对比研究[M]．上海：上海外语教育出版社，2001.

[8]刘辰诞．教学篇章语言学[M]．上海：上海外语教育出版社，1999.

[9]张维为．英汉同声传译[M]．北京：中国对外翻译出版公司，1999.

语境与 yes/no 的翻译

首都经济贸易大学外国语学院　宫照丽

摘　要：Yes 和 no 这两个词在字典里的意思非常明确，没有任何歧义，但是在真实语境中，yes 和 no 的意义远远不能用“是”或“不是”来简单翻译。本文从语言内语境和语言外语境两个方面出发，研究各种不同语境下的 yes 和 no 的翻译。

关键词：语境；语言内语境；语言外语境；yes/no 的翻译；语篇分析；语用对等

Abstract: In dictionary, "yes" and "no" have very clear and unambiguous definitions. However, words are also subject to many factors other than the relatively invariant abstract semantic meanings, e. g. , the linguistic context (i. e. , the indexical information implied by the linguistic context), and the socio-cultural context (i. e. , the empirical feelings and understandings of readers from a different cultural background), etc. Therefore, this paper tends to study the translation of "yes" and "no" in different contexts through the analysis of both lingual context and extra-lingual context.

Key Words: context; lingual context; extra-lingual context; the translation of yes/no; discourse analysis; pragmatic equivalence

The nature of translation is to convey the meaning of words from one language into another. The famous American translation theorist Eugene A. Nida, in his book *From One Language to Another* said: "Translation means translating meaning." He made meaning the core of language function. However, the meaning of any isolated word, phrase, sentence, or even paragraph may be quite variable if not put in a definite context. Therefore, context serves as a basis for people to understand and interpret discourses and context analysis plays a very important role in the entire process of translation.

Ⅰ. The Concept of Context

Bronislaw Kaspar Malinowski (1884—1942), the British socio-anthropologist and one of the founders of functionalism, was the first scholar to put out the notion of context. He said:"They regard context as the sole determiner of meaning without which meaning does not exits." (Liu RunQing et al., 1998, Book II, 64 ~ 65) After him, John Rupert Firth (1890—1960), a British linguist, accepted and developed his idea, and regarded meaning as the function that language segments have in a specific context. He extended the notion of context put forward by Malinowski, and pointed out that besides the linguistic context, the whole society, culture etc are all factors of context (or situational context) (ibid, 85 ~ 86). M. A. K. Halliday, a famous modern linguist further developed Firth's theory. He held that language variations, according to their different use, could be classified into different registers, thus categorizing situational factors restricting language features into mode, field, and discourse (ibid, 164).

Ⅱ. The Classification of Context

Context could be classified into two kinds: linguistic and extra-linguistic.

1. Linguistic context

Linguistic context, again, could be subdivided into linguistic context and paralinguistic context.

Linguistic context refers to the previous or following words or sentences of the word or sentence studied. In a broader sense, linguistic context may be used to refer to paragraphs, chapters, even the whole book. Linguistic context can not only eliminate the ambiguity of the segment studied, but also help the readers to determine what the pronouns refer to, even load the segment studied with meanings that are not possibly be expressed by the segment itself. Just like Firth said: "Each word when used in a new context is a new word."

Paralinguistic context can be classified into two categories: verbal and nonverbal. Verbal paralinguistic context refers to the tone, intonation etc. of the speaker, whereas the non-verbal paralinguistic context refers to the expression, manner, gesture etc. of the speaker. Just like the famous linguist Abercorombe once said: "We speak with our vocal organs, but we converse with our entire bodies... the conversational use of spoken language cannot be properly understood unless paralinguistic context are taken into account."

2. Extra-linguistic

Extra-linguistic context could be subdivided into socio-cultural context, environmental context and stylistic context. All these categories of context are necessary in understanding the actual meaning of the language segment studied. However, the following study of "Yes" and "No" will mainly focus on the linguistic context. Therefore, the writer will not elaborate on the details of these categories.

Ⅲ. Context and the Translation of Yes/No

In dictionary, "yes" and "no" have very clear and unambiguous definitions. Viewed from the perspective of pure semantics, they do not have any complicated collocations, metaphors or any associations with socio-culture. Therefore, it seems that they would not make any trouble for the translators. However, from the above analysis, we can see that words are also subject to many factors other than the relatively invariant abstract semantic meanings, e. g., the linguistic context (i. e., the indexical information implied by the linguistic context), and the socio-cultural context (i. e., the empirical feelings and understandings of readers from a different cultural background), etc. The actual meaning of a word changes with these pragmatic factors on which the text relies to state its intention by manipulating words and sentences. Dictionaries are not to blame, since limited by all kinds of conditions, they can only provide the readers with the abstract or basic meaning of the words. It is impossible for a dictionary to list all the specific meanings of a word in real pragmatic contexts. Therefore, it is quite difficult for translators to convey the actual meanings of "Yes" and "No" in specific contexts though they are such simple words.

The understanding of a discourse, i. e., the speaker's communicative purpose and intention, is the starting point of the process of translation. As the meaning of a discourse is determined by contexts, contexts play a key role in understanding the communicative meaning of a discourse, hence the importance of context analysis. Therefore, when putting "yes" and "no" into Chinese, we should disregard the rigid surface-level equivalence they are in with "是" and "不是", make full use of discourse analysis and the information provided by words and contexts to make out their profound meanings in different contexts, and then put these profound pragmatic meanings into appropriate words from the target language.

On many occasions, the seemingly simple "yes" and "no" convey meanings other than the simple and direct "是" and "不是". Rather, they are tinged with strong emotions and may all by themselves show the emotions, feelings and attitudes etc. of the speaker in a specific context. The following is a detailed study on the context and translation of "yes" and "no".

1. Context and the Translation of "Yes"

a. *He starts on Monday as a Canal Bank Renovation Supervisor... If he worked for a thousand years he will never get it cleaned of all the old bikes and prams and weeds and Coca Cola tins! I told my father that he was in a no-win situation, but he said, "On the contrary, in one years time it will be a beauty spot."*

"*Yes! And I am Nancy Reagan, Dad!*" (*from The Adrian Mole Diaries* by Sue Townsend)

The father who has been appointed Canal Bank Renovation Supervisor, is very optimistic about his new job and predicts that in less than a year, he would change the bank full of trash into a beauty spot. However, his son insists that his father is just fighting a losing war, and answers back sarcastically: "Yes! And I am Nancy Reagon, Dad!" Here "yes" shows that the son was quite against his father's groundless confidence and unrealistic optimism. Apparently "yes" is loaded with a very clear sense of irony. Moreover, from the contextual clues of the text, the following "and" marks a turning point in the meaning of the sentence, and implies a sense of "要是……那么". Through the above analysis, we come to a full understanding of "yes" in this specific context. Therefore, it is not difficult now for us to put the profound information that "yes" carries, i. e., a sense of irony, into Chinese: "爸! 你要有这本事,我就是总统夫人了!" Taken literally, the translation seems quite different from the basic meaning of "yes", but how can a single "是" convey all the communicative information of "yes" here? Equivalence more often than not refers to the equivalence of meaning rather than form.

b. *I was shocked at this sexist attitude and told him that I was in love with Pandora because of her brains and compassion for lesser mortals. My father gave a nasty laugh and said, "Oh yeah! And if Pandora was as ugly as sin, you would not have noticed her bloody IQ and bleeding heart in the first place."* (*ibid*)

This is a heart-to-heart talk between the father and the son. The son tells the father that he falls in love with his classmate Pandora, because she is smart and kind. But the father thinks otherwise. He holds that his son is only fascinated by the girl's beauty and says sarcastically: "Oh, yearh." This obviously is also an irony. In rendering it into Chinese, consideration shall be taken in retaining the ironic tone of it. The word-for-word translation "确实是" cannot express the strong emotion that "yeah" implies to its full extent. Therefore, in accordance with the real connotation of "Oh, yearh" in this context and the stylistic clues the text provides, we might as well render it into: 父亲冷笑一声说:"说得好听啊! 要是潘多拉是个丑八怪,你根本不会看上她的那个智商和仁爱之心。"

c. *Last night some irresponsible people down our street had bonfire parties in their own back gardens!*

Yes! (*ibid*)

Some neighbors could actually have bonfire parities in their back gardens! Such reckless and socially immoral behavior shocks Andrian, a lad who concerns himself with the trend of human morality. Such a great grievance at that moment is poured into the word "yes". Moreover, "yes" by itself constitutes one paragraph, which evidently shows the intensity of his dissatisfaction.

Translation:

"昨晚街坊中一些不负责任的邻里竟然在各自的花园里开起了篝火晚会!"

"岂有此理!"

In just one phrase "岂有此理", the translation successfully conveys the information that the original text intends to pass onto the readers to its full extent.

2. Context and the Translation of "No"

Similarly, the negative "no" is also heavily loaded with the communicative information that the speaker intends to convey. Therefore, it also has different pragmatic meanings in different contexts. For example: An adolescent wants to watch special movies for adults only. But the box-office clerk refuses to sell him the ticket. The following is the conversation between them:

d. *A:May I have a ticket?*

B:Are you eighteen?

A:No.

B:No.

In this conversation, the first "no" is the adolescent's answer to the box-office clerk's question, i. e., whether he is eighteen. Whereas the second one is a firm refusal to sell the ticket to him uttered by the clerk, since he gets to know that he is not yet an adult. Therefore, basing on the pragmatic meaning of "no", we can put this conversation into Chinese like this:

A:我想买一张票。

B:你满十八岁了吗?

A:还没有。

B:不能卖给你。

However, in the following example, "no" is used as a negation and retort to other's blame on the speaker. It has a very strong tone. So a single "不" cannot convey all the information "no" is loaded.

e. *When Smith pointed out that he had spread the rumor, he vehemently retorted: "No! No!"*

Translation:

当史密斯指出他散布谣言时,他拼命地反驳说:"没那么回事! 没那么回事!"(柯平译)

Through a repetition of "没那么回事", the Chinese translation appropriately shows what the speaker is quite annoyed and eager to speak for himself. In a certain context, "no" often serves as a means to express strong emotions, and its actual meaning can only be obtained fully through contextual clues and discourse analysis.

f. *Husband (H):Honey. I gotta talk to you.*

Wife (W):Sure. Is something wrong?

H:Well,sort of. Yes.

W:Bob,something in your voice scares me. Have I done anything?

H:No. It's me. I've done it. Sheila,remember when you were pregnant with Paula?

W:Yes?

H:I had to fly to Europe-Montpellier to give that paper...

W:And?

H:I had an affair.

W:No. This is some terrible joke. Isn't it?

H:No. It's true. I-I'm sorry.

This example is taken from *Man,Woman and Child*,a novel written by Erich Segal, a famous American writer and professor at Yale. The husband and wife have had 18 years' happy marriage life. But one day the husband confesses to his wife that he had a short-term affair after their marriage, which stuns the wife. They are on the verge of breaking up. At first,the husband speaks with such seriousness in his tone that it seems he had something of great importance to talk to his wife. The wife asks agitatedly:"出什么事了?" Though stammering,still the husband says in confirmation:"嗯,有点儿,是出了点事儿。" The wife is even more agitated,and says:"我做错什么了吗?" The answer the husband gives her,"No,it's me",is simple but powerful. "No" in itself is a complete sentence,which shows the husband's seriousness and sincerity to acknowledge his mistake. If we,without studying this "No" carefully,simply put it into "不,是我", then we would not only weaken the tone of the source text,but also make the translation monotonous and charmless. Therefore,we should take the actual meaning of "no" in this specific context as the starting point of translation,and then convey the original tone of this sentence by rendering it into"做错事的是我,不是你". The wife is stunned by her husband's confession, and says: "No. This is some terrible joke. " Here a simple interjection "no" implies her shock,uneasiness,and irritation. It is too difficult for her to face the truth. But the husband, with a leaden heart, continues to confess: "No. It's true. " "No" here is different from the one uttered by his wife. It is no longer an interjection,but a negation which denotes the firmness and resolution that mark his tone. It completely shatters the wife's last ray of hope. We can render "no" in these two sentences in this way:

——我有过一段那种事。

——不——! 你这是在开玩笑吧?(A dash shows her surprise.)

——不是开玩笑,是事实。(Repetition is used here to fulfill the emphasizing function of "no" in the source text.)

g. He had been anxiously looking round him for an aristocratic face, in order that he might tell him what he thought, but could not recognize lord this or duke that. No! No!

Translation:

他着急地四处张望,想找出一位贵族面孔,好向这个贵族谈谈他的看法,但是他认不出这位勋爵或那位公爵。认不出! 认不出!(柯平译)

Through the repetition of "认不出", the Chinese version fully expresses the eagerness and worry of the man that the source text means to convey by the repetition of "No".

Here is another instance: in Shakespeare's *King Lear*, when King Lear gets to know that his beloved daughter Cordelia is hanged under an unjust charge, he is in great grief. All his inner remorse, sorrow and regret burst out and find their way out in the several "no" and "never" he utters:

Lear: And my poor fool is hanged. No, no, no life! Why should a dog, a horse, a rat, have life, and thou no breath at all? Thou'll come no more.

Never, never, never, never, never!

Translation:

Version 1:我的傻孩子被绞杀了! 没、没、没有命了! 为什么一条狗、一匹马、一只老鼠都有命,而你偏没有气息了呢? 你永不再来了,永不、永不、永不、永不、永不!(梁实秋译)

Version 2:我可怜的傻瓜被绞死了。没命了、没命了、没命了! 为什么狗、马、老鼠都有生命,唯独你却没有一丝呼吸呢? 你再也不会回来了,永远、永远、永远、永远、永远不会回来了!(范家材译)

In version 1, "No, no, no life" is put into "没、没、没有命了!", which gives the target language readers a feeling that the King is speaking incoherently. However, the repetition of "no" in the source text is meant to show that though the King is in profound sorrow, he doesn't lose his reason. The translator of version 2 had an appropriate understanding of the contextual meanings of "No" here, and through the repetition of "没命了", created a chance for the target language readers to have a full understanding of the strong emotion implied in the source text.

All in all, once simple words like "yes" and "no" are viewed carefully from a pragmatic perspective, it would be clear that the actual meanings they are loaded with are not so simple and clear as they seem to be, but are complicated and would change with the changes of context. Therefore, it is safe to say that "yes" and "no" inherently possess a high probability of free translation. In translating them, we should free ourselves from their rigid surface-level Chinese equivalence "是" and "不是", take their context into full consideration, and convey their original flavor to its full extent.

References

[1]Eugene, A. Nida. *From One Language to Another*[M]. Nashville-Camden-New-York, 1986.

[2]卞正东. 语境与翻译[J]. 无锡教育学院学报, 2001.

[3]段自力. 语境与翻译[J]. 外语教学与研究, 2003.

[4]韩彩英. 语境的制约功能及其表现形式[J]. 语言文字应用, 2001.

[5]冀宁华. 语境与翻译[J]. 中州大学学报, 2001.

[6]柯平. 英汉与汉英翻译教程[M]. 北京:北京大学出版社, 1993.

[7]刘润清等. 语言学入门[M]. 北京:人民教育出版社, 1988.

[8]西槙光正. 语境研究论文集[M]. 北京:北京语言学院出版社, 1992.

汉字科学系统论

首都经济贸易大学　蒋立珠　佳木斯退休高级教师　蒋辅文

摘　要:传统的形声字理论(部首偏旁)不能指导汉字上网互联。音码受识字量限制和同音字太多而叹息,形码因违背汉字规律而说不。孔子汉字网首次发现汉字部件音位(汉语拼音首字母)等同于ASCII码,是汉字的序,是汉字形、音、义属性之外的第四属性;以之为核心,实现汉字教学和信息处理之互动,建立起汉字科学系统;弥补了钱学森教授于1993年主持制订的系统科学体系没有汉字汉语一项的遗憾。

关键词:汉字部件;汉字部件音位;汉字第四属性序;部件音位码;汉字科学系统

Abstract: The old theory of phonogram or characters and character components, is not efficiently operated online due to too many homophones and the limits of one's characters. The authors find the phonemes of each Chinese character (the initial letter in Pinyin) are equal to the ASCII (American Standard Code for Information Interchange), which are the order of Chinese characters and the fourth nature of Chinese characters besides form, sound and meaning. Based on the component phoneme theory, Chinese character teaching can be easily learned and Chinese information can be easily operated so that a scientific system of Chinese characters is formed and is making up for the lack of no Chinese character system in the systematic science.

Key Words: Chinese character components; Chinese character component phonemes; order—the fourth Chinese character nature; component phoneme codes; Chinese character scientific system

一、导言

(一)什么是科学系统

按照系统研究开创者奥地利人贝塔朗菲的定义:“系统是相互作用的多元素之复合体。”①这个定义中多元素是指若干具有差异性的同类事物,按照可辨认的特

① 许国志《系统科学》第17页,上海:上海科技教育出版社,2000年第一版。

有方式相互联系在一起,成为一个新的整体并产生新的功能;这样的一个集合称作系统。其形式化表达式为:$S = <A,R>$①。其中 A 为组成系统 S 的全部组分和元素的集合。单个组分和元素之间的关系式为 r,R 是全部关系式集合。组分的关联方式即是该系统的结构,结构是组成该系统的纽带。

科研人员运用数学和计算机技术,在规划、设计、研究、测试、应用等环节,对该事物内部结构的组分(组成成分)和元素,环境中物质、能量、信息的输入和输出等方面,进行调节、协同、优化、整合,称为系统工程。

经验证,对事物有全面的、综合的、整体性的认识,结构达到最优状态,实现了有序,则称系统,即科学系统。

(二)汉字不是科学系统

我国两院院士、系统工程总设计师钱学森教授于 1993 年主持制订的系统科学体系结构,11 个学科中没有汉字汉语。② 我们认为,汉字是用工具在平面载体上(如刀凿在木石上,笔在纸上)做成,有形、音、义、序的属性,属自然科学;它是五千年中华文化的基因和载体,汉民族思维和交际最重要的书面语符号,属人文科学。它的属性如半导体一样是双重的,或可称之为阴阳体。它以字(词素)为基本使用单位。当把字比喻为物质的分子,则字的上一级词/词组为大分子,字的下一级部件为原子,它由笔画组成;笔画是构成汉字的基础材料。传统的汉字使用限于平面载体(主要是纸)上的读写,进入信息时代主要以在计算机上输入输出为主,增加了信息处理的内涵。

国家语委副主任李宇明分析汉字国情时说:“很多字形的输入法拆字主要是考虑技术,与教育领域相关的语言文字传承常常有差距,语文教育讲究字理。这样就出现了学校的信息化教育与语文教学之间的不协调,老师和学生用的软件和课堂上讲的文字原理差别很大。”③他还指出,“汉字编排和检索,实际上就是信息处理。汉字分成多少部是一个问题,哪个字归到哪个部也是问题。东汉许慎在《说文解字》中首创 540 部。明代《字汇》是 214 部,清代《康熙字典》也是 214 部。《新华字典》第 9 版之前是 189 部。这给教育、辞典编纂、信息检索都带来一些困难。”④

当前常用的字处理软件是汉语拼音(全拼)输入。这个方法提供的是一个个

① 许国志《系统科学》第 18 页。

② 许国志《系统科学》第 14 页。

③ 引自光明网刊载李玉兰记者的文章《新规范如何定义汉字拆分》,2009. 3。

④ 同①。

音节,同码字多,需要挑选。yi 音节 303 字,翻页 30 次 ×9 字,眼睛十分疲劳。而字形输入法讲究文字原理,以形声字为汉字基本特征,由形旁和声旁两部分组成,犹如两股道上的车,无法走向统一。电报流水码是人为规定的:“域”的代码是 1008,无论在码本上,还是发送或接收的电文里,只要见到 1008,则必然代表“域”字。这给我们一个启示:字典的部首和检索方式虽然多样,但如果每个字都有自己的代码,则放在哪本字典、哪个部首里,检索结果都是一样的。所以,为汉字编出教学和信息处理的共用代码,是解决问题的关键。

(三)建立汉字科学系统的前提——编形码

1. 非英语文字都要编码

系统相似原理规定,在不改变系统内部结构的前提下,通过改变输入功能而获得好的输出功能,把不相容问题变为相容。由于汉字不含有字母和数字信息,不能直接上网。但人类信息 80% 是靠语言文字传递的(李宇明语),而且当前的键盘处理还是绝大部分,所以必须编码,使之等同于计算机上的 ASCII 码,即数字和字母。同理,任何非英语文字也需要编码才能被计算机处理。例字:

文种	字	组字成分	能上网否	编码/翻译	结果
汉字	诗	讠土寸	否	ytc	成功上网
俄文	Стихй	Сти-хй	否	poem	成功上网

TB 131　非英语文字的编码

2. 汉字编码从娃娃抓起

人教版小学语文第一二册识字量为 400 + 550 = 950 个,从学习任务和学生接受能力来看,加入编码教学和训练不成问题:

(1)汉语拼音码

字的拼式就是汉字的拼音码。在识字、写字的同时记住它的拼式。如:下 xia,中 zhong;厦 xia,种 zhong。

使用拼音码的问题:1. 拼音码只关联汉字音节,一个音节对应 1 至数百字不等,选字非常麻烦;2. 识字量的限制,小学生超过 3000,成人超过 3500,不会认读就不能使用拼音码。

(2)孔子汉字部音码

由孔子汉字网开发的形码,用部件的音位(汉语拼音首字母)打字,基本上不选字:

字	拆为部件	部件拼音	部件音位码	识字谜语
学	⺍冖子	Xiao men zi	Xmz	小门口前有个孩子
校	木六乂(读叉)	Mu liu cha	Mlc	一棵树六个叉
语	讠五口	Yan u kou	Yuk	五张嘴巴齐发言

TB 132　小学生学汉字形码

郑码、五笔字型也是形码。郑码以传统的部首和偏旁为字根,处理上分第一主根、第二主根和普根;五笔字型以肢解的部首、偏旁为字根;两者都依据形声字理论。从系统学说看,形声字具有两类结构成分:形旁和声旁,即具有两个不同的子系统。计算机要同时处理两种不同成分的子系统根本不可能。2009 年国家规范把部首、偏旁统称为部件(包括 9 个笔画),成为元素,只有一个成分。部音码用部件的拼音头作码,即等于 ASCII 码,因而可直接上网互联。

二、汉字系统的特点

(一)汉字集合不是一个简单系统

简单系统没有层次,其内部成分各自独立。如:电子计算机硬件{主机 显示器 键盘 打印机};战斗班成员{张三 李四 王五 于得水}。汉字不是简单系统。

(二)汉字是一个简单巨系统

汉字所包含的子系统(即单字)数目多,从数千到 10 万左右;而且字的内部包含着层次结构。每个汉字都是具有自己独特形、音、义、序信息的综合体,属于简单巨系统。

(三)汉字的内部结构关系

1. 笔画叠加组成部件,有三种结构方式:相离关系如“二、八、氵”,相接关系如“工、丁、厂、口”,相交关系如“十、力、廴”;

2. 笔画与部件叠加组成字,如“王、中、由、甲、史、福”;

3. 部件叠加组成字,如“吕、品、古、胡、湖、福”。

由于叠加的方式多种多样,造成字的结构形态纷繁,出现了分不清部件的穿插形式,如“戠、噩、爽”……

(四)汉字的外部环境

汉字是中文的基本使用单位,它有着强大的扩展功能。字与其扩展形式词、词组、短语和句,共同构成了千变万化的五级书面语(其实也是口语)形态:

结构级别	1	2	3	4	5
结构形态	字(词素)	词	词组	短语	句
单句	我	早先	在中华武术学校	当教练。	(整句)
扩展句	现在的我	希望	到湖北武汉中华武术学校	为外国人开办的培训班授中国功夫课。	(整句)

TB 24　汉语书面语形态

单句和扩展句都根据句意由字连缀而成。口说的句子与书面语完全一样。孔子汉字网总结汉字、汉语的关系时有句言简意赅的话:汉字连续读、说出来就是汉语,即汉字语言。由于说话者讲求速效,任意断句,增添词语,因而与书面语往往有些差别。从实质上看,句子是字的有理扩展和衔接。

(五)汉字的三级结构形态

笔画(材料)——→部件——→单字

TB 25　字的三级结构形态

含义:笔画组成部件,部件组成单字。其中部件是核心,是基本结构单位,汉字教学和信息处理都以部件为纲。笔画不是三级结构中的一个层级,而是组字的结构材料,也可作部件。社会上通称的5种笔画,因折笔含有三个起始方向横折、竖折、撇折,而且各自包孕一些类似笔形,在系统上不统一,所以素质教育和信息处理大多改用九笔画:基本笔形6个加3个折笔:一丨丿㇏丶㇀㇕㇄𠃋。笔画总数:基本笔形6个,加派生笔形26个共32个。①

组字的过程是:一些有关的笔画组成笔画块(非字部件)和部件,一些意义相关的成字部件或再加非字部件共同组成字。

(六)汉字的结构方式

汉字结构历来以"六书"为基础;有的直接把"六书"当作汉字结构。清代学者把"六书"区分为"四体二用"之说,以后学者们又创立"三书说"和"新六书说"。著名学者王宁有创立"汉字构形学"的深厚功底,深谙历时的和共时的汉字结构,熟悉中外汉语教学的规律,他指出,汉字结构是指部件构成汉字的方式和规则。"古人造字是先造出独体的文,然后扩展为合体的字,具有表音、表意两重功能的独体字,承担了基础构件的职责,成为音与义的载体,二度拼合或三度拼合,组成了数万之多的合体字,且把形、音、义的信息带进合体字。"②

① 北京语言大学张静贤《现代汉字笔形论》,《第二届国际汉语教学讨论会论文选》,第499页。
② 王宁《论汉字简化的必然趋势及其优化的原则》,《语文建设》,1992年第2期20页。

(七)汉字的结构类型

把部件之间的界沟作为识别条件,采用一次性平面切分,可直接获得部件;归纳为 9 类(以部件数分类,现代汉字简繁体最多有 9 个部件)15 种基本结构类型,如下:

1　一部字(独体字):在常用字范围内有 256 个:一 二 小 我 丞 燕
2　二部字左右结构:休 匡 旭 酽(严是常用字部件)
3　　　　上下结构:杏 呆 凼 困 瞽(鼓是传统部件)
4　三部字左右结构:树 框 匯
5　　　　上下结构:同 周 凤 函
6　　　　品形结构:架 部 陪
7　四部字上下结构:零 耋 爱 睿
8　　　　混合结构:雕 棱 鬻(鬲是传统部件)
9　五部字上下结构:夐
10　　　　混合结构:赢 噩 樊
11　六部字上下结构:藑
12　　　　混合结构:懿 攀 壑
13　七部字混合结构:疆
14　八部字混合结构:籲 欞
15　九部字混合结构:齉(鼻的部件:自田丌,囊的部件:𠮛冖口口𡗗亻)

TB 27　汉字的结构类型

值得注意的是,通常所说上三包围如"冈"、下三包围如"函"、上左包围如"屠"、上右包围如"司"、下左包围如"过",这 5 种形式从字形重心来看,可用上下结构解释。左三包围如"匠",解释为左右结构的变形;全包围结构如"圆",框架结构如"巫、噩",在不拆部件的前提下解释为上下结构。这样使汉字结构类型简明,可听其名而知其结构成分。

这种改变是否触犯人们的认知习惯呢?科学发展观认为,世界上万事万物都是与时俱进的。著名语言学家王力说:"其实依语言学的观点来看,一般人不追究文字的历史却是对的,因为撇开了历史,然后显得出文字在现代的价值。"①从汉字发展史看,甲、金、篆、隶、楷,简、繁,各种字体即使有变异,也始终保持着形声字的基本格局。

① 王力《汉语言语法纲要》第 18 页,上海教育出版社,1982 年 2 月。

分析汉字结构还采用二岔树分析法:第一级部件组合模式和末级部件组合模式。两者都认定“把、保、朝、凯、揄”这些字是左右结构;“要、骂、药、然”是上下结构。这种分析法对传统的认字、写字有一定的指导作用;而对信息处理的查字、打字、检索,没有什么使用价值。

三、汉字的科学排序

(一)序是检验系统的唯一标准

如何把数千乃至数万汉字排序成易于查找的形式,是汉民族苦苦探寻的大课题。从《说文解字》到《康熙字典》,经历了1900多年才找到部首—笔画数查字法,沿用至今。然而它在计算机网络面前却寸步难行。

英文字词存在着数学上的偏序——科学的序,查字时,按着字母找,一次到位;插入或撤销字词,不影响原来的序列。英文字母是音素,一种单信息符号,它本身就是一种序。正因为这种资质,它才和数字一起被计算机网络采用,成为世界通用的信息工具。

序是宏观可辨认的量度,有序的事物才可以分辨和认识。《辞海》指出,序是“按次第区分、排列”,[①]通过排序把事物内部组分和元素的先后次序确定。序是造成系统的核心因素,是检验系统(包括汉字系统)的唯一标准。

(二)建立汉字系统的基础

国家于2009年颁布了《现代常用字部件及部件名称规范》《通用规范汉字表》《常用字表》和《汉字部首表》这4个文献,是继《说文解字》初立部首、《字汇－康熙字典》采用部首—笔画数查字法之后,汉字发展史上第三座高峰,是中华文化史上的伟大创举。其重大意义在于从4个方面为汉字系统之建立奠定基础:

首先,确立汉字的定量。通用规范字符集8300字规定为汉字的使用平台,按频度分为三级。第一级常用字3500个(国际汉语教学第一级为3000个);第二级次常用字3000个;第三级科技人名地名字1800个。另外还有国标扩字符集21003字,以及拥有27484个字的18030字符集,以满足大字量需要者。

其次,确立汉字的定形。颁布的540个部件是组成汉字的基本结构成分。换句话说,全部汉字由这540个部件组成。汉字是方块形的,每个汉字的形体就由所属的部件按结构类型固定下来。“汉字是形声字”这个历史惯语,升华为“汉字由部件(含非字部件和笔画)组成”这个定义。

---

① 许国志《系统科学》第180页,上海:上海科技教育出版社,2000年第一版。

第三,引导汉字的定序。部件包括非字部件都具有类似字一样的形、义、音信息;音是双重的:音节和音位。看、读字的一个部件,如“培”字里面的“土”,首先听到的音响是音节 tu,仔细品味,这个音节的爆发力是“t”,叫作音位,即“能够区别意义的最简单的语音单位”(《现汉》语)。孔子汉字网首次发现,部件音位是汉字的新属性,即字的序,因而汉字有了形、义、音之外的第四属性。“培”的部件是土、立、口,部件音位是 tlk,那么 tlk 就是“培”字的代码,是它的序。序是事物包括汉字成为系统的唯一条件。当全部汉字有序之时,便是汉字科学系统建成之日。

第四,引导汉字的定性。汉字的性质首先由西方人根据字的形态和功能定性为表意文字。随后国内外学者以字的三级结构为视点,定名多种汉字性质:

⊙以词为视点的有:象形文字(王凤阳、成中英),表意文字(胡裕树),表词文字(王德春)。

⊙以单字为视点的有:意音文字、词素文字、词素—音节文字、语素文字、语素—音节文字、语素—意符文字(赵元任、吕叔湘、刘庆俄、苏培成)……

⊙以部件为视点的有:意符音符记号文字(裘锡奎),新会意字(安子介);改革开放以来,由于汉字第四属性——字序的发现,孔子汉字网宣称汉字性质是“以部件音位排序的表意文字,简称部音文字”。

(三)笔画是汉字的基本元素

笔画是汉字大厦最底层的结构材料,是造成汉字形体的基本元素。其生成过程是:笔画叠加即涌现(突现)一个新的整体(层次)。当它再次与笔画叠加,或与另一个整体叠加,即再涌现一个层次。这样的过程多次出现,使字的结构形态即字的数量增多。许慎《说文解字》对文字孳乳的解释:先造出一至多个笔画的独体“文”,然后孳乳出由多个“文”合成的合体“字”。每一新层次产生,都给整字带来新的意蕴,使整字所包含的音、形、义信息,超出原有笔画和部件任何一个、两个或多个之和,按科学说法就是“整体大于部分之和”。

随着笔画与部件无极限的涌现,字的笔画数从 1 增加到 64 画,总字数达到十万。《说文解字》以义类检索,1900 年后《字汇—康熙字典》建立起部首 × 笔画数 × 五种笔形的三重信息的综合排序,延续到现在。不必说从《康熙字典》找字如大海捞针,就连最大众化的《新华字典》,也须经过两次转换、7 个步骤,找到的还不是唯一(参见附 2)。汉字无序的主要原因是笔画。

(四)字谜引路字序

汉民族历来有拆字做谜的传统。2500 年前我国第一部史书《左传》记载:“止戈为武,虫皿为蛊。”明确析出二字的结构成分及其含义,“止戈”是停止干戈,即反对战争;"虫皿"是虫蛀器皿,引申为蛊惑人心。此后诸如"千里草,十日卜",暗示汉朝末年权臣董(千里草)卓(十日卜),诅咒他"不得生"。"黄绢幼妇外孙齑臼",是三国魏才子杨修对曹娥碑文的解读。黄绢即色丝,丝色合成"绝"字;幼妇即少女,女少合成"妙"字;外孙,是女儿的子,女子合成"好"字;齑臼,齑是葱姜蒜等辛味,臼是钵盂,是受器,受、辛合成"辞"(繁体是辤,等于辭)字。这4个字赞美曹娥碑文是一篇"绝妙好辞"。越到近代,拆字认字的越多。清代文字学家王筠首次提出拆字教学理念:"人之不识字也,病于不能分。苟分一字为数字,则易学而难忘矣!"①直至现在,人们在日常生活和素质教育中说一个姓字时,把拼音头(音位)也说出来,这种由古代"射覆"嬗变而来的猜谜式语言,帮助听话者快而准地找到目标,是利用汉字本身的序来传接信息的典范。例字:

口语	含义	听到的部件音节	部件音位码	在全汉字中的序
弓长张	弓长组成"张"字	gong chang	gc	gc
木子李	木子组成"李"字	mu zi	mz	mz
禾口王程	禾口王组成"程"字	he kou wang	hkw	hkw
立口阝部	立口阝组成"部"字	li kou er	lke	lke

TB 34　语言生活诠释字序的例

正当"山穷水尽疑无路"之时,出现了"山开旷望旋平陆"的明朗前景。用部件音位法把各个字符集以至全汉字集的单字进行编码,是实现汉字有序之路。

(五)部件音位码体现汉字本身的序

通用字符集有三个连续的集合:1级字、2级字、3级字,各是一个子系统。既然汉字无序,则由单字构成的三个字符集也不会有序。它们相加可以成为一个大的汉字集合,但因无序,决不会成为系统。

一个单字也是一个集合,一个子系统。它有两个结构层次:单字和部件,两者各有自己的集合,不存在数学上的偏序关系(即序),因而两者不能直接关联。

当前汉字字词典大多采用部首笔画数查字法。这种方法要处理部首、笔画数和笔顺三种信息包含7个步骤,其中笔顺还要区分5种笔画的25种两两排列。鉴于其步骤繁复,通用字符集和常用字部件表只采用笔画数一种信息。其实所谓一种信息也并不单一。某个笔画数之下如何排序,还要按五种笔形排列。"简",

① 见于被誉为清代"《说文》四大家"之一的王筠《文字蒙求·自序》。

13 画，首二笔为丿一。这样的序列已难于记忆，何况“13 画、首二笔为丿一”的字，在通用字符集中有错、锚等 62 个。看来用部首、笔画数查字，不过是权宜之计。

“汉字无序”是从字形方面说的，而从汉语拼音方面来探讨汉字的序没有意义。因为汉语拼音只关联字的音节，对音节下的同音字不予区分，也无法区分。

汉字部件音位码简称孔子码或部音码，在国家语委“根据字理、从形出发”这一原则拆字，在音位学说的指引下抽绎出部件音位（汉语拼音首字母）作代码，在长期的查字、打字实践中几乎无同码，可以作为汉字的身份标志——序。“兼”：独体字，字的音位 j ＋首笔点 d ＋次笔撇 p，组成字代码 jdp；“简”：合体字，首部件竹 z＋次部件门 m＋三部件日 r，组成字代码 zmr。于是“兼”“简”这两个同音字有了各自的序，在任何汉字词典、资料目录、古今汉字文献以及计算机各种传媒之中，都代表这两个字。推而广之，可获得全部汉字的序。

（六）字的统一编码

TB 361

此编码模式示意从字到码的转换过程：由部件组成的二维平面型方块单字，取前 4 个部件为一维线型部件集，转换成一维线型部件音位代码。编码公式是：

$$Hz = a \pm b \pm c \pm d \cdots\cdots \pm n$$ TB 362

其中：＋表堆叠，－表平排，a、b、c……n 为部件的码。

例字：瀛（全部件编码）＝氵－｛亡＋口＋［月－女－凡］｝＝$d-\{w+k+[v-n-f]\}=dwkvnf$

瀛（查字打字码，取 1 2 3 4 码）＝氵＋亡＋口＋月＝d w k v

四、以部件音位为核心建成汉字科学系统

（一）部件音位码促进汉字教学

1. 认字：用字谜辅助认识字形

以部件的音义编字谜，其形象性和趣味性促进了国内外学生的积极性而提高习得效率。如北京语言大学对外汉语教学《汉语教程》一年级上下册生字共 382 个，编出字谜 105 个，占总字数的 27.5%，其中含“口”的字谜有十多个：

五张嘴巴齐说话(语)　千张嘴巴齐发言(话)　水多可饮千张嘴(活)
小门口前有土堆(堂)　小门口下晒毛巾(常)　人有一张嘴(合)
人有一口一只手(拿)　四方操场王子点兵(国)

2. 读字:抓住标音字

传统形声字的偏旁有示音作用,但不准确。部音码从中挑选出一些示音准确的来辅助教学,称标音字。

⊙准确标音的100多个:

○由一个部件指示,如"妻"组:凄、棲。

○由两个部件组合的偏旁指示,如"代"组:贷、岱。

○由三个部件组合的偏旁指示,如"胡"组:湖、葫。

○由四个部件组合的偏旁指示,如"爱(愛)"组:暧、嫒。

⊙基本准确提示字音的(不计声调)200多个:

○由一个部件提示,如"东(東)"组:冻、栋。

○由两个部件组合的偏旁提示,如"匡"组:框、筐。

○由三个部件组合的偏旁提示,如"居"组:锯、剧。

○由四个部件组合的偏旁提示,如"蒙"组:檬、朦。

当一个人会读300多个常用字,就已经超过扫盲标准2500字的十分之一。这是值得追求的目标。

但要警惕!国内俗语"秀才先生读半边"是个误导,一读就错。比如以"合"为部件的字有10多个读音,只有盒、颌、郃、饸这4个字读hé,其他字请你试一下,看看能读准多少?(答案见[附1]。)

3. 写字:用三步写字法

把笔画叠架的传统写字方式,改为由笔画—部件—整字的三步写字法:

⊙第一步,学写笔画。从学画圆圈到写笔画,掌握笔画构字的三种基本类型。

⊙第二步,学写由笔画构造成字部件(即独体字)和非字部件。掌握256个独体字。

⊙第三步,学写由部件构成合体字。由于写字教材标明了合体字的部件及其编码方式,对查字、打字提供了码本启示。

[附2]教育科学出版社小学一年级(上)《写字练习册》第18页。

(二)部件音位码提高汉字信息处理效率

1. 打字

合体字:打1~4个部件音位码(拼音头);独体字:击音位,或再加首、次、三笔的音码。部音码与五笔字型比较,效率提高2倍多,总比率为238∶100。

2. 查字

以部件的音位码查字，基本上可以一次查到。

用查字力度对部音码和新华字典部首查字法对比，效率为 7.2∶1，超出近 7 倍。[附 3]

3. 检索

举凡字词典的字词、信息资料、物资管理，都可用部音码代替部首笔画数法检索，国家和地方的大小会议代表姓名排序，也可以用部音码代替姓氏笔画数排序；按 2 字词、3 字词、4 字以上词打字即可。

（三）部件的形/音转换双重性功能

历来归结汉字的特征是形声字，由部首和偏旁两部分组成，包含各自系统的两种信息，因而不能直接关联。

2009 年国家规范把部首、偏旁统称作部件。它同字一样，也是形音义序信息的综合体。它的形包含着音的信息，具有形/音转换的双重性；读部件，抓住音位（汉语拼音首字母），就是部件音位码。这是一种等同于数学偏序的字母序，其功能如同英文字母。原来拼形的汉字与拼音的英文不相容的问题完全冰释，实现了汉字键盘输入与英文一致：

中文：词（形）——字（形）——部件（形/音）

≠　　≠　　‖　　TB 43

英文：词（音）——词素（音）——字母（音）

‖

键盘字母

（四）汉字部音码是汉字的科学系统

经过长期的实践，孔子汉字网向社会宣告一个关于汉字性质的假说："汉字是以部件音位排序的表意文字，简称部音文字。"它概括了汉字共时的、历时的实践经验，升华传统的人工处理汉字信息方法，优化汉字教学，并把汉字教学作为汉字信息处理的基础，使信息处理获得高效，反过来又促进汉字教学，两者相辅相成。

历来汉字研究都是在形声字理论上踯躅。创新引出"部音文字"理论，挖掘出古今汉字的序，抹平中外文字的鸿沟，跃上计算机和网络的信息高速路。

汉字结构以部件为基本成分，汉字信息在部件音位。部件是字之魄，部件音位是字之魂，魂魄一体，载负着中华文化搏激流而勇进。

自《说文解字》近两千年来，汉民族孜孜探寻汉字科学排序，而今修成适用于古今汉字的正果。汉字部音码解决了汉字无序的千古难题，经汉字教学和信息处理的严峻洗礼而成为科学系统,必将促进中华文化之发达,助圆中国梦。

[附1]有共同的偏旁(以“合”为例)但读音极少相同的字例16个:盦 an1　姶(姓)e4　鸽 ge1　合 he2/ge2　韐 ge2　鞈 ge2　鮯 ge2　蛤 ge2/ha2　閤 ge2　䶎 ge2　弇 yan3　拿 na2　龕 kan1　翕 xi1　给 gei3/ji3　颌 he2

[附2]教育科学出版社小学一年级上《写字练习册》第18页,合体字下标有部件。

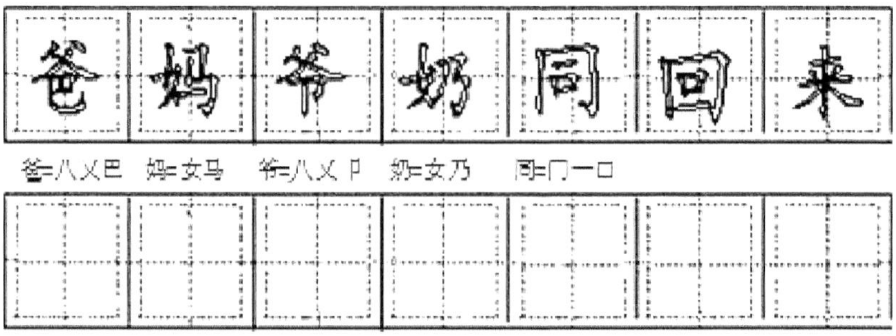

[附3]部音法查字与新华字典部首法查字比较

○《新华字典》部首法查字(7个步骤)

步　骤		1.	2.	3.	4.	5.	6.	7.		
目标字	查找的内容	查哪个部首?在何页?	该部首有几画	该部首在部首目录何处	该部首在检字表何处	该字除去部首有几画	该字在该部的何处	该字在正文的页码	与部音码信息量之比	与部音码效率之比
江	信息	氵	3画	3画28#	P58	3画	3画第5	p223	44:6	7.3:1
	在何页	P16				P58				
	信息量	2	3	28	1	4	5	1		
妹	信息	女	3画	3画42#	P47	5画	5-4	P329	59:5	11.8:1
	在何页	P16				P47				
	信息量	2	3	42	1	6	4	1		
爱	信息	爫	4画	4画38#	P65	6画	爫-9	P3	62:9	6.8:1
	在何页	P17				p65				
	信息量	2	4	38	1	7	9	1		
合计									165:23	7.17:1

《新华字典》部首法查字数据

○部音码查字(3 个步骤)

	步骤	1.	2.	3.	小计	小计
目标字		拆分部件	换拼音头 (斜体为区别码)	在正文的 页码	与部首法 信息量之比	与部首法 效率之比
江	信息	氵工	dg*i*	p559	7 : 44	1 : 6.3
	在何页	x				
	信息量	3	3	1		
妹	信息	女未	nu	P201	6 : 59	1 : 9.83
	在何页	y				
	信息量	3	2	1		
爱	信息	爫冖ナ又	zmsi	P3	10 : 62	1 : 6.2
	在何页	z				
	信息量	5	4	1		
合计					23 : 165	1 : 7.17

孔子部音码查字数据

手语词任意性的实例分析

首都经济贸易大学外国语学院　刘润楠

摘　要：直接描写10个常用的形象性程度比较高的北京动物手语词的打法并分析、探讨其任意性，即这10个动物手语词有可能被不懂手语的人猜测成其他含义。如果不使用现在的手势表示"鼠"、"熊"、"骆驼"、"象"、"猩猩"和"河马"这6种动物，还可以采用其他的手势同样形象地、生动地、具有理据性地表示这些动物。证明了虽然手语词的理据性明显、形象性强，但手语符号同样具有任意性，手语之所以能够成为聋人交流的工具不是因为它的理据性，而是因为它的任意性和规约性。

关键词：手语；任意性；理据性；实例

Abstract: This thesis describes the forms of ten Peking Sign Language words, which are highly iconic. It analyzes the arbitrariness of the ten words through showing other various possible meanings about the forms of the ten words. And it also illustrates other forms which can be used to iconically mean the six animals: mouse, bear, camel, elephant, chimpanzee and hippopotamus. Though Peking Sign Language is highly iconic, it is also arbitrary. Peking Sign Language can be used as a commutation media not for its iconicity, but for its arbitrariness.

Key Words: sign language; arbitrariness; iconicity; examples

一、引言

长久以来，聋人手语给人们的印象一直是图画似的、具体的、哑剧似的和形象的。甚至很多语言研究者都认为手语是一系列图画似手势的集合。如果这种图画似的语言只是对事物的形象化描绘或模拟、只具有理据性不具有任意性，人们的确有理由质疑手语的语言性质——因为语言学界一直公认符号的任意性是人类语言的本质属性之一。如果聋人手语不具有任意性，那它从本质上同有声语言（如汉

本文是2011年国家社科基金项目"再论聋人手语的语言地位——基于手语符号任意性的实验研究"（项目号11CYY020）的研究成果之一。

语、英语)的确是完全不同的。

事实的确如此吗?1979年两位美国学者Klima(克利马)和Bellugi(贝卢吉)针对手语的任意性进行了卓有成效的研究。首先,他们注意到同一个概念在各国手语中常常反映为不同的表现形式。比如"树"这个概念,美国手语、丹麦手语和中国手语分别抽取树的不同特征进行模仿。美国手语一只手横于胸前,另一只手垂直其上,五指张开,手腕及前臂扭动,模仿树干、树枝及树在风中摇摆的情态;丹麦手语双手对称在胸前划环状勾画树冠轮廓,再向下划勾画树干轮廓;中国手语则将双手围成树干形状并向上运动。这三种手语不仅选取不同的特征对树进行模仿,对同一特征模仿的形式也有差别。

各国手语对同一概念的不同表现形式说明了手语的多样性,也从一个方面证明了手语的形式和意义之间不具有天然的联系——它们之间的关系是约定俗成的。

接下来,Klima和Bellugi通过实验证明了没有手语背景的听力正常人很难正确猜出手语词的意思,说明了手语符号不仅具有象似性、理据性,同时具有任意性。在Klima和Bellugi以后,以Clayton Valli(克莱顿·瓦利)和Ceil Lucas(西尔·卢卡斯)为代表,国外研究者普遍认为手语词同时具有理据性和任意性,即一部分手语词表现出明显的理据性,另一部分手语词则表现出更多的任意性。

徐望模仿Klima和Bellugi的实验,以上海手语为研究对象得出了同Klima和Bellugi相同的研究结果,即手语符号具有任意性。中国大陆对手语任意性做过研究的还有蔡浩中,他指出聋人手语和有声语言一样,其"形式和意义之间没有必然的、本质的联系,两者的结合完全由社会'约定俗成'"。傅逸亭、梅次开和赵锡安介绍了一些概念在几个国家手语中的不同打法,客观上也反映了手语符号的任意性。

本文的研究与以往的研究不同,以北京地区手语为研究对象,通过直接描写10个常用的形象性比较高的动物手语词的打法和分析、探讨其任意性和理据性试图论证手语符号任意性的存在。为了论证这10个动物手语词的任意性,阐明这些动物词的手势和它们表示的意义之间不存在必然的联系,本文主要从两个方面展开论述:一方面本文分析了这10个手势有可能被不懂手语的人猜测成的其他含义;另一方面针对"鼠"、"熊"、"骆驼"、"象"、"猩猩"和"河马"6个手势还探讨了如果不用这些手势表示这6种动物,还有没有其他的手势也可以同样形象地、生动地、具有理据性地表示这些动物,即论证这些动物手语词的打法和其含义之间不是天然的一对一的关系。

二、10 个常用动物手语词的任意性和理据性分析

(一)虎

打法:

第一个手势:双手五指伸出并弯曲,成"抓"状,掌心向下,置于胸前,向前挠动两下。

第二个手势:左手中指、无名指和小拇指平伸,其余两指指尖捏合,掌心朝后,置于额头前方。右手食指竖起,其余四指指尖捏合,掌心朝左,也置于额头前方,并且置于左手的内侧。同时,右手食指的侧面与左手平伸的三指搭成"王"的形状。

图 1 "虎"的第一个手势

图 2 "虎"的第二个手势

理据性:第一个手势模仿动物的前爪;第二个手势中在额头前搭成的"王"字模仿虎头上的"王"形花纹,这和虎是百兽之王也有关联。

任意性:

(1)虽然第一个手势看起来很像是模仿动物的前爪在挠动,但是有爪子的动物除了"虎"以外还有很多种,而且这个手势也很像"树根"。

(2)首先,如果事先知道这两个手势代表某种动物,不懂手语的中国人基本可以猜出这个手语词表示"虎"。但如果没有被预先告知这个手势表示某种动物,看到后可能会被猜成汉字"王"。其次,对于不懂手语的外国人来说,这个手势更不一定和"虎"挂上钩。因为,第一,他们不认识"王"这个汉字。第二,在他们的文化当中可能不认为虎的头上有"王"形花纹。第三,他们更不大可能认同虎是百兽之王。基于这几点,他们便不可能由"三横一竖"想到虎。

（二）鼠

图3 “鼠”

打法：右手拇指、中指和无名指指尖捏合，食指和小拇指翘起，掌心向下，从胸前向前滑动。

理据性：“右手的拇指、中指和无名指指尖捏合，食指和小拇指翘起，掌心朝下”好像模仿鼠的小脑袋、耳朵和尖嘴巴。“从胸前向前滑动”是模仿鼠窜的样子。

任意性：

（1）“拇指、中指和无名指指尖捏合，食指和小拇指翘起”也很像兔、鹿、牛的头或者蜗牛的头，或者采摘时的手形。“从胸前向前滑动”也很像兔子、鹿或者牛在伸头。

（2）其他可能被用来表示这个手语词的方式：右手五指并拢并翘起食指、中指、无名指和小拇指的指根，形成一个三角形的空心拳，置于左手掌心之上——这个手势通过模仿老鼠的外形来表示鼠；也可以通过模仿老鼠的尖嘴巴来表示鼠，右手的拇指、食指和中指伸直，指尖捏合，其余两指缩回至掌心，形成一个锥形，并置于口部的前方。

（三）猴

图4 “猴”

打法:右手四指并拢并弯曲,拇指自然伸出,右臂弯曲。

理据性:这个手势是借用和模仿生活中表示猴子或者“孙悟空”的动作。

任意性:首先,如前文对手语词“虎”的任意性的分析,如果事先知道这个手势表示某种动物,不懂手语的中国人基本能猜出这个手势表示“猴”。但如果事先没有被告知是动物,可能会被猜成“孙悟空”或者“猴子、孙悟空在远眺”。其次,对于一个不了解“孙悟空”文化的外国人来说,这个手势很难和“猴”联系起来。在他们眼里,这个手势可能代表“鹤”——因为弯曲的右手好像鹤的头,而弯曲的手臂好像鹤的长脖子;也可能表示某个动作,如照镜子、用手遮挡太阳光等。

(四)狼

图5 “狼”

打法:右手五指张开,从口前向前方拉出并捏合指尖。

理据性:右手在口前方捏合好像模仿狼的尖嘴巴。

任意性:这个动作也很像模仿“面罩”及其相连的导管,或者能让人联想到焦点、聚集等意思。而且,即便这个动作是模仿尖嘴巴,也不一定是狼的尖嘴巴,因为很多动物的嘴巴都是长而尖的,例如狐狸。

(五)熊

打法:

第一个手势:右手拇指、食指弯曲,指尖抵在鼻子的两边。

第二个手势:双手自然平伸,一前一后交替移动。同时,上身随着交替的双手有节奏地左右晃动。

理据性:

第一个手势很像是指点熊的两个大鼻孔。

第二个手势像是模仿熊走路沉重而笨拙的样子。

图6 “熊”的第一个手势

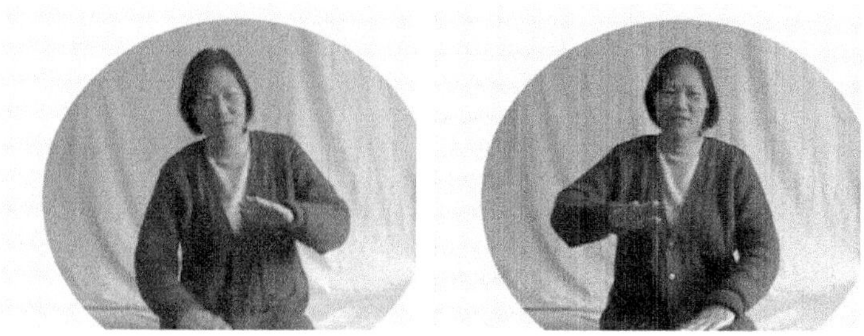

图7 “熊”的第二个手势

任意性：

(1)对于不懂手语的人来说，第一个手势不大容易让人猜到表示熊的鼻孔。即使想到了它有可能指鼻孔，也有可能被猜成“牛或马的鼻孔”——因为它们的鼻孔也很大而且人们对“牛”和“马”更熟悉。另外，这个动作也有可能被看成是暗示某个人的鼻子大或者鼻子的两边长了东西或者干脆就是指鼻子两边的两个穴位。

(2)第二个手势有可能被理解为“拍球”。

(3)其他可能被用来表示这个手语词的方式：举起双臂，在高于头顶约一掌的位置，双手自然张开，掌心朝前，来回晃动上身。这个动作是通过模仿熊举起熊掌的样子来表示“熊”的概念。

(六)猫

打法：双手的拇指和食指指尖捏合，其余三指伸出并使指间保持一定距离，指尖稍微倾斜，指向斜上方，掌心朝后，从口部向两边平拉。

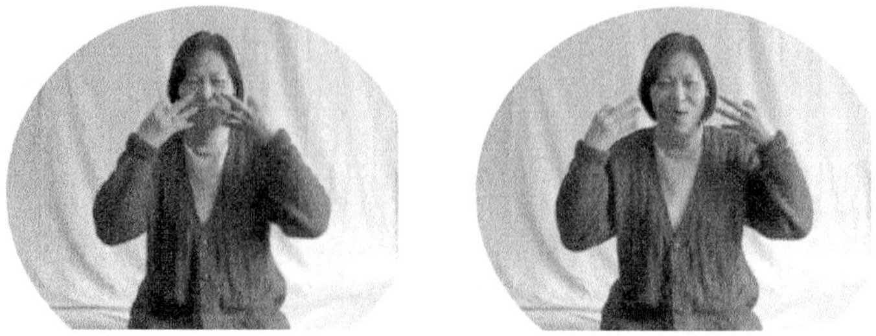

图 8 “猫”

理据性:这个手势是模仿“猫的胡须”和日常生活中表示猫的动作。

任意性:如同前面的手语词“猴”和“虎”的任意性的分析,如果事先知道这个手势代表某种动物,没学过手语的人会说这个手势表示“猫”。但是如果事先不知道,也可能会被猜成嘴的两边留着大胡子的人物,例如“张飞”或“李逵”;也可能会被猜成“做美容”——因为这个手势很像做面部美容时美容师的动作手法。另外,对于不熟悉中国文化的外国人来说,即使他们知道这个手势代表某种动物,他们也不一定会猜对。因为只有在中国文化中或者在中国的卡通画中,猫的典型特征才是“嘴两边各画三根胡须”,而在其他文化中情况未必如此。例如,全球著名的美国动画《猫和老鼠》,其中的明星人物——名为“汤姆”的一只猫,它的嘴两边各有两根胡须。

(七)骆驼

图 9 “骆驼”

打法:右手五指聚在一起,左手自然平伸,掌心朝上,托住右臂的肘关节,右前臂以肘关节为轴前后晃动。

理据性:这个手势好像是模仿骆驼的头和脖子在晃动着。

任意性：

(1)这个手势看起来可能更像是“蛇的头和脖子在前后移动”。也很像鸵鸟、仙鹤等某种鸟的头和长脖子在晃动。

(2)其他可能被用来表示这个手语词的方式：先用右手拍一下后背，然后，用右手的食指或者右手在胸部前方的空中画一个类似“m”的图形。这个手势通过模仿骆驼的驼峰来指代骆驼。

(八)象

图10 “象”

打法：双手自然伸出，左手心朝右，左手手指顶住右肘内侧，右臂和右手来回晃动。

理据性：这个手势好像在模仿大象来回晃动的长鼻子。

任意性：

(1)这个手势可能会给不懂手语的人很多的联想。人们可能会猜这个手势表示“牛或马”——因为这个动作很像它们用尾巴赶走苍蝇的动作；人们也可能会猜成是胳膊受了伤或骨折了。

(2)其他可能表示这个手语词的方式：右手伸出食指，其余四指缩回，右手的食指尖抵在鼻尖上，然后呈一条弧线向下拉出约30厘米，并在末端向内弯曲。这个动作也是通过模仿大象的长鼻子来表示“象”。

(九)猩猩

打法：挺胸，双手成拳状，交替捶打前胸。

理据性：这个手势是模仿大猩猩捶打前胸的手势。

任意性：

(1)这个手势也很像生气、发怒或捶胸顿足；也可能被不懂手语的人猜成“自己很有力量”的意思。

(2)其他可能被用来表示这个手语词的方式：前臂向前探出，双手缩回，五指

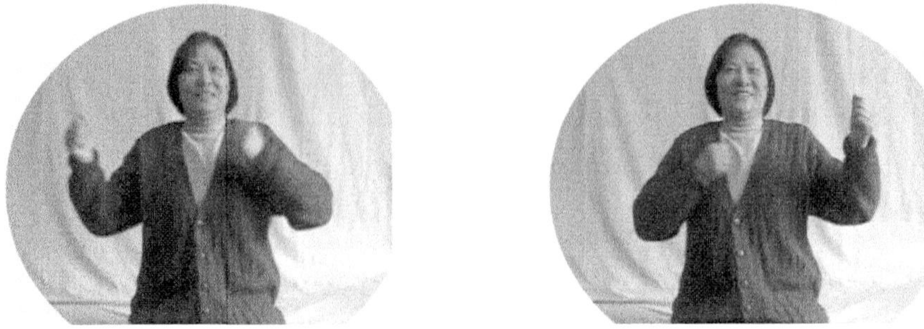

图 11 “猩猩”

弯曲——这个动作是通过模仿猩猩双臂拄地的样子来表示猩猩的;也可以通过把聋人手语“星星”和聋人手语“动物的爪子”组合起来表示“猩猩”。

(十)河马

图 12 “河马”

打法:双手五指张开并弯曲,掌心相对并扣合在一起,置于口的前方。之后,以手掌的末端为轴,双手向上下分开,同时尽量张大嘴。

理据性:这个手势是模仿河马的大嘴张开和闭合。

任意性:

(1)这个手势有可能被不懂手语的人猜测为鳄鱼、虎、豹等大嘴动物;或者被猜成“青蛙”,张开、闭合的双手象征青蛙发出的“呱呱”声。

(2)其他可能被用来表示这个手语词的方式:把聋人手语“河”和聋人手语“马”组合起来。

三、结语

通过对 10 个常用的北京动物手语词打法的描述和理据性、任意性的分析和探讨,一方面我们看到这10个动物手语词的形象性确实很高,临摹性极强,具有很明显的理据性。但是另一方面它们同样具有任意性,它们的打法或者形式和意义之间,即手语符号的能指和所指之间不存在必然联系——在这一点上,手语和汉语、英语等其他有声语言是一样的。这既肯定了手语作为人类自然语言的地位,同时也再次验证了任意性是人类语言的共性。

对于没有接触过本文分析的这些动物手语词的人来说,他们很难一下子百分之百地猜中这些手势所模仿的动物。就算是"虎"、"猫"和"猴"这几个看来理剧性极强的手语词,也不是在任何情况下都可以被完全猜对的。因为这几个手语词的打法中有很深的文化烙印,所以对于不懂手语的外国人来说要正确猜出其含义更加困难。如前文对手语词"猴"的任意性的分析,对于不知道"孙大圣"为何许人也的外国人来说,他们很难从模仿"孙大圣"招牌动作的手势联想到"猴"的意思。

另一方面,这些动物手语词的打法并不是唯一"合理"的选择。我们完全可以使用前文任意性分析中提出的其他的手势动作表示这些动物——这些手势动作同样形象、生动,具有理据性。换而言之,这些动物手语词的打法之所以成为现在的样子,而不是其他的样子,起决定作用的不是它们的形象性、理据性而恰恰是它们的任意性和规约性。如果不经过像学习其他外语的过程,例如英语,我们仅靠"猜"是"猜"不出手语表示的真正含义的。

参考文献:

[1]Klima,Edward S. and Bellugi,Ursula. *The Signs of Language*[M]. Cambridge:Harvard University Press,1979:10.

[2]Valli,Clayton and Ceil Lucas. *Linguistics of American Sign Language*[M]. Washington D. C:Gallaudet University Press,2000.

[3]徐望. 上海手语常用词象似性实验分析[D]. 复旦大学,2005.

[4]蔡浩中. 聋人手势语的语言资格[A]. 聋人手语概论(附录)[M]. 上海:学林出版社,1986:125-126.

[5]傅逸亭、梅次开等. 聋人手语概论[M]. 上海:学林出版社,1986:89-91.

[6]赵锡安. 中国手语研究[M]. 北京:华夏出版社,1999:68.

向心理论的应用与发展

首都经济贸易大学外国语学院　刘欣

摘　要：向心理论是从语篇注意焦点出发，关注处理语篇指称方式和语篇连贯问题的理论。国内外学者对向心理论进行了验证和修正，并广泛应用该理论于语篇局部连贯研究、回指消解和文本自动生成等领域。本文将在介绍向心理论的基础上，对向心理论的应用与发展进行梳理，并指出相关问题。

关键词：向心理论；局部连贯；参数研究；回指消解；语篇生成

Abstract: Centering Theory is a theory focusing on discourse center of attention and concerning discourse referential mode and discourse coherence. Scholars home and abroad test and improve this theory and apply it to fields like discourse local coherence, anaphora resolution and text automatic generation. This article is an introduction about Centering Theory and its appliance and development with relevant problems being discussed.

Key Words: Centering Theory; local coherence; parametric study; anaphora resolution; text generation

一、引言

向心理论（Centering Theory）是20世纪80年代由美国语言学家和认知科学家提出的关于语篇局部结构和语篇处理的理论。该理论描述了语篇的注意焦点、指称方式的选择和语篇连贯性之间的关系，利用“中心”概念对语篇片段的连贯性进行解释（洪明，2011）。该理论对语篇回指研究、语篇局部连贯的计算机识别以及文本自动生成等方面都有实际的指导意义，因此自提出以来便得到学术界的广泛关注，研究成果也十分丰富。本文在介绍该理论框架的基础上，试图对国内外对该理论的应用、修正和发展完善进行简单梳理，并重点关注其在语篇局部连贯分析的发展，以期推动对计算机处理自然语言连贯性的研究。

二、向心理论的理论基础

向心理论是在语篇焦点理论和语篇向心模式理论的基础上发展起来的。语篇焦点理论(Grosz 1977;Sidner 1979,1983;Grosz and Sidner 1986)的两位创始人是 Grosz(格罗希)和 Sidner(希德勒)。他们将认知的观点引入语篇分析中,关注语篇的注意焦点。Grosz 认为语篇存在整体焦点和局部焦点。整体焦点是与语篇整体相关的一系列实体,它们由情景语境决定。局部焦点是单个句子中的聚焦实体,会随着语段的推进产生变化。语句焦点的延续保持或转换会影响语篇的连贯性,同时影响受话者对语句的理解。Sidner 又将局部焦点分为当前焦点(current discourse focus)和潜在焦点(potential focus),并建立了一系列规则,通过计算可以识别回指的指称对象。在此基础上,Grosz & Sinder 提出了语篇结构理论。语篇结构包括三个成分:语言结构、意向结构和注意状态。语言结构包括语段如何组织成语篇片段、各片段之间的关系以及句法等外部语言特征。意向结构包括语篇的整体交际意图和片段意图。语言结构最终取决于意向结构。注意状态指的是语篇任一点上由意向结构和语言结构所决定的语篇参与者的注意焦点。总体而言,意图结构影响注意状态的变化,注意状态的变化通过语言结构表现出来。

语篇向心模式理论(Joshi and Kuhn 1979;Joshi and Weinstein 1981)是由 Joshi & Weinstein 提出的。他们认为语篇具有一元倾向(monadic tendency),如果对语段进行一元谓词演算,势必会降低语篇推理难度。他们提出了语篇片段中的前瞻中心(forward-looking center)和回指中心(backward-looking center)的概念,前瞻中心确定句子与下文的连接,回指中心决定句子与上文的连接,其中的回指中心就是突出的谓词诸论元中的一个。通过对回指中心的研究,可以推断句子的局部连贯,并将单句含义与语篇整体联系起来。

基于这两个理论体系,Grosz(1995)最终提出向心理论的框架,包括了三条制约条件和两条规则。Walker(沃尔克勒,1998)完善了向心理论体系。

三、向心理论基本框架

语篇所谈论的对象是语篇实体,作为一种心理表征,语篇实体在具体的语篇中体现为各种指代成分,如名词、代词等。在语篇的任何一个点上,某一个语篇实体可以与上文的实体发生联系,充当回指中心(简称 Cb),同时,这一实体也可以和下文产生联系,充当下指中心(简称 Cf)。语篇中每个话语 U_n 都包含一个下指中心集,记为 Cf(U_n),其中的实体是按照显著度呈等级排序的。每一个非篇首话语中的某个实体被认作为它的回指中心,即 Cb(U_n)。一般来说,Cf(U_n)中包括 U_n 中所有实体,其中包括 Cb(U_n)。在英语中,下指中心的显著度按语法功能排序为:主语 > 直接宾语 > 间接宾语 > 其他。下指中心中显著度最高的成分被称作优选中心(preferred center,简称 Cp),它将优选为下一个话语的 Cb,即 Cb(U_{n+1})。

例如:(1)a. Jeff helped Dick wash the car.

b. He washed the windows as Dick waxed the car.

c. He soaped a pane.

在(1a)中下指中心集包括 Jeff、Dick、car。其中优选中心为 Jeff。Jeff 在(1b)和(1c)中均为回指中心,由代词 he 来替代。通过下指中心和回指中心,话语呈现出连贯的关系。

向心理论还包括三个制约条件和两条规则。其制约条件为:

对于由语段 U_1……U_m组成的语篇片段 D 中的每一个语段 U_i:

(1)只有一个回指中心 Cb(U_i,D)。

	Cb(U_i) = Cb(U_{i-1})或 Cb(U_{i-1}) = [?]	Cb(U_i) ≠ Cb(U_{i-1})
Cb(U_i) = Cp(U_i)	延续	流畅转换

(2)下指中心集合 Cf(U_i,D)的每一个成分都必须在 U_i中实现。

(3)回指中心 Cb(U_i,D)是在 U_i中实现的下指中心 Cf(U_{i-1},D)中显著度最高的那个成分。

第一条件规定了回指中心只能有一个。第二个条件中"实现"的意义在于所有下指中心都必须在该语段表现为某种形式的指代成分,比如代词、零代词、名词短语等。第三个条件说明一个语段的优选中心 Cp(U_i)会预期成为下一个语段的回指中心 Cb(U_{i+1})。

向心理论的两条规则为:

对于由语段 U_1……U_m组成的语篇片段 D 中的每一个语段 U_i:

规则 1:如果下指中心 Cf(U_n)的某一成分在 U_{n+1}中体现为代词,那么 Cb(U_{n+1})也必须体现为代词;

规则 2:延续(continue)过渡优于保持(retain)过渡,保持过渡优于转换(smooth-shift)过渡。

规则 1 是对中心的实现的制约。除非 Cb 也体现为代词,否则话语中的其他成分不能体现为代词。这条规则体现了代词指称的作用,Cb 用代词表现说明谈话人要表明谈话主题的一致性。

例如:(2)a. He has been acting quite odd. (Cb = John = "he")

b. He called up Mike yesterday. (Cb = John = "he")

c. John wanted to meet him urgently. (Cb = John;"him" = Mike)

(转引自 Grosz et al. ,1995:215)

	$Cb(U_i)=Cb(U_{i-1})$ 或 $Cb(U_{i-1})=[?]$	$Cb(U_i)\neq Cb(U_{i-1})$
$Cb(U_i)=Cp(U_i)$	延续	流畅转换
$Cb(U_i)\neq Cp(U_i)$	保持	非流畅转换

在(2c)中,Cb John 没有体现为代词,而非 Cb 的 Mike 却实现为了代词,这就是对规则 1 的违反,对语段的连贯性造成了阻碍。

规则 2 是通过衡量过渡方式来分析语篇的局部连贯程度。当中心处于延续过渡方式时,谈话人的焦点没有转移,受话人理解语篇就相应减少认知推理的负担。具体来说,向心理论对语篇局部连贯的考察依靠回指中心和优选中心之间的关系,具体表现在以下 4 类:

其中 $Cb(U_{i-1})=[?]$表示在上一个语段中没有回指中心 $Cb(U_{i-1})$的情况,比如在语篇的开始。

根据向心理论的制约条件、规则、过渡状态,我们可以对例(3)和例(4)的语篇做如下分析:

(3) a. John went to his favorite music store to buy a piano.

[Cfs = John, store, piano, Cb = none, 过渡方式 = 无]

b. He had frequented the store for many years.

[Cfs = John, store, Cb = John, 过渡方式 = 延续]

c. He was excited that he could finally buy a piano.

[Cfs = John, piano, Cb = John, 过渡方式 = 延续]

d. He arrived just as the store was closing for the day.

[Cfs = John, store, Cb = John, 过渡方式 = 延续]

(4) a. John went to his favorite music store to buy a piano.

[Cfs = John, store, piano, Cb = none, 过渡方式 = 无]

b. It was a store John had frequented for many years.

[Cfs = store, John, Cb = John, Cb(John) ≠ Cp(store), 过渡方式 = 保持]

c. He was excited that he could finally buy a piano.

[Cfs = John, piano, Cb = John, 过渡方式 = 延续]

d. It was closing just as John arrived.

[Cfs = store, John, Cb = John, Cb(John) ≠ Cp(store), 过渡方式 = 保持]

(转引自 Grosz et al., 1995:206)

例(3)的语段多采用延续过渡手段,因而篇章的连贯性较好,而例(4)的语段过渡方式在保持和延续间转换,中心不断变换,使得篇章的连贯性差于例(3)。

四、向心理论的应用与发展

向心理论在问世以来引起国内外学者的广泛关注,对该理论的应用、修正与发展也体现在各个领域,主要包括语篇的局部连贯研究、回指消解、参数化研究、文本自动生成和作文评分系统等。

(1)局部连贯研究

向心理论对局部连贯的自动化考察是有重要意义的。Miltsakaki(2000)等应用向心理论对学生作文进行统计分析,发现非流畅转换方式使用得越多,作文的质量越差,说明向心理论的转换方式可以作为衡量语篇连贯性的标准,通过计算,对语篇质量进行评价。

然而研究者们在检测向心理论的使用中也发现很多问题。Poesio et al.(2004)以博物馆描述展品和介绍展品制作者的语篇以及药品说明为语料,发现主流四分法定义的过渡方式只占总数的16.7%,而出现最多的是无过渡,占47.9%,其次为中心过渡,占18.8%,零过渡占16.7%。他因此将主流的四分法扩充为七分法。即增加了以下三种过渡类型:

中心确立:$Cb(U_i) = Cp(U_i)$,且 $Cb(U_{i-1}) = 0$;

无过渡:$Cb(U_{i-1}) = 0$,且 $Cb(U_i) = 0$;

零过渡:$Cb(U_{i-1}) \neq 0$,且 $Cb(U_i) = 0$

Kibble(1999)认为向心理论制约条件中Cp对Cb的预测性并没有在过渡规则中有所考虑。Strube and Hahn(1996:275;1999:332-4)经过对英语和德语文学语料分别进行分析研究后提出以低价性原则(Cheapness)代替规则2:如果前一语句的优选中心能够正确预测当前语句的回指中心,即 $Cb(U_i) = Cp(U_{i-1})$,那么这对相邻语句之间的过渡是低价的;否则即为高价。低价性过渡优先于高价性过渡,因为低价性原则将语句序列处理的推理成本降至最低。Kibble(2001:585)认为满足低价性原则可以弥补片段首句无法体现显著性的缺陷,将规则2修改为:低价过渡语句对优先于高价过渡语句对。这个原则能够更好地衡量指称的连贯性。

Kibble(1999)还指出,主流四分法中提出的保持过渡优先于流畅转换的情况是没有事实根据的。已有学者(Di Eugenio 1998;Passonneau 1998;Hurewitz 1998,转引自 Kibble 1999:74)证明连贯语篇中流畅转换的比例高于保持过渡,Passonneau(1998)甚至在口语语料中发现转换多于延续过渡。基于此,Kibble(2001)提出如下四项原则取代规则2:

延续性(continuity):优先过渡方式为 $Cf(U_i) \cap Cf(U_{i-1}) \neq ?$

显著性(salience):优先过渡方式为 $Cb(U_i) = Cp(U_i)$

低价性(cheapness):优先过渡方式为 $Cb(U_i) = Cp(U_{i-1})$

衔接性(cohesion):优先过渡方式为 $Cb(U_i) = Cb(U_{i-1})$

国内学者洪明(2011)对以上三种向心理论局部连贯模式进行了对比分析,并通过大学生作文的语料库,对主流模式、七分法和四项原则对语篇连贯量化分析的有效性进行了对比,最后发现 Kibble(基布尔)的四项原则相对更加完善。许宁云(2010)针对语篇中零回指、零过渡的问题,以“诗歌语段对”为例,总结了三种费力衔接过渡类型,弥补向心理论的不足。

(2)回指消解

向心理论对语篇中的回指研究,特别是回指的形式化提供了理论基础。在此基础上 Brennan(布伦南,1987)提出了 BFP 模式,即依据下指中心和回指中心的判定,对所有下指中心集和回指中心组合进行过滤,然后进行切换、排序,最终确定最佳回指。这套方法成为向心理论应用于回指消解的基础,但因其复杂缭乱的操作模式等问题而引发研究者们寻求更为经济简单的方式。

Beaver(比沃,2004)将向心理论与优选论(Optimality Theory)结合,形成了 COT(Centering Optimality Theory)中心优选论。熊学亮(2005)认为 COT 虽然较 BFP 简洁,用主题概念替换了下指中心和回指中心,但解释面有限,对很多语料的解释无能为力,因而其应用性受限。

国内学者许宁云(2006)和王德亮(2004)利用向心理论进行了汉语零回指现象的解析,王德亮(2011)还对汉语回指的消解算法进行了推导。如何完善向心理论,应用于回指消解,特别是汉语语篇的回指研究,还有广阔的空间可为。

(3)参数化研究

向心理论是作为语篇研究的抽象理论提出的,因而对其中一些基本概念的界定并不明确。应用向心理论进行不同语言的语篇分析和计算时,就会因为这些概念的不确定性而出现不同的结果,从而影响了向心理论的有效性。研究者们因此针对向心理论所涉及的各类参数进行研究,以证明参数的调整对向心理论的应用会产生何种影响。

研究最多的参数为下指中心 Cf 的排序。早期向心理论是以英语为研究对象,且以语法角色来设定 Cf 的排序(见上文),Miltsakaki(2003)研究了主句和从句各成分的排序,结论认为主句各成分的显著性高于从句。国内学者段嫚娟(2009)等将语法角色的显著度大体分为三个等级:第一等级为主题、主语以及存现动词引导的名词及其修饰语;第二等级为焦点成分、直接宾语、间接宾语及其修饰语;最后一个等级为旁语、状语及其修饰语;在每一等级中,名词的显著度高于其修饰语。研究者们还发现在词序相对自由的语言中,不适用于依据语法角色进行下指中心显著度的排序。Iida(伊达,1998)发现日语中下指中心中显著度最高的应为主题,其顺序应为主题 > 移情代词 > 主语 > 宾语 > 其他。Rambow(兰博,1993)认为在德语中,语篇实体的出现顺序会影响 Cf 的显著度排列顺序。以语法角色为基础,研究者们可以展开针对不同语言的研究,探索有效的排序方式。

除了对下指中心排序的研究,“实现”和“语句”的定义也是向心理论参数研究的重点。早期向心理论,将语句默认为是整个句子。但是自然语篇中的句子往往比较复杂,包含不同类型的小句。Kameyama(1998)提出将语句定义为“时态小句”,并将语句分两类:一类是并列小句和状语小句,一类是内嵌小句,不对焦点的改变产生持续影响。而 Miltsakaki 却认为,句子的主句才能成为存在焦点的语句。国内学者孙珊珊、许云龙等(2013)对英汉代词回指消解的研究发现,将语句设定为小句要比自然句更有利于零型代词消解。鉴于过去的研究都是对单个参数的考察,研究不构成系统性,Poesio 等对各种版本的研究进行交叉研究,对所有参数进行了综合考察,发现将语句设定为句子更支持向心理论。参数研究对向心理论的完善和应用有重要意义,对语篇分析和回指研究等也有重要价值,但这方面的综合研究还很少,国内只有许余龙和段嫚娟等几位学者从事该方面的研究。

(4)文本自动生成

向心理论在文本自动生成领域最大的应用即是有效的排列信息,增强语篇连贯性。李等人(Roh & Lee,2003)借鉴向心理论生成 4 个连贯评价指标:中心转换顺序、推理成本、相似最大化和事实权重。按照这些指标对语料语句进行排序,结果与原语篇相似度高达 64%。这说明向心理论对增强自动生成文本的连贯性方面有很大意义。

Hasler(汉斯勒,2004)对计算机自动生成缩写(summary)和人工缩写进行对比,发现延续过渡的使用是最佳语篇的统一特点。因此,向心理论中延续过渡的原则可以作为自动生成语篇连贯性的参考依据。

基布尔和波沃尔(2004)认为自然语篇的生成可以分为语篇规划、句子规划和语言实验三个步骤。他们将向心理论的四项原则作为各步骤的制约条件进行实验。研究表明四项原则有助于语篇生成中的小句排列和论元排列。

向心理论在文本自动生成中还可大有作为,但国内这方面的研究还几乎是空白。

五、结语

向心理论对语篇的连贯分析、回指消解和文本自动生成都有非常重要的指导意义。国外相关研究已经较为成熟和深入，主要是对向心理论本身进行验证、补充、修正和完善。但国内这方面的研究还屈指可数，主要集中在几位研究者对于回指消解、参数研究和文本连贯研究方面。向心理论的研究还有待进一步深入，尤其是不同语言、不同体裁的语篇如何利用向心理论进行处理。国内学者可以将向心理论引入汉语的自然语言处理当中，验证其在汉语自然语言处理中的价值。

参考文献：

[1]段嫚娟，许余龙，付相君．前瞻中心的排序对指代消解的影响——一项向心理论参数化实证研究[J]．外国语．2009．(3)：20－27.

[2]孙珊珊等．"语句"和"代词"的设定对英汉指代消解影响的对比分析[J]．外国语．2013，Vol. 36(2)：13－21.

[3]洪明．向心理论的发展与应用研究[J]．学术界．2011(4)：173.

[4]洪明．向心理论在英语写作连贯性量化评价中的应用[J]．外语电化教学．2011(139)：67－72.

[5]王德亮．汉语零形回指解析——基于向心理论的研究[J]．现代外语．2004．Vol. 27(4)：350－359.

[6]王德亮．汉语回指消解算法推导[J]．外语教学．2011，Vol. 32(3)：42－61.

[7]熊学亮，翁依琴．回指的优选解析[J]．外语教学与研究．2005，Vol. 37(6)：432－438.

[8]许宁云．关于向心理论中过渡类型问题的探讨[J]．学术界．2010(2)：76－82.

[9]许宁云．汉语篇章零回指的解析与生成：一项基于语料的向心研究[D]．复旦大学博士学位论文，2006.

[10] Beaver, D. I. *The Optimization of Discourse Anaphora* [J]. Linguistics and Philosophy，2004，27 (3)：3－56.

[11]Brennan S et al. 1987. *A Centering Approach to Pronouns*[C]. In proceedings of the 25th Annual Meeting of the Association for Computational Linguistics. Stanford，CA，1987：155－162.

[12] Grosz, B. J. *The Representation and Use of Focus in Dialogue Understanding* [R]. Technical Report No. 151. SRI International, Menlo Park, California. 1977.

[13] Grosz, B. J. and C. L. Sidner. *Attentions, Intentions and Structure of Discourse* [J]. Computational Linguistics. 1986. 12:175 - 204.

[14] Grosz, B. J, A. K. Joshi & S. Weinstein. *Centering: a Framework for Modeling the Local Coherence of Discourse* [J]. Computational Linguistics. 1995, 21 (2): 203 - 225.

[15] Hasler, L. *An Investigation into the Use of Centering Transitions for Summarization* [C]. In Proceedings of the 7th Annual CLUK Research Colloquium. University of Birmingham, 2004. 100 - 107.

[16] Iida, M. *Discourse Coherence and Shifting Centers in Japanese texts* [A]. In M. A. Walker, A. K. Joshi& E. F. Prince (eds). Centering in Discourse Oxford. Clarendon Press, 1998, 161 - 182.

[17] Joshi, A. K. and S. Kuhn. *Centered Logic: the Role of Entity Centered Sentence Representation in Natural Language Inferencing* [C]. In Proceedings of the 6th International Joint conference on Artificial Intelligence. 1979. 435 - 9. Tokyo.

[18] Joshi, A. K. and S. Weinstein. *Control of Inference: Role of Some Aspects of Discourse Structuring—Centering* [C]. In Proceedings of the 7th International Joint Conference on Artificial Intelligence. 1981. 385 - 7. Vancouver.

[19] Kameyama. *Intra Sentential Centering a Case Study* [A]. In M. A. Walker, A. K, Joshi& E. F. Prince (eds.). Centering in Discourse Oxford. Clarendon Press, 1998, 89 - 112.

[20] Kibble, R. *Optimizing Referential Coherence in Text Generation* [J]. Computational Linguistics, 2004, 30(4): 401 - 416.

[21] Kibble, R. *A Reformulation of Rule 2 of Centering Theory* [J]. Computational Linguistics, 2001. 27(4), 579 - 87.

[22] Kibble, R. *Using Centering Theory to Plan Coherent Texts* [C]. In proceedings of the 12th Amsterdam Colloquium, Amsterdam, The Netherlands: 187 - 192.

[23] Miltsakaki, E, Kukich K. *Automated Evaluation of Coherence in Student Essays* [C]. In proceedings of the Workshop on Language Resources and Tools in Educational Applications, LREC. Athens Greek. 2000, 7 - 14.

[24] Miltsakaki, E. *The Syntax-discourse Interface Effects of the Main Subordinate*

Distinction on Attention Structure[D]. University of Pennsylvania,2003.

[25]Passonneau,R. *Interaction of Discourse Structure with Explicitness of Discourse Anaphoric Noun Phrases* [A]. In M. A. Walker et al. (eds.). Centering Theory in Discourse. Oxford: Clarendon Press,1998.

[26]Poesio, M, Stevenson R, Eugenio B. D, Hitzeman J. *Centering: a Parametric Theory and Its Instantiations*[J]. Computational Linguistics,2004 (3):309 -363.

[27]Rambow, O. *Pragmatics Aspects of Scrambling and Topicalization in German* [C]. Proc of the Workshop on Centering Theory in Naturally Occurring Discourse, Philadelphia,IRCS,1993.

[28] Roh, Ji-Eun & J. H. Lee. Coherent Textgeneration Using Entity—Based Coherence Measures ICCPOL Shen-Yang China,2003. 243 -249.

[29]Sidner,C. L. *Toward a Computational Theory of Definite Anaphora Comprehension in English*. Technical Report No. AI-TR-537,MIT,Cambridge,MA. 1979.

[30]Strube,M. & U. Hahn. *Functional Centering*[C]. In proceedings of the 34th Annual Meeting of Association for Computational Linguistics, Santa Cruz, 1996. CA: 270 -7.

[31]Strube,M. & U. Hahn. *Functional Centering—Grounding Referential Coherence in Information Structure*[J]. Computational Linguistics,1999. 25(3),309 -44.

[32]Walker, M. A, A. K. Joshi & E. F. Prince. *Centering in Naturally Occurring Discourse an Overview*[C]. In M. A. Walker,A. K. Joshi & E. F. Prince(eds). Centering Theory in Discourse. Oxford Clarendon Press,1998:1 -2.

概念转喻理论与翻译研究

首都经济贸易大学外国语学院　索绪香

摘　要：翻译首先是对语符形式的意义构建，因为“所谓翻译的本质，就是意义的语际转换”。译者对源语文本进行解读，在理解的基础上形成概念和意义，建构认知信息，然后在目的语中将该认知信息用语言形式表征出来。在翻译过程中，对原文本的解读体现了“部分代整体”的转喻思维。在挑选和建构的过程中，人们往往是通过认知某个显著的、易理解的部分来代表整个范畴，或者以一个凸显的典型特征来认识整个实体，由此构成形式和意义之间的“部分代整体”的转喻关系。转喻“部分代整体”是各种意义建构的原则之一。

关键词：概念转喻；翻译研究；翻译策略

Abstract: During the translation process, it's impossible for the translator to make a direct inheritance of the imagery and metaphor relationship from the source text like the Information Inheritance Integration Model. In order to achieve the equivalence between the source text and the target text, the translator will make a substitution of information, the result of which is that the information of the target text and the source text are not equal in appearance, but the metaphorical intention and the intrinsic relationship of the two are equal. In this kind of model, the source text information space usually contains has the unique characteristics of metaphorical imagery in culture's cognition of the source language.

Key Words: Conceptual metonymy; translation studies; translation strategies

一、概念转喻理论

（一）转喻的内涵

首先，我们来回顾传统的转喻观。转喻几乎都被视为一种修辞手法，并在汉语界等同于“借代”修辞格，如“转喻是一种修辞格，在这种辞格中，用某一事物的名称替代与该事物相关或由该事物联想到的另一个事物”（Webster's New World College Dictionary 1997:854）。借代（转喻）：修辞学的辞格之一。甲事物同乙事物不相类似，但有不可分离的关系，利用这种关系，以乙事物的名称来代替甲事物。

(《辞海》一卷本 1999:303)在传统修辞学中,转喻是 A 与 B(B 与 A 有一定的邻近联系)之间的替代关系,这里的 A 和 B 都停留在语言层面上。

随着认知语言学的发展,人们普遍意识到转喻的认知本质。它不单是一种修辞工具,也是一种认知机制。认知语言学认为转喻的本质与隐喻一样是人类基本的认知手段,转喻是概念、思维层面上的问题,对于人类推理起着重要的作用(Lakoff & Johnson 2003[1980]:36~39)。正是由于转喻的概念本质,认知语言学家称之为"概念转喻"(conceptual metonymy)。

A. George Lakoff(乔治·拉考夫)和 Mark Johnson(马克·约翰逊)的转喻定义

"转喻主要具有一种指代功能,即,它允许我们用一种实体代替另一种实体。……同时,转喻也具有理解功能"(Lakoff & Johnson 2003[1980]:35)。在谈到转喻和隐喻的区别时,Lakoff & Turner(拉考夫和丢勒,1989:103)指出转喻映射发生在单一认知域中,不涉及跨域映射。

B. William Croft(威廉·克罗夫特)的转喻定义

基于兰艾克(1987:147)"认知矩阵"的概念,Croft(1993:347)认为一个概念通常涉及的并不是一个单一的认知域,而是复杂的认知域矩阵。如"人类"这个概念就分别属于"生命体"、"物理体"、"有意志的施事"等认知域,因此,与"人类"这个概念相关的转喻就不是只涉及一个认知域,而是涉及由多个相关认知域组成的一个认知域矩阵。于是,Croft 对 Lakoff & Turner 的转喻定义做了如下修正:

转喻映射发生在单一的认知矩阵中,不涉及跨域或跨矩阵映射。同时,Croft(1993:348)利用域凸显(domain highlighting)来阐释概念转喻。他在同一认知域矩阵(domain matrix)中考察转喻的认知本质,认为概念转喻是次认知域和主认知域(主认知域即一个认知域矩阵,由许多次认知域构成)之间的凸显关系,例如:

[1]鲁迅非常难读。

这个转喻表达的意思是鲁迅的作品很难读懂。在我们关于鲁迅的概念中,相对于作家鲁迅而言,他的作品则处于一个次要的位置,属于次认知域,因为提到"鲁迅"我们首先想到的是鲁迅这个人。该转喻表达就是将次认知域"作品"放在了"作家鲁迅"认知域矩阵中凸显的位置,从而传达出了想要表达的意义。

C. Ronald Langacker(罗纳德·兰艾克)的转喻定义

Langacker(1993:30)在认知语法框架内利用认知参照点来阐释概念转喻。"转喻从根本上讲是一种参照点现象。更准确地讲,通常用转喻表达的实体作为参照点为所需的目标实体(即实际所指的实体)提供心理通道"(Langacker,2000:

199)。

[2]a. 红领巾走过来了。

b. 花白胡子一面说,一面走到康大叔面前。

a 表达的意义是“戴红领巾的人走过来了”。“红领巾”是此人身上高度凸显的物体,这里作为认知参照点来激活,唤醒人们大脑中凸显度较低的目标实体“戴红领巾的人”,使听者或读者与目标实体进行概念接触;b 句中“花白胡子”同样作为认知参照点为目标实体“长着花白胡子的人”提供了心理通道。

以上定义都视转喻为概念框架内的认知过程,代表了概念转喻定义的主流。

(二)转喻的分类

转喻的分类向来是学术界关注的焦点,涉及对转喻本质的理解。传统修辞学的分类是尽可能地归纳出各种具体的转喻表达,这种分类法非常繁芜、缺乏概括性;Ullmann(乌尔曼,1962)基于他对邻近性的三分法,将转喻大致分为空间邻近性转喻、时间邻近性转喻和逻辑邻近性转喻;般瑟尔和索恩伯格(1999:335)从转喻的语用功能出发,将其分为指称转喻、述谓转喻和言语行为转喻;塞托(1999:98)根据转喻出现的领域将转喻分为空间转喻、时间转喻和抽象转喻;布朗克(1999:178)利用共现性(copresence)和连续性(succession)来划分转喻等。众多概念转喻的分类中,拉登和威塞斯(1999:24 ~43)的分类最为系统、全面(李福印,2008),根据理想化认知模式中转喻喻体和转喻目标之间关系他们将转喻分为两大类:整体与其部分之间的转喻和整体中不同部分之间的转喻。具体分类如下:

1. 整体与其部分之间的转喻

这类转喻可以进一步细分为 7 小类:

(1)事物与部分之间的转喻

这类转喻主要包括整体转指部分和部分转指整体两种情况。例 3a 句中需要清洗的是车身,这里 car 作为整体转指车身部分,是整体转指部分;b 句用“四海”转指“全世界”,属于部分转指整体。

[3]a. The *car* needs washing.(这车需要清洗了。)

b. 马列主义是放之四海而皆准的真理。

(2)标量(scale)转喻

标量是由标量单位构成的整体。标量可作为整体用以表示其上限,也可用其上限代表标量整体。例 4a 句中速度标量作为整体转指上限“快速”;例 4b 句用年龄标量的上限 old(老)转指年龄标量整体,此用法中我们很少用标量下限来表示整体标量,如,我们不用 How young are you 或者“你多小了”。

[4]a. Henry is speeding again.(亨利又把车开得很快。)

b. How old are you?(你多大了?)

(3)构成(constitution)转喻

事物是由材料、物质构成的整体。这种转喻类型中,事物可代表它所含的物质和材料,材料、物质也可表示其构成的事物整体。例5a句用构成的材料 steel 转指凶器,b句用整个"钻戒" 转指其中的"钻石"材料。

[5]a. And as he plucked the cursed *steel* away…(当他拔出那可恶的凶器时……)

b. 他买了枚3克拉的钻戒。

(4)事件(event)转喻

事件是由众多同时发生或相继发生的分事件(subevent)组成的整体,分事件和事件整体之间相互代替产生事件转喻。这类转喻还涉及助动词间的替代关系,如,现在时态和将来时态、可能语气与确定语气之间的转指等等。例6句中,会说某种语言通常包括听、说、读、写四项技能,这里用分事件"说法语"表达玛丽懂法语这门语言整个事件。

[6]Mary speaks French.(玛丽会说法语。)

(5)范畴和成员之间的转喻

范畴与成员之间以及总称和特指之间的转喻关系也属于整体与其部分之间的转喻。例如,英语国家通常用 aspirin 转指"止痛片"整个范畴。例7a、b句中分别用特称"雷锋"、"华佗"来替代泛称范畴"具有雷锋精神英雄人物"以及"具有华佗医术的医生"。

[7]a. 千万个雷锋又站起,一代新人接班来。

b. 绿水青山枉自多,华佗无奈小虫何。

(6)范畴及其特征之间的转喻

范畴定义通常反映其主要特征。因此,可以用整体范畴来表示其主要特征,如用 jerk 表示 stupidity 这一特性;也可用其主要特征来替代整个范畴,如,我们常用 black 转指 black people。

(7)缩减转喻

这里转喻是用某一语言形式的部分来替代整个语言形式。最常见的例子就是首字母缩写形式,如 UN 替代 United Nations;汉语中也存在缩减转喻,如"中国" 转指"中华人民共和国"等。

2. 整体中不同部分之间的转喻

这类转喻主要包含9个小类:

(1)行为(action)转喻

行为理想化认知模式含有施事、受事、工具、行为本身、行为结果、时间等,这些因素之间存在行为转喻关系。如例 8 中,a 句用时间转指"度过夏天"这一行为,b 句以行为施事转指"写书"行为。

[8]a. We *summered* at the seashore.(我们在海边度过了夏天。)

b. John finally *authored* his third book.(约翰最终写出了他的第三本书。)

(2)感知(perception)转喻

人们的感知和所感知的事物之间存在感知转喻关系。例 9a 句用人们感到疼痛的身体部分"膝盖" 转指"疼痛感";同时,也可用人们的感知转指所感知的事物,b 句中 *sight* 这一视觉感知转指"所看到的景观" 。

[9]a. There goes my *knee*.(我膝盖痛。)

b. The sunrise at the seaside was quite a *sight* to behold.(海滨日出真是个奇观。)

(3)因果(causation)转喻

因果关系中,人们常用结果表示造成该结果的人或事,如例 10a 句表示"某一事物或事件使她难过",b 句是用"化蝶"的结果替代原因"睡梦";也可用原因替代事件结果,c 句表示执笔以便作诗绘画,"命笔"是原因,转指结果"作诗或绘画" 。

[10]a. She was upset.(她很沮丧。)

b. 化蝶方酣枕,闻鸡又著鞭。

c. 他欣然命笔。

(4)生产(production)转喻

生产、创作活动涉及生产(创作)者、产品、生产工具、产地、生产机构、产品名称等,这些因素之间相互替代产生生产转喻。例 11a 句中"杜康"是古代酿酒名师之名,转指"好酒",b 句用作者转指其著作。

[11]a. 何以解忧,唯有杜康。

b. 当代大学生应多读些马列。

(5)控制(control)转喻

控制关系中的控制者和受控者之间相互替代产生控制转喻。例 12a 句中"布什"代表他统率、控制的美国军队;b 句用受控物"福特汽车" 转指驾驶者。

[12]a. 布什轰炸了伊拉克。

b. The *Ford* has arrived.(那辆福特已经到了。)

(6)所属(possession)转喻

所属者和所属物之间相互替代产生所属转喻。例 13 属于所属物转指所属者，money 表示有钱的人；也存在所属者转指所属物的情况，如，我们用 That's me 表示 That's my car 的意义。

[13]He married *money*.（他娶了个有钱人。）

（7）容器（containment）转喻

容器转喻包括容器代表容纳内容以及容纳内容代替容器两种类型。例 14a 句指壶中的水开了；b 句指把盛牛奶的容器盖上。

[14]a. 壶开了。

b. 你记得要把牛奶盖上。

（8）地点（location）转喻

地点与处于该地的人、机构、事件等密切相关，这些因素之间的替代属于地点转喻。例 15 用地名 Cambridge 转指 Cambridge Press。

[15]*Cambridge* will publish his works.（剑桥将出版他的作品。）

（9）符号（sign）和指称（reference）转喻

Kovecses（威塞斯）和 Radden（拉登）将语言形式和所指概念之间的认知关系归为符号转喻类型，如“书”的字形转指“书”这一概念。同时他们认为语言形式、概念和指称的事物（事件）之间存在指称转喻，如，“牛”的字形和概念可分别转指“牛”这一事物。Kovecses、Radden 的分类将转喻的范围扩展得很广，以试图揭示语言的转喻本质。

（三）转喻的制约原则

概念转喻的生成受到以下原则的制约（Barcelona 2002:230 ~ 231）：

A. 转喻喻体和转喻目标需要满足转喻映射的某一默认类型，即 Kovecses、Radden 转喻分类中的任一类型。

B. 原则 A 中的默认类型受到多种认知原则和交际原则的制约（Kovecses & Radden 1998:62 ~ 71）。（a）认知原则：人们趋向于选择与自身有关的、具体的、有生命的、易完形感知的、典型的、具有使用功能等的事物作为转喻喻体转指与人无关的、抽象的、无生命的、不易完形感知的、非典型的、无使用功能等的转喻目标。转喻表达的喻体和目标越多地符合以上条件，其规约性就越强，越容易被人们接受。（b）交际原则：为了满足交际的准确性和交际的“经济原则”，人们通常选取清楚明白的、相关性强的事物来转指模糊不清、相关性弱的事物。

C. 原则 A 中的默认类型受到一些文化、社会、美学原则的制约（Kovecses & Radden 1998:71 – 74；Taylor 1995[1989]:123），原则 B 与原则 C 矛盾时，通常优先考虑后者。

二、概念转喻理论与翻译

(一)转喻翻译研究回顾

在传统修辞学中,转喻的翻译研究侧重转喻的表达形式,关注的是两种语言结构与词汇的转换,即探究如何理解源语文本中的转喻表达,然后在目的语中寻求与之对等的表达式。与隐喻翻译相比,转喻翻译的研究成果较少,且大多聚焦于转喻表达的翻译策略研究,如余立三、康旭平、韩启毅、郑雅丽、张光明等。在现有的转喻翻译研究文献中,韩启毅(2000)探讨了借代格(即作为修辞格的转喻)的理解及其翻译问题,并提出了"直译"、"意译"、"增译"和"注释"4 种翻译方法;郑雅丽(2004)在探讨借代格的翻译时,提出了"直译"、"引申"(即采用"译者按"或"篇末加注"的方法)和"意译"(即舍弃借代格)三种方法。二者主要探讨了修辞转喻的翻译转换问题,未能涵盖认知转喻的翻译转换,因而他们的研究带有一定的局限性(卢卫中,2011)。这些研究秉承修辞学的转喻观,倾向于把转喻作为具体的语言表达式来处理,从而导致人们把转喻等同于转喻表达,转喻翻译也就变成了转喻表达的翻译策略研究。认知科学的发展带来了转喻研究的认知转向,人们开始重新审视转喻的翻译(吴淑琼,2013)。肖坤学、邓国栋、张志慧、谭业升、卢卫中、刘敏等都尝试运用认知语言学理论来解决转喻翻译的实际问题。邓国栋(2007)在韩启毅(2000)研究的基础上,从认知语言学的角度探讨了转喻的认知机制和转喻翻译的认知观,并提出了如下四种转喻翻译策略,即"转喻认知模式的对等激活"、"转喻认知模式的附加激活"、"转喻认知模式的对等激活加注"和"转喻认知模式激活的归化";张志慧(2009)在论述转喻的基本概念的基础上,提出了演讲中的转喻翻译的两种模式,即:基于认知语言学体验原则的喻体等值翻译和基于关联原则的喻体诠释性翻译。

(二)转喻理论与翻译研究

1. 翻译是具有转喻性的认知活动

王寅提出:"翻译是一种认知活动,是以现实体验为背景的认知主体所参与的多重互动作用为认知基础的。"基于体验哲学,他认为翻译具有体验性,正是体验性构成了不同语言之间具有互译性的认知基础。翻译的体验性一方面表现为原文本是作者对现实世界的体验和认知,另一方面为译者对原文本的认知和理解。"翻译是用某一语言社团的体验来说明或理解另一语言社团的体验的一种认知活动。"翻译的目的在于把源语的全部信息在译语中再现并取得最大限度的等值效果,因此翻译中的等值是经验结构的相似性,换言之,翻译要求的是概念对等,而不是字词对等。

翻译首先是对语符形式的意义构建,因为“所谓翻译的本质,就是意义的语际转换”。译者对源语文本进行解读,在理解的基础上形成概念和意义,建构认知信息,然后在目的语中将该认知信息用语言形式表征出来。语言符号仅仅具有产生某种意义的潜势,具体的意义还要依赖人们的思维方式进行推理才能获得。这种意义的不确定性正是“部分激活整体”的转喻思维。因此,在翻译过程中,对原文本的解读体现了“部分代整体”的转喻思维。在挑选和建构的过程中,人们往往是通过认知某个显著的、易理解的部分来代表整个范畴,或者以一个凸显的典型特征来认识整个实体,由此构成形式和意义之间的“部分代整体”的转喻关系。转喻“部分代整体”是各种意义建构的原则之一。由此可见,翻译过程中对文本的理解和表达都体现了“部分代整体”转喻思维,翻译是具有转喻性的认知活动(吴淑琼,2013)。

2. 概念转喻是一种翻译策略

在翻译过程中,作为认知机制的转喻也是一种翻译策略。转喻作为翻译策略主要体现在以下三个方面。其一,原文中没有使用转喻思维,但在翻译过程中采用转喻思维机制,从而使译文更加生动形象。其二,对于同一个目标概念,两种语言可能会选取实体的不同部分或属性来表征该事物。因为邻近关系在不同语言中的凸显程度是不一样的,因此在源语中用事物的某一属性或特征来通达该事物,而在目的语中可能选取的是事物的另一属性或特征,但这些属性或特征处于同一个认知框架中,构成“部分代部分”的转喻关系。其三,在翻译过程中,源语中的整体概念在目的语中可能用部分概念来表达,或者源语中的事物在目的语中用其特征或属性来表达。换言之,在为目标概念提供心理可及的过程中,源语中的源概念和目的语中的源概念构成整体和部分的转喻关系。

3. 概念转喻理论对转喻翻译的启示

概念转喻是用同一认知框架中的一个概念实体为另一概念实体提供心理可及的认知过程,两个概念实体可及的心理基础是邻近关系。邻近关系的不同凸显程度导致转喻喻体的不同选择。因此,在翻译的过程中,源语中通达目标的源概念与目的语中通达目标的源概念可能不一致,这导致不同语言的主体可能会选取不同的语言载体表达同样的目标。换言之,对于源语中的心理可及过程,译文可能选取不同的实体来激活目标。因此,衡量转喻翻译是否成功是看译文与原文在心理可及的认知过程上是否一致。转喻翻译不是语法结构和词汇的简单对应,也不是单纯的喻体转换过程,而是一个从思维到语言的互动过程。

4. 转喻翻译的原则

转喻是概念之间的一种心理可及过程,转喻的翻译就是在目的语中再现从源概念到目标概念的心理可及过程。因此,在转喻翻译过程中,如果译语中从源概念到目标概念的心理可及过程与原文中的心理可及过程基本保持一致,那么翻译就是成功的。这种翻译过程强调的是认知上的对等,不同于在语言中寻找对等物的传统对等观。

(三)概念转喻的翻译策略

简单地说,转喻由喻体和喻标(即"本体")构成。人类语言的共性决定着不同语言之间存在着对应的转喻形式,即用相同的喻体表达相同的喻标;但因环境和文化等因素之不同,不同语言中同时又存在着用不同的转喻形式(即不同的喻体)表达相同的喻标的情况;第三种情形是,在两种语言中,一种语言里存在着某一转喻形式,而在另一种语言里却不存在对应的形式。

卢卫中(2011)在综合已有研究的基础上认为,对于源语中使用的转喻,译者可以分别采用以下翻译转换策略:(1)对于第一种情况,可以直接采用目的语的对应喻体;(2)对于第二种情况,可以采用目的语的特有喻体;(3)对于第三种情况,至少有三种选择:为了保留源语的文化特色,可以采用"源语喻体+喻标"或者"源语喻体+注解/译者按语"的方法;否则,对于不宜采用这两种处理方式的情况,译者可以舍弃源语的喻体,而直接将源语的喻标翻译出来。具体而言,对于源语中使用的转喻喻体,译者可以根据具体的语境采取以下5种翻译方法,即"采用目的语的对应喻体"、"采用目的语的特有喻体"、"采用源语喻体+喻标"、"采用源语喻体+注解/译者按"和"舍弃源语喻体"。

在翻译过程中,译者在识别出具体的转喻用法之后应该首先分析该转喻用法背后的概念转喻,以便对该转喻用法做出正确的把握和理解,然后在进行跨语言比较的基础上选择以下5种翻译方法中的一种,继而进行贴切的翻译转换。

1. 采用目的语的对应喻体

对于跨语言共性程度高的源语转喻用法来说,译者可以采用直译法,即直接采用目的语的对应喻体,从而向目的语读者传递与源语读者相同的信息。例如:

[16]I can't play basketball today,I haven't got any shoes.

译文:因为没有鞋子,我今天不能打篮球。

在运动语境中,英、汉语里作为上义词的"鞋子"都可以转指其下义词"运动鞋",属于范畴代成员的概念转喻,所以例16中的直译是贴切的,对于目的语读者来说是可以接受的。

[17]他们纷纷投笔从戎,奔赴前方。

译文:They *threw aside the writing brush and joined the army* one after another and hurried to the front.

例17中,“投笔从戎”指代“弃文从武”,是“具体代一般”的转喻操作。译文采用了直译法,翻译为threw aside the writing brush and joined the army,译文中源概念激活并通达目标概念的认知路径与原文几乎对等,译文读者能获得相似的认知体验。

2. 采用目的语的特有喻体

对于两种语言之间用不同喻体表达相同喻标的情况,译者需用目的语喻体翻译源语喻体,以便向目的语读者传递相同或者相近的信息。例如:

[18]*She is in a family way.*

译文:她有了。

在例18中,英语斜体部分是借怀孕的伴随方式转指“怀孕”,属于结果代原因的概念转喻;而汉语译文中的楷体部分是用泛指的“有了”转指具体的“有身孕了”,属于范畴代成员的概念转喻。尽管两种语言选用了不同的喻体,但所表达的委婉含义却是相同的。

[19]“咱们吃大宾馆还是吃小饭店?”

译文:“Shall we *go to a big guest house* or to *some small restaurant*?”

在例19中,原文中的“吃大宾馆”和“吃小饭店”体现了“容器代内容”的转喻操作,“大宾馆”和“小饭店”分别转喻“大宾馆的饭菜”和“小饭店的饭菜”。译文却采用了“动作代结果”的转喻思维,即用动作“go to a big guest house or to some small restaurant”来指代结果“have a meal in a big guest house or in some small restaurant”。

3. 采用“源语喻体+喻标”

原文中的转喻喻体蕴含丰富的文化内涵,包含特有的生活习惯、民俗风情、典故、传说、历史事件、人物、政治宗教等,在另一种文化中用对等的喻体进行翻译时,往往无法再现原文的文化信息。对于具有民族文化色彩的转喻形式,为了既保留源语的文化特色,同时又能向目的语读者传递源语的文化信息,译者可以采用这样的方法,即在直译源语喻体的同时,将源语喻标翻译出来。例如:

[20]中国还有一句成语,“三个臭皮匠,合成一个诸葛亮。”这就是说,群众有伟大的创造力。

译文:Still another Chinese proverb says,“Three cobblers with their wits combined would equal Zhuge Liang the master mind." It simply means the masses have great creative power.

在例20涉及的源语文化中,古典名著《三国演义》中的人物"诸葛亮"用来转指"智者",属于个别代一般的概念转喻用法。这是个文化负载词,因此翻译过程中最好予以保留,但直译的拼音是英语族人无法理解的,所以宜在后面附加其喻标含义"the master mind"。

[21]这对年轻夫妇并不相配,一个是西施,一个是张飞。

译文:This young couple is not well matched, one is a *Xi Shi—a famous Chinese beauty*, while the other is a *Zhang Fei—a well-known ill-tempered brute.*

4. 采用"源语喻体+注解/译者按"

"源语喻体+喻标"的译法是跨文化交际翻译中一种有效的方法,但对于那些民族文化色彩浓重的转喻用法来说,这种方法不足以将源语的文化信息传递出来,在这种情况下译者应该改用"源语喻体+注解"或"源语喻体+译者按语"的翻译方法。在以下例22中,译者采用了"源语喻体+译者按语"的方法:

[22]Cassandra's warnings, she thought bitterly. Pat won't listen to me.

译文:真是卡桑德拉的警告(译者按:传说太阳神阿波罗向卡桑德拉求爱不遂,大怒,令她成为先知来惩罚她。从此,卡桑德拉赋有预见未来的本领,但没人相信她的话,甚至到处被人讥笑奚落。)——她闷闷不乐,自忖碧儿不会听她的。

[23]We have enrolled every local *Cicero*.

译文:我们把各地西塞罗似的雄辩家都找来了。(Cicero:西塞罗,古罗马雄辩家、政治家、哲学家。)

5. 舍弃源语喻体

由于英汉语言表达习惯不同,两种语言之间在转喻用法上存在不对称的情况,即目的语中没有与源语相对应的转喻形式。在这种情况下,可以舍弃源语喻体,而直接将其喻标含义翻译出来,从而传递出源语句子的含义。例如:

[24]Great minds think alike.

译文:英雄所见略同。

[25]Wet floor!

译文:(小心)地滑!

在例24中,源语中的转喻用法"Great minds"属于属性代人的概念转喻,但在目的语中没有相同或相似的喻体,所以译文直接将目的语中的喻标"英雄"译了出来。在例25中,源语句子采用了原因代结果(即"地湿"代"地滑")的概念转喻结构。因为目的语中没有类似的转喻用法,所以译文舍弃了源语喻体,而直接将喻标翻译了出来。

[26]从根本上说,手头东西多了,我们在处理各种矛盾和问题时就有主动权。

译文:Fundamentally speaking when we gain in *economic strength*, we will gain the initiative in handling contradictions and problems.

例26中,原文用具体概念"手头东西"激活抽象概念"经济实力",体现了"具体代一般"的转喻思维。但在译文中无法找到一个对等的源概念,这种情况下通常采用意译法,直接翻译出转喻的目标概念,即 economic strength。

综上所述,为了保持与原文一致的心理可及过程,我们认为,转喻翻译必须尽量保留原文的转喻特征,这包含以下两方面的含义:

一是译文要尽可能让译文读者获得与原文读者相同的心理反应。换言之,在翻译的过程中,译文应尽量保留源概念为目标概念提供心理可及的转喻思维过程。这种心理可及的过程是概念层面的。因此,在不同的语言中,通达目标概念的源概念的语言表达形式可能不一样,但认知过程是一致的。

二是译文要尽可能再现转喻的修辞功能,维持原文的形式美和意蕴美。"转喻的认知研究并不意味着应该忽视其修辞效果。"转喻通常是以凸显的或具体的事物来为不凸显的或抽象事物提供心理桥梁,把两种表面上关联不大的对象联系起来,引起读者的联想、思考和感悟,从而获得语言的美感。同时,转喻通过简单的措辞来传达复杂的意义,以达到认知和表达的经济性。因此,转喻翻译除了保持信息的忠实与文字的通顺外,译文还要实现原文修辞效果的对等再现,让译文读者能够欣赏或领略到原文转喻的风采。

在转喻翻译过程中,要尽量保持原文的转喻特征,包括原文的转喻思维和修辞意蕴。只有这样,译文读者和原文读者才能获得一致的心理反应。

生态视域下的公示语翻译管理研究

首都经济贸易大学外国语学院　张春玲

摘　要:公示语是公共场所展示的语言信息文字,是社会语言文化的一部分。作为一种交际手段,它具有广泛的社会功能。目前对公示语翻译的研究已取得可喜成就,但从翻译管理方面,其研究仍有很大的空间有待开拓。公示语的翻译是一项很庞杂的工作,它综合了译者程度、翻译策略、译者本质、标牌制作者、社会监视等多种因素。本文试图从生态视角来研讨公示语翻译管理中所存在的问题和解决办法。

关键词:生态翻译学;公示语翻译;管理

Abstract:As a part of social language culture and means of communication,"Public Signs" has a wide social function. Though the translation of public signs has obtained gratifying achievements,the study on translation management of public signs still has much space to be explored. The translation of public signs is a very complex work. It is influenced by a variety of factors such as the translator's degree,the nature of the translator,the governance of the government,the producer of the signs,and the social surveillance. The essay is to discuss the problems and solutions of the translation management of public signs from the ecological perspectives.

Key Words:eco-translatology;public signs translation;management

一、前言

"公示语是一种较为独特的应用文体,公示语及其英语翻译体现了一个城市的社会开放化程度和文化品位,是都市国际语言环境的重要组成部分。要了解一个时代、一个社会、一个国家或一个城市的风貌,往往从这个时代、社会、国家或城市的语用水平中获得初步的印象。"(何自然,1997)因此,公共场合使用合适的英语表达,清晰传达信息,不仅是国际大都市公共服务之需要,更是国家与城市良好形

本文为首都经济贸易大学校内专项"生态视域下公示语翻译管理研究"(项目编码:02491654490209)资助研究。

象之展现。然而,公示语翻译的发展却不尽人意,在实际使用过程中,可能由于译者的英语表达能力、中外语言和文化的差异所限,欠妥当、欠规范甚至是错误的公示语英译不时出现在城市的街头,有的误译甚至影响了外国人的生活,更不利于给国家树立良好的国际形象。公示语是城市对外宣传的“名片”,也是城市文化环境,语言环境的重要组成部分,改进公示语质量对提升城市良好形象十分重要。而如何对已有公示语进行梳理,形成统一规范?如何对错误的公示语翻译进行修正?如何让新的公示语制作有据可依?理顺翻译生态中的各种关系,提升翻译质量,使公示语翻译生态能和谐健康发展,需要一定程度上的翻译综合管理。

二、生态视域下公示语翻译

翻译从本质上来说,是语言的转换,而语言又是文化的载体,文化又是人类活动乃至整个自然界的重要内容,所以整个翻译过程可以看成是一个翻译生态系统,与自然生态在许多方面具有类似性和同构性(胡庚申,2010),正如自然生态环境中的“适者生存”、“优胜劣汰”、“互利共生”等生态平衡现象一样,在翻译生态环境里,翻译过程中也存在大量的适应、选择、生存、淘汰等现象。

生态学视角下的翻译研究可以理解为一种生态学途径的翻译研究,是关于译者与翻译生态环境互动的整体性研究。翻译即是以“译者适应翻译生态环境的选择活动”的主题概念为基调。翻译生态环境指的是原文、源语和译语所呈现的世界,即语言、交际、文化、社会,以及作者、读者、委托者等互联互动的整体(胡庚申,2008)。

语言是文化的一部分,它受文化的影响与控制。公示语翻译的最大障碍就是不同语言文化的差异。在跨文化交际过程中,不同国度和民族的人,他们的文化背景、宗教信仰、价值观和思维方式等不尽相同,所以在进行交际的时候,总是倾向于根据各自的文化背景去理解对方和判断对方,这就难免会产生分歧、误解甚至于冲突,造成交际障碍,影响跨文化交际的效率和效果。所以公示语汉英翻译工作者一定要对两种语言的文化异同有比较深入的了解,才能做到译文在保证跨文化交际的顺利进行方面发挥应有的作用。

生态学翻译理论主张以“译者为中心”的翻译理念,是一种能够对翻译本体作出新解的翻译理论范式。强调翻译者要更关注信息接受者的感受;翻译实践要更贴近现实,理论研究要更创新求真。由于英汉思维方式不同,在语言表达层面上存在很大的差异。因此在了解整个翻译生态环境之后,译者应以多维度适应翻译生态环境的不同层次、不同方面为基础,进而依此做出与生态环境相适应的不同的选择转换。

三、公示语的翻译问题

公示语作为国家国际化的名片和城市的标签广泛地树立在我们的周围,公示语翻译是我国对外交流水平和文化环境优劣的重要体现。然而,汉英双语公示语在实际使用过程中并没有朝着服务、便利公众的方向发展。由于没有受到足够的重视,全国各地已有的公示语的英语翻译质量总体水平低下,翻译不规范、不准确现象十分严重。尤其是由于缺乏有效的管理措施和统一的翻译标准,各地公示语翻译存在许多问题。主要表现在以下几个方面。

(一)不统一问题

生态学认为生态系统中不同个体是相互联系的。公示语翻译中每则公示语之间也是相互联系的,特别是当几则公示语里面都出现同一专有名词时,须注意规范统一。尽管近年来对公示语翻译的研究不断深入,关注点也从基本信息服务转向整体语言及人文环境建设,但由于国家相关译写标准尚未出台、地区开放程度不均衡等因素,在翻译公示语时,生搬硬套、东拼西凑的现象仍屡见不鲜。且由于公示语宣传涉及的职能部门相当多,如语委、文化局、旅委等,缺乏有效的协调和对公示语进行梳理,造成一词多译,错误频出的现象。

(二)准确问题

公示语有着比较多的种类与广泛的范围,其功能包括示意与语用两种。由于译者没有正确把握公示语的翻译原则,出现了信息偏差、信息错误和信息交际障碍。主要分为三种类型:词汇错误、句法错误和语用错误。其中词汇错误又可分为拼写错误和用词不当两种类型;句法错误可分为语法错误和词序不当两种类型;而语用错误可分为婉转表达、信息冗余、非常见表达和文化干扰 4 种类型。随着中外交流的深入发展,中外语际交流的困难已经成为国人的共识,对公示语的任何歧义、误解、滥用、误译,都会导致不良后果(朱慧芬,2013)。

从生态翻译学视角,把原文本放到"翻译生态环境"中去考察和解读,适时地运用生态翻译学中的翻译生态环境、译者适应与选择以及语言维、文化维和交际维等多维度层面对公示语文本进行适应性选择以及跨语际转换,从而取得适应选择度较高的英译文(胡庚申,2009)。

(三)缺乏系统分析和研究

"优胜劣汰"或者"汰弱留强"是生态翻译学在翻译的具体操作层面上的主张。生态翻译学认为,在翻译过程中译者会尽可能地通过修改把译者认为不好的、劣质

的东西去掉，而留下优秀的。这样不断地选择、推敲和淘汰的过程也就是不断提高和完善的过程，只有这样才能达到更佳的翻译效果，得到最好的翻译文本（许建中，2009）。然而，目前的研究主要集中在纠正翻译错误上，缺乏用系统分析和研究公示语翻译。与此同时，分析的内容通常是语言方面的，缺乏有力的数据支持。而且仅靠相关学者学术方面对公示语的提高，其力度还是有限。

（四）缺乏管理与协调机制

公示语翻译质量的提升，不仅关系到翻译理论和技巧，更有翻译管理的问题。虽然译界学者对公示语翻译进行了卓有成效的理论研究，但由于缺乏完善的公示语翻译管理与协调机制，现状仍不容乐观。主要表现在由于缺乏统一有序的公示语协调部门和相关制度，翻译的差错没有相关的责任追究制度。现存公示语的错误尽管大量被指出来了，但是，没有能够得到及时有效的改正，沟通渠道还不够畅通。

（五）公示语制作，处于无序状态

当前，城市公示语的来源没有规范的途径，只要需要制作公示语的公共区域，都可以制作公共语标识牌，对其内容没有人在意，因此，汉英公示语的标识牌任由采购组织自行决定，没有管理制度的约束，专业人员的水平也参差不齐。

（六）缺乏严格的审核

虽然译界尝试建立相关标准去规范公示语翻译，但这只是学术上的探讨，根本没有涉及政府管理层面。部分地方性的公示语翻译规范只能由本地公示语译者提供指导，不具有普适性，这造成双语公示语既没有政府相关部门的严格审核，也没有管理部门对公示语语言准确性的确定。

（七）经费不充足

在财政上还没有形成专项费用，更多地只能靠民间的力量进行纠错和呼吁。

四、公示语翻译管理对策

（一）促进翻译专业人才培养，加强翻译职业化建设

翻译教学的生态发展离不开教育生态环境，就是指以翻译教学为中心，将教学置身于自然环境、社会环境及文化环境中，开展多种形式的公示语翻译培训，提高公示语翻译人员专业素质。赵小沛指出语用失误经常出现，说明了语用教学在我国外语教学中的重要性。教师有责任唤起学生的语用意识，明确地传授有关语用方面的知识，以减少语用失误的现象，使学生尽快适应中国与世界接轨的局势。提高英语教学质量，培养学生英语的语言实际应用能力。

(二)与国际接轨建立公示语翻译标准体系

生态翻译学认为:“翻译是一个整合一体的、和谐统一的系统。”翻译活动的各个环节并不是孤立的,和生态自然系统一样是一个有机的整合体。“和谐统一”的特征也贯穿于翻译活动的各个环节(胡庚申,2009)。

公示语翻译不能只局限在翻译的水平上,要从政府管理的视角提出应对策略,从政府的管理制度上来探讨,尽快出台国家公示语翻译标准,对城市公共场所英译进行统一规范的管理。根除城市公示语混乱现象以解决当前公示语的相关研究与实践脱节问题。公示语翻译一旦有章可循,有法可依,可以在很大程度上杜绝低级错误的出现。实践公共场所英文使用“发现错误”和“纠正错误”两套标准化工作流程;关注地方标准和国家标准的衔接问题,有效处理地方差异。在标准制定工作中,要充分吸收英语翻译领域的学术研究成果,确保译写的标准化、规范化;保证翻译生态的动态性和时效性。扩大宣传,提升规范在翻译界的认知度和影响力。

坚持“标准”先行原则,规范公示语翻译。刘法公教授曾指出,公示语汉英翻译的“统一”原则有三层含义:现成的惯用的公示语,直接借鉴,统一到国际惯例;译名固定,即名从主人;没有可借鉴的公示语根据权威性的官方网站、报刊和辞典来统一。在标准制定工作中,要充分吸收英语翻译领域的学术研究成果,确保译写的标准化、规范化。

(三)建立相应的管理机构与机制,提高公示语翻译质量

成立专门的管理机构,设立公示语翻译评审与监督管理系统。协调各部门之间的沟通,做好总体规划和管理。政府管理部门要积极支持建立规范的公示语翻译评审制度,组织高校和相关专家建立公示语翻译专家咨询委员会,以此提高政府公共服务的国际化水准。由中外专家结合进行研究是满足外籍人员公示语信息需求的最佳翻译工作组合模式。由于公示语在全球范围内具有通用性,要参照、借鉴国外公示语,建立公示语翻译语料库、加强管理服务监督、提高社会关注度。采取各种有效形式及时对错误的公示语翻译进行修正,如公示语外语纠错大赛、志愿者活动、专家寻访等,收集错误,并监督改正。同时,加强行业间的沟通和探讨,对公示语汉英翻译进行规范与管理,以保证翻译质量,净化语言环境,提升城市的文明程度和国家形象。

参考文献:

[1]何自然. 语用学与英语学习[M]. 上海:上海外语教育出版社,1997.

[2]胡庚申. 生态翻译学解读[J]. 中国翻译,2008(6).

[3]胡庚申．傅雷翻译思想的生态翻译学诠释[J]．外国语,2009(2).

[4]胡庚申．翻译适应选择论[M]．武汉:湖北教育出版社,2004.

[5]李敬科．公示语翻译现状与管理对策[J]．西南农业大学学报,2012(4).

[6]刘法公．汉英、英汉译名统一与翻译规范研究[M]．北京:人民出版社,2010.

[7]吕和发．公示语功能特点与汉英翻译研究[J]．术语标准化与信息技术,2005(2).

[8]罗海鹏,魏福利．汉英公示语标准化与城市经济建设[J]．中外企业家,2009(5).

[9]许建忠．翻译生态学[M]．北京:中国三峡出版社,2009.

[10]赵小沛．公示语翻译中的语用失误探析[J]．南京理工大学学报,2010(5).

[11]朱慧芬．生态视域下的商务英语翻译理论与实践研究[M]．北京:北京理工大学出版社,2013.

[12]应远马,朱慧芬,陈晓远．杭州市公示语翻译管理的问题与对策[J]．杭州研究,2012(2).

大学英语翻译教学现状及翻译技巧

首都经济贸易大学外国语学院　王立华

摘　要：翻译教学是大学英语教学的重要组成部分，不管是 CET（College English Test, Band 4 and Band 6）还是研究生入学考试，都是学生必考的题目，也是存在问题比较多的部分。学生不了解西方的文化，英译汉的翻译明显带有“西化”倾向，汉译英中的英语又不符合外国人表达的习惯。本文对大学英语翻译教学做些简单分析，提供些翻译技巧，希望对学生有所帮助。

关键词：大学英语；翻译教学；翻译问题；翻译技巧

大学英语和中文一样，有听、说、读、写 4 方面的能力，而“译”又是作为一门单独能力而存在，学习一门外语，要学会翻译成国语，才能使这门外语的学习更有意义和价值，反过来还能懂得如何去学习这门外语，所以翻译的重要性是不言而喻的。而大学英语的教学大纲则要求教师的教学要以语言知识的应用能力、学习能力、翻译能力、跨文化交际能力并重为主要教学内容。很多教师也意识到了翻译在教学中的重要性，但是还缺乏良好的翻译教学方法。所以本文就此讲述了一些翻译技巧。

一、大学英语翻译教学中存在的问题

（一）大学英语教材的局限性

目前很多高校使用的大学英语教材都没有翻译的基础理论，也没有常用的翻译方法和翻译技巧，就算很多教材课后有几个翻译句子，但那也是为了巩固或强调课文中的单词、短语、语法、句型等知识，并不是为了训练翻译能力，所以，这样的翻译不是真正意义上的翻译，只能算是单词、短语、语法、句型的综合练习题而已。大学英语的覆盖面很广，范围很宽，1996 年以前的 CET 过级考试没有翻译这个题型，完全忽略了翻译对英语学习的重要性，进而导致英语教师和学生对英语翻译的轻视。目前很多教师和学生都是以四、六级为学习目标，单纯地为了考试而学习，也导致很多高分学生没有实际运用语言的能力。

（二）翻译的理论知识传授得不够

理论是实践的指导者，翻译需要良好的翻译理论作为基础保障，也只有具备较深的翻译理论基础，翻译才可能会有声有色，但是学校却忽略了对学生传授翻译的理论知识，进而导致教师很少给学生讲授翻译理论和翻译技巧，只是教学生“直译法”，所以就算学生拥有很大的词汇量和大量的语法知识，翻译出来的结果也非常生硬，没有情感。目前，很多人都把外语翻译作为一种社会现象，认为它是一种跨文化活动，也是一种国际间的交际手段，这拓宽了翻译的边界，无形中增加了翻译的对象。有学者指出，翻译理论与实践的脱节是当前翻译存在的严重问题，而对于正在求知的大学生更甚，使他们把翻译理论和实践混为一谈，不能分清两者之间的关系，或不能找到翻译理论和实践的切合点，翻译时，困难多多。

（三）教学模式的落后

大学的课时相对较少，而翻译基本完全来自课堂，课堂上也基本上是以教师为中心，教师布置几道脱离实际语境的翻译作业，然后进行批改点评，这对学生的翻译能力没有多大的帮助，最多也就让学生多记得一些词汇或短语，收获少之又少，而学生觉得这种翻译没有多大用处，进而不重视翻译教学。

（四）针对性不够强

在《大学英语课程教学要求》中，明确提出了翻译的三个层次要求，其中，最一般的要求相当于大学英语的四级水平，较高要求指的是能够摘译所学专业的英语文献资料，而最高要求是能够翻译所学专业的文献资料，同时，也对翻译速度做出了明确的规定。

二、翻译技巧

（一）词义的选择和引申技巧

英汉两种语言都有一词多类和一词多义的现象。一词多类就是指一个词往往属于几个词类，具有几个不同的意义；一词多义就是同一个词在同一词类中又往往有几个不同的词义。在英译汉的过程中，我们在弄清原句结构后，就要善于运用选择和确定原句中关键词词义的技巧，以使所译语句自然流畅，完全符合汉语习惯的说法；选择确定词义通常可以从两方面着手：

1. 根据词在句中的词类来选择和确定词义

They are as like as two peas. 他们相似极了。（形容词）

He likes mathematics more than physics. 他喜欢数学甚于喜欢物理。（动词）

Wheat, oat, and the like are cereals. 小麦、燕麦等等皆系谷类。（名词）

2. 根据上下文联系以及词在句中的搭配关系来选择和确定词义。

He is the last man to come. 他是最后来的。

He is the last person for such a job. 他最不配干这个工作。

He should be the last man to blame. 怎么也不该怪他。

This is the last place where I expected to meet you. 我怎么也没料到会在这个地方见到你。

词义引申是我们英译汉时常用的技巧之一。翻译时,有时会遇到某些词在英语辞典上找不到适当的词义,如果任意硬套或逐词死译,就会使译文生硬晦涩,不能确切表达原意,甚至会造成误解。这时就应根据上下文和逻辑关系,从该词的根本含义出发,进一步加以引申,引申时,往往可以从三个方面来加以考虑。

(1)词义转译。当我们遇到一些无法直译或不宜直译的词或词组时,应根据上下文和逻辑关系,引申转译。

The energy of the sun comes to the earth mainly as light and heat. 太阳能主要以光和热的形式传到地球。

(2)词义具体化。根据汉语的表达习惯,把原文中某些词义较笼统的词引申为词义较具体的词。

The last stage went higher and took the Apollo into orbit round the earth. 最后一级火箭升得更高,把"阿波罗号"送进围绕地球运行的轨道。

(3)词义抽象化。根据汉语的表达习惯,把原文中某些词义较具体的词引申为词义较抽象的词,或把词义较形象的词引申为词义较一般的词。

Every life has its roses and thorns. 每个人的生活都有甜有苦。

(二)词类转译技巧

在英译汉过程中,有些句子可以逐词对译,有些句子则由于英汉两种语言的表达方式不同,不能逐词对译,只有将词类进行转译之后,方可使译文显得通顺、自然;对词类转译技巧的运用须从4个方面加以注意。

(1)转译成动词。英语中的某些名词、介词、副词,翻译时可转译成汉语中的动词。

The lack of any special excretory system is explained in a similar way.

植物没有专门的排泄系统,可用同样的方式加以说明。(名词转译)

As he ran out ,he forgot to have his shoes on. 他跑出去时,忘记了穿鞋子。

(2)转译成名词。英语中的某些动词、形容词,翻译时可转换成汉语中的名词。

The earth on which we live is shaped a ball. 我们居住的地球,形状像一个大球。

（动词转译）

The doctor did his best to cure the sick and the wounded. 医生尽了最大的努力来治疗病号和伤员。（形容词转换）

（3）转译成形容词。英语中有些作表语或宾语的抽象名词，以及某些形容词派生的名词，往往可转译成汉语中的形容词。另外，当英语动词转译成汉语名词时，原来修饰该动词的副词也往往随之转译成汉语中的形容词。

It is no use employing radar to detect objects in water. 使用雷达探测水下目标是没有用的。（作表语的名词转译）

The sun affects tremendously both the mind and body of a man. 太阳对人的身体和精神都有极大的影响。（副词转译）

（4）转译成副词。英语中的某些名词、形容词，翻译时可转译成汉语中的副词。

When he catches a glimpse of a potential antagonist, his instinct is to win him over with charm and humor. 只要一发现有可能反对他的人，他就本能地要用他的魅力和风趣将这些人争取过来。（名词转译）

（三）汉译的增词技巧

英译汉时，按意义上、修辞上或句法上的需要加一些词，使译文更加忠实通顺地表达原文的思想内容；但是，增加的词并不是无中生有，而是要增加原文中虽无其词却有其意的一些词，这是英译汉中常用的技巧之一。增词技巧一般分作两种情况。

（1）根据意义上或修辞上的需要，可增加下列 7 类词。

Flowers bloom all over the yard. 朵朵鲜花满院盛开。（增加表示名词复数的词）

After the banquets , the concerts and the table tennis exhibitor , he went home tiredly. 在参加宴会、出席音乐会、观看乒乓球表演之后，他疲倦地回到了家里。（增加动词）

He sank down with his face in his hands. 他两手蒙着脸，一屁股坐了下去。（增加副词）

I had known two great social systems. 那是以前，他就经历过两大社会制度。（增加表达时态的词）

As for me , I didn't agree from the very beginning. 我呢，从一开始就不赞成。（增加语气助词）

The article summed up the new achievements made in electronic computers , artificial satellites and rockets. 本文总结了电子计算机、人造卫星和火箭这三方面的

新成就。(增加概括词)

(2)根据句法上的需要增补一些词汇。

Reading makes a full man;conference a ready man;writing an exact man. 读书使人充实,讨论使人机智,写作使人准确.(增补原文句子中所省略的动词)

All bodies on the earth are known to possess weight. 大家都知道地球上的一切物质都有重量。(增补被动句中泛指性的词)

(四)正反、反正汉译技巧

正反、反正汉译技巧是指翻译时突破原文的形式,采用变换语气的办法处理词句,把肯定的译成否定的,把否定的译成肯定的。运用这种技巧可以使译文更加合乎汉语规范或修辞要求,且不失原意。这种技巧可分 5 个方面加以陈述。

(1) 肯定译否定

The above facts insist on the following conclusions. 上述事实使人们不能不得出以下结论。

(2)否定译肯定

She won't go away until you promise to help her. 她要等你答应帮助以后才肯走。

(3) 双否定译肯定

There can be no sunshine without shadow 有阳光就有阴影。

但是,如果翻译时保留英语原来的"否定之否定"的形式并不影响中文的流畅时,则应保留。这样还可突出原文中婉转的语气。如 He is not unequal to the duty. 他并非不称职。

(4)正反移位

I don't think he will come. 我认为他不会来了。

(5) 译为部分否定

Not all minerals come from mines. 并非所有矿物都来自矿山。

Both of the substances do not dissolve in water. 不是两种物质都溶于水。

三、结论

英语是世界上较为普及的一门语言,学好英语可以让学生的未来有着更光明的前景。翻译是英语能力的重要部分之一,良好的翻译技能可以使学生流利地用英语和外国人交流,实现学习英语的真正用处。所以大学师生应该分析目前的翻译教学现状,掌握翻译技巧,做到学以致用。